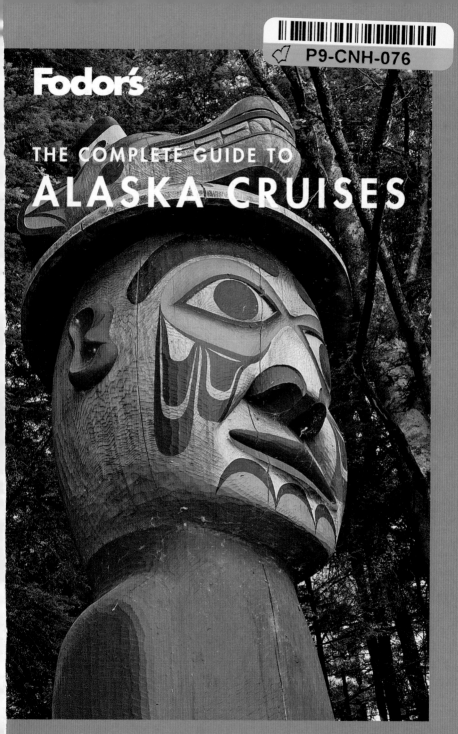

Fodor's

THE COMPLETE GUIDE TO
ALASKA CRUISES

Portions of this book appear in *Fodor's Alaska*.

Fodor's THE COMPLETE GUIDE TO ALASKA CRUISES

Publisher: Amanda D'Acierno, *Senior Vice President*

Editorial: Arabella Bowen, *Editor in Chief*; Linda Cabasin, *Editorial Director*

Design: Fabrizio La Rocca, *Vice President, Creative Director*; Tina Malaney, *Associate Art Director*; Chie Ushio, *Senior Designer*; Ann McBride, *Production Designer*

Photography: Melanie Marin, *Associate Director of Photography*; Jessica Parkhill and Jennifer Romains, *Researchers*

Maps: Rebecca Baer, *Senior Map Editor*; Mark Stroud (Moon Street Cartography), David Lindroth, *Cartographers*

Production: Linda Schmidt, *Managing Editor*; Evangelos Vasilakis, *Associate Managing Editor*; Angela L. McLean, *Senior Production Manager*

Sales: Jacqueline Lebow, *Sales Director*

Marketing & Publicity: Heather Dalton, *Marketing Director*; Katherine Fleming, *Senior Publicist*

Business & Operations: Susan Livingston, *Vice President, Strategic Business Planning*; Sue Daulton, *Vice President, Operations*

Fodors.com: Megan Bell, *Executive Director, Revenue & Business Development*; Yasmin Marinaro, *Senior Director, Marketing & Partnerships*

Copyright © 2014 by Fodor's Travel, a division of Random House LLC.

Writer: Linda Coffman

Editor: Douglas Stallings

Editorial Contributors: Teeka Ballas, Amy Fletcher, Sarah Henning, Lisa Hupp, Chris McBeath, E. Readicker-Henderson

Production Editor: Elyse Rozelle

Fodor's is a registered trademark of Random House LLC. All rights reserved. Published in the United States by Fodor's Travel, a division of Random House LLC, New York, a Penguin Random House Company, and in Canada by Random House of Canada Limited, Toronto. No maps, illustrations, or other portions of this book may be reproduced in any form without written permission from the publisher.

1st Edition

ISBN 978-0-8041-4189-5

ISSN 2330-4421

All details in this book are based on information supplied to us at press time. Always confirm information when it matters, especially if you're making a detour to visit a specific place. Fodor's expressly disclaims any liability, loss, or risk, personal or otherwise, that is incurred as a consequence of the use of any of the contents of this book.

SPECIAL SALES

This book is available at special discounts for bulk purchases for sales promotions or premiums. For more information, e-mail specialmarkets@randomhouse.com

PRINTED IN COLOMBIA

10 9 8 7 6 5 4 3 2 1

CONTENTS

Keepers of the Deep:
A Look at Alaska's Whales. 209

Native Handicrafts 233

Alaska's Glaciers:
Notorious Landscape Architects 278

Gold! Gold! Gold! 289

CONTENTS

ABOUT
THIS GUIDE

Fodor's Recommendations

Everything in this guide is worth doing—we don't cover what isn't—but exceptional sights, hotels, and restaurants are recognized with additional accolades. Fodor'sChoice★ indicates our top recommendations; and **Best Bets** call attention to notable hotels and restaurants in various categories. Care to nominate a new place? Visit Fodors.com/contact-us.

Trip Costs

We list prices wherever possible to help you budget well. Hotel and restaurant price categories from $ to $$$$ are noted alongside each recommendation. For hotels, we include the lowest cost of a standard double room in high season. For restaurants, we cite the average price of a main course at dinner or, if dinner isn't served, at lunch. For attractions, we always list adult admission fees; discounts are usually available for children, students, and senior citizens.

Hotels

Our local writers vet every hotel to recommend the best overnights in each price category, from budget to expensive. Unless otherwise specified, you can expect private bath, phone, and TV in your room. For expanded hotel reviews, facilities, and deals visit Fodors.com.

Restaurants

Unless we state otherwise, restaurants are open for lunch and dinner daily. We mention dress code only when there's a specific requirement and reservations only when they're essential or not accepted. To make restaurant reservations, visit Fodors.com.

Credit Cards

The hotels and restaurants in this guide typically accept credit cards. If not, we'll say so.

Top Picks
★ Fodor'sChoice

Listings
⊠ Address
⊠ Branch address
☎ Telephone
🖷 Fax
⊕ Website
✉ E-mail
🎫 Admission fee
☉ Open/closed times
Ⓜ Subway
⊹ Directions or Map coordinates

Hotels & Restaurants
🖭 Hotel
⇌ Number of rooms
🍽 Meal plans
✗ Restaurant
🀪 Reservations
👗 Dress code
🚫 No credit cards
$ Price

Other
⇨ See also
☞ Take note
🏌 Golf facilities

EXPERIENCE AN ALASKA CRUISE

WHAT'S WHERE

1 Southeast Alaska.
Southeast Alaska ("the Panhandle" or "Southeast") includes the Inside Passage. Only Haines and Skagway have roads to "the Outside." Juneau, the state capital, and Sitka, the former Russian hub, are here. At Glacier Bay National Park you can get close to massive tidewater glaciers, and the Alaska Chilkat Bald Eagle Preserve draws more than 4,000 of these birds to the Haines area. Long fjords snake between the mountains, timbered slopes plunge to the rocky shores, and marine life abounds. You're almost certain to spend at least some time here on your cruise.

2 Anchorage. With nearly half the state's population, Anchorage is Alaska's biggest city and a common arrival or departure point for cruisers—even if you'll likely be traveling to either Seward or Whittier where your ship is docked. The restaurants, art and history museums, copious espresso stands, and performing arts have earned the city the sobriquet "Seattle of the North." Alaskans often deride the place as "Los Anchorage," but the occasional moose ambling down a bike trail hints at the nearby wilderness.

Chukchi Sea

Icy Cape

Barrow Point Barrow

Harrison Bay

NORTH SLOPE

Point Hope

LISBURNE PENINSULA

Anaktuvuk Pass

Arctic Circle

B R O O K S

CHUKOTKA

Cape Espenberg

Kotzebue

Bettles

Nunyagmo

SEWARD PENINSULA

ProvidEniya

RUSSIA
U.S.

Bering Strait

Teller

Taylor

Nome

Galena

Manley Hot Springs

River

4

Savoonga

Norton Sound

Unalakleet

Denali National Park & Preserve

Saint Lawrence Island

St Marys

Takotna

Mt. McKinley 20,320ft

Cape Romanzof

YUKON DELTA

A L A S K A

Saint Matthew Island

Bethel

2

Nunivak Island

1

Dillingham

Homer

Saint Paul Island

Kuskokwim Bay

Naknek

KENAI PENINSULA

Pribilof Islands

Cape Newenham

Kodiak

Saint George Island

Bristol Bay

Kodiak Island

Bering Sea

Port Heiden

Shelikof Strait

PENINSULA

SEE INSET AT RIGHT

Cold Bay

ALASKA

Sand Point

ALEUTIAN ISLANDS

Unimak Island

Unalaska Island

Umnak Island

PACIFIC OCEAN

0   300 mi

0   300 km

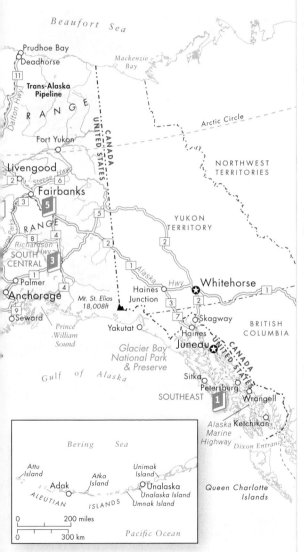

3 **South Central Alaska.**
This is the place for great fishing, hiking, rafting, and wildlife-viewing. Prince William Sound is a top destination for these activities and is a common cruise stop. Your ship might call at Seward or Homer on the Kenai Peninsula, two laid-back towns with great museums. Kodiak is a lesser-called-at port known for its green-carpeted mountains and Kodiak brown bears; if you're one of the lucky few who visits, charter outfits can take you to remote wilderness spots.

4 **Denali National Park.**
Home to Mt. McKinley— the highest peak in North America—Denali National Park and Preserve comprises 6 million acres of Alaska's best wildlife, scenery, and adventures. If you do one land extension before or after your cruise, make it this one.

5 **The Interior.** Bound by the Brooks Range to the north and the Alaska Range to the south, the interior is home to Denali National Park and Preserve. The region's major city is Fairbanks; Canada's Yukon Territory is within striking distance.

ALASKA PORTS OF CALL
TOP ATTRACTIONS

Skagway's Gold Rush Relics

(A) On deck at sailaway (cruise-speak for when you leave your port of embarkation), you might hear the musical theme from the John Wayne movie *North to Alaska* as a reminder that there was gold in them thar hills. Waves of fortune-seekers passed through Skagway during the gold rush of 1898, inflating the population of the small town on the northern end of Lynn Canal to more than 10,000. Today's White Pass and Yukon Railroad follows their trail from Skagway to the goldfields of the Klondike. The spirit of the gold rush lives on in town, with wooden sidewalks, horse-drawn carriages, and old-fashioned saloons that once also housed bordellos.

Glacier Bay

(B) With approximately 5,000 glaciers in Alaska it may seem peculiar that such a fuss is made about Glacier Bay, but part of its allure is the abundant wildlife, including seals, bears, and even humpback whales. Another source of its mystique is its inaccessibility. Until 1870 it was frozen behind a wall of ice a mile high. Today, it's designated as a national park and only a limited number of permits per season are issued to the many cruise ships plying Alaska's coastal waters. If your cruise experience won't be complete without seeing Glacier Bay, choose your ship and itinerary with care.

Ketchikan's Frontier History

(C) Alaskans are a hardy breed and many still consider hunting and fishing an important part of everyday life. Ketchikan is almost a time capsule devoted to frontier living, offering the best salmon fishing possible, wilderness hikes, a hilarious lumberjack show that kids love, and the restored gold rush–era Creek Street with buildings on pilings over a stream. Head to Creek Street for boutiques, eateries, and the

infamous Dolly's House; Dolly practiced the world's oldest profession and her home stands as a bawdy museum where period-costumed docents bid passersby to enter—for a price.

Whale-Watching

(D) Aside from an up-close encounter with a bear, humpback whale sightings are perhaps the most thrilling wildlife encounter to be had in Alaska. To spot whales, look for their blow—a waterspout that can rise 10 feet high. Whales typically blow several times before rising gently to reveal their hump backs for a few moments. Before they start a deep dive, when they might disappear for a few minutes or nearly half an hour, they may "wave" with their fluke (tail) in the air.

Flightseeing

(E) Much of the grandeur of Alaska can only be seen from the air, and flightseeing by small plane or helicopter delivers a view of otherwise inaccessible sights, such as Misty Fjords and expansive glacial ice fields. Helicopter excursions usually make a glacier landing where, depending on your tour, you might do some glacial ice-trekking or visit a dog-mushing camp to participate in a dogsled ride over the snow-covered glacier.

Denali National Park

(F) Anchored by North America's highest mountain, 20,320-foot Mt. McKinley, Denali is a must-see for cruisers who intend to visit Alaska only once and want a land-and-sea experience either before or after their north- or southbound cruise. Almost a million people a year enter the area by bus or train, making it Alaska's most visited wilderness area. Aside from the spectacular scenery, Denali is the place to see wildlife. It is home to 161 species of birds, 37 species of mammals, and at least 450 plant species. Look closely for bears, caribou, and the official state bird, the willow ptarmigan.

IF YOU LIKE

Glaciers

Every Alaska cruise includes a day of glacier viewing; it's practically a law. Tidewater glaciers—those that come right up to the water's edge—are known to rumble with a thunderous creak just before calving off icebergs with a showy splash.

Glacier Bay. Considered the best place to view glaciers, ships will most likely sidle up to Marjerie and Lamplugh glaciers during a typical nine-hour day spent in the bay; they'll only enter John Hopkins Glacier inlet in late season because sea lions are usually giving birth there the rest of the time. Un-Cruise Adventures is a good bet for a small-ship cruise with numerous Glacier Bay itineraries; Holland America Line and Princess Cruises are the two large ship lines with the most permits to enter.

Mendenhall Glacier. Known as "the drive-up glacier," Mendenhall glacier is one of Alaska's most accessible. Hop on the refurbished blue school bus pier-side in Juneau for an inexpensive 13-mile ride to the glacier. Park rangers are on duty at the U.S. Forest Service visitor center to answer any questions you might have after viewing the exhibits and video. To get even closer to the glacier, there is a ½-mile nature trail.

Tracy Arm, Sawyer Glacier. Waterfalls and craggy cliffs outline the long, narrow, ice-strewn Tracy Arm fjord that ships slowly creep through to reach Sawyer Glacier. Why are they creeping? Because Sawyer Glacier constantly sheds huge blocks of ice, and navigating the passage can be difficult. Depending on conditions you might not reach the glacier's face, but Tracy Arm is a good bet for iceberg and sea lion photo ops.

People and Culture

Alaska's unique people and culture have been shaped by the region's history. Migrations over the Bering Land Bridge about 14,000 years ago were followed by millennia of settlement by dozens of culturally distinct Alaska Native peoples. Russian occupation followed in the 18th and 19th centuries, and that gave way to homesteaders after the eventual acquisition of the Alaska Territory by the United States from Russia for $7.2 million in 1867. Each wave of newcomers adds a layer of cultural identity to the region, most recently the gold fever of the early 20th century and Alaska's designation as the 49th state in 1959.

Alaska Natives. You won't find them living in igloos, though you might sail by some people tending their family's summer fish camps on remote stretches of shore. Alaska Natives share their heritage in centers such as Ketchikan's Saxman Native Village, where visitors can see the tribal house and a performance by dancers in the theater, and Totem Bight, a publicly accessible fish camp set in the rain forest with ceremonial clan house and totem poles.

Gold history. Alaska might have never made it to statehood without the Yukon Gold Rush of 1896 and the thousands of gold seekers who flooded the territory. Although there was no gold in Skagway, it became the jumping-off point for a journey on the Chilkoot Trail and possible riches. The quest for gold is illustrated here in the Klondike Gold Rush National Historical Park visitor center.

Living off the land. Many who choose to live in Alaska do so because they love being outside both for work and for play. Fishing, hunting, and logging have all played a part in the area's commerce.

You're unlikely to visit a working logging camp, but you can go salmon fishing, crab fishing, or pet sled dogs at a musher's camp.

Wildlife

Alaska really is where the wild things are. Although most creatures are abundant throughout the state, they are often elusive. To get close, consider a small-ship cruise, such as one with Lindblad Expeditions, American Cruise Lines, or Un-Cruise Adventures. Some larger ships offer excursions that will get you close to the wildlife, too.

Bald eagles. With a wingspan of 6 to 8 feet, these grand Alaska residents are often spotted soaring through the air in Glacier Bay and circling cruise ships docked in Juneau. When they swoop close to the water, you're likely to get a glimpse of them catching a fish for lunch.

Bears. Early in the Alaska cruising season, bears are likely to be scarce along the shoreline—they've just awakened from their annual hibernation. Late-season cruisers are more likely to spot them feeding near the water in preparation for their long winter's sleep.

Salmon. Fishermen are in luck almost any month during the Alaska cruise season. If you just want to get a look, many rivers and streams are so thick with salmon in late summer that you can almost walk across them. Just watch out for bears that might join you for lunch.

Whales. Beluga whales live along much of the coast, but you're more likely to see humpback whales in Alaska. To guarantee that you'll get more than just a glimpse of them off in the distance, take a whale-watching excursion in Juneau's Stephens Passage.

Dine and Drink

Cruise lines pride themselves on their cuisine and you'll find an abundant variety of food on hand, including regional Alaska favorites, but don't limit yourself to meals on board or you'll miss some authentic, and tasty, local dining and drinking experiences.

Baked Alaska. Complete with parading waiters and flaming meringue, Baked Alaska has long been a festive cruise-ship tradition. Presented with a flourish, it's a staple that Holland America raises to new heights by serving it sprinkled with edible gold.

Beer. Mention beer during your Alaska cruise and the Alaskan Amber brand is sure to enter the conversation. A short cab ride from downtown Juneau, Alaskan Brewing Co. offers complimentary tours and samples for guests over the age of 21 at its tasting bar.

Duck Fart. No visit to Alaska is complete without a trip to an authentic saloon to sample the state drink, a Duck Fart. Don't let the name put you off—even locals order this concoction of Kahlúa, Bailey's Irish Cream, and Crown Royal.

Salmon. Although Alaskan king crab legs may be offered only once, freshly caught Alaskan salmon will be a frequent menu item at restaurants in port and aboard every cruise ship. Holland American Line offers a different version every night.

BEST BETS

Best Cruise Line: Mainstream

■ **Carnival Cruise Lines.** With its adults-only Serenity area, water park–style slides, and Vegas-style entertainment (not to mention all the other activities), the line's ships are designed to appeal to the widest range of travelers.

■ **Norwegian Cruise Line.** Noted for their family-friendly accommodations, specialty dining, and outstanding entertainment, the line gets high marks from passengers of all ages.

■ **Royal Caribbean International.** The line appeals to families with its high-energy entertainment, extensive sports facilities, youth programs, and even nurseries for toddlers and babies.

Best Cruise Line: Premium

■ **Princess Cruises.** Sophisticated styling includes piazza-style atriums, many different specialty restaurants, quiet enclaves, and fast-paced dance clubs. Spas are noted for their facilities and service.

■ **Holland America Line.** Traditional cruise enthusiasts find that HAL hits the right note with gracious, art-filled ships that also include all the latest high-tech gadgets.

■ **Celebrity Cruises.** For sheer beauty and excellent cuisine, Celebrity ships deliver a quality experience in modern surroundings.

Best Cruise Line: Luxury

■ **Silversea Cruises.** Butlers assigned to every suite add an extra level of pampering on luxuriously appointed vessels.

■ **Regent Seven Seas Cruises.** In the luxury segment Regent offers the most all-inclusive cruises, even including all shore excursions in the fare.

Best Cruise Ship: Large

■ *Celebrity Solstice,* **Celebrity Cruises.** *Celebrity Solstice* offers a dozen places to dine, with half of them included in the fare, and a serene atmosphere for total relaxation.

■ *Crown Princess,* **Princess Cruises.** *Crown Princess* incorporates all the line's signature elements, including a stunning atrium with a sidewalk café atmosphere.

■ *Norwegian Pearl* and *Jewel,* **Norwegian Cruise Line.** The sister ships offer more than a dozen dining options and nonstop activities, including bowling.

Best Cruise Ship: Medium

■ *Seven Seas Navigator,* **Regent Seven Seas Cruises.** With complimentary gourmet specialty restaurants and shore excursions, *Seven Seas Navigator* is a stylish choice for discerning travelers.

■ *Oceania Regatta,* **Oceania Cruises.** With only 684 passengers onboard, *Regatta* scores high marks for its country club casual ambience in intimate spaces with beautifully appointed accommodations, unobtrusive service, and fine dining.

■ *Statendam,* **Holland America Line.** Accommodations filled with amenities are some of the most comfortable at sea, and the specialty dining charge is the most reasonable you will find without sacrificing quality.

Best Cruise Ship: Small

■ *Safari Endeavour,* **Un-Cruise Adventures.** The luxury adventure yachts offer a nearly all-inclusive experience on vessels with well-appointed public areas and accommodations.

- *Silver Whisper,* **Silversea Cruises.** High-end specialty restaurants, expansive decks and lounges, and a theater for superior entertainment are just some of the luxury features aboard *Silver Whisper.*

Best Regular Outside Cabins
- *Coral Princess,* **Princess Cruises.** All cabins feature niceties such as a refrigerator and generous storage for even the largest wardrobe.

- *Statendam,* **Holland America Line.** Comfort is key, and all cabins have DVD players, flat-screen televisions, lighted magnifying makeup mirrors, and comfortable bedding.

Best Inside Cabins
- *Amsterdam,* **Holland American Line.** The largest inside cabin category measures in at a whopping 293 square feet—some of the most spacious inside accommodations at sea.

- *Disney Wonder,* **Disney Cruise Line.** Designed with families in mind, *Disney Wonder*'s inside cabins have all the space needed for a comfortable cruise.

Best Regular Dining Room Cuisine
- **Holland America Line.** Under the leadership of Master Chef Rudi Sodamin, the culinary staff of Holland America Line creates dishes high in quality and taste.

- **Regent Seven Seas Cruises.** Creative dishes and wines chosen to complement all menus are a hallmark of Regent Seven Seas. Service is attentive, but not hovering or intrusive.

- **Silversea Cruises.** A true gourmet meal is hard to come by on land, let alone at sea, but Silversea chefs accomplish just such a feat with dishes prepared à la minute and appropriate wines chosen to accompany them.

Best Ships for Families
- *Carnival Miracle,* **Carnival Cruise Lines.** Facilities for teens and tots have to be seen to be believed. Pools and the disco are elaborate, and even picky kids should find the active programs enticing.

- *Radiance of the Seas,* **Royal Caribbean International.** Well-conceived areas for children and teens, plus facilities that invite family members to play together, are bonuses for parents who want to spend quality family time with the kids.

- *Disney Wonder,* **Disney Cruise Line.** Designed from the keel up with family fun in mind, *Disney Wonder* delivers fun for all with entertainment and age-appropriate activities and facilities.

Best Ships for Spa Lovers
- *Celebrity Solstice,* **Celebrity Cruises.** Attractive, tranquil decor and a full complement of wraps, massages, and deluxe treatments are features of the AquaSpa. The expansive Persian Garden thermal suite includes cold and hot rooms as well as a Turkish hammam.

- *Oosterdam,* **Holland America Line.** Massages and facials take a backseat to the elaborate pleasures of a soothing whirlpool and indoor relaxation areas worthy of a fine European spa resort.

- *Celebrity Millennium,* **Celebrity Cruises.** In addition to offering a wide range of massages and spa treatments, the utterly decadent spa on this ship has a complimentary hydrotherapy pool and café.

Best Ships for Travelers with Disabilities

■ *Celebrity Solstice,* **Celebrity Cruises.** Although accommodations designed for accessibility are some of the best at sea, equally as desirable are the line's "easy" shore excursion options.

■ *Amsterdam,* **Holland America Line.** At the forefront of accessible cruise travel, the ship has a variety of services for passengers with mobility, sight, and breathing impairments. All shore tenders are equipped with wheelchair-accessible platforms.

■ *Grand Princess,* **Princess Cruises.** Not only are accessible staterooms and suites available in a wide range of categories but there is also shore-side wheelchair access to appropriate tours on vehicles equipped with lifts.

Best Ships for Service

■ *Volendam,* **Holland America Line.** The Filipino and Indonesian stewards and servers go out of their way to provide gracious service with a sincere smile and genuine warmth.

■ *Seven Seas Navigator,* **Regent Seven Seas Cruises.** Staff efforts almost go unnoticed, yet even out-of-the-ordinary requests are handled with ease. Butlers provide personalized service to guests in the top-category suites.

■ *Silver Whisper,* **Silversea Cruises.** The mostly European staff don't seem to understand the word no. Every attempt is made to satisfy even the most unusual request by butlers assigned to every suite.

Best Enrichment Programs

■ **Un-Cruise Adventures.** Naturalists and expedition guides are knowledgeable about the history, cultures, and wildlife of Alaska.

■ **Holland America Line.** Guest lecturers cover a wide range of topics and the Culinary Arts Center offers hands-on cooking classes, gourmet food presentations, and tasting events.

Best Ports for Strolling

■ **Sitka.** One of the best Inside Passage ports to explore on foot, Sitka exhibits its long Native Tlingit and Russian history in a fairly compact area. A walk will take you past St. Michael's Cathedral, the Sheldon Jackson Museum, Castle Hill, and Sitka National Historical Park. A must-see stop is the Alaska Raptor Center, where 100 to 200 birds are rehabilitated each year in the avian hospital. Only a 20-minute walk from the center of town, it gives you a bird's-eye view of eagles and other raptors.

■ **Haines.** There's no need to board a tour bus in Haines since nearly everything to see in town is within walking distance. After a leisurely stroll along the small boat harbor, visit the nearby Sheldon Museum and Cultural Center, which contains an extensive collection of Native artifacts and gold rush memorabilia as well as a model of a Tlingit tribal house.

■ **Victoria, B.C.** The walk into town from the port is rather long, so a better option is to catch the Hop-On/Hop-Off double-decker bus that makes stops at some of the city's most interesting sights. Once you are there, however, a walk through the inner harbor as you make your way to the Empress Hotel for tea or just a look around the impressive interiors and beautiful grounds can make a nice morning. And there are plenty of other sights to see, including Craigdarroch Castle, Market Square, and Fisherman's Wharf.

Best Splurge Excursions

■ **Taku Lodge Feast and Glacier Seaplane Tour, Juneau.** Everyone has a window seat aboard the seaplane, and headsets are provided for a narration of the sights below. After landing in front of the Hole in the Wall glacier at the isolated Taku Lodge, which is on the National Register of Historic Places, salmon roasted over alder wood is served with all the trimmings. Following lunch, a guided trail walk is offered before the return flight to Juneau.

■ **White Pass and Yukon Route, Skagway.** The scenic White Pass and Yukon Route train tour explores the Yukon by motorcoach and train—one mode of transport out to the Yukon and the other on the way back. Once aboard the narrow-gauge train, you are treated to some of the most amazing scenery in North America. Train cars are comfortable, with large windows, complimentary drinking water, and bathroom facilities. A small outdoor viewing platform is located between cars and is a popular spot for shutterbugs. However, since this excursion crosses the Canadian border, a passport is required.

Best Ports for Shoppers

■ **Ketchikan.** For salmon lovers, there are shops on nearly every block that stock the famous wild Alaska salmon as well as halibut. (The salmon can be shipped to your home overnight, but a better bet is to purchase it smoked since you probably won't be home the next day.) Have it shipped to your home and it should arrive within a day or so of your return. Most merchants also stock seasonings, specialty items, and even salmon cat treats.

■ **Juneau.** In Alaska's capital city you will find shopping that runs the gamut from souvenir T-shirts to jewelry and designer clothing. Many of the stores are branches of those also found in many Caribbean ports of call, so for more authentic goods look for shops owned by local merchants where handcrafted items and artwork created by Native Alaskans are on offer.

Best Ports for Active Excursions

■ **Skagway.** A 2-mile hike along the rugged Chilkoot Trail winds through rain forest alive with animals, birds, and wild flowers. The trail is an important piece of gold rush history and the main route to the Klondike. Upon reaching the Taiya River, you can board an 18-foot raft to return you to civilization past snow-capped peaks and hanging glaciers.

■ **Juneau.** A helicopter whisks you off to a glacier adventure that includes three hours of hiking and climbing over the icy glacial terrain. Outerwear and mountaineering gear is provided as well as some basic training. Experience is not required, but you should be in good physical condition to participate.

■ **Icy Strait Point.** You can soar above a majestic rain forest at speeds of 60 miles an hour for almost a mile on Alaska's longest zipline.

FLORA AND FAUNA OF ALASKA

FAUNA

(A) Arctic Ground Squirrel (*Spermophilus parryii*): These yellowish-brown, gray-flecked rodents are among Alaska's most common and widespread mammals. Ground squirrels are known for their loud, persistent chatter. They may often be seen standing above their tundra den sites, watching for grizzlies, golden eagles, and weasels.

(B) Arctic Tern (*Sterna paradisaea*): These are the world's long-distance flying champs; some members of their species make annual migratory flights between the high Arctic and the Antarctic. Sleekly beautiful, the bird has a black cap and striking blood-red bill and feet. They often can be seen looking for small fish in ponds and coastal marshes.

(C) Bald Eagle (*Haliaeetus leucocephalus*): With a wingspan of 6 to 8 feet, these grand Alaska residents are primarily fish eaters, but they will also take birds or small mammals when the opportunity presents itself. The world's largest gathering of bald eagles occurs in Southeast Alaska each winter, along the Chilkat River near Haines.

(D) Beluga Whale (*Dephinapterus leucas*): Belugas are gray at birth, bluish gray as adolescents, and white as adults (the word *byelukha* is Russian for "white"). Though they seem to favor fish, belugas' diet includes more than 100 different species, from crabs to squid. They live along much of the coast, from the Beaufort Sea to the Gulf of Alaska.

(E) Black-capped Chickadee (*Parus atricapillus*): This songbird is one of Alaska's most common residents. As with two close relatives, the chestnut-backed and boreal chickadees, the black-cap gets through the winters by lowering its body temperature at night and shivering through the long hours of darkness.

(F) Caribou (*Rangifer tarandus*): Sometimes called the "nomads of the north," caribou are long-distance wandering mammals. They are also the most abundant of the state's large mammals; in fact, there are more caribou in Alaska than people! The Western Arctic Caribou Herd numbers more than 400,000, while the Porcupine Caribou Herd has ranged between 110,000 and 180,000 over the past decades. Another bit of caribou trivia: they are the only members of the deer family in which both sexes grow antlers. Those of bulls may grow up to 5½ feet long with a span of up to 3 feet.

(G) Common Loon (*Gavia immer*): Some sounds seem to be the essence of wilderness: the howl of the wolf, the hooting of the owl, and the cry of the loon. The common loon is one of five *Gavia* species to inhabit Alaska (the others are the Arctic, Pacific, red-throated, and yellow-billed). Common loons are primarily fish eaters. Excellent swimmers, they are able to stay submerged for up to three minutes.

(H) Common Raven (*Corvus corax*): A popular character in Alaska Native stories, the raven in indigenous culture is both creator and trickster. Entirely black, with a wedge-shaped tail and a heavy bill that helps distinguish it from crows, the raven is Alaska's most widespread bird.

(I) Common Redpoll (*Carduelis flammea*): Slightly larger than the chickadee, the common redpoll and its close cousin, the hoary redpoll (*Carduelis hornemanni*), are among the few birds to inhabit Alaska's Interior year-round. Though it looks like a sparrow, this red-capped, black-bibbed songbird is in the finch family.

FLORA AND FAUNA OF ALASKA

Dall Sheep (*Ovis dalli dalli*): One of four types of wild sheep to inhabit North America, the white Dall is the only one to reside within Alaska. Residents of high alpine areas, the sheep live in mountain chains from the St. Elias Range to the Brooks Range. Though both sexes grow horns, those of females are short spikes, while males grow grand curls that are "status symbols" displayed during mating season.

Dolly Varden (*Salvelinus malma*): This sleek, flashy fish inhabits lakes and streams throughout Alaska's coastal regions. A member of the char family, it was named after a character in Charles Dickens's novel *Barnaby Rudge* because the brightly colored spots on its sides resemble Miss Dolly Varden's pink-spotted dress and hat. Some members of the species remain in freshwater all their life, while sea-run dollies may live in the ocean for two to five years before returning to spawn.

Golden Eagle (*Aquila chrysaetos*): With a wingspan of up to 7½ feet, this inland bird can often be spotted spiraling high in the sky, riding thermals. The bird usually nests on cliff faces and feeds upon small mammals and ptarmigan. The plumage of adult birds is entirely dark, except for a golden head. These migratory eagles spend their winters as far away as Kansas and New Mexico.

Great Horned Owl (*Bubo virginianus*): The best known of Alaska's several species of owls, its call is a familiar one here. It is a large owl with prominent ear tufts and a white throat with barred markings. Residing in forests from Southeast Alaska to the Interior, it preys on squirrels, hares, grouse, and other birds.

Harbor Seal (*Phoca vitulina*): Inhabiting shallow marine waters and estuaries along much of Alaska's southern coast, harbor seals may survive up to 30 years in the wild on a diet of fish, squid, octopus, and shrimp. They, in turn, may be eaten or killed by orcas, sea lions, or humans. Solitary in the water, harbor seals love company on land, and will gather in large colonies. They weigh up to 250 pounds and range in color from black to white.

Hermit Thrush (*Catharus guttatus*): Some Alaskans argue that there is no northern song more beautiful than the flute-like warbling of the hermit thrush and its close relative, the Swainson's thrush (*Catharus ustulatus*). The two birds are difficult to tell apart except for their songs, the hermit's reddish brown tail, and the color of their eye rings. Among the many songbird migrants to visit Alaska each spring, they begin singing in May while seeking mates and defending territories in forested regions of southern and central Alaska.

Horned Puffin (*Fratercula corniculata*): Named for the black, fleshy projections above each eye, horned puffins are favorites among birders. Included in the group of diving seabirds known as alcids, puffins spend most of their life on water, coming to land only for nesting. They are expert swimmers, using their wings to "fly" underwater and their webbed feet as rudders. Horned puffins have large orange-red and yellow bills. A close relative, the tufted puffin (*Fratercula cirrhata*) is named for its yellow ear tufts.

Lynx (*Lynx canadensis*): The lynx is the only wild cat to inhabit Alaska. It's a secretive animal that depends on stealth and quickness. It may kill birds, squirrels, and mice, but the cat's primary prey

is the snowshoe hare (*Lepus americanus*), particularly in winter; its population numbers closely follow those of the hare's boom-bust cycles. Large feet and a light body help the lynx run through deep snowpack.

Moose (*Alces alces gigas*): The moose is the largest member of the deer family, the largest bulls standing 7 feet tall at the shoulders and weighing up to 1,600 pounds. The peak of breeding occurs in late September. Females give birth to calves in late May and early June; twins are the norm. Bulls enter the rut in September, the most dominant engaging in brutal fights. Though most commonly residents of woodlands, some moose live in or just outside Alaska's cities.

Mountain Goat (*Oreamnos americanus*): Sometimes confused with Dall sheep, mountain goats inhabit Alaska's coastal mountains. As adults, both males and females have sharp-pointed horns that are short and black (sheep have buff-colored horns). They also have massive chests and comparatively small hindquarters, plus bearded chins.

Musk Ox (*Ovibos moschatus*): The musk ox is considered an Ice Age relic that survived into the present at least partly because of a defensive tactic: they stand side by side and form rings to fend off predators such as grizzlies and wolves. Unfortunately for the species, that tactic didn't work very well against humans armed with guns. Alaska's last native musk oxen were killed in 1865. Musk oxen from Greenland were reintroduced here in 1930; they now reside on Nunivak Island, the north slope of the Brooks Range, and in the Interior. The animal's most notable physical feature is its long guard hairs, which form "skirts" that nearly reach the ground. Inupiats called the musk ox *oomingmak*, meaning "bearded one." Beneath those coarser hairs is fine underfur called *qiviut*, which can be woven into warm clothing.

Pacific Halibut (*Hippoglossus stenolepis*): The halibut is the largest of the flatfish to inhabit Alaska's coastal waters, with females weighing up to 500 pounds. Long-lived "grandmother" halibut may survive 40 years or more, producing millions of eggs each year. Bottom dwellers that feed on fish, crabs, clams, and squid, they range from the Panhandle to Norton Sound. Young halibut generally stay near shore, but older fish have been found at depths of 3,600 feet.

Pacific Salmon (*Oncorhynchus*): Five species of Pacific salmon spawn in Alaska's waters, including the king, silver, sockeye, pink, and chum. Hundreds of millions of salmon return to the state's streams and lakes each summer and fall, after spending much of their lives in saltwater. They form the backbone of Alaska's fishing industry and draw sport-fishers from around the world.

Rainbow Trout (*Salmo gairdneri*): A favorite of anglers, the rainbow trout inhabits streams and lakes in Alaska's coastal regions. The Bristol Bay region is best known for large 'bows, perhaps because of its huge returns of salmon. Rainbows feed heavily on salmon eggs as well as the deteriorating flesh of spawned-out salmon. Sea-run rainbows, or steelhead, grow even larger after years spent feeding in ocean waters. The state record for steelhead/rainbow trout is 42 pounds, 3 ounces.

FLORA AND FAUNA
OF ALASKA

(A) **Red fox** (*Vulpes vulpes*): Though it's called the red fox, this species actually has four color phases: red, silver, black, and cross (with a cross pattern on the back and shoulders). An able hunter, the red fox preys primarily on voles and mice, but will also eat hares, squirrels, birds, insects, and berries.

(B) **Sandhill crane** (*Grus canadensis*): The sandhill's call has been described as "something between a French horn and a squeaky barn door." Though others may dispute that description, few would disagree that the crane's calls have a prehistoric sound. And, in fact, scientists say the species has changed little in the 9 million years since its earliest recorded fossils. Sandhills are the tallest birds to inhabit Alaska; their wingspan reaches up to 7 feet. The gray plumage of adults is set off by a bright red crown. Like geese, they fly in Vs during migratory journeys.

(C) **Sea otter** (*Enhydra lutris*): Sea otters don't depend on blubber to stay warm. Instead, hair trapped in their dense fur keeps their skin dry. Beneath their outer hairs, the underfur ranges in density from 170,000 to one million hairs per square inch. Not surprisingly, the otter takes good care of its coat, spending much of every day grooming. Otters also spend a lot of time eating. In one study, researchers found that adult otters consumed 14 crabs a day, equaling about one-fourth of their body weight.

(D) **Sitka black-tailed deer** (*Odocoileus hemionus sitkensis*): The Panhandle's rain forest is the primary home of this deer, though it has been transplanted to Prince William Sound and Kodiak. Dark gray in winter and reddish brown in summer, it's stockier than the whitetails found in the Lower 48. The deer stay at lower elevations during the snowy months of winter, then move up to alpine meadows in summer.

(E) Snowy owl (*Nyctea scandiaca*): Inhabiting the open coastal tundra, the snowy owl is found from the western Aleutian Islands to the Arctic. Adults are largely white (though females have scattered light brown spots) and immature birds are heavily marked with brown. Their numbers rise and fall with swings in the population of lemmings, their primary prey. Rather than hoots, the snowy emits loud croaks and whistles.

(F) Steller sea lion (*Eumetopias jubatus*): Its ability—and tendency—to roar is what gives the sea lion its name. Because they can rotate their rear flippers and lift their bellies off the ground, sea lions can get around on land much more easily than seals can. They are also much larger, the males reaching up to 9 feet and weighing up to 1,500 pounds. They feed primarily on fish, but will also eat sea otters and seals. They have been designated an endangered species because their populations north of the Panhandle have suffered huge declines.

(G) Walrus (*Odobenus rosmarus*): The walrus's ivory tusks can be dangerous weapons; there are stories of walruses killing polar bears when attacked. Weighing up to 2 tons, the walrus's primary food includes clams, mussels, snails, crabs, and shrimp.

(H) Willow ptarmigan (*Lagopus lagopus*): One of three species of ptarmigan (the others are the rock and the white-tailed), the willow is the most widespread. It is also Alaska's state bird. It tends to live in willow thickets, where it feeds and hides from predators. Aggressively protective parents, willow ptarmigan have been known to attack humans to defend their young.

FLORA AND FAUNA OF ALASKA

Wolf (*Canis lupus*): The largest and most majestic of the Far North's wild canines, wolves roam throughout all of mainland Alaska. They form close-knit family packs, which may range from a few animals to more than 30. Packs hunt a variety of prey, from small mammals and birds to caribou, moose, and Dall sheep. They communicate with each other through body language, barks, and howls.

Wolverine (*Gulo gulo*): Consider yourself lucky if you see a wolverine, because they are among the most secretive animals of the North. They are also fierce predators, with enormous strength and endurance. Denali biologists once reported seeing a wolverine drag a Dall sheep carcass more than 2 miles; an impressive feat, since the sheep likely weighed four times what the wolverine did. They have been known to run 40 mph through snow when chased by hunters. Though they look a lot like bears and have the ferocity of a grizzly, wolverines are in fact the largest members of the weasel family.

Wood frog (*Rana sylvatica*): One of the few amphibians to inhabit Alaska, and the only one to live north of the Panhandle, these frogs range as far north as the Arctic, surviving winters through the help of a biochemical change that keeps them in a suspended state while frozen. Come spring, the bodies revive after thawing. Though they mate and lay eggs in water, wood frogs spend most of their lives on land.

FLORA

Balsam poplar and black cottonwood (*Populus balsamifera* and *Populus trichocarpa*): These two closely related species sometimes interbreed and are difficult, if not impossible, to tell apart. Mature trees of both species have gray bark that is rough and deeply furrowed. In midsummer they produce cottony seedpods. They also have large, shiny, arrowhead-shaped leaves.

Birch (*Betula*): Ranging from Kodiak Island to the Brooks Range, birch trees are important members of Alaska's boreal forests. Deciduous trees that prefer well-drained soils, they have white bark and green heart- to diamond-shaped leaves with sharp points and toothed edges. One species, the paper birch (*Betula papyrifera*), is easily distinguished by its peeling, paperlike bark.

Blueberry (*Vaccinium*): A favorite of berry pickers, blueberries are found throughout Alaska, except for the farthest northern reaches of the Arctic. They come in a variety of forms, including head-high forest bushes and sprawling tundra mats. Pink, bell-shaped flowers bloom in spring, and dark blue to almost black fruits begin to ripen in July or August, depending on the locale.

Cow parsnip (*Heracleum lanatum*): Also known to some as Indian celery, cow parsnip resides in open forests and meadows. The plant may grow several feet high, with dull green leaves the size of dinner plates; thick, hairy, hollow stalks; and clusters of white flowers. Anyone who harvests—or walks among—this species must take great care. Oils on the stalks, in combination with sunlight, can produce severe skin blistering.

Devil's club (*Echinopanax horridum*): This is a prickly shrub that grows 4 to 8 feet high and forms dense, spiny thickets in forests ranging from the Panhandle to South Central. Hikers need to be wary of this plant: its large, maple-like leaves (which can be a foot or more across) have spines, and needles cover its pale brown trunk. In late summer, black bears enjoy its bright red berries.

Salmonberry (*Rubus spectabilis*): The salmonberry canes, on which the leaves and fruits grow, may reach 7 feet tall; they grow in dense thickets. The juicy raspberrylike fruits may be either orange or red at maturity; the time of ripening is late June through August.

Spruce (*Picea*): Three species of spruce grow in Alaska. Sitka spruce (*Picea sitchensis*) is an important member of coastal rain-forest communities; white spruce (*Picea glauca*) prefers dry, well-drained soils in boreal forests that stretch from South Central to the Arctic; black spruce (*Picea mariana*) thrives in wet, boggy areas.

Tall fireweed (*Epilobium angustifolium*): The fireweed is among the first plants to reinhabit burn areas and, in the proper conditions, it grows well. Found throughout much of Alaska, it's a beautiful plant, with fuchsia flowers that bloom from the bottom to the top of stalks; it's said that the final opening of flowers is a sign that winter is only weeks away. Spring fireweed shoots can be eaten raw or steamed, and its blossoms can be added to salads. A related species is dwarf fireweed (*Epilobium latifolium*); also known as "river beauty," it is shorter and bushier.

Wild prickly rose (*Rosa acicularis*): Serrated leaves grow on prickly spines, and fragrant five-petal flowers begin blooming in late spring. The flowers vary from light pink to dark red. Appearing in late summer and fall, bright red rose hips rich in vitamin C can be harvested for jellies, soups, or pie.

Willow (*Salix*): An estimated three dozen species of willow grow in Alaska. Some, like the felt-leaf willow (*Salix alaxensis*), may reach tree size; others form thickets; still others, like the Arctic willow (*Salix arctica*), hug the ground in alpine terrain. They often grow thickest in the subalpine zone between forest and tundra. Whatever the size, willows produce soft "catkins" (pussy willows), which are actually columns of densely packed flowers without petals.

DID YOU KNOW?

Whether your small ship picks its way carefully through icebergs to the face of Endicott Arm's Dawes Glacier or your large ship organizes a flotilla of excursion vessels to the face of Tracy Arm's Sawyer Glacier, keep your eyes out for mama and baby harbor seals lounging on icebergs during pupping season (early summer).

PLANNING YOUR ALASKA CRUISE

By Linda
Coffman

Alaska is one of cruising's showcase destinations. Itineraries give passengers more choices than ever before—from traditional loop cruises of the Inside Passage, to round-trips from Vancouver or Seattle, to one-way Inside Passage–Gulf of Alaska cruises.

Though Alaska cruises have generally attracted an older-passenger demographic, more young people and families are setting sail for the 49th state, and children are a common sight aboard ship. Cruise lines have responded with youth programs and shore excursions that appeal to youngsters and their parents. Shore excursions have become more active, too, often incorporating activities families can enjoy together, such as bicycling, kayaking, and hiking. Many lines also offer pre- or post-cruise land tours as an optional package trip, and onboard entertainment and learning programs are extensive. Most also hire naturalists, historians, or local experts to lead discussions stimulated by the local environment.

Cruise ships may seem like floating resorts, but you can't check out and go elsewhere if you don't like your ship. The one you choose will be your home—it determines the type of accommodations you have, the kind of food you eat, the style of entertainment you see, and even the destinations you visit. If you don't enjoy your ship, you probably won't enjoy your cruise. That is why the most important choice you'll make when booking a cruise is the combined selection of cruise line and cruise ship.

CHOOSING YOUR CRUISE

Which cruise is right for you depends on numerous factors, notably your budget, the size and style of ship you choose, and the itinerary.

ITINERARIES

Cruise ships typically follow one of two itineraries in Alaska: round-trip Inside Passage loops and one-way Inside Passage–Gulf of Alaska cruises. Itineraries arc usually seven days, though some lines offer longer trips. ■ TIP→ Keep in mind that the landscape along the Inside Passage changes dramatically over the course of the summer cruise season. In May and June, you'll see snowcapped mountains and dramatic waterfalls from snowmelt cascading down the cliff faces, but by July and August most of the snow and some waterfalls will be gone.

The most popular Alaskan ports of call are Haines, Juneau, Skagway, Ketchikan, and Sitka. Lesser-known ports in British Columbia, such as Victoria and the charming fishing port of Prince Rupert, have begun to see more cruise traffic.

Small ships typically sail within Alaska, setting sail from Juneau or other Alaskan ports, stopping at the popular ports as well as smaller, less visited villages. Some expedition vessels focus on remote beaches and fjords, with few, if any, port calls.

ROUND-TRIP INSIDE PASSAGE LOOPS

A seven-day cruise typically starts and finishes in Vancouver, British Columbia, or Seattle, Washington. The first and last days are spent at sea, traveling to and from Alaska along the mountainous coast of British Columbia. Once in Alaska waters, most ships call at a different port on each of four days, and reserve one day for cruising in or near Glacier Bay National Park or another glacier-rich fjord.

ONE-WAY INSIDE PASSAGE–GULF OF ALASKA ITINERARIES

These cruises depart from Vancouver, Seattle, or, occasionally, San Francisco or Los Angeles, and finish at Seward or Whittier, the seaports for Anchorage (or vice versa). They're a good choice if you want to explore Alaska by land, either before or after your cruise. For this itinerary, you'll need to fly into and out of different cities (into Vancouver and out of Anchorage, for example), which can be pricier than round-trip airfare to and from the same city.

SMALL-SHIP ALASKA-ONLY ITINERARIES

Most small ships and yachts home port in Juneau or other Alaskan ports and offer a variety of one-way and round-trip cruises entirely within Alaska. A typical small-ship cruise is a seven-day, one way or round-trip from Juneau, stopping at several Inside Passage ports—including smaller ports skipped by large cruise ships.

SMALL-SHIP INSIDE PASSAGE REPOSITIONING CRUISES

Alaska's small cruise ships and yachts are based in Juneau or other Alaskan ports throughout the summer. In September they sail back to their winter homes in the Pacific Northwest; in May they return to Alaska via the Inside Passage. These repositioning trips are usually about 11 days and are sometimes discounted, because they take place during the shoulder season.

OTHER ITINERARIES

Although mainstream lines stick to the popular seven-day Alaskan itineraries, some smaller luxury or excursion lines add more exotic options. For example, you may find an occasional voyage across the Bering Sea to Japan and Asia. You can also create your own itinerary by taking an Alaska Marine Highway System ferry to ports of your choosing.

FERRY TRAVEL IN ALASKA

The cruise-ship season is over by October, but for independent, off-season ferry travel, November is the best month. After the stormy month of October, it's still relatively warm on the Inside Passage (temperatures will average about 40°F), and it's a good month for wildlife-watching. In particular, humpback whales are abundant off Sitka, and bald eagles congregate by the thousands near Haines.

INLAND CRUISE TOURS

Most cruise lines offer the option of independent, hosted, or fully escorted land tours before or after your cruise. Independent tours give you a preplanned itinerary with confirmed hotel and transportation arrangements, but you're free to follow your interests in each town. Hosted tours are similar, but tour-company representatives are available along the route for assistance. On fully escorted tours you travel with a group, led by a tour director. Activities are preplanned (and typically prepaid), so you have a good idea of how much your trip will cost (not counting some meals and incidentals) before departure. Most lines offer cruise-tour itineraries that include a ride aboard the Alaska Railroad.

Running between Anchorage, Denali National Park, and Fairbanks are Holland America Line's *McKinley Explorer,* Princess Tours' *Denali Express* and *McKinley Express,* and Royal Caribbean's *Wilderness Express,* which offer unobstructed views of the passing terrain and wildlife from private glass-dome railcars. Princess Cruises and Holland America Line have the most extensive Alaska cruise tours, owning and operating their own coaches, railcars, and lodges.

In addition to rail trips to Denali, Holland America offers tours into the Yukon, as well as river cruises on the Yukon River. Princess's cruise tours include trips to the Yukon and the Kenai Peninsula. Both lines offer land excursions across the Arctic Circle to Prudhoe Bay. Several cruise lines also offer pre- and post-cruise tours of the Canadian Rockies. Of the traditional cruise-ship fleets, Carnival Cruise Lines and Disney Cruise Line do not offer cruise-tour packages in Alaska at this writing. Many cruise lines also offer pre- or post-cruise hotel and sightseeing packages in Vancouver, Seattle, or Anchorage lasting one to three days.

SMALL-SHIP LINES

Most small-ship lines offer hotel add-ons, but not land tours.

DO-IT-YOURSELF LAND SEGMENTS

Independent travel by rental car or RV before or after a cruise is another option. Passengers who wish to do so generally begin or end their cruise in Anchorage, the most practical port city to use as a base for exploring Alaska. Almost any type of car or recreational vehicle can be rented here.

WHEN TO GO

Cruise season runs from mid-May to late September. The most popular sailing dates are from late June through August, when warm days are apt to be most plentiful. In spring, wildflowers are abundant, and you'll likely see more wildlife along the shore because the animals haven't yet migrated to higher elevations. May and June are traditionally drier than July and August. Alaska's early fall brings the splendor of autumn hues and the first snowfalls in the mountains. Animals return to low ground, and shorter days bring the possibility of seeing the northern lights. Daytime temperatures in May, June, and September are in the 50s and 60s. July and August averages are in the 60s and 70s, with occasional days in the 80s. Cruising in the low and shoulder seasons provides other advantages besides discounted fares: availability of ships and particular cabins is greater, and ports are almost completely free of tourists.

CRUISE COSTS

Average fares for Alaskan itineraries vary dramatically depending on when you sail, which ship and grade of cabin you choose, and when you book. Published rates are highest during June, July, and August; you'll pay less—and have more space on ship and ashore—if you sail in May or September.

Whenever you choose to sail, remember that the brochure price is the highest fare the line can charge for a given cruise. Most lines offer early-booking discounts. Although these vary tremendously, many lines will offer at least 10% off if you book ahead of time, usually by the end of January for a summer cruise. Sometimes you can book a discounted last-minute cruise if the ship hasn't filled all its cabins, but you won't get your pick of ships, cabins, or sailing dates. However, since some cruise lines will, if asked, refund the difference in fare or offer other credits and/or upgrades if the price drops after you've paid your deposit and before you make your final payment, there's little advantage in last-minute booking. Your travel agent should be your advocate in such instances.

TIPS

One of the most delicate—yet frequently debated—topics of conversation among cruise passengers involves the matter of tipping. Whom do you tip? How much? What's "customary" and "recommended"? Should parents tip the full amount for children, or is just half adequate? Why do you have to tip at all?

When transfers to and from your ship are a part of your air-and-sea program, gratuities are generally included for luggage handling. In that

CLOSE UP

Recommended Gratuities by Cruise Line

Each cruise line has a different tipping policy. Some allow you to add tips to your shipboard account, and others expect you to dole out the dollars in cash on the last night of the cruise. Here are the suggested tipping amounts for each line covered in this book. Gratuity recommendations are often higher if you're staying in a suite with extra services, such as a butler.

American Cruise Lines: $125 per person per week

Carnival Cruise Lines: $11.50 per person per day

Celebrity Cruises: $12–$15.50 per person per day

Disney Cruise Line: $12 per person per day

Holland America Line: $11.50–$12 per person per day

Lindblad Expeditions: $12–$15 per person per day

Norwegian Cruise Line: $12 per person per day

Oceania Cruises: $15–$22 per person per day

Princess Cruises: $11.50–$12 per person per day

Regent Seven Seas Cruises: No tipping expected

Royal Caribbean International: $12–$14.25 per person per day

Silversea Cruises: No tipping expected

Un-Cruise Adventures: 10% of the fare

case, do not worry about the interim tipping. However, if you take a taxi to the pier and hand over your bags to a stevedore, be sure to tip him. Treat him with respect and pass along at least $5.

During your cruise, room-service waiters generally receive a cash tip of $1 to $3 per delivery. A 15% to 18% gratuity will automatically be added to each bar bill during the cruise. If you use salon and spa services, a similar percentage might be added to the bills there as well. If you dine in a specialty restaurant, you may be asked to provide a one-time gratuity for the service staff.

Nowadays, tips for cruise staff generally add up to about $11.50 to $22 per person per day, depending on the category of your accommodations. You tip the same amount for each person who shares the cabin, including children, unless otherwise indicated. Most cruise lines now either automatically add gratuities to passengers' onboard charge accounts or offer the option.

EXTRAS

Cruise fares typically include accommodation, onboard meals and snacks, and most onboard activities. Not normally included are airfare, shore excursions, tips, soft drinks, alcoholic drinks, or spa treatments. Port fees, fuel surcharges, and sales taxes are generally added to your fare at booking.

CABINS

In years gone by, cabins were almost an afterthought. The general attitude of both passengers and the cruise lines used to be that a cabin is a cabin and is used only for changing clothes and sleeping. That's why the cabins on most older cruise ships are skimpy in size and short on amenities.

Most cabin layouts on a ship are identical or nearly so, but cabins with a commanding view fetch higher fares. But you should know that they are also more susceptible to side-to-side movement; in rough seas you could find yourself tossed right out of bed. On lower decks, you'll pay less and find more stability, particularly in the middle of the ship, but even upper-level cabins in the middle of the ship are more steady than others.

Forward cabins have a tendency to be oddly shaped, as they follow the contour of the bow. They are also likely to be noisy; when the ship's anchor drops, you won't need a wake-up call. In rough seas you can feel the ship's pitch (its upward and downward motion) more in the front.

Should you go for the stern location instead? You're more likely to hear engine and machinery noise there, but you may also feel the pitch and possibly some vibration. However, many passengers feel the view of the ship's wake (the ripples it leaves behind as its massive engines move it forward) is worth any noise or vibration they might encounter there.

Above all, don't be confused by all the categories listed in cruise-line brochures—the categories more accurately reflect price levels based on location than any physical differences in the cabins themselves (keep repeating: prefabricated). Shipboard accommodations fall into four basic configurations: inside cabins, outside cabins, balcony cabins, and suites.

INSIDE CABINS

An inside cabin has no window or porthole. These are always the least expensive cabins and are ideal for passengers who would rather spend their vacation funds on excursions or other incidentals than on upgraded accommodations. Inside cabins are generally just as spacious as outside cabins, and decor and amenities are similar. Parents sometimes book an inside cabin for their older children and teens, while their own cabin is an outside across the hall with a window or balcony.

OUTSIDE CABINS

A standard outside cabin has either a picture window or porthole. To give the illusion of more space, these cabins might also rely on the generous use of mirrors for an even airier feeling. Two twin beds can be joined together to create one large bed. Going one step further, standard and larger outside staterooms on modern ships are often out-fitted with a small sofa or loveseat with a cocktail table or small side table. Some larger cabins may have a combination bathtub–shower instead of just a shower.

BALCONY CABINS

A balcony—or veranda—cabin is an outside cabin with floor-to-ceiling glass doors that open onto a private deck. Although the cabin may have large expanses of glass, the balcony is sometimes cut out of the cabin's square footage (depending on the ship). Balconies are usually furnished with two chairs and a table for lounging and casual dining

DECIPHER YOUR DECK PLAN

LIDO DECK

The Lido Deck is a potential source of noise–deck chairs are set out early in the morning and put away late at night; the sound of chairs scraping on the floor of the Lido buffet can be an annoyance.

Music performances by poolside bands can often be heard on upper-deck balconies located immediately below.

UPPER DECK AFT

Take note of where lifeboats are located–views from some outside cabins can be partially, or entirely, obstructed by the boats.

Upper-deck cabins, as well as those far forward and far aft, are usually more susceptible to motion than those in the middle of the ship on a low deck.

Cabins near elevators or stairs are a double-edged sword. Being close by is a convenience; however, although the elevators aren't necessarily noisy, the traffic they attract can be.

Balcony cabins are indicated by a rectangle split into two sections. The small box is the balcony.

MAIN PUBLIC DECK

Cabins immediately below restaurants and dining rooms can be noisy. Late sleepers might be bothered by early breakfast noise, early sleepers by late diners.

Theaters and dining rooms are often located on middle or lower decks.

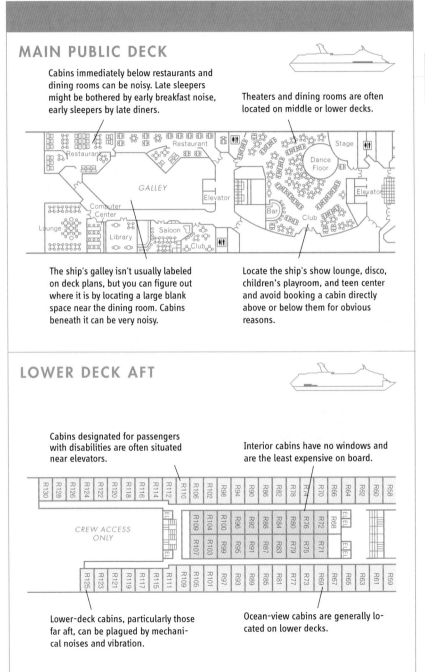

The ship's galley isn't usually labeled on deck plans, but you can figure out where it is by locating a large blank space near the dining room. Cabins beneath it can be very noisy.

Locate the ship's show lounge, disco, children's playroom, and teen center and avoid booking a cabin directly above or below them for obvious reasons.

LOWER DECK AFT

Cabins designated for passengers with disabilities are often situated near elevators.

Interior cabins have no windows and are the least expensive on board.

Lower-deck cabins, particularly those far aft, can be plagued by mechanical noises and vibration.

Ocean-view cabins are generally located on lower decks.

outdoors. However, you should be aware that balconies are not always completely private; sometimes your balcony is visible both from balconies next door and also from balconies above. The furnishings and amenities of balcony cabins are otherwise much like those in standard outside cabins.

SUITES

Suites are the most lavish accommodations afloat, and although suites are always larger than regular cabins, they do not always have separate rooms for sleeping. Suites almost always have amenities that standard cabins do not have. Depending on the cruise line, you may find a small refrigerator or minibar stocked with complimentary soft drinks, bottled water, and the alcoholic beverages of your choice. Top suites on some ships include complimentary laundry service and complex entertainment centers with large flat-screen TVs, DVD players, and CD stereo systems. An added bonus to the suite life is the extra level of services many ships offer. Little extras might include afternoon tea and evening canapés delivered to you and served by a white-gloved butler.

Although minisuites on most contemporary ships have separate sitting areas with a sofa, chair, and cocktail table, don't let the marketing skill of the cruise lines fool you: so-called minisuites are usually little more than slightly larger versions of standard balcony cabins and seldom include the extra services and elaborate amenities you can get in regular suites. They're still generally a good value for the price if space matters.

ACCESSIBILITY ISSUES

All major cruise lines offer a limited number of staterooms designed to be wheelchair- and scooter-accessible. Booking a newer vessel will generally assure more choices. On newer ships, public rooms are generally more accessible, and more facilities have been planned with wheelchair users in mind. Auxiliary aids, such as flashers for the hearing impaired and buzzers for visually impaired passengers, as well as lifts for swimming pools and hot tubs, are available. However, more than the usual amount of preplanning is necessary for smooth sailing if you have special needs.

For example, when a ship is unable to dock—as is the case in Sitka—passengers are taken ashore on tenders that are sometimes problematic even for the able-bodied to negotiate. Some people with limited mobility may find it difficult to embark or disembark the ship when docked because of the steep angle of the gangways during high or low tide at certain times of day. In some situations, crew members may offer assistance that involves carrying guests, but if the sea is choppy when tendering is a necessity, that might not be an option.

Passengers who require continuous oxygen or have service animals have further hurdles to overcome. You can bring both aboard a cruise ship, but you should be prepared to present up-to-date records for your service animal if they are requested.

BOOKING YOUR CRUISE

As a rule, the majority of cruisers plan their trips four to six months ahead of time. It follows, then, that a four- to six-month window should give you the pick of sailing dates, ships, itineraries, cabins, and flights to the port city. If you're looking for a standard itinerary and aren't choosy about the vessel or dates, you could wait for a last-minute discount, but they are harder to find than in the past.

2

If particular shore excursions are important to you, consider booking them when you book your cruise to avoid disappointment later.

USING A TRAVEL AGENT

Whether it is your first or 50th sailing, your best friend in booking a cruise is a knowledgeable travel agent. The last thing you want when considering a costly cruise vacation is an agent who has never been on a cruise, calls a cruise ship "the boat," or—worse still—quotes brochure rates. The most important steps in cruise-travel planning are research, research, and more research; your partner in this process is an experienced travel agent. Booking a cruise is a complex process, and it's seldom wise to try to go it alone, particularly the first time. But how do you find a cruise travel agent you can trust?

The most experienced and reliable agent will be certified as an Accredited Cruise Counselor (ACC), Master Cruise Counselor (MCC), or Elite Cruise Counselor (ECC) by CLIA (the Cruise Lines International Association). These agents have completed demanding training programs, including touring or sailing on a specific number of ships. Your agent should also belong to a professional trade organization. In North America, membership in the American Society of Travel Agents (ASTA) indicates that an agency has pledged to follow the code of ethics set forth by the world's largest association for travel professionals. In the best of all worlds, your travel agent is affiliated with both ASTA and CLIA.

Contrary to what conventional wisdom might suggest, cutting out the travel agent and booking directly with a cruise line won't necessarily get you the lowest price. Approximately 90% of all cruise bookings are still handled through travel agents. In fact, cruise-line reservation systems simply are not capable of dealing with tens of thousands of direct calls from potential passengers. Without an agent working on your behalf, you're on your own. Do not rely solely on Internet message boards for authoritative responses to your questions—that is a service more accurately provided by your travel agent.

Travel Agent Professional Organization American Society of Travel Agents (*ASTA* ☎ *703/739–2782, 800/965–2782 24-hr hotline* ⊕ *www.travelsense.org*).

Cruise Line Organizations Cruise Lines International Association (*CLIA* ☎ *754/224–2200* ⊕ *www.cruising.org*).

BOOKING YOUR CRUISE ONLINE

In addition to local travel agencies, there are many hardworking, dedicated travel professionals working for websites. Both big-name travel sellers and mom-and-pop agencies compete for the attention of cyber-savvy clients, and it never hurts to compare prices from a variety of these sources. Some cruise lines even allow you to book directly with them through their websites.

As a rule, Web-based and toll-free brokers will do a decent job for you. They often offer discounted fares, though not always the lowest, so it pays to check around. If you know precisely what you want and how much you should pay to get a real bargain—and you don't mind dealing with an anonymous voice on the phone—by all means make your reservations when the price is right. Just don't expect the personal service you get from an agent you know. Also, be prepared to spend a lot of time and effort on the phone if something goes wrong.

BEFORE YOU GO

To expedite your preboarding paperwork, some cruise lines have convenient forms on their websites. As long as you have your reservation number, you can provide the required immigration information (usually your citizenship information and passport number), reserve shore excursions, and even indicate any special requests from the comfort of your home. Less-wired cruise lines might mail preboarding paperwork to you or your travel agent for completion after you make your final payment and request that you return the forms by mail or fax. No matter how you submit them, be sure to make hard copies of any forms you fill out and bring them with you to the pier to smooth the embarkation process.

WHAT TO PACK

Don't forget your valid passport; American and Canadian citizens are now required to provide proof of citizenship regardless of whether their Alaska cruise is crossing international boundaries. Although disposable and small digital cameras are very handy for candid shots, they are not much good for catching wildlife from afar. A good zoom lens can be heavy, but can make all the difference. Even if you have a high-quality camera, pack binoculars for everyone. Be sure to take bug spray during the summer months, as the mosquitoes are large, plentiful, and fierce.

WHAT TO WEAR

When preparing for your Alaska cruise, remember this first rule of Alaskan thumb: be an onion. Never leave the ship without dressing in layers. Your first layer should be thin and airy so that if it gets warm, your skin can breathe. Every layer over that, however, should aim to keep you warm and dry. In Alaska it is quite common for a hot and sunny day to change abruptly. For onboard dress, follow your cruise line's suggestions about what to bring for the evening or two you might need to wear something formal to dinner.

CLOSE UP

Before You Book

If you've decided to use a travel agent, ask yourself these 10 simple questions, and you'll be better prepared to help the agent do his or her job.

1. Who will be going on the cruise?

2. What can you afford to spend for the entire trip?

3. Where would you like to go?

4. How much vacation time do you have?

5. When can you get away?

6. What are your interests?

7. Do you prefer a casual or structured vacation?

8. What kind of accommodations do you want?

9. What are your dining preferences?

10. How will you get to the embarkation port?

INSURANCE

It's a good idea to purchase travel insurance, which covers a variety of possible hazards and mishaps, when you book a cruise. Any policy should insure you for travel and luggage delays. A travel policy will ensure that you can get to the next port of call should you miss your ship, or replace delayed necessities secure in the knowledge that you will be reimbursed for those unexpected expenditures. Save your receipts for all out-of-pocket expenses to file your claim, and be sure to get an incident report from the airline at fault.

Insurance should also cover you for unexpected injuries and illnesses. The medical insurance program you depend on at home might not extend coverage beyond the borders of the United States (many Alaska cruises stop in Canada). Medicare assuredly will not cover you if you are hurt or sick while abroad. It is worth noting that all ships of foreign registry are considered to be "outside the United States" by Medicare.

Nearly all cruise lines offer their own line of insurance. Compare the coverage and rates to determine which is best for you. Keep in mind that insurance purchased from an independent carrier is more likely to include coverage if the cruise line goes out of business before or during your cruise. Although it is a rare and unlikely occurrence, you do want to be insured in the event that it happens.

U.S. Travel Insurers Allianz Travel Insurance (800/284–8300 www.allianztravelinsurance.com). **CSA Travel Protection** (800/711–1197 www.csatravelprotection.com). **HTH Worldwide** (610/254–8700 or 888/243–2358 www.hthworldwide.com). **Travelex Insurance** (800/228–9792 www.travelex-insurance.com). **Travel Guard International** (715/345–0505 or 800/826–4919 www.travelguard.com). **Travel Insured International** (800/243–3174 www.travelinsured.com).

ARRIVING AND EMBARKING

Most cruise-ship passengers fly to the port of embarkation. If you book your cruise far enough in advance, you'll be given the opportunity to purchase an air-and-sea package, which may—or may not—save you money on your flight. You might get a lower fare by booking your air independently, so it's a good idea to check for the best fare available. Independent air arrangements might save you enough to cover the cost of a hotel room in your embarkation port so you can arrive early. It's not a bad idea to arrive a day early to overcome any jet lag and avoid the possibility of delayed flights.

If you buy an air-and-sea package from your cruise line, a uniformed cruise-line agent will meet you at baggage claim to smooth your way from airport to pier. You will need to claim your own bags and give them to the transfer driver so they can be loaded onto the bus. On arrival at the pier, luggage is automatically transferred to the ship for delivery to your cabin. The cruise-line ground transfer system can also be available to independent fliers. However, be sure to ask your travel agent how much it costs; you may find that a taxi or shuttle service is less expensive and more convenient.

GETTING TO THE PORT

Even if you opt to purchase your own airfare without an air-and-sea package, you can usually still access the cruise's transfer service, but it might cost more than a cab or shuttle.

BOARDING

The lines at check-in can be long (up to an hour of wait time) if you are boarding a large cruise ship. You'll be issued a boarding card that doubles as your stateroom key and shipboard charge card. Either before you enter the check-in area or before proceeding to the ship, you and your hand luggage will pass through a security checkpoint. Once you're on board, you'll produce your boarding card once more before heading to your cabin. On a small-ship cruise, embarkation is much more relaxed and relatively line-free.

ON BOARD

Check out your cabin to make sure that everything is in order. Try the plumbing and set the thermostat to the temperature you prefer. Your cabin may feel warm while docked but will cool off when the ship is under way. You should find a copy of the ship's daily schedule in the cabin. Take a few moments to look it over—you will want to know what time the lifeboat (or muster) drill takes place (a placard on the back of your cabin door will indicate directions to your emergency station), as well as meal hours and the schedule for various activities and entertainments.

ONBOARD EXTRAS

As you budget for your trip, keep these likely additional costs in mind.

Cocktails: $6–$10

Wine by the glass: $7–$9

Beer: $5–$6

Bottled water: $2.50–$4

Soft drinks: $2–$2.50

Specialty ice cream and coffee: $4–$6

Laundry: $1–$10 per piece (where self-launder facilities are unavailable)

Spa treatments: $125–$199

Salon services: $30–$100

Casino gambling: 5¢ to $10 for slot machines; $5 and up for table games

Bingo: $5–$10 per card for multiple games in each session

Rented tuxedoes are either hanging in the closet or will be delivered sometime during the afternoon; bon voyage gifts sent by your friends or travel agent should appear as well. Be patient if you are expecting deliveries, particularly on megaships. Cabin stewards participate in the ship's turnaround and are extremely busy, although yours will no doubt introduce himself at the first available opportunity. It will also be a while before your checked luggage arrives, so your initial order of business is usually the buffet, if you haven't already had lunch. Bring along the daily schedule to check over while you eat.

While making your way to the Lido buffet, no doubt you'll notice bar waiters offering trays of colorful bon voyage drinks, often in souvenir glasses that you can keep. Beware—they are not complimentary! If you choose one, you will be asked to sign for it. Like the boarding photos, you are under no obligation to purchase.

Do your plans for the cruise include booking shore excursions and indulging in spa treatments? The most popular tours sometimes sell out, and spas can be busy during sea days, so your next stops should be the Shore Excursion Desk to book tours and the spa to make appointments if you didn't already book your spa visits and excursions in advance.

Dining room seating arrangements are another matter for consideration. If you aren't happy with your assigned dinner seating, speak to the maitre d'. The daily schedule will indicate where and when to meet with him. If you plan to dine in the ship's specialty restaurant, make those reservations as soon as possible to avoid disappointment.

PAYING FOR THINGS ON BOARD

Because cashless society prevails on cruise ships, during check-in an imprint is made of your credit card or you place a cash deposit for use against your onboard charges. Most onboard expenditures are charged to your shipboard account (via a swipe of your key card) with your signature as verification, with the exception of some casino gaming.

Drinking and Gambling Ages

Many underage passengers have learned to their chagrin that the rules that apply on land are also adhered to at sea. On most mainstream cruise ships you must be 21 to imbibe alcoholic beverages. There are exceptions—for instance, on cruises departing from countries where the legal drinking age is typically lower than 21. On some cruise lines, a parent who is sailing with his or her son(s) and/or daughter(s) who is between the ages of 18 and 20 may sign a waiver allowing the 18- to 20-year-old to consume alcoholic beverages, generally limited to beer and wine. However, by and large, if you haven't achieved the magic age of 21, your shipboard charge card will be coded as booze-free, and bartenders won't risk their jobs to sell you alcohol.

Gambling is a bit looser, and 18-year-olds can try their luck on cruise lines such as Carnival, Celebrity, Holland America, Norwegian, Royal Caribbean, and Silversea; most other cruise lines adhere to the age-21 minimum. Casinos are trickier to patrol than bars, though, and minors who look old enough may get away with dropping a few coins in an out-of-the-way slot machine before being spotted on a hidden security camera. If you hit a big jackpot, you may have a lot of explaining to do to your parents.

You'll get an itemized bill listing your purchases at the end of the voyage, and any discrepancies can be discussed at the purser's desk. To save time, check the balance of your shipboard account before the last day by requesting an interim printout of your bill from the purser to ensure accuracy. On some ships you can even access your account on your stateroom television.

DINING

All food, all the time? Not quite, but it is possible to literally eat away the day and most of the night on a cruise. A popular cruise directors' joke is "You came on as passengers, and you will be leaving as cargo." Although it is meant in fun, it does contain a ring of truth. Food—tasty and plentiful—is available 24 hours a day on most cruise ships, and the dining experience at sea has reached almost mythic proportions. Perhaps it has something to do with legendary midnight buffets and the absence of menu prices, or maybe it's the vast selection and availability.

RESTAURANTS

Every ship has at least one main restaurant and a Lido, or casual buffet alternative. Increasingly important are specialty restaurants. Meals in the primary and buffet restaurants are included in the cruise fare, as are round-the-clock room service, midday tea and snacks, and late-night buffets. Most mainstream cruise lines levy a surcharge for dining in alternative restaurants that may also include a gratuity, although there generally is no additional charge on luxury cruise lines.

You may also find a pizzeria or a specialty coffee bar on your ship— increasingly popular favorites cropping up on ships old and new.

Although pizza is complimentary, expect an additional charge for specialty coffees at the coffee bar and, quite likely, in the dining room as well. You will also likely be charged for sodas and drinks other than iced tea, regular coffee, tap water, and fruit juice during meals.

There is often a direct relationship between the cost of a cruise and the quality of its cuisine. The food is sophisticated on some (mostly expensive) lines, among them Regent Seven Seas and Silversea. In the more moderate price range, Celebrity Cruises has always been known for its fine cuisine, and Oceania Cruises scores high marks as well. The trend toward featuring specialty dishes and even entire menus designed by acclaimed chefs has spread throughout the cruise industry; however, on most mainstream cruise lines the food is of the quality that you would find in any good hotel banquet—perfectly acceptable but certainly not great.

DINNER SEATINGS

If your cruise ship has traditional seatings for dinner, the one decision that may set the tone for your entire cruise is your dinner seating. Which is best? Early dinner seating is generally scheduled between 6 and 6:30 pm, and late seating can begin from 8:15 to 8:45 pm.

Families with young children and older passengers often choose an early seating. Early-seating diners are encouraged not to linger too long over dessert and coffee, because the dining room has to be readied for late seating. Late seating is viewed by some passengers as more romantic and less rushed.

Cruise lines understand that strict schedules no longer satisfy the desires of all modern cruise passengers. Most cruise lines now include alternatives to the set schedules in the dining room, including casual dinner menus in their buffet facilities where more flexibility is allowed in dress and mealtimes. Open seating is the norm on more upscale lines; it allows passengers the flexibility to dine any time during restaurant hours and be seated with whomever they please.

However, led by Norwegian Cruise Line and Princess Cruises, more contemporary and premium cruise lines offer adaptations of open seating to offer variety and a more personalized experience for their passengers.

SPECIALTY RESTAURANTS

A growing trend in shipboard dining is the emergence of sophisticated specialty restaurants that require reservations and frequently charge a fee. From as little as $25 per person for a complete steak dinner to $200 per person for an elaborate gourmet meal including vintage wines paired with each course, specialty restaurants offer a refined dining option that cannot be duplicated in your ship's main restaurants. If you anticipate dining in your ship's intimate specialty restaurant, make reservations as soon as possible to avoid disappointment.

SPECIAL DIETS

Cruise lines make every possible attempt to ensure dining satisfaction. If you have special dietary considerations—such as low-salt, kosher, or food allergies—be sure to indicate them well ahead of time and check to be certain your needs are known by your waiter once on board. In addition to the usual menu items, so-called "spa," low-calorie, low-carbohydrate, or low-fat selections, as well as children's menus, are usually available. Requests for dishes not featured on the menu can often be granted if you ask in advance.

ALCOHOL

On all but the most upscale lines, you pay for alcohol aboard the ship, including wine with dinner. Wine typically costs about what you would expect to pay at a nice lounge or restaurant in a resort or in a major city. Wine by the bottle is a more economical choice at dinner than ordering it by the glass. Any wine you don't finish will be kept for you and served the next night. Gifts of wine or champagne ordered from the cruise line (either by you, a friend, or your travel agent) can be taken to the dining room. Wine from any other source will incur a corkage fee of approximately $10 to $25 per bottle. Some (though not all) lines will allow you to carry wine aboard when you embark for the first time; almost no line allows you to carry other alcohol on board.

ENTERTAINMENT

It's hard to imagine, but in the early years of cruise travel, shipboard entertainment consisted of little more than poetry readings and passenger talent shows. Those days are long gone. These days, seven-night cruises usually include two original production shows. One of these might be a Las Vegas–style extravaganza and the other a best-of-Broadway show featuring old and new favorites from the Great White Way. Other shows highlight the talents of individual singers, dancers, magicians, comedians, and even acrobats.

Real treats are the folkloric shows or other entertainments arranged to take place while cruise ships are in port. Local performers come aboard, usually shortly before the ship sails, to present traditional songs and dances. It's an excellent way to get a glimpse of their performing arts.

Most ships also have movie nights or in-cabin movies, or you may be able to rent or borrow movies to watch on your in-cabin DVD player, if you have one. The latest twist in video programming can be found on some Princess, Disney, and Carnival ships—huge outdoor LED screens where movies, music video concerts, news channels, and even the ship's activities are broadcast for passengers lounging poolside.

Enrichment programs have also become a popular pastime at sea. It may come as a surprise that port lecturers on many large contemporary cruise ships offer more information on shore tours and shopping than insight into the ports of call. If more cerebral presentations are important to you, consider a cruise on a line that features stimulating enrichment programs and seminars at sea. Speakers can include destination-oriented historians, popular authors, business leaders, radio or television personalities, and even movie stars.

CLOSE UP

Will I Get Seasick?

Many first-time passengers are anxious about whether they'll be stricken by seasickness, but there is no way to tell until you actually sail. Modern vessels are equipped with stabilizers that eliminate much of the motion responsible for seasickness. On an Alaska cruise you will spend most of your time in calm, sheltered waters, so unless your cruise includes time out in the open sea (say, between San Francisco and Vancouver), you may not even feel the ship's movement—particularly if your ship is a megaliner. You may feel slightly more movement on a small ship, but not by much, as these ships ply remote bays and coves that are even more sheltered than those traveled by regular cruise ships.

If you have a history of seasickness, don't book an inside cabin. For the terminally seasick, it will begin to resemble a movable coffin in short order. If you do become seasick, you can use common drugs such as Dramamine and Bonine. Some people find anti-seasickness wristbands helpful; these apply gentle pressure to the wrist in lieu of drugs. Worn behind the ear, the Transderm Scop patch dispenses a continuous metered dose of medication, which is absorbed into the skin and enters the bloodstream. Apply the patch four hours before sailing and it will continue to be effective for three days.

LOUNGES AND NIGHTCLUBS

You'll often find live entertainment in the ship lounges after dinner (and even sometimes before dinner). If you want to unleash your inner American Idol, look for karaoke. Singing along in a lively piano bar is another shipboard favorite for would-be crooners.

Other lounges might feature easy-listening or jazz performances or live music for pre- and post-dinner social dancing. Later in the evening, lounges pick up the pace with music from the 1950s and 60s; clubs aimed at a younger crowd usually have more contemporary dance music during the late-night hours.

CASINOS

On most ships, lavish casinos pulsate with activity. On ships that feature them, the rationale for locating casinos where most passengers must pass either through or alongside them is obvious—the unspoken allure of winning. In addition to slot machines in a variety of denominations, cruise-ship casinos usually have table games. Casino hours vary based on the itinerary or location of the ship; most are required to close while in port, whereas others may be able to offer 24-hour slot machines and simply close table games. Every casino has a cashier, and you may be able to charge a cash advance to your onboard account, for a fee.

SPORTS AND FITNESS

Onboard sports facilities might include a court for basketball, volleyball, tennis—or all three—a jogging track, or even an in-line skating track. Some ships are even offering innovative and unexpected features, such as rock-climbing walls, bungee trampolines, and surfing pools on some Royal Caribbean ships. For the less adventurous, there's always table tennis and shuffleboard.

Naturally, you will find at least one swimming pool, and possibly several. Cruise-ship pools are generally on the small side—more appropriate for cooling off than doing laps—and the majority contain filtered salt water. But some are elaborate affairs, with waterslides and interactive water play areas for family fun. Princess Grand–class ships have challenging, freshwater "swim against the current" pools for swimming enthusiasts who want to get their low-impact exercise while on board.

Shipboard fitness centers have become ever more elaborate, offering state-of-the-art exercise machines, treadmills, and stair steppers, not to mention weights and weight machines. As a bonus, many fitness centers with floor-to-ceiling windows have the world's most inspiring sea views. Most ships offer complimentary fitness classes, but you might also find classes in Pilates, spinning, or yoga (usually for a fee). Personal trainers are usually on board to get you off on the right foot, also for a fee.

On small-ship lines in Alaska you are likely to find fitness equipment outside on the top deck where your ship may also have a hot tub, but you'll rarely, if ever, find a swimming pool. Treks ashore and kayaking are often the preferred exercise options.

SPAS

With all the usual pampering and service in luxurious surroundings, simply being on a cruise can be a stress-reducing experience. Add to that the menu of spa and salon services at your fingertips and you have a recipe for total sensory pleasure. Spas have also become among the most popular of shipboard areas. Steiner Leisure is the largest spa and salon operator at sea (the company also operates the Mandara and the Greenhouse spa brands), with facilities on more than 100 cruise ships worldwide.

In addition to facials, manicures, pedicures, massages, and sensual body treatments, other hallmarks of Steiner Leisure are salon services and products for hair and skin. Founded in 1901 by Henry Steiner of London, a single salon prospered when Steiner's son joined the business in 1926 and was granted a Royal Warrant as hairdresser to Her Majesty Queen Mary in 1937. In 1956 Steiner won its first cruise-ship contract to operate the salon on board the ships of the Cunard Line. By the mid-1990s Steiner Leisure began taking an active role in creating shipboard spas offering a wide variety of wellness therapies and beauty programs for both women and men.

CLOSE UP

Safety at Sea

Safety begins with you, the passenger. Once settled into your cabin, locate your life vests if they are stored there, and review the posted emergency instructions. Make sure the vests are in good condition, and learn how to secure them properly. Make certain the ship's purser knows if you have a physical infirmity that may hamper a speedy exit from your cabin, so that in an emergency he or she can quickly dispatch a crew member to assist you. If you're traveling with children, be sure that child-size life jackets are placed in your cabin.

Before your ship leaves the embarkation port, you'll be required to attend a mandatory lifeboat drill. Do so and listen carefully. If you're unsure about how to use your vest, now is the time to ask. Some cruise lines no longer require you to bring your vest to the muster drill and instead store them near the muster station, but crew members are more than willing to assist if you have questions. Only in the most extreme circumstances will you need to abandon ship—but it has happened. The time you spend learning the procedure may serve you well in a mishap.

In actuality, the greatest danger facing cruise-ship passengers is fire. All cruise lines must meet international standards for fire safety, which require sprinkler systems, smoke detectors, and other safety features. Fires on cruise ships are not common, but they do happen, and these rules have made ships much safer. You can do your part by *not* using an iron in your cabin and taking care to properly extinguish smoking materials. Never throw a lighted cigarette overboard—it could be blown back into an opening in the ship and start a fire.

OTHER SHIPBOARD SERVICES

COMMUNICATIONS

Just because you are out to sea does not mean you have to be out of touch. However, ship-to-shore telephone calls can cost $2 to $15 a minute, so it makes more economic sense to use email to remain in contact with your home or office. Most ships have basic computer systems, and some newer vessels offer more high-tech connectivity—even in-cabin hookups or wireless connections for either your own laptop computer or one you can rent on board. Expect to pay an activation fee and subsequent charges in the 75¢- to $1-per-minute range for the use of these Internet services. Ships usually offer some kind of package so that you get a reduced per-minute price if you pay a fee up front.

The ability to use your own mobile phone for calls from the high seas is an alternative that is gaining in popularity. It's usually cheaper than using a cabin phone if your ship offers the service; however, it can still cost $2.50 to $5 a minute. A rather ingenious concept, the ship acts as a cell "tower" in international waters—you use your own cell phone and your own number when roaming at sea, and you can even send and receive text messages and email with some smartphones (albeit with a surcharge in addition to any roaming fees). Before leaving home, ask your cell-phone service provider to activate international roaming on

FODOR'S CRUISE PREPARATION TIME LINE

3 TO 4 MONTHS BEFORE SAILING

■ Check with your travel agent or the State Department for the identification required for your cruise.

■ Gather the necessary identification you need. If you need to replace a lost birth certificate, apply for a new passport, or renew one that's about to expire, start the paperwork now. Doing it at the last minute is stressful and often costly.

60 TO 75 DAYS BEFORE SAILING

■ Make the final payment on your cruise fare. Though the dates vary, your travel agent should remind you when the payment date draws near. Failure to submit the balance on time can result in the cancellation of your reservation.

■ Make a packing list for each person you'll be packing for.

■ Begin your wardrobe planning now. Try things on to make sure they fit and are in good repair (it's amazing how stains can magically appear months after something has been dry cleaned). Set things aside.

■ If you need to shop, get started so you have time to find just the right thing (and perhaps to return or exchange just the right thing). You may also need to allow time for alterations.

■ Make kennel reservations for your pets. (If you're traveling during a holiday period, you may need to do this even earlier.)

■ Arrange for a house sitter.

If you're cruising, but your kids are staying home:

■ Make child care arrangements.

■ Go over children's schedules to make sure they'll have everything they need while you're gone (gift for a birthday party, supplies for a school project, permission slip for a field trip).

■ If you have small children, you may want to put together a small bag of treats for them to open while you're gone—make a tape of yourself reading a favorite bedtime story or singing a lullaby (as long as it's you, it will sound fantastic to them).

30 DAYS BEFORE SAILING

■ If you purchased an air-and-sea package, call your travel agent for the details of your airline schedule. Request seat assignments.

■ If your children are sailing with you, check their wardrobes now (do it too early and the really little kids may actually grow out of garments).

■ Make appointments for any personal services you wish to have before your cruise (for example, a haircut or manicure).

■ Get out your luggage and check the locks and zippers. Check for anything that might have spilled inside on a previous trip.

■ If you need new luggage or want an extra piece to bring home souvenirs, purchase it now.

2 TO 4 WEEKS BEFORE SAILING

■ Receive your cruise documents through the travel agent or print them from the cruise line's website.

■ Examine the documents for accuracy (correct cabin number, sailing date, and dining arrangements); make sure names are spelled correctly. If there's something you do not understand, ask now.

■ Read all the literature in your document package for suggestions specific to your cruise. Most cruise lines include helpful information.

■ Pay any routine bills that may be due while you're gone.

■ Go over your personalized packing list again. Finish shopping.

2

1 WEEK BEFORE SAILING
■ Finalize your packing list and continue organizing everything in one area.

■ Buy film or digital media and check the batteries in your camera.

■ Refill prescription medications with an adequate supply.

■ Make two photocopies of your passport or ID and credit cards. Leave one copy with a friend and carry the other copy separately from the originals.

■ Get cash and/or traveler's checks at the bank. If you use traveler's checks, keep a separate record of the serial numbers. Get a supply of one-dollar bills for tipping baggage handlers (at the airport, hotel, pier, etc.).

■ You may also want to put valuables and jewelry that you won't be taking with you in the safety deposit box while you're at the bank.

■ Arrange to have your mail held at the post office or ask a neighbor to pick it up.

■ Stop newspaper delivery or ask a neighbor to bring it in for you.

■ Arrange for lawn and houseplant care or snow removal during your absence (if necessary).

■ Leave your itinerary, the ship's telephone number (plus the name of your ship and your stateroom number), and a house key with a relative or friend.

■ If traveling with young children, purchase small games or toys to keep them occupied while en route to your embarkation port.

3 DAYS BEFORE SAILING
■ Confirm your airline flights; departure times are sometimes subject to change.

■ Put a card with your name, address, telephone number, and itinerary inside each suitcase.

■ Fill out the luggage tags that came with your document packet, and follow the instructions regarding when and how to attach them.

■ Complete any other paperwork that the cruise line included with your documents (foreign customs and immigration forms, onboard charge application, etc.). Do not wait until you're standing in the pier check-in line to fill them in!

■ Do last-minute laundry and tidy up the house.

■ Pull out the luggage and begin packing.

THE DAY BEFORE SAILING
■ Take pets to the kennel.

■ Water houseplants and lawn (if necessary).

■ Dispose of any perishable food in the refrigerator.

■ Mail any last-minute bills.

■ Set timers for indoor lights.

■ Reorganize your wallet. Remove anything you will not need (local affinity cards, department store or gas credit cards, etc.), and put them in an envelope.

■ Finish packing and lock your suitcases.

DEPARTURE DAY
■ Adjust the thermostat and double-check the door locks.

■ Turn off the water if there's danger of frozen pipes while you're away.

■ Arrange to be at the airport a minimum of two hours before your departure time (follow the airline's instructions).

■ Have photo ID and/or your passport ready for airport check-in.

■ Slip your car keys, parking claim checks, and airline tickets into your carry-on luggage. Never pack these items in checked luggage.

CLOSE UP

Crime on Ships

Crime aboard cruise ships has occasionally become headline news, thanks in large part to a few well-publicized cases. Most people never have any type of problem, but you should exercise the same precautions aboard ship that you would at home. Keep your valuables out of sight—on big ships virtually every cabin has a small safe. Don't carry too much cash ashore, use your credit card whenever possible, and keep your money in a secure place, such as a front pocket that's harder to pick. Single women traveling with friends should stick together, especially when returning to their cabins late at night. When assaults occur, it often comes to light that excessive drinking of alcohol is a factor. Be careful about whom you befriend, as you would anywhere, whether it's a fellow passenger or a member of the crew. Don't be paranoid, but do be prudent.

Your cruise is a wonderful opportunity to leave everyday responsibilities behind, but don't neglect to pack your common sense. After a few drinks it might seem like a good idea to sit on a railing or lean over the rail to get a better view of the ship's wake. Passengers have been known to fall. "Man overboard" is more likely to be the result of carelessness than criminal intent.

your account. When in port, depending on the type of cell phone you own and the agreements your mobile service-provider has established, you may be able to connect to local networks in Alaska. Most GSM phones are also usable in Canada. Rates for using the maritime service, as well as any roaming charges from Alaskan and Canadian cities, are established by your mobile service carrier and are worth checking into before your trip. To avoid excessive charges, it's a good idea to turn off your phone's data roaming option while at sea.

LAUNDRY AND DRY CLEANING

Most cruise ships offer valet laundry and pressing (and some also offer dry-cleaning) service. Expenses can add up fast, especially for laundry, since charges are per item and the rates are similar to those charged in hotels, unless your ship offers a fixed-price laundry deal (all you can stuff into a bag they provide for a single fee). If doing laundry is important to you and you do not want to send it out to be done, many cruise ships have a self-service laundry room (which usually features an iron and ironing board in addition to washer and dryer). If you book one of the top-dollar suites, laundry service may be included for no additional cost. Upscale ships such as those in the Regent Seven Seas Cruises and Silversea Cruises fleets have complimentary self-service launderettes. On other cruise lines, such as Princess Cruises, Oceania Cruises, Carnival Cruise Lines, and Holland America Line (except Vista-class and Signature-class ships), you can do your own laundry for about $3 or less per load. None of the vessels in the Norwegian, Royal Caribbean, or Celebrity Cruises fleets has self-service laundry facilities.

DISEMBARKATION

All cruises come to an end eventually, and the disembarkation process actually begins the day before you arrive at your ship's final port. During that day your cabin steward delivers special luggage tags to your stateroom, along with customs forms and instructions on some itineraries.

The night before you disembark, you'll need to set aside clothing to wear the next morning when you leave the ship. Many people dress in whatever casual outfits they wear for the final dinner on board, or change into travel clothes after dinner. Also, do not forget to put your passport or other proof of citizenship, airline tickets, and medications in your hand luggage. The luggage tags go onto your larger bags, which are placed outside your stateroom door for pickup during the hours indicated. Your cruise line may offer self-assist debarkation, and in that case, you do not have to put your luggage outside your stateroom the night before departure and may leave the ship early if you can take all your luggage with you.

A statement itemizing your onboard charges is delivered before you arise on disembarkation morning. Plan to get up early enough to check it over for accuracy, finish packing your personal belongings, and vacate your stateroom by the appointed hour. Any discrepancies in your onboard account should be taken care of before leaving the ship, usually at the purser's desk. Breakfast is served in the main restaurant as well as the buffet on the last morning, but room service usually isn't available. Disembarkation procedures vary by cruise line, but you'll probably have to wait in a lounge or on deck for your tag color or number to be called.

Then you take a taxi, bus, or other transportation to your post-cruise hotel or to the airport for your flight home. If you are flying out the day your cruise ends, leave plenty of time to go through the usual check-in, passport control/immigration, and security procedures at the airport.

CUSTOMS AND DUTIES

U.S. CUSTOMS

If your cruise includes a stop in Canada, each individual or family must fill out a customs declaration form, which will be provided before your ship docks. Be sure to keep receipts for all purchases made outside the United States; you may also be asked to show officials what you've bought. After showing your passport to Canadian immigration officials upon debarkation, you must collect your luggage from the dock. If your ship sails round-trip from Vancouver, you will not go through U.S. Customs and Immigration until you reach the Vancouver airport. Once you've completed the process there, you will board what is essentially a "domestic" flight to the United States with no further U.S. Customs and Immigration procedure upon arrival.

ALLOWANCES

You're always allowed to bring goods of a certain value back home without having to pay any duty or import tax. But there's a limit on the amount of tobacco and liquor you can bring back duty-free. The values of so-called "duty-free" goods are included in these amounts. When you shop abroad, save all your receipts, as customs inspectors may ask to see them as well as the items you purchased. If the total value of your goods is more than the duty-free limit, you'll have to pay a tax (most often a flat percentage) on the value of everything beyond that limit. For U.S. citizens who have been out of the country for at least 48 hours, the duty-free exemption is $800. For visits of less than 48 hours, the allowance is only $200. But the duty-free exemption includes only one carton of 200 cigarettes, 100 cigars, and 1 liter of alcohol (this includes wine); above these limits, you have to pay duties, even if you didn't spend more than the limit allowed.

2

ALASKA CRUISE SHIPS AND ITINERARIES			
SHIP	EMBARKATION PORT	DURATION IN NIGHTS	ITINERARY AND PORTS OF CALL
American Cruise Lines			
American Spirit	Juneau	7	Round-trip: Skagway, Glacier Bay, Icy Strait Point, Haines, Petersburg, Sawyer Glacier
	Seattle	11	Northbound: Anacortes, WA, Friday Harbor, WA, Ketchikan, Wrangell, Petersburg, Tracy Arm, Angoon, Icy Strait Point, Juneau
	Juneau	11	Southbound: Ketchikan, Wrangell, Petersburg, Tracy Arm, Angoon, Icy Strait Point, Anacortes, WA, Friday Harbor, WA, Seattle
Carnival Cruise Lines			
Carnival Miracle	Seattle	7	Round-trip: Juneau, Skagway, Ketchikan, Victoria, BC, Sawyer Glacier
Celebrity Cruises			
Celebrity Solstice	Seattle	7	Round-trip: Ketchikan, Juneau, Skagway, Victoria, BC, Sawyer Glacier
Celebrity Century	Vancouver	7	Round-trip: Ketchikan, Juneau, Icy Strait Point, Hubbard Glacier
Celebrity Millennium	Vancouver	7	Northbound: Skagway, Juneau, Ketchikan, Icy Strait Point, Hubbard Glacier
	Seward	7	Southbound: Skagway, Juneau, Ketchikan, Icy Strait Point, Hubbard Glacier
Disney Cruise Line			
Disney Wonder	Vancouver	7	Round-trip: Ketchikan, Juneau, Skagway, Sawyer Glacier
Holland America Line			
Amsterdam	Seattle	14	Round-trip: Ketchikan, Juneau, Skagway, Sawyer Glacier, Hubbard Glacier, Sitka, Icy Strait Point, Anchorage, Homer, Kodiak, Victoria, BC
	Seattle	7	Round-trip: Juneau, Sitka, Ketchikan, Sawyer Glacier, Victoria, BC
Oosterdam	Vancouver	7	Northbound: Juneau, Ketchikan, Skagway, Glacier Bay, Seward
	Seward	7	Southbound: Glacier Bay, Haines, Juneau, Ketchikan, Vancouver
Statendam	Vancouver	7	Northbound: Skagway, Juneau, Ketchikan, Glacier Bay
	Seward	7	Southbound: Haines, Juneau, Ketchikan, Glacier Bay

ALASKA CRUISE SHIPS AND ITINERARIES			
SHIP	EMBARKATION PORT	DURATION IN NIGHTS	ITINERARY AND PORTS OF CALL
Volendam	Vancouver	7	Round-trip: Skagway, Juneau, Ketchikan, Sawyer Glacier, Glacier Bay
Westerdam	Seattle	7	Round-trip: Juneau, Sitka, Ketchikan, Victoria, BC, Glacier Bay
Zaandam	Vancouver	7	Round-trip: Juneau, Skagway, Ketchikan, Sawyer Glacier
Zuiderdam	Vancouver	7	Round-trip: Skagway, Juneau, Ketchikan, Sawyer Glacier, Glacier Bay
Lindblad Expeditions			
National Geographic Sea Bird and Sea Lion	Sitka	7	Northbound: Point Adolphus, Glacier Bay, Petersburg, Frederick Sound, Dawes or Sawyer Glacier, Juneau
	Juneau	7	Southbound: Dawes or Sawyer Glacier, Petersburg, Frederick Sound, Glacier Bay, Point Adolphus, Sitka
	Seattle	11	Northbound: Gulf Islands, Alert Bay, Misty Fjords, Petersburg, Glacier Bay, Dawes or Sawyer Glacier, Juneau, Sitka
	Sitka	11	Southbound: Baranof or Chichagof Island, Glacier Bay, Juneau, Petersburg, Dawes or Sawyer Glacier, Misty Fiords, Alert Bay, Gulf Islands, Seattle
Norwegian Cruise Line			
Norwegian Pearl	Seattle	7	Round-trip: Juneau, Skagway, Ketchikan, Victoria, BC, Glacier Bay
Norwegian Jewel	Seattle	7	Round-trip: Juneau, Skagway, Ketchikan, Victoria, BC, Sawyer Glacier
Norwegian Sun	Whittier	7	Southbound: Hubbard Glacier, Icy Strait Point, Juneau, Skagway, Ketchikan, Sawyer Glacier, Vancouver, BC
	Vancouver	7	Northbound: Ketchikan, Juneau, Skagway, Glacier Bay, Hubbard Glacier, Whittier
Oceania Cruises			
Regatta	San Francisco	10	Northbound: Astoria, OR, Ketchikan, Juneau, Sitka, Hubbard Glacier, Victoria, BC, Vancouver, BC
	Vancouver	9	Round-trip: Ketchikan, Juneau, Sitka, Skagway, Hoonah, Hubbard Glacier
	Vancouver	10	Southbound: Sitka, Juneau, Skagway, Hoonah, Ketchikan, Hubbard Glacier, Victoria, BC, Seattle

2

ALASKA CRUISE SHIPS AND ITINERARIES			
SHIP	EMBARKATION PORT	DURATION IN NIGHTS	ITINERARY AND PORTS OF CALL
	Seattle	7	Round-trip: Ketchikan, Wrangell, Prince Rupert, BC, Sawyer Glacier
	Seattle	10	Round-trip: Ketchikan, Skagway, Juneau, Hoonah, Sitka, Wrangell, Victoria, BC, Hubbard Glacier
	Vancouver	10	Southbound: Ketchikan, Juneau, Sitka, Hubbard Glacier, Victoria, BC, Astoria, OR, San Francisco
Princess Cruises			
Coral Princess	Vancouver	7	Northbound: Ketchikan, Juneau, Skagway, Glacier Bay, College Fjord
	Whittier	7	Southbound: Ketchikan, Juneau, Skagway, Glacier Bay, Hubbard Glacier
Crown Princess	Vancouver	7	Northbound: Ketchikan, Juneau, Skagway, Glacier Bay, College Fjord
	Whittier	7	Southbound: Ketchikan, Juneau, Skagway, Glacier Bay, Hubbard Glacier
Golden Princess	Seattle	7	Round-trip: Juneau, Skagway, Ketchikan, Victoria, BC, Glacier Bay
Grand Princess	Seattle	7	Round-trip: Juneau, Skagway, Ketchikan, Victoria, BC, Sawyer Glacier
Island Princess	Vancouver	7	Northbound: Ketchikan, Juneau, Skagway, Glacier Bay, College Fjord
	Whittier	7	Southbound: Ketchikan, Juneau, Skagway, Glacier Bay, Hubbard Glacier
Pacific Princess	Vancouver	7	Round-trip: Juneau, Skagway, Ketchikan, Glacier Bay or Sawyer Glacier
Star Princess	San Francisco	11	Round-trip: Juneau, Skagway, Ketchikan, Victoria, BC, Glacier Bay or Sawyer Glacier
Regent Seven Seas Cruises			
Seven Seas Navigator	Vancouver	7	Northbound: Sitka, Juneau, Skagway, Ketchikan, Hubbard Glacier, Sawyer Glacier, Seward
	Seward	7	Southbound: Sitka, Juneau, Skagway, Ketchikan, Hubbard Glacier, Sawyer Glacier, Vancouver, BC
	Vancouver	7	Round-trip: Wrangell, Juneau, Prince Rupert, BC, Ketchikan
	San Francisco	12	Northbound: Astoria, OR, Ketchikan, Juneau, Skagway, Sitka, Icy Strait Point, Hubbard Glacier, Victoria, BC, Vancouver, BC

| ALASKA CRUISE SHIPS AND ITINERARIES | | | |
SHIP	EMBARKATION PORT	DURATION IN NIGHTS	ITINERARY AND PORTS OF CALL
	Vancouver	12	Southbound: Sitka, Icy Strait Point, Ketchikan, Juneau, Skagway, Hubbard Glacier, Victoria BC, Astoria, OR, San Francisco
Royal Caribbean International			
Radiance of the Seas	Vancouver	7	Northbound: Ketchikan, Juneau, Skagway, Icy Strait Point, Hubbard Glacier
	Seward	7	Southbound: Ketchikan, Juneau, Skagway, Icy Strait Point, Hubbard Glacier
	Vancouver	7	Round-trip: Juneau, Ketchikan, Icy Strait Point, Sawyer Glacier
Rhapsody of the Seas	Seattle	7	Round-trip: Juneau, Skagway, Victoria, BC, Sawyer Glacier
	Vancouver	7	Round-trip: Juneau, Skagway, Ketchikan, Sawyer Glacier
Silversea Cruises			
Silver Shadow	Vancouver	9	Round-trip: Ketchikan, Juneau, Skagway, Sitka, Prince Rupert, BC. Victoria, BC
	Vancouver	10	Round-trip: Skagway, Juneau, Sitka, Ketchikan, Sawyer Glacier, Prince Rupert, BC, Victoria, BC
	Vancouver	11	Round-trip: Skagway, Juneau, Sitka, Ketchikan, Wrangell, Sawyer Glacier, Prince Rupert, BC, Victoria, BC
	Vancouver	7	Northbound: Ketchikan, Juneau, Skagway, Sitka, Hubbard Glacier, Seward
	Seward	7	Southbound: Ketchikan, Juneau, Skagway, Sitka, Hubbard Glacier, Vanouver
	Vancouver	11	Southbound: Skagway, Juneau, Sitka, Ketchikan, Prince Rupert, BC, Victoria, BC, Astoria, OR, San Francisco
Un-Cruise Adventures			
Wilderness Adventurer, Wilderness Discoverer	Ketchikan	7	Northbound: El Capitan Passage, Klawock, Chatham Strait, Frederick Sound, Stephen's Passage, Ford's Terror, Endicott Arm, Dawes Glacier, Juneau
	Juneau	7	Southbound: Sawyer Glacier, Frederick Sound, Thomas Bay, Wrangell Narrows, Wrangell, Behm Canal, Misty Fiords, Ketchikan

ALASKA CRUISE SHIPS AND ITINERARIES

SHIP	EMBARKATION PORT	DURATION IN NIGHTS	ITINERARY AND PORTS OF CALL
Wilderness Adventurer, Wilderness Discoverer, Wilderness Explorer	Sitka	7	Northbound: Glacier Bay (3 days), Icy Strait Point, Chichagof and Baranof Islands, Peril Strait, Sergius Narrows, Juneau
	Juneau	7	Southbound: Glacier Bay (3 days), Icy Strait, Chichagof and Baranof Islands, Peril Strait, Sergius Narrows, Sitka
Safari Quest, Safari Explorer, Safari Endeavour	Juneau	7	Round-trip: Glacier Bay (2 days), Icy Strait, Chichagof and Baranof Islands, Frederick Sound, Stephen's Passage, Ford's Terror, Endicott Arm
Legacy	Ketchikan	7	Northbound: Wrangell, Petersburg, Frederick Sound, Sitka, Chichagof Island, Icy Strait, Glacier Bay, Haines, Skagway, Juneau
	Juneau	7	Southbound: Wrangell, Petersburg, Frederick Sound, Sitka, Chichagof Island, Icy Strait, Glacier Bay, Haines, Skagway, Ketchikan
	Seattle	11	Northbound: Friday Harbor, Ketchikan, Wrangell, Petersburg, Sitka, Icy Strait, Glacier Bay, Haines/Skagway, Juneau
	Juneau	11	Southbound: Haines/Skagway, Glacier Bay, Icy Strait, Sitka, Petersburg, Wrangell, Ketchikan, Friday Harbor, Seattle
Safari Endeavour, Safari Explorer, Safari Quest, Wilderness Adventurer, Wilderness Discoverer, Wilderness Explorer	Seattle	12	Northbound: Friday Harbor/Salish Sea, Misty Fiords, Ketchikan, Tongass National Forest/El Capitan Passage, Klawock Native Village, Chatham Strait, Frederick Sound, Brothers Islands/Stephen's Passage, Endicott Arm, Juneau
	Juneau	11	Southbound: Tracy Arm, Thomas Bay, Wrangell, Behm Canal, Misty Fiords, Ketchikan, Friday Harbor, Seattle

2

CRUISE LINES AND CRUISE SHIPS

After the Caribbean and Europe, more ships sail in Alaska than in any other region of the world, offering passengers a wide range of choices, from mainstream to luxury, from large megaliners to small yachtlike vessels. The size of the ship will in part dictate where it can go and how passengers will enjoy their vacation. So just as with other popular cruise destinations, picking the right cruise ship is the most important decision you will make in choosing your cruise, particularly if you stick with a large ship.

Make no mistake about it: cruise ships have distinct personalities. Norwegian's lack of formality and range of dining choices and entertainment makes these ships the favorites of some and the bane of others. Even those belonging to the same class and nearly indistinguishable from one another have certain traits that make them stand out.

That is why the most important choice you'll make when booking a cruise is the combined selection of cruise line and cruise ship. Cruise lines set the tone for their fleets, but since the cruise industry is relatively fluid, some new features introduced on one ship may not be found on all the ships owned by the same cruise line. For instance, you'll find ice-skating rinks only on the biggest Royal Caribbean ships. However, most cruise lines attempt to standardize the overall experience throughout their fleets (for example, you'll find a rock-climbing wall on *every* Royal Caribbean ship).

ABOUT THE CRUISE LINES

Just as cruise ships differ by size and style, so do the cruise lines themselves, and finding a cruise line that matches your personality is as important as finding the right ship. Some cruise lines cater to families, others to couples, active singles, and even food and wine aficionados. Selecting the right one can mean the difference between struggling with unmet expectations and enjoying the vacation of a lifetime. Although some of the differences are subtle, most of today's cruise lines still fall into three basic categories: Mainstream, Premium, and Luxury.

MAINSTREAM LINES

Mainstream cruise lines usually have a little something for everyone: Ships tend to be the big, bigger, and biggest at sea, carrying the highest number of passengers per available space. Cabins can be basic or fancy since most mainstream lines also offer more upscale accommodations categories, including suites. Some mainstream lines still offer traditional dining, with two assigned seatings in the main restaurant for dinner. But increasingly, most mainstream cruise lines have introduced variations of open seating dining and alternative restaurant options that allow passengers to dine when and with whom they please, though almost all alternative restaurants carry an extra charge.

PREMIUM LINES

Premium lines usually offer a more subdued atmosphere and refined style: Ships tend to be newer midsize to large vessels that carry fewer passengers than mainstream ships and have a more spacious feel. Staterooms still range from more basic to more upscale, but even the basic accommodations tend to have more style and space. Cuisine on these ships tends to be a bit better, and most of these ships have à la carte options for more upscale dining for an extra charge, often higher than those on mainstream lines. There are still extra charges on the ship.

LUXURY LINES

The air on these deluxe vessels is as rarified as the champagne and caviar: Ships range from megayachts for only a hundred or so privileged guests to midsize vessels, which are considered large for this category. Space is so abundant that you might wonder where the other passengers are hiding. Spacious staterooms are frequently all suites; at the least, they are the equivalent to higher-grade accommodations on mainstream and premium ships. Open seating is the norm, and guests dine where and with whom they please during dinner hours. There are relatively few extra charges on these ships, except for premium wines by the bottle, spa services, and excursions, but some lines even include excursions and airfare in their prices.

SMALL-SHIP LINES

A casual, relaxed atmosphere in intimate spaces prevails on these yacht-like vessels for fewer than a hundred passengers. Emphasis is placed on unique and flexible itineraries to off-the-beaten-path destinations with exploration leaders guiding the way to insightful encounters ashore. Accommodations are proportionately small, but basic amenities are provided. Meals often feature fresh local ingredients and are served in open seating, buffet, or family style. The dress code is always comfortable casual, and evenings on board may include a lecture, but socializing with other passengers is the most common activity. Exercise equipment is usually found on board, but kayaking and nature hikes are offered for a more adventurous workout.

SMALL-SHIP CRUISES

We cover the most recognized small-ship lines sailing in Alaska, but that is by no means exhaustive. Other great small ships sailing the Inside Passage include Fantasy Cruises' *Island Spirit* (⊕ *www.smallalaskaship.com*), owned and operated by Captain Jeff Behrens. Captain Behrens is committed to rapport-building with and respect for the area's smallest communities; as a result, 32-passenger *Island Spirit* can make off-the-beaten-path port calls like Tenakee Springs (⊕ *www.tenakeespringsak.com*), Five Finger Lighthouse (⊕ *www.5fingerlighthouse.com*), and Baranof Warm Springs, in addition to scenic anchorages like Ford's Terror that only small ships can access. Charters and photography-focused cruises are also available.

Alaska Sea Adventures (⊕ *www.yachtalaska.com*) focuses on charters and single-theme cruises on wildlife photography, birding, research, archaeology, whale migration, or fish spawning. Its two ships, *Northern Song* and *Alaska Legend*, can accommodate up to eight passengers each.

ABOUT THE SHIPS

LARGE CRUISE SHIPS

Large cruise lines account for the majority of passengers sailing to Alaska. These typically have large cruise ships in their fleets with plentiful deck space and, often, a promenade deck that allows you to stroll around the ship's perimeter. In the newest vessels, traditional meets trendy with resort-style innovations; however, they still feature cruise-ship classics, such as afternoon tea and complimentary room service. The smallest cruise ships in the major cruise lines' fleets carry as few as 400 passengers, whereas the biggest can accommodate between 1,500 and 3,000 passengers—enough people to outnumber the residents of many Alaskan port towns. Large ships are a good choice if you're looking for nonstop activity and lots of options; they're especially appealing for groups and families with older kids. If you prefer a gentler pace and a chance to get to know your shipmates, try a smaller ship.

SMALL SHIPS

Compact expedition-type vessels bring you right up to the shoreline to skirt the face of a glacier and pull through narrow channels where big ships don't fit. These cruises focus on Alaska, and you'll see more wildlife and call into smaller ports, as well as some of the better-known towns. Enrichment talks—conducted by naturalists, Native Alaskans, and other experts in the state's natural history and Native cultures—are the norm. Cabins on expedition ships can be tiny, sometimes with no phone or TV, and bathrooms are often no bigger than cubbyholes. The dining room and lounge are usually the only public areas on these vessels; however, some are luxurious with cushy cabins, comfy lounges and libraries, and hot tubs. You won't find much nightlife aboard, but what you trade for space and onboard diversions is a unique and unforgettable glimpse of Alaska.

Many small ships are based in Juneau or another Alaska port and sail entirely within Alaska. Twice annually, some offer an Inside Passage cruise as the ships reposition to and from their winter homes elsewhere.

Small-ship cruising can be pricey, as fares tend to be inclusive (except for airfare), but there are few onboard charges, and, given the size of ship and style of cruise, fewer opportunities to spend on board.

ABOUT THESE REVIEWS

3

For each cruise line described, ships that regularly cruise in Alaska are grouped by class or similar configuration. Some ships owned by the cruise lines listed do not include regularly scheduled Alaska cruises on their published itineraries as of this writing and are not reviewed in this book. *For a complete listing of the ships and the itineraries they are scheduled to follow in the 2014 cruising season, see the chart in Chapter 2.*

Many ships are designed with an eye to less-than-perfect weather. For that reason, you're likely to find indoor swimming pools featured on their deck plans. Except in rare cases, these are usually dual-purpose pools that can be covered when necessary by a sliding roof or magrodome to create an indoor-swimming environment. Our reviews indicate the total number of swimming pools found on each ship, with such permanently or temporarily covered pools included in the total and also noted as "# indoors" in parentheses.

When ships belong to the same class—or are basically similar—they're listed together in the subhead under the name of the class; the year each was introduced is also given in the same order in the statistics section. Capacity figures are based on double occupancy, but when maximum capacity numbers are available (the number of passengers a ship holds when all possible berths are filled), those are listed in parentheses. Many larger ships have three- and four-berth cabins that can substantially increase the total number of passengers on board when all berths are booked.

Unlike other cruise guides, we not only describe the features but also list the cabin dimensions for each accommodation category available on the ships reviewed. Dimensions should be considered approximate and used for comparison purposes, since they sometimes vary depending on the actual location of the cabin. For instance, although staterooms are largely prefabricated and consistent in size and configuration, those at the front of some ships may be oddly curved to conform to the shape of the bow.

When you're armed with all the right information, we're sure you'll be able to find one that not only fits your style but offers you the service and value you expect.

AMERICAN CRUISE LINES

Since its relaunch in 2000, American Cruise Lines has specialized in a unique style of small-ship cruising along the inland waterways and rivers of the United States. Typical itineraries include the Pacific Northwest, Maine, New England Islands, Hudson River, Chesapeake

American Spirit at sea

Bay, the Historic South and Golden Isles, Florida, and the Mississippi River. One of its ships, *American Spirit*, is designed specifically for cruising the inside passage.

☎ *800/460–4518*
⊕ *www.american cruiselines.com.*
☞ *Cruise Style: Small-ship.*

In 2012, American Cruise Lines added Alaska to its itinerary roster with one-week, round-trip Inside Passage cruises from Juneau and 11-night repositioning cruises between Seattle and Juneau at the beginning of the season—and from Juneau to Seattle at season's end. With no more than 100 passengers on board, the small ship allows passengers to experience each port of call up close and personal. Itineraries are designed to explore some of Alaska's most popular ports as well as remote wilderness areas.

To enhance the cruise experience, American Cruise Lines invites carefully selected experts to join each voyage. Through informal lectures, open discussions, and activities, they bring local history, nature, and culture alive with their knowledge and passion for American heritage. These naturalists and historians also lead shore excursions while in port to give you behind-the-scenes tours of some of Alaska's best-kept secrets and favorite treasures. Basic shore excursions are included in the fare in Alaska, and alternative tours are available for purchase.

Food

Using the freshest ingredients available, menus are inspired by regional and local specialties and take advantage of fresh meats and seafood and in-season fruits and vegetables. Special menus are available to passengers on restricted diets. Every evening before dinner, a complimentary cocktail hour is hosted with a bar setup and hors d'oeuvres. Dinner is served with complimentary wine and beer.

Entertainment

American Cruise Lines provides unique, regional entertainment on its cruises, so don't look for splashy entertainers or a casino on board. Activities are designed to highlight the areas through which you are sailing, including local musicians, demonstrations, minor theatrical performances, and games. Activities and lectures are as rich in history and culture as the ports themselves.

Fitness and Recreation

Exercise equipment and a putting green to hone your game are featured on board. Walks ashore led by the ship's naturalist offer a more rigorous workout. There is no spa or salon, but the reception desk may be able to recommend possibilities to you in ports.

Your Shipmates

Typical passengers are older, well-traveled individuals looking for a destination-focused adventure where they will have the opportunity to explore the history, culture, natural scenery, and wildlife of the unique areas visited.

Dress Code

Casual sportswear is suggested during the day. Attire should include clothing for layering when the weather turns cool. Comfortable walking shoes, a windbreaker, and light rainwear are also recommended items. Evening attire is always country club casual.

Junior Cruisers

Families are more than welcome, but it is rare to see children on board. There are no youth facilities; however, the cruise director will plan appropriate activities when children are sailing.

Service

With the services of an American crew, your needs will be satisfied in an attentive, if not overly polished, manner and without a language barrier.

KNOWN FOR

■ **All-American:** The large fleet of American-built, flagged, and crewed small ships is also environmentally friendly and entirely nonsmoking.

■ **Budget-Conscious Beverage Policy:** Although not all alcoholic beverages are included in the fare, your own alcohol is welcome on board, and a complimentary cocktail hour is hosted every evening. Wine and beer are served with lunch and dinner at no additional charge.

■ **Accessibility:** With elevator service to all decks, the ships are accessible to the mobility impaired.

■ **United States Passenger Advantage:** All departure ports and ports of call are located in the United States; a passport is recommended for Alaska cruises but not usually required.

Top: Whale-watching
Bottom: Standard cabin

3

AMERICAN CRUISE LINES

Top: Shopping for crafts
Middle: View from the bridge
Bottom: Dinner on informal
night

Tipping

Tips are entirely at your personal discretion and generally average about $125 per person on a seven-night cruise.

Past Passengers

After your first cruise you will receive an invitation to join the Eagle Society in the mail. If you are already a past passenger and would like to join, you can do so on board your next cruise or by calling a cruise specialist and requesting an invitation. Past passenger benefits include complimentary standard shore excursions after having taken 3 cruises—after your 3rd cruise you will never have to pay for standard shore excursions again; special gifts on subsequent cruises; a complimentary 11th cruise—after you complete 10 cruises, the 11th cruise is be free; invitations to Eagle Society cruises and select sailings; Eagle Society luggage tags and name tags; and members-only savings and promotions. In addition, when a ship is in port near a member's hometown, American Cruise Lines extends an invitation to come aboard for lunch or dinner and when in port during a sailing, members may invite friends or family aboard for a tour of the ship or to join them for meals.

Ships of the Line

American Cruise Lines offers small-ship cruises along the inland waterways and rivers of the United States, from the Mississippi River to New England, and Alaska.

American Spirit. Built to provide maximum relaxation and amenities that are often unexpected on ships this size, the casual and inviting public areas of American Cruise Line's 100-passenger *American Spirit* reflect the company's American heritage in spaces that are comfortable and stylish.

Outside you'll find plenty of space on the 1,200-gross-ton ship's partially covered Observation deck to view the passing scenery, either at the rail or from a deck chair. The covered areas are where you'll find exercise equipment as well. You won't miss Alaska's scenic wonders from inside the ship either—both the

CHOOSE THIS LINE IF ...

You are a discriminating traveler looking for the intimacy of a small ship.

You appreciate learning about the history and culture of the ports you visit.

You prefer a relaxed and casual atmosphere.

main lounge and dining salon feature walls of windows that bring the outside in. Lounges, sundecks, and dining salons are accessible by wheelchairs or other walking aid devices. The ship is also equipped with an elevator for ease of movement between decks. Wireless Internet access is available shipwide, but you'll have to be close to shore to receive a signal for cell phone use.

Each evening before dinner you are invited to mingle with your fellow passengers to share the day's adventures over complimentary cocktails and hors d'oeuvres.

Meals are served in the open seating dining salon, which is large enough to accommodate all passengers at once. The day's menu is announced in advance and special menus are available to passengers on restricted diets. Breakfast is prepared to order on most mornings and lunches are light and casual. Coffee, nonalcoholic beverages, and snacks are available 24 hours a day and there is room service upon request.

Spacious cabins feature flat-screen televisions with DVD players, a sitting area, and more than half have a balcony. While storage space is plentiful in the cabin itself, it is somewhat tight in the bathroom. Bedding configurations are either king or two twin beds. Cabins without a balcony have large picture windows that open to the sea air. Amenities include hair dryers as well as basic toiletries. Some cabins are available as either a double or single and a handful are interconnecting. One cabin is designated as wheelchair-accessible.

HELPFUL HINTS

■ Each ship has a large resource library, including books and videos, as well as naturalists and historians on board for each sailing.

■ Complimentary guided walking tours are offered on port days.

■ The main lounge has panoramic windows to view the scenery when the weather is not ideal, but the Observation deck is also partially covered.

■ It's a good idea to arrive in the embarkation port a day before sailing as cruises leave early in the day. Departures are at 1:30 pm (sometimes earlier if all passengers have arrived), and embarkation begins at 10 am. Passengers need to be on board by 12:30.

3

AMERICAN CRUISE LINES

DON'T CHOOSE THIS LINE IF ...

You must be entertained with splashy production shows and nonstop activity.

You must smoke—it is prohibited on board.

You would rather spend time in a casino than attend an evening lecture.

CARNIVAL CRUISE LINES

The world's largest cruise line originated the Fun Ship concept in 1972 with the relaunch of an aging ocean liner, which got stuck on a sandbar during its maiden voyage. In true entrepreneurial spirit, founder Ted Arison shrugged off an inauspicious

Lobby Bar on board *Carnival Fantasy*

beginning to introduce superliners a decade later. Sporting red-white-and-blue flared funnels, which are easily recognized from afar, new ships are continuously added to the fleet and rarely deviate from a successful pattern. If you find something you like on one vessel, you're likely to find something similar on another.

☎ *305/599–2600 or 800/227–6482*
⊕ *www.carnival.com*
☞ *Cruise Style: Mainstream.*

Each vessel features themed public rooms, ranging from ancient Egypt to futuristic motifs, although many of those elements are being replaced with a more tropical decor as older ships are upgraded and new ones enter service. Carnival is also introducing features that are branded by the line itself, such as the poolside Blue Iguana Tequila Bar with an adjacent burrito cantina and the Red Frog Rum Bar that also serves Carnival's own brand of Thirsty Frog Red beer. In partnership with well-known brands such as EA SPORTS, teh line has also created EA SPORTS Bars at sea and Guy's Burger Joint, in partnership with Food Network star Guy Fieri. Implementation of the new features is scheduled for completion in 2015.

Food

Carnival ships have both flexible dining options as well as casual alternative restaurants. Although the tradition of two set mealtimes for dinner prevails on Carnival ships, the line's open seating concept—Your Time Dining—is available fleet-wide.

Choices are numerous, and the skill of Carnival's chefs has elevated the line's menus to an unexpected level. Although the waiters still sing and dance, the good-to-excellent dining room food appeals to American tastes. Upscale steak houses on certain ships serve cuisine comparable to the best midrange steak houses ashore.

Carnival serves the best food of the mainstream cruise lines. In addition to the regular menu, vegetarian, low-calorie, low-carbohydrate, low-salt, and no-sugar selections are available. A children's menu includes such favorites as macaroni and cheese, chicken fingers, and peanut-butter-and-jelly sandwiches. If you don't feel like dressing up for dinner, the Lido buffet serves full meals, including sandwiches, a salad bar, rotisserie chicken, Asian stir-fry, and excellent pizza.

Entertainment

More high-energy than cerebral, the entertainment consists of lavish Las Vegas–style revues presented in main show lounges by a company of singers and dancers. Other performers might include magicians, jugglers, acrobats, passengers performing in the talent show, or karaoke. Live bands play a wide range of musical styles for dancing and every ship has a nightclub, a piano bar, and a comedy club. Adult activities, particularly the competitive ones, tend to be silly and hilarious and play to full houses. With Carnival's new branding initiative, look for the introduction of Hasbro, The Game Show, and performances created by Playlist Productions.

Fitness and Recreation

Manned by staff members trained to keep passengers in shipshape form, Carnival's trademark spas and fitness centers are some of the largest and best equipped at sea. Spas and salons are operated by Steiner Leisure, and treatments include a variety of massages, body wraps, and facials; salons offer hair and nail services and even tooth whitening. Fitness centers have state-of-the-art cardio and strength-training equipment, a jogging track, and basic exercise classes at no charge. There's a fee for personal training, body composition analysis, and specialized classes such as yoga and Pilates.

Your Shipmates

Carnival's passengers are predominantly active Americans, mostly couples in their mid-thirties to mid-fifties. Many families enjoy Carnival cruises in the Caribbean year-round. Holidays and school vacation periods are very popular with families, and you'll see lots of kids in summer. More than 710,000 children sailed on Carnival ships in 2012—a sixfold increase in just 12 years.

KNOWN FOR

■ Diversions: Casinos, spas, and fitness centers are some of the most extensive at sea.

■ Fun: Not surprisingly, the fleet delivers a high-energy cruise vacation for passengers of all ages.

■ Kid's Stuff: Each Carnival ship has a water-park area and children's facilities and programs designed to appeal to the pickiest youngsters as well as their parents.

■ Lack of Hierarchy: Every Carnival passenger enjoys the same service and attention, including nightly turn-down service, room service, and 24-hour pizzerias.

■ Quieter Zones: For adults only, each ship has a Serenity Deck dedicated to kid-free relaxation.

3

CARNIVAL CRUISE LINES

Top: *Carnival Victory* dining room

Top: *Carnival Triumph*
walking and jogging track
Middle: *Carnival Elation*
at sea
Bottom: *Carnival Destiny*
penthouse suite

Dress Code

Two "cruise elegant" nights are standard on seven-night cruises; one is the norm on shorter sailings. Although men should feel free to wear tuxedos, dark suits (or sport coats) and ties are more prevalent. All other evenings are "cruise casual," with jeans and dress shorts permitted in the dining rooms. All ships request that no short-shorts or cutoffs be worn after 6 pm, but that policy is often ignored.

Junior Cruisers

Camp Carnival, run year-round by professionals, earns high marks for keeping young cruisers busy and content. Dedicated children's areas include great playrooms with separate splash pools. Toddlers from two to five years are treated to puppet shows, sponge painting, face painting, coloring, drawing, and crafts. As long as diapers and supplies are provided, staff will change toddlers. Activities for ages six to eight include arts and crafts, pizza parties, computer time, T-shirt painting, a talent show, and fitness programs. Nine- to 11-year-olds can play Ping-Pong, take dance lessons, play video games, and participate in swim parties, scavenger hunts, and sports. Tweens ages 12 to 14 appreciate the social events, parties, contests, and sports in Circle C. Every night they have access to the ships' discos, followed by late-night movies, karaoke, or pizza.

Club O2 is geared toward teens 15 to 17. Program directors play host at the spacious teen clubs, where kicking back is the order of the day between scheduled activities. The fleet-wide Y-Spa program for older teens offers a high level of pampering. Staff members also accompany teens on shore excursions designed just for them.

Daytime group babysitting for infants two and under allows parents the freedom to explore ports of call without the kids until noon. Parents can also pursue leisurely adults-only evenings from 10 pm to 3 am, when slumber party–style group babysitting is available for children from ages 6 months to 11 years. Babysitting is available for a fee.

CHOOSE THIS LINE IF ...

You want an action-packed casino with a choice of table games and rows upon rows of clanging slot machines.

You don't mind standing in line—these are big ships with a lot of passengers, and lines are not uncommon.

You don't mind hearing announcements over the public-address system reminding you of what's next on the schedule.

Service

Service on Carnival ships is friendly but not polished. Stateroom attendants are not only recognized for their attention to cleanliness but also for their expertise in creating towel animals—cute critters fashioned from bath towels that appear during nightly turndown service. They've become so popular that Carnival publishes an instruction book on how to create them yourself.

Tipping

A gratuity of $11.50 per passenger per day is automatically added to passenger accounts, and gratuities are distributed to stewards and waitstaff. Passengers may adjust the amount based on the level of service experienced. All beverage tabs at bars get an automatic 15% addition.

Past Passengers

After sailing on one Carnival cruise, you'll receive a complimentary subscription to the company email magazine, and access to your past sailing history on the Carnival website. You are recognized on subsequent cruises with color-coded key cards determined by points or the number of days you've sailed—Red (starting on your second cruise), Gold (when you've accumulated 25–74 points); Platinum (75–199 points); and Diamond (200-plus points)—which serve as your entrée to a by-invitation-only cocktail reception. Platinum and Diamond members are eligible for benefits including priority embarkation and debarkation, priority dining assignments, supper club and spa reservations, a logo item gift, and limited complimentary laundry service.

3

CARNIVAL CRUISE LINES

HELPFUL HINTS

■ The line's Fun Ship 2.0 improvements are toning down the noisy, brash style in lieu of something more relaxed and tropical.

■ New features introduced in partnership with recognized brands (Hasbro, The Game Show, a diner crafted by Guy Fieri) have stepped up the complimentary elements of the onboard experience.

■ Casinos are good, and you can use your onboard charge card for casino play.

■ Carnival's great online planning tool (⊕ *www. carnivalconnections.com*) offers planning tips, cruise reviews, and a message board.

■ Most activities for children are free, but fees attached to their late-night party program can add up, in addition to the charges for video games.

DON'T CHOOSE THIS LINE IF ...

You want an intimate, sedate atmosphere. Carnival's ships are big and bold.

You want elaborate accommodations. Carnival suites are spacious but not as feature-filled as the term *suite* may suggest.

You're turned off by men in tank tops. Casual on these ships means casual indeed.

SPIRIT-CLASS
Carnival Spirit, Pride, Legend, Miracle

CREW MEMBERS	930
ENTERED SERVICE	2001, 2001, 2002, 2004
GROSS TONS	88,500
LENGTH	960 feet
NUMBER OF CABINS	1,062
PASSENGER CAPACITY	2,124 (2,667 max)
WIDTH	105.7 feet

700 ft.

500 ft.

300 ft.

Spirit-class vessels may have seemed to be a throwback in size on their introduction, but these sleek ships have the advantage of fitting through the Panama Canal and, with their additional length, include all the trademark characteristics of their larger fleetmates. They're also racehorses with the speed to reach far-flung destinations. *Carnival Spirit*—for which the class is named—makes its home port in Australia, primarily serving the Australian and New Zealand markets.

A rosy red skylight in the front bulkhead of the funnel—which houses the reservations-only upscale steak house—caps a soaring, 11-deck atrium. Lovely chapels are available for weddings, either on embarkation or while in a port of call, and are also used for occasional shipboard religious services.

The upper and lower interior promenade decks are unhampered by a midship restaurant or galley, which means that passenger flow throughout the ships is much improved over earlier, and even subsequent, designs.

Cabins

Layout: Cabins on Carnival ships are spacious, and these are no exception. Nearly 80% have an ocean view and, of those, more than 80% have balconies. Suites and some ocean-view cabins have private balconies outfitted with chairs and tables; some cabins have balconies at least 50% larger than average. Every cabin has adequate closet and drawer–shelf storage, as well as bathroom shelves. High-thread-count linens and plush pillows and duvets are a luxurious touch in all accommodations. Suites also have a whirlpool tub and walk-in closet. Decks 5, 6, and 7 each have a pair of balcony staterooms that connect to adjoining interior staterooms that are ideal for families because of their close proximity to children and teen areas.

Decor: Light-wood cabinetry, soft pastels, mirrored accents, a small refrigerator, a personal safe, a hair dryer, and a seating area with sofa, chair, and table are typical for ocean-view cabins and suites. Inside cabins have ample room but no seating area.

Bathrooms: Extras include shampoo and bath gel provided in shower-mounted dispensers and an array of sample toiletries, as well as fluffy towels and a wall-

Top: *Carnival Legend* at sea
Bottom: Spirit-class balcony stateroom

mounted magnifying mirror. Bathrobes for use during the cruise are provided for all.

Accessibility: Sixteen staterooms are designed for wheelchair accessibility.

Restaurants

One formal restaurant serves open seating breakfast and lunch; it also serves dinner in two traditional assigned evening seatings or an open seating option. The casual Lido buffet with stations offers a variety of food choices (including a deli, salad bar, dessert station, and different daily regional cuisines); at night it becomes the Seaview Bistro for casual dinners. There's also an upscale steak house that requires reservations and an additional charge, a pizzeria, poolside outdoor grills for burgers, hot dogs, and the trimmings, a specialty coffee bar and patisserie, a complimentary sushi bar and Taste Bar serving bite-size appetizers before dinner, and 24-hour room service with a limited menu of breakfast selections, sandwiches, and snacks.

Spas

Steiner Leisure operates the 14,500 square-foot spas that offer an indoor therapy pool as well as such indulgences as a variety of massages, body wraps, and facials for adults and teens. Complimentary steam rooms and saunas in men's and women's changing rooms feature glass walls for sea views. Salons offer tooth whitening in addition to hair and nail services.

Bars and Entertainment

Pride and *Legend* received newly branded bars and comedy club features in 2013. All have high-energy shows by resident singers and dancers or guest performers in the main show room, spirited piano bars, and nightclubs featuring music for dancing and listening. Comedy clubs, karaoke, and deck parties add to the fun of nighttime activities.

Pros and Cons

Pros: the enclosed space located forward on the promenade deck is quiet and good for reading; for relaxation, his-and-hers saunas and steam rooms have glass walls and sea views; complimentary self-serve ice-cream dispensers are on the Lido deck.

Cons: these are long ships, and some cabins are quite far from elevators; connecting staterooms are relatively scarce; the video arcade is almost hidden at the forward end of the ship.

Cabin Type	Size (sq. ft.)
Penthouse Suites	370 (average)
Suite	275
Ocean View	185
Interior	185

FAST FACTS

- 12 passenger decks
- Specialty restaurant, dining room, buffet, ice cream parlor, pizzeria
- Wi-Fi, safe, refrigerator
- 3 pools (1 indoor), children's pool
- Fitness classes, gym, hot tubs, sauna, spa, steam room
- 7 bars, casino, 2 dance clubs, library, show room, video game room
- Children's programs
- Laundry facilities, laundry service
- Internet terminal
- No-smoking cabins

Carnival Miracle Gatsby's Garden

CELEBRITY CRUISES

The Chandris Group, owners of budget Fantasy Cruises, founded Celebrity in 1989. Initially utilizing an unlovely, refurbished former ocean liner from the Fantasy fleet, Celebrity gained a reputation for professional service and fine food despite the shabby-chic

Swim-up bar under the stars

vessel on which it was elegantly served. The cruise line eventually built premium sophisticated cruise ships. Signature amenities followed, including large standard staterooms with generous storage, fully equipped spas, and butler service. Valuable art collections grace the fleet.

☎ 800/647–2251
⊕ *www.celebrity cruises.com*

☞ *Cruise Style: Premium.*

Although spacious accommodations in every category are a Celebrity standard, Concierge-class, an upscale element on all ships, makes certain premium ocean-view and balcony staterooms almost the equivalent of suites in terms of service. A Concierge-class stateroom includes numerous extras, such as chilled champagne, fresh fruit, and flowers upon arrival; exclusive room-service menus; evening canapés; luxury bedding, pillows, and linens; upgraded balcony furnishings; priority boarding and luggage service; and other VIP perks. At the touch of a single telephone button, a Concierge-class desk representative is at hand to offer assistance. Suites are still the ultimate, though, and include the services of a butler to assist with unpacking, booking spa services and dining reservations, shining shoes, and even replacing a popped button.

Food

Aside from the sophisticated ambience of its restaurants, the cuisine has always been a highlight of a Celebrity cruise. Happily, every ship in the fleet has a highly experienced team headed by executive chefs and food and beverage managers who have developed their skills in some of the world's finest restaurants and hotels.

Alternative restaurants throughout the fleet offer fine dining and a variety of international cuisines in splendid surroundings. A less formal evening alternative is offered in Lido restaurants, where you'll find made-to-order sushi, stir-fry, pasta, pizza, and curry stations, as well as a carving station, an array of vegetables, "loaded" baked potatoes, and desserts. The AquaSpa Cafés serve light and healthy cuisine from breakfast until evening. Cafés serve a variety of coffees, teas, and pastries that carry an additional charge. Late-night treats served by white-gloved waiters in public rooms throughout the ships can include mini–beef Wellingtons and crispy tempura.

To further complement the food, Celebrity's extensive wine collection features more than 500 choices, including vintages from every major wine-producing region.

Entertainment

Entertainment has never been a primary focus of Celebrity Cruises, although every ship offers a lineup of lavish production shows. In addition, ships have guest entertainers and music for dancing and listening, and you'll find lectures on every Celebrity cruise. Presentations may range from financial strategies, astronomy, wine appreciation, photography tips, and politics to the food, history, and culture of ports of call. Culinary demonstrations, bingo, and art auctions are additional diversions throughout the fleet. There are plenty of activities outlined in the daily program of events. There are no public-address announcements for bingo or hawking of gold-by-the-inch sales. You can still play and buy, but you won't be reminded repeatedly.

Fitness and Recreation

Celebrity's AquaSpa by Elemis and fitness centers are some of the most tranquil and nicely equipped at sea, with complimentary access to thalassotherapy pools on Millennium-class ships. Spa services are operated by Steiner Leisure, and treatments include a variety of massages, body wraps, and facials. Trendy and traditional hair and nail services are offered in the salons.

State-of-the-art exercise equipment, a jogging track, and basic fitness classes are available at no charge. There's a fee for personal training, body composition analysis, and specialized classes such as yoga and Pilates. Golf pros offer hands-on instruction, and game simulators allow passengers to play world-famous courses. Each ship also has an Acupuncture at Sea treatment area staffed by licensed practitioners of Oriental medicine.

KNOWN FOR

- **AquaSpa:** The AquaSpa facilities on Celebrity ships are considered some of the finest at sea.

- **Art:** Celebrity's contemporary style is complemented by stunning modern art collections.

- **Food:** Sophisticated cuisine and menu options make Celebrity's dining experience outstanding at this level of cruising.

- **Service:** With a high ratio of staff to guests, Celebrity offers personal and intuitive, yet unobtrusive service.

Top: The Millennium AquaSpa
Bottom: Millennium-class cinema and conference center

Top: *Century* Rendezvous Lounge
Middle: Lounge in climate-controlled comfort
Bottom: Lounging on deck

Your Shipmates

Celebrity caters to American cruise passengers, primarily couples from their mid-thirties to mid-fifties. Many families enjoy cruising on Celebrity's fleet during summer months and holiday periods, particularly in the Caribbean. Lengthier cruises and exotic itineraries attract passengers in the over-sixty age group.

Dress Code

Two formal nights are standard on seven-night cruises. Men are encouraged to wear tuxedos, but dark suits or sport coats and ties are more prevalent. Other evenings are designated "smart casual and above." Although jeans are discouraged in formal restaurants, they are appropriate for casual dining venues after 6 pm. The line requests that no shorts be worn in public areas after 6 pm, and most people observe the dress code of the evening, unlike on some other cruise lines.

Junior Cruisers

Each Celebrity vessel has a dedicated playroom and offers a four-tier program of age-appropriate games and activities designed for children ages 3 to 5, 6 to 8, and 9 to 11. Younger children must be toilet trained to participate in the programs and use the facilities; however, families are welcome to borrow toys for their non–toilet-trained kids. A fee may be assessed for participation in children's dinner parties, the Late-Night Slumber Party, and Afternoon Get-Togethers while parents are ashore in ports of call. Evening in-cabin babysitting can be arranged for a fee. All ships have teen centers, where tweens and teenagers (ages 12 to 17) can hang out and attend mock-tail and pizza parties.

Service

Service on Celebrity ships is unobtrusive and polished. Concierge-class adds an unexpected level of service and amenities that are usually reserved for luxury ships or passengers in top-category suites on other premium cruise lines.

CHOOSE THIS LINE IF ...

You want an upscale atmosphere at a really reasonable fare.

You don't mind paying extra for exceptional specialty dining experiences.

You want to dine amid elegant surroundings in some of the best restaurants at sea.

Tipping

Gratuities are automatically added daily to onboard accounts in the following amounts (which may be adjusted at your discretion): $12 per person per day for passengers in stateroom categories; $12.50 per person per day for Concierge-class and Aqua-class staterooms; and $15.50 per person per day for suites. An automatic gratuity of 15% is added to all beverage tabs, minibar purchases, and salon and spa services.

Past Passengers

Once you've sailed with Celebrity, you become a member of the Captain's Club and receive benefits commensurate with the number of cruises you've taken, including free upgrades, the chance to make dining reservations before sailing, and other benefits. Classic members have been on at least one Celebrity cruise. Select members have sailed at least six cruises and get more perks, including an invitation to a senior officer's cocktail party. After 10 cruises you become an Elite member and can take advantage of a private departure lounge. Royal Caribbean International, the parent company of Celebrity Cruises, also extends the corresponding levels of their Crown & Anchor program to Celebrity Captain's Club members.

HELPFUL HINTS

■ Wine/dining packages are a comparative bargain since fees for specialty restaurants are so high, but they are only offered in limited numbers; book them early.

■ The line offers stateroom bar setups and flat-rate beverage packages to help you avoid per-drink charges.

■ Ship's photographers will cover individual special events if asked.

■ Service animals are welcome on board all ships, including those sailing to the United Kingdom if they are in compliance with DEFRA regulations.

■ Celebrity's private shore excursions (in 50 ports) offer personalized travel in the comfort of a private car or van.

3

CELEBRITY CRUISES

DON'T CHOOSE THIS LINE IF ...

You need to be reminded of when activities are scheduled. Announcements are kept to a minimum.

You look forward to boisterous pool games and wacky contests. These cruises are fairly quiet and sophisticated.

You think funky avant-garde art is weird. Abstract modernism abounds in the art collections.

SOLSTICE-CLASS
Solstice, Equinox, Eclipse, Silhouette, Reflection

CREW MEMBERS	
1,253	
ENTERED SERVICE	
2008, 2009, 2010, 2011, 2012	
700 ft. **GROSS TONS**	
122,000, 126,000 (*Reflection*)	
LENGTH	
1,033 feet, 1,047 feet (*Reflection*)	
500 ft. **NUMBER OF CABINS**	
1,425, 1,515 (*Reflection*)	
PASSENGER CAPACITY	
2,850, 3,046 (*Reflection*)	
300 ft. **WIDTH**	
121 feet, 123 feet (*Reflection*)	

Solstice-class ships are the largest in the Celebrity fleet. While the ships are contemporary in design—even a bit edgy for Celebrity—the line included enough spaces with old-world ambience to satisfy traditionalists. The atmosphere is not unlike a hip boutique hotel yet filled with grand spaces, as well as intimate nooks and crannies. *Celebrity Reflection* adds an additional deck for more high-end suite accommodations.

The Lawn Club, a half acre of real grass on deck 15, is where you can play genteel games of croquet, practice golf putting, indulge in lawn games and picnics, or simply take barefoot strolls. In a nearby open-air "theater" on *Solstice, Eclipse,* and *Equinox,* artisans demonstrate glassmaking in the Hot Glass Show. A similar space on *Silhouette* and *Reflection* houses an outdoor grill restaurant, and those ships also have private cabanas in the Lawn Club (for a fee). These ships have a lot to offer families, with a family pool and the most extensive children's facilities in the Celebrity fleet.

Cabins
Layout: Although cabins are larger than those on other Celebrity ships, closet and drawer storage is barely adequate. On the other hand, bathrooms are generous and have plentiful storage space. An impressive 85% of all outside accommodations have balconies. With sofa–trundle beds, many categories are capable of accommodating third and fourth occupants. Connecting staterooms are also available. Family staterooms have a second bedroom with bunk beds.

Suites: Most suites have a whirlpool tub, DVD, and walk-in closet, while all have butler service, personalized stationery, and a logo tote bag. Penthouse suites have guest powder rooms; Penthouse and Royal suites have whirlpool tubs on the balconies. *Celebrity Reflection* introduces several additional suite categories.

Amenities: A refrigerator, TV, personal safe, hair dryer, seating area with sofa and table, bathroom toiletries (shampoo, soaps, and lotion), and bathrobes for use during the cruise are standard.

Accessibility: Thirty staterooms are designed for wheelchair accessibility.

Top: Blu, the AquaClass specialty restaurant
Bottom: Lawn bowling

Restaurants

The main restaurant serves open seating breakfast and lunch; dinner is served in two traditional assigned seatings or an open seating option. A second dining room, reserved for Aqua-class passengers, serves lighter cuisine. There are also a casual Lido buffet, pizza, a sushi bar, the AquaSpa Café with healthy selections, a luncheon grill, a café that offers crepes (cover charge), and specialty coffee, tea, and gelato bar (extra charge). Three upscale alternative restaurants require dinner reservations and charge extra for contemporary French, Asian fusion, and Italian. *Eclipse, Silhouette,* and *Reflection* replaced the Asian restaurant with one serving modern American food. Additionally, *Silhouette,* and *Reflection* feature the Lawn Club Grill for evening alfresco dining (cover charge) and the Porch for light breakfast and lunch fare (cover charge). Available 24 hours, room service rounds out the dining choices.

Spas

The AquaSpa by Elemis is one of the most tranquil at sea with spa services operated by Steiner Leisure. In addition to treatments that include a variety of massages, body wraps, and facials, each ship also has an acupuncture treatment area and Medi-Spa Cosmetic services. A relaxation room and thermal suite with dry and aromatherapy steam rooms and a hot Turkish bath are available to Aqua-class passengers and those who have booked a treatment or purchased a pass. Changing rooms for men and women have complimentary saunas.

Bars and Entertainment

Production companies and guest entertainers perform in the show lounges. Bars and lounges are designed as unique destinations on board with drink menus offering not only a selection of classics, but also "signature" and trendier cocktails. Some drinks are a reflection of the regions you are visiting. Live bands or DJs provide music for listening and dancing.

Pros and Cons

Pros: an interactive TV system allows you to book shore excursions and order room service; Aqua-class has its own staircase direct to the spa; a Hospitality Director oversees restaurant reservations.

Cons: closet space is skimpy in standard cabins; there are no self-service laundries; dining choices are plentiful, but pricey.

Cabin Type	Size (sq. ft.)
Penthouse/ Refection Suite	1,291/ 1,636
Royal Suites	590
Celebrity/ Signature Suites	394/441
Sky/Aqua-Class Suites	300
Family Ocean-View Balcony	575
Ocean-View Balcony	194
Sunset Veranda	194
Ocean View	177
Inside	183–200

FAST FACTS

- 13 passenger decks (14 *Celebrity Reflection*)
- 4 specialty restaurants (5 *Celebrity Reflection*), 3 dining rooms, buffet, ice cream parlor, pizzeria
- Wi-Fi, safe, refrigerator, DVD (some)
- 3 pools (1 indoor)
- Fitness classes, gym, hot tubs, sauna, spa
- 11 bars, casino, dance club, library, show room, video game room
- Children's programs
- Dry-cleaning, laundry service
- Internet terminal
- No-smoking cabins

The solarium on *Solstice*

MILLENNIUM-CLASS
Millennium, Summit, Infinity, Constellation

CREW MEMBERS	999
ENTERED SERVICE	2000, 2001, 2001, 2002
GROSS TONS	91,000
LENGTH	965 feet
NUMBER OF CABINS	1069, 1079, 1085, 1085
PASSENGER CAPACITY	2,138, 2,158, 2,170, 2,170
WIDTH	105 feet

700 ft.

500 ft.

300 ft.

Millennium-class ships are among the largest and most feature-filled in the Celebrity fleet. The ships include show lounges reminiscent of splendid opera houses, and an alternative restaurant with a classic ocean liner theme. The spas are immense and house a complimentary hydrotherapy pool and café. These ships have a lot to offer families, with some of the most expansive children's facilities in the Celebrity fleet. Recent upgrades have introduced more accommodation categories and dining venues similar to those found on Solstice-class ships.

Rich fabrics in jewel tones mix elegantly with the abundant use of marble and wood accents throughout public areas. The atmosphere is not unlike a luxurious European hotel filled with grand spaces that flow nicely from one to the other.

Cabins

Layout: As on most Celebrity ships, cabins are thoughtfully designed, with ample closet and drawer/shelf storage, as well as bathroom shelves. Some ocean-view cabins and suites have balconies. Penthouse suites also have guest powder rooms. Most staterooms and suites have convertible sofa beds, and many can accommodate third and fourth occupants. Connecting staterooms are also widely available. Family staterooms have huge balconies, and some have two sofa beds. Aqua-class accommodations with direct spa access are a relatively new addition.

Amenities: A small refrigerator, personal safe, hair dryer, and a seating area with sofa, chair, and table are typical standard amenities. Extras include bathroom toiletries (shampoo, soaps, and lotion) and bathrobes. Suite luxuries vary, but most include a whirlpool tub, a DVD, an Internet-connected computer, and a walk-in closet, while all have butler service, personalized stationery, and a logo tote bag. Penthouse and Royal suites have outdoor whirlpool tubs on the balconies.

Accessibility: Twenty-six staterooms are designed for wheelchair accessibility.

Top: *Millennium* Cova Café
Bottom: *Millennium* Ocean Grill

Restaurants

The formal two-deck restaurant serves open seating breakfast and lunch, while dinner is served in two assigned seatings or open seating. The casual Lido buffet offers breakfast and lunch; for dinner, it has made-to-order entrées, a carving station, and an array of side dishes. A poolside grill offers fast food, while a spa café serves lighter fare. Each ship has an upscale alternative restaurant that specializes in table-side food preparation; each also has a demonstration kitchen and wine cellar (reservation and cover charge). Each also has a café that offers crepes and other light items (cover charge), and an extra-charge specialty coffee, tea, and gelato bar. All ships feature a second specialty restaurant serving modern American food except *Constellation*, which serves Italian cuisine. Pizza delivery and 24-hour room service augment dining choices.

Spas

The AquaSpa by Elemis is one of the most nicely equipped at sea with spa services operated by Steiner Leisure. In addition to treatments that include a variety of massages, body wraps, and facials, each ship also has an acupuncture treatment area and offers Medi-Spa Cosmetic services. A relaxation room and thermal suite with a dry sauna, aromatherapy steam room, and a Turkish bath are available to Aqua-class passengers and those who have booked a treatment or purchased a pass. Changing rooms for men and women have complimentary saunas, and a large hydrotherapy pool is available to all adults at no charge.

Bars and Entertainment

Production companies and guest entertainers perform in the show lounges. Bars and lounges are designed as unique destinations on board with drink menus with both classic and also "signature" and trendier cocktails. Some drinks are a reflection of the regions you are visiting. Live bands or DJs provide music for listening and dancing.

Pros and Cons

Pros: stylishly appointed Grand Foyers have sweeping staircases; there's no charge for use of the thalassotherapy pool in the Solarium; the AquaSpa Café serves complimentary light and healthy selections.

Cons: these ships just have too many passengers to offer truly personal service; wines in the specialty restaurants are pricey; there are no self-service laundries.

Cabin Type	Size (sq. ft.)
Penthouse Suite	1,432
Royal Suite	538
Celebrity Suite	467
Sky Suite	251
Family Ocean View	271
Concierge-Class	191
Ocean View/ Interior	170

FAST FACTS

- 11 passenger decks
- 3 specialty restaurants, dining room, buffet, ice cream parlor, pizzeria
- Internet (*Constellation*), Wi-Fi, safe, refrigerator, DVD (some)
- 3 pools (1 indoor), children's pool
- Fitness classes, gym, hot tubs, sauna, spa, steam room
- 7 bars, casino, dance club, library, show room, video game room
- Children's programs
- Dry-cleaning, laundry service
- Internet terminal
- No-smoking cabins

Millennium-class conservatory

3

CELEBRITY CRUISES

CENTURY-CLASS
Century

CREW MEMBERS	858
ENTERED SERVICE	1995
GROSS TONS	70,606
LENGTH	815 feet
NUMBER OF CABINS	907
PASSENGER CAPACITY	1,814
WIDTH	105 feet

700 ft.

500 ft.

300 ft.

Top: Formal dining on *Century*
Bottom: *Century* Shipmates
Fun Factory

Although quietly elegant, *Celebrity Century* has an eclectic air, due in part to the fine collections of modern and classical art displayed throughout public rooms. A 2006 refit added a stunning specialty restaurant, an ice-topped martini bar, 14 suites, and 10 staterooms (both inside and outside), not to mention 314 verandas—the most ever added to an existing cruise ship at that time.

Century has facilities for children and teens, but adults fare much better on board with a spectacular spa and sophisticated lounges dedicated to a variety of tastes. The dining room is nothing short of gorgeous. Overall, the first impression is that this is a fine resort hotel that just happens to float.

Cabins

Layout: As on all Celebrity ships, cabins are thoughtfully designed with ample closet and drawer/shelf storage and bathroom shelves. Some ocean-view cabins and suites have balconies with chairs and tables. Penthouse and Royal suites have a whirlpool bathtub and separate shower as well as a walk-in closet; Penthouse suites have a guest powder room. *Century* also has Family Veranda Staterooms.

Amenities: Light-wood cabinetry, mirrored accents, a refrigerator, a personal safe, a hair dryer, and a seating area with sofa, chair, and table are typical standard amenities. Extras include bathroom toiletries (shampoo, soaps, and lotion) and bathrobes for use during the cruise. Penthouse and Royal suites have an elaborate entertainment center with a large TV, while all suites include butler service, personalized stationery, DVD, and a tote bag.

Accessibility: Eight staterooms are designed for wheelchair accessibility.

Restaurants

The formal two-deck restaurant serves open seating breakfast, lunch, and evening meals in two assigned seatings; however, Celebrity Select Dining, an open seating option, allows participants to be seated any time the main restaurant is open. Formal dining is supplemented by a casual Lido restaurant offering buffet-style breakfast and lunch. By night, the Lido restaurant offers made-to-order entrées, a carving station, and an array of side dishes. *Century* has both a complimentary spa café and an upscale, reservations-only restaurant that specializes in table-side preparation and has an extra cover charge. Poolside grills offer burgers and other fast-food favorites and specialty coffees, teas, and pastries are available for an additional charge in the café. Room service is available 24 hours and includes pizza delivered to your door.

Spas

The AquaSpa by Elemis facilities are nicely equipped with services operated by Steiner Leisure. In addition to treatments that include a variety of massages, body wraps, and facials, each ship also has an acupuncture treatment area and offers Medi-Spa Cosmetic services. A thermal suite with dry sauna and aromatherapy steam rooms and a hot Turkish bath is available to passengers who have booked a treatment or purchased a pass. Changing rooms for men and women have complimentary saunas.

Bars and Entertainment

Bars and lounges are designed as unique destinations on board with drink menus offering not only a selection of classics, but also "signature" and trendier cocktails. Some drinks are a reflection of the regions you are visiting. Production shows and guest entertainers are a staple in the show lounge and live bands or DJs provide music for listening and dancing.

Pros and Cons

Pros: Michael's Club, once a cigar lounge, is now a smoke-free piano bar; the food and service is more than worth the price; you can descend a fairly grand staircase to dine in the tradition of great ocean liners.

Cons: the trendsetting thalassotherapy pool has been removed; there is no dedicated swimming pool for small children; a downside for smokers is that smoking is not allowed in most indoor spaces or on balconies.

Cabin Type	Size (sq. ft.)
Penthouse Suite	1,101
Royal Suite/Sky Suite	537/246
Century Suite/ Family Stateroom	190/192
Concierge, Veranda/Ocean View	170–175/172–175
Interior	171–174

FAST FACTS

- 10 passenger decks
- Specialty restaurant, dining room, buffet, ice cream parlor, pizzeria
- Wi-Fi, safe, refrigerator, DVD (some)
- 2 pools
- Fitness classes, gym, hot tubs, sauna, spa
- 7 bars, casino, dance club, library, show room, video game room
- Children's programs
- Dry-cleaning, laundry service
- Internet terminal
- No-smoking cabins

DISNEY CRUISE LINE

With the launch of Disney Cruise Line in 1998, families were offered yet another reason to take a cruise. The magic of a Walt Disney resort vacation plus the romance of a sea voyage are a tempting combination, especially for adults who discovered Disney

Disney ships have a classic style

movies and the Mickey Mouse Club as children. Mixed with traditional shipboard activities, who can resist scheduled opportunities for the young and young-at-heart to interact with their favorite Disney characters?

☎ 407/566–3500 or 888/325–2500
⊕ www.disneycruise.com
☞ Cruise Style: Mainstream.

Although Disney Cruise Line voyages stuck to tried-and-true Bahamas and Caribbean itineraries in their formative years, and sailed exclusively from Port Canaveral, Florida, where a terminal was designed especially for Disney ships, the line has branched out to other regions, including Europe.

Food

Don't expect top chefs and gourmet food. This is Disney, and the fare in each ship's casual restaurants is all-American for the most part. A third restaurant is a bit fancier, with French-inspired dishes on the menus. Naturally, all have children's menus with an array of favorite sandwiches and entrées. Vegetarian and healthy selections are also available in all restaurants. A bonus is complementary soft drinks, lemonade, and iced tea throughout the sailing. A beverage station in the buffet area is always open; however, there is a charge for soft drinks ordered from the bars and room service.

Palo, the adults-only restaurant serving northern Italian cuisine, requires reservations for a romantic evening of fine dining. Although there's a cover charge for dinner, it's a steal and reservations go fast. A brunch also commands a surcharge. More upscale and pricey, Remy on *Disney Dream* and *Disney Fantasy* serves French cuisine in an elegant atmosphere.

Entertainment

Shipboard entertainment leans heavily on popular Disney themes and characters. Parents are actively involved in the audience with their children at production shows, movies, live character meetings, deck parties, and dancing in the family nightclub. Teens have a supervised, no-adults-allowed club space in the forward fake funnel, where they gather for activities and parties. For adults, there are traditional no-kids-allowed bars and lounges with live music, dancing, theme parties, and late-night comedy, as well as daytime wine-tasting sessions, game shows, culinary arts and home entertaining demonstrations, and behind-the-scenes lectures on animation and filmmaking. This is Disney, so there are no casinos.

A giant LED screen is affixed to the forward funnels of both the original ships and their newer fleetmates. Passengers can watch movies and special broadcasts while lounging in the family pool area.

Fitness and Recreation

Three swimming pool areas are designated for different groups: children (Mickey's Pool, which has a waterslide and requires a parent to be present); families (Goofy Pool); and adults (Quiet Cove). Young children who aren't potty trained can't swim in the pools but are invited to splash about in the fountain play area near Mickey's Pool. Be sure to bring their swim diapers.

The salon and spa feature a complete menu of hair- and nail-care services as well as facials and massages. The Tropical Rainforest is a soothing coed thermal suite with heated tile lounges. It's complimentary for the day if you book a spa treatment or available on a daily or cruise-long basis for a fee. SpaVillas are indoor–outdoor treatment suites that feature a veranda with a hot tub and an open-air shower. In addition to a nicely equipped fitness center and aerobics studio are a jogging track and basketball court.

Your Shipmates

Disney Cruises appeal to kids of all ages—the young and not so young, singles, couples, and families. Multigeneration family groups are the core audience for these ships, and the facilities are ideal for family gatherings. What you might not have expected are the numerous newlywed couples celebrating their honeymoons on board.

KNOWN FOR

- Character Interaction: Disney characters make frequent appearances.

- Classic Ships: Classic ship design (Disney's are the first passenger ships since the 1950s to have two funnels).

- Entertainment: Some of the best entertainment at sea for guests of all ages.

- Fireworks: Among the few ships that are allowed to host fireworks at sea.

- Kid Stuff: Excellent facilities for children and teens.

3

DISNEY CRUISE LINE

Top: Dining in Palo, the adults-only restaurant
Bottom: Relax in a Mickey-approved spa

Top: Sweet treats await you
on board
Middle: Enjoy a quarter-mile
track for walking or jogging
Bottom: *Disney Magic* and
Disney Wonder at sea

Dress Code

One-week cruises schedule a semiformal evening and
a formal night, during which men are encouraged to
wear tuxedos, but dark suits or sport coats and ties are
acceptable for both. Resort casual is the evening dress
code for dinner in the more laid-back dining rooms.
A sport coat is appropriate for the restaurants designated as fancier, as well as the adults-only specialty
restaurants, where a jacket is required at Remy and
suggested for Palo.

Junior Cruisers

As expected, Disney ships have extensive programs
for children and teens, including shore excursions
designed for families to enjoy together. Parents are
issued a pager for peace of mind while their children
are participating in onboard activities and to alert
them when their offspring need them. Complimentary
age-appropriate activities are scheduled from 9 am to
midnight in the Oceaneer Club and Oceaneer Lab for
ages 3 to 12. While some activities are recommended
for certain age groups, participation is based on the
child's interest level and maturity. Activities include
arts projects, contests, computer games, pool parties,
interactive lab stations, and opportunities for individual and group play. The emphasis is on fun over
education, but subtle educational themes are certainly there. Coffeehouse-style tween (ages 11–14) and
teen (ages 14–17) clubs offer music, a dance floor,
big-screen TV, and Internet café for the younger set.
Scheduled activities include challenging games, photography lessons, sporting contests, beach events, and
parties, but they are also great places to just hang out
with new friends in an adult-free zone.

An hourly fee is charged for child care in Floun-
der's Reef Nursery, which is open during select hours
for infants as young as three months through three
years. Supply your own diapers, and nursery attendants will change them. Private, in-cabin babysitting
is not available.

CHOOSE THIS LINE IF ...

You want to cruise with the
entire family—Mom, Dad, the
kids, and grandparents.

You enjoy having kids around.
(There are adults-only areas
to retreat to when the fun
wears off.)

Your family enjoys Disney's
theme parks and can't
get enough wholesome
entertainment.

Service

Friendly service is extended to all passengers, with particular importance placed on treating children with the same courtesy extended to adults.

Tipping

Suggested gratuity amounts are calculated on a per-person per-cruise rather than per-night basis and can be added to onboard accounts or offered in cash on the last night of the cruise. Guidelines include gratuities for your dining-room server, assistant server, head server, and stateroom host/hostess on the basis of $12 per night in the following amounts: $36 for three-night cruises, $48 for four-night cruises, and $84 for seven-night cruises. Tips for room-service delivery, spa services, and the dining manager are at the passenger's discretion. An automatic 15% gratuity is added to all bar tabs.

Past Passengers

Castaway Club membership is automatic after completing a Disney cruise. Benefits include a complimentary gift (such as a tote bag or beach towel), communication about special offers, priority check-in, invitations to shipboard cocktail parties during subsequent cruises, and a special toll-free reservation telephone number (☎ *800/449–3380*) for convenience.

HELPFUL HINTS

■ There are hidden Mickeys all over the ships, just as in the theme parks.

■ Consider buying pins and autograph books at a Disney store before your cruise.

■ You can reserve many services and make dinner reservations prior to sailing.

■ Roomier than average standard cabins can easily handle four occupants.

■ Alcohol may be brought on board but must be hand-carried on embarkation by an adult, age 21 or older.

3

DISNEY CRUISE LINE

DON'T CHOOSE THIS LINE IF ...

You want to spend a lot of quality time bonding with your kids. Your kids may not want to leave the fun activities.

You want to dine in peace and quiet. The dining rooms and buffet can be boisterous.

You want to gamble. There are no casinos, so you'll have to settle for bingo.

DISNEY MAGIC, DISNEY WONDER

CREW MEMBERS	950
ENTERED SERVICE	1998, 1999
GROSS TONS	83,000
LENGTH	964 feet
NUMBER OF CABINS	877
PASSENGER CAPACITY	1,754 (2,400 max)
WIDTH	106 feet

700 ft.

500 ft.

300 ft.

Reminiscent of classic ocean liners, Disney vessels have two funnels (the forward one is nonfunctional) and high-tech interiors behind their art deco and art nouveau styling. Whimsical design accents cleverly incorporate images of Mickey Mouse and his friends without overpowering the warm and elegant decor. Artwork showcases the creativity of Disney artists and animators. The atmosphere is never stuffy.

More than 15,000 square feet—nearly an entire deck—are devoted to children's activity centers, outdoor activity areas, and swimming pools. Theaters cater to family entertainment with large-scale production shows, movies, dances, lively game shows, and even 3-D movies.

Adults-only hideaways include an avenue of theme bars and lounges tucked into the area just forward of the lobby atrium; the Promenade Lounge, near the aft elevator lobby; and Cove Café, a quiet spot adjacent to the adult pool to relax with coffee or a cocktail, surf the Internet, or read.

Cabins

Layout: Designed for families, Disney ships have some of the roomiest, most functional staterooms at sea. Natural woods, imported tiles, and a nautical flavor add to the decor, which even includes the touch of Disney-inspired artwork on the walls. Most cabins can accommodate at least three people and have a seating area and unique bath-and-a-half arrangement. Three-quarters of all accommodations are outside cabins, and 44% of those include private balconies with kid-proof door handles and higher-than-usual railings for safety. All cabins have adequate closet and drawer/shelf storage, as well as bathroom shelves.

Suites: Suites are truly expansive, with master bedrooms separated from the living areas for privacy. All suites have walk-in closets, a dining table and chairs, a wet bar, a DVD player, and a large balcony.

Amenities: Though not luxurious, Disney cabins are comfortably furnished. Each has a flat-screen TV, a small refrigerator, a personal safe, and a hair dryer; bathrobes are provided for use during the cruise in the top-category staterooms. All suites have concierge service.

Top: Friendships are forged on a cruise
Bottom: Dreams come true on a Disney cruise

Accessibility: Sixteen cabins are wheelchair accessible.

Restaurants

In a novel approach to dining, passengers (and their waiters) rotate through the three main dining rooms in assigned seatings. Parrot Cay (*Disney Wonder*), Carioca's (*Disney Magic*) and Animator's Palate are casual, while Triton's (*Disney Wonder*) and Lumière's (*Disney Magic*) are a bit fancier. Palo is a beautifully appointed northern Italian restaurant for adults only that requires reservations for brunch, dinner, or tea and carries an extra charge. Breakfast and lunch are open seating in dining rooms. Disney characters make an appearance at a character breakfast on seven-night cruises. Breakfast, lunch, and dinner are also offered in the casual pool-deck buffet, while poolside pizzerias, snack bars, grills, and ice-cream bars serve everything from pizza, burgers, and hot dogs to fresh fruit, wraps, and frozen treats during the day. Specialty coffees are available in the adults-only Cove Café for an extra charge. Room service is available around the clock.

Spas

Spas feature a complete menu of facials and massages. The Tropical Rainforest is a soothing coed thermal suite with heated tile lounges and is complimentary for the day if you book a spa treatment; it's available on a daily or cruise-long basis for a fee. SpaVillas, indoor–outdoor treatment suites, each have a veranda with a hot tub and an open-air shower.

Bars and Entertainment

After the energetic production shows, deck parties, and activities designed for the entire family, adults can slip off to bars and lounges reserved for them after dark, including a sports bar or nightclub where the entertainment staff offers activities such as karaoke or themed dance parties. For quiet conversation and a drink under the stars, there's a cozy bar alongside the adult pool.

Pros and Cons

Pros: there are plenty of connecting cabins that fit three up to seven; soft drinks at meals and beverage stations are complimentary; for adults, each ship has a piano bar/jazz.

Cons: only the splash play areas are available for youngsters who wear swim diapers; although a Disney cruise isn't all Disney all the time, it can get tiring if you aren't really into the atmosphere; there's no library on board.

Cabin Type	Size (sq. ft.)
Royal Suites	1,029
Two-Bedroom Suite	945
One-Bedroom Suite	614
Deluxe Family Balcony	304
Deluxe Balcony	268
Ocean View	226
Deluxe Inside	214
Standard Inside	184

Dimensions include the square footage for balconies.

FAST FACTS

- 11 passenger decks
- Specialty restaurant, 3 dining rooms, buffet, ice cream parlor, pizzeria
- Wi-Fi, safe, refrigerator, DVD (some)
- 2 pools, children's pool
- Fitness classes, gym, hot tubs, sauna, spa
- 6 bars, dance club, 2 show rooms, video game room
- Children's programs
- Dry-cleaning, laundry facilities, laundry service
- Internet terminal
- No kids under 12 weeks
- No-smoking cabins

Goofy touches up the paint on *Disney Magic*

3

DISNEY CRUISE LINE

HOLLAND AMERICA LINE

Holland America Line has enjoyed a distinguished record of traditional cruises, world exploration, and transatlantic crossings since 1873—all facets of its history that are reflected in the fleet's multimillion-dollar shipboard art and antiques collections. Even

A day on the Lido Deck

the ships' names follow a pattern set long ago: all end in the suffix *dam* and are either derived from the names of various dams that cross Holland's rivers, important Dutch landmarks, or points of the compass. The names are even recycled when vessels are retired, and some are in their fifth and sixth generation of use.

☎ *206/281–3535 or 800/577–1728*
⊕ *www.holland america.com*
☞ *Cruise Style: Premium.*

Noted for focusing on passenger comfort, Holland America Line cruises are classic in design and style, and with an infusion of younger adults and families on board, they remain refined without being stuffy or stodgy. Following a basic design theme, returning passengers feel as at home on the newest Holland America vessels as they do on older ones.

Food

Holland America Line chefs, led by Master Chef Rudi Sodamin, utilize more than 500 different food items on a typical weeklong cruise to create the modern Continental cuisine and traditional favorites served to their passengers. Vegetarian options as well as health-conscious cuisine are available, and special dietary requests can be handled with advance notice. But the food quality, taste, and selection have greatly improved in recent years. A case in point is the reservations-required Pinnacle Grill alternative restaurants, where fresh seafood and premium cuts of Sterling Silver beef are used to prepare creative specialty dishes. The $25-per-person charge for dinner would be worth it for the Dungeness crab cakes starter and dessert alone. Other delicious traditions are afternoon tea, a

Dutch Chocolate Extravaganza, and Holland America Line's signature bread pudding.

Flexible scheduling allows for early or late seatings in the two-deck, formal restaurants. An open seating option from 5:15 to 9 has been introduced fleetwide.

Entertainment

Entertainment tends to be more Broadway-stylish than Las Vegas–brash. Colorful revues are presented in main show lounges by the ships' companies of singers and dancers. Other performances might include a range of cabaret acts: comedians, magicians, jugglers, and acrobats. Live bands play a wide range of musical styles for dancing and listening in smaller lounges and piano bars. Movies are shown daily in cinemas that double as the Culinary Arts Centers.

Holland America Line may never be considered cutting-edge, but their innovative Signature of Excellence concept sets it apart from other premium cruise lines. An interactive Culinary Arts Center offers cooking demonstrations and wine-tasting sessions; Explorations Café (powered by the *New York Times*) is a coffeehouse, library, and Internet center; the Explorations Guest Speakers Series is supported by in-cabin televised programming on flat-screen TVs in all cabins; the traditional Crow's Nest observation lounge has a nightclub-disco layout, video wall, and sound-and-light systems; and facilities for children and teens have been greatly expanded.

Fitness and Recreation

Well-equipped and fully staffed fitness facilities contain state-of-the-art exercise equipment; basic fitness classes are available at no charge. There's a fee for personal training, body composition analysis, and specialized classes such as yoga and Pilates.

Treatments in the Greenhouse Spa include a variety of massages, body wraps, and facials. Hair styling and nail services are offered in the salons. All ships have a jogging track, multiple swimming pools, and sports courts; some have hydrotherapy pools and soothing thermal suites.

Your Shipmates

No longer just your grandparents' cruise line, today's Holland America sailings attract families and couples, mostly from their late thirties on up. Holidays and summer months are peak periods when you'll find more children in the mix. Retirees are often still in the majority, particularly on longer cruises. Families

KNOWN FOR

■ **Comfort:** Ships in the fleet are noted for their cozy and warm atmosphere.

■ **Consistency:** From afternoon tea to the chimes that announce dinner, each ship in the fleet delivers the expected experience.

■ **The Promenade:** A trademark of each ship is its wraparound promenade deck for walking, jogging, or stretching out in the shade on a padded steamer chair.

■ **Service:** It's not unusual for crew members to remember passengers' names, even if they haven't seen them for years.

■ **Tradition Rules:** Holland America Line is one of the most traditional cruise lines, and the line's history is an important part of the experience.

Top: Casino action
Bottom: Stay fit or stay loose

Top: Soak up some sun on the outdoor deck
Middle: Production showtime
Bottom: Spa relaxation

cruising together who book five or more cabins receive perks such as a fountain-soda package for each family member, a family photo for each stateroom, and complimentary water toys at Half Moon Cay (for Caribbean itineraries that call at the private island). If the group is larger than 10 cabins, the Head-of-Family is recognized with an upgrade from outside stateroom to a veranda cabin. It's the best family deal at sea, and there's no extra charge.

Dress Code

Evenings on Holland America Line cruises fall into two categories: smart casual and formal. For the two formal nights standard on seven-night cruises, men are encouraged to wear tuxedos, but dark suits or sport coats and ties are acceptable, and you'll certainly see them. On smart-casual nights, expect the type of attire you'd see at a country club or upscale resort. It's requested that no T-shirts, jeans, swimsuits, tank tops, or shorts be worn in public areas after 6 pm.

Junior Cruisers

Club HAL is Holland America Line's professionally staffed youth and teen program. Age-appropriate activities planned for children ages 3 to 7 include storytelling, arts and crafts, ice cream or pizza parties, and games; for children ages 8 to 12 there are arcade games, Sony PlayStations, theme parties, on-deck sports events, and scavenger hunts. Club HAL After Hours offers late-night activities from 10 pm until midnight for an hourly fee. Baby food, diapers, cribs, high chairs, and booster seats may be requested in advance of boarding. Private in-cabin babysitting is sometimes available if a staff member is willing.

Teens ages 13 to 17 have their own lounge, with activities including dance contests, arcade games, sports tournaments, movies, and an exclusive sundeck on some ships. Most Caribbean itineraries offer water park–type facilities and kid-friendly shore excursions to Half Moon Cay, Holland America Line's private island in the Bahamas.

CHOOSE THIS LINE IF ...

You crave relaxation. Grab a padded steamer chair on the teak promenade deck and watch the sea pass by.

You like to go to the movies, especially when the popcorn is free.

You want to bring the kids. Areas designed exclusively for children and teens are hot new features on all ships.

Service

Professional, unobtrusive service by the Indonesian and Filipino staff is a fleet-wide standard on Holland America Line. Crew members are trained in Indonesia at a custom-built facility called the MS *Nieuw Jakarta*, where employees polish their English-language skills and learn housekeeping in mock cabins.

Tipping

Gratuities of $11.50 per passenger per day, or $12 per passenger per day for suite passengers, are automatically added to shipboard accounts, and distributed to stewards and waitstaff. Passengers may adjust the amount based on the level of service experienced. Room-service tips are usually given in cash (it's at the passenger's discretion here). Gratuities for spa and salon services can be added to the bill or offered in cash. An automatic 15% gratuity is added to bar-service tabs.

Past Passengers

All passengers who sail with Holland America Line are automatically enrolled in the Mariner Society and receive special offers on upcoming cruises, as well as insider information concerning new ships and product enhancements. Mariner Society benefits also include preferred pricing on many cruises; Mariner baggage tags and buttons that identify you as a member during embarkation; an invitation to the Mariner Society champagne reception and awards party hosted by the captain; lapel pins and medallions acknowledging your history of Holland America sailings; a special collectible gift delivered to your cabin; and a subscription to *Mariner,* the full-color magazine featuring news and Mariner Society savings.

HELPFUL HINTS

■ Charges for specialty dining on Holland America Line ships are some of the most reasonable at sea.

■ All passengers are presented with a complimentary canvas tote bag imprinted with the line's logo.

■ Narrated iPod art tours of the ships' art collections can be borrowed from the library on each vessel.

■ A wide variety of shore excursions that fit lifestyles ranging from easygoing to active adventure can be booked before sailing.

■ A reservation may be canceled for any reason whatsoever up to 24 hours prior to departure and a refund of 80% to 90% of eligible amounts will be paid.

3

HOLLAND AMERICA LINE

DON'T CHOOSE THIS LINE IF ...

You want to party hard. Most of the action on these ships ends relatively early.

Dressing for dinner isn't your thing. Passengers tend to ramp up the dress code most evenings.

You have an aversion to extending tips. The line's "tipping not required" policy has been dropped.

ROTTERDAM, AMSTERDAM

CREW MEMBERS	600, 615
ENTERED SERVICE	1997, 2000
GROSS TONS	61,859/62,735
LENGTH	780 feet
NUMBER OF CABINS	702, 690
PASSENGER CAPACITY	1,404, 1,380
WIDTH	106 feet

700 ft.

500 ft.

300 ft.

The most traditional ships in the fleet, the interiors of sister ships *Amsterdam* and *Rotterdam* display abundant wood appointments in the public areas on promenade and lower promenade decks and priceless works of art throughout.

The Ocean Bar, Explorer's Lounge, Wajang Theater, and Crow's Nest are familiar lounges to longtime Holland American passengers. Newer additions include the spa's thermal suite, a culinary-arts demonstration center in the theater, Explorations Café, and expansive areas for children and teens. Multimillion-dollar collections of art and artifacts are showcased throughout both vessels. In addition to works commissioned specifically for each ship, Holland America Line celebrates its heritage by featuring antiques and artworks that reflect the theme of worldwide Dutch seafaring history.

Cabins

Layout: Staterooms are spacious and comfortable, although fewer have private balconies than newer fleetmates. Lanai cabins were added during *Rotterdam*'s latest upgrade. Every cabin has adequate closet and drawer/shelf storage, as well as bathroom shelves. Some suites also have a whirlpool tub, powder room, and walk-in closet. Connecting cabins are available in a range of categories, as well as a number of triple and a few quad cabins.

Suites: Extras include duvets on beds, a fully stocked minibar, and personalized stationery. Penthouse and Deluxe Verandah suites have exclusive use of the Neptune Lounge, concierge service, canapés before dinner, binoculars and umbrellas for use during the cruise, an invitation to a VIP party with the captain, and complimentary laundry, pressing, and dry-cleaning services.

Amenities: All staterooms and suites are appointed with pillow-top mattresses, 250-thread-count cotton bed linens, magnifying halo-lighted mirrors, hair dryers, a fruit basket, flat-panel TVs, and DVD players. Bathrooms have Egyptian cotton towels, nice toiletries, plus deluxe bathrobes to use during the cruise.

Accessibility: Twenty-one staterooms are designed for wheelchair accessibility on *Amsterdam*, 22 on *Rotterdam*.

Top: Pinnacle Grill dining
Bottom: *Rotterdam* at sea

Restaurants

The formal dining room offers open seating breakfast and lunch, as well as two assigned seatings or open seating for dinner. Pinnacle Grill (reservation, cover charge) serves lunch and dinner. A casual Lido restaurant serves buffet breakfast and lunch; at dinner, the Lido offers waiter service. Italian fare is served in the adjacent Canaletto Restaurant (reservation, cover charge). Poolside lunch at the Terrace Grill includes fast food and sandwiches. The extra-charge Explorations Café offers specialty coffees and pastries. There's daily afternoon tea service. Complimentary hors d'oeuvres are served by waiters during cocktail hour, hand-dipped chocolates are offered after dinner in the Explorer's Lounge, and a late-night buffet and chocolate extravaganza is served in the Lido restaurant during every cruise. Room service is available 24 hours.

Spas

Treatments in the Greenhouse Spa include a variety of massages, body wraps, and facials, as well as acupuncture and tooth-whitening services. A thermal suite with heated ceramic lounges for relaxation and dry sauna and steam rooms is available for a fee or complimentary for use when a spa appointment is booked. Changing rooms for men and women have complimentary saunas.

Bars and Entertainment

Popular spots before dinner are the Ocean Club and Explorers Lounge, where servers pass through with canapés. Later, those bars are quiet spots for drinks and conversation. For livelier action aboard *Amsterdam*, there's a Sports and Piano Bar; on *Rotterdam*, try Mix—where champagne, martinis, ales, and spirits are served near the piano. The late-night dance spot on both is the Crow's Nest.

Pros and Cons

Pros: *Rotterdam* has the Retreat, a resort-style pool on the aft Lido deck; as the line's flagships, *Rotterdam* and *Amsterdam* have the fleet's most elegant interior decor; realistic landscapes with surreal touches accent walls in *Amsterdam*'s Pinnacle Grill.

Cons: one-way window glass in outside cabins on lower promenade deck does not offer occupants complete privacy; there is little shipboard nightlife more than an hour after dinner; despite excellent facilities designed for kids and teens, family cabins are limited.

Cabin Type	Size (sq. ft.)
Penthouse Suite	1,159
Deluxe Verandah Suite	556
Verandah Suite	292
Lanai	197 (Rotterdam only)
Ocean View	197
Inside	182

Dimensions include the square footage for balconies.

FAST FACTS

- 9 passenger decks
- Specialty restaurant, dining room, buffet
- Wi-Fi, safe, refrigerator, DVD
- 2 pools (1 indoor), 2 children's pools
- Fitness classes, gym, 2 hot tubs, sauna, spa
- 6 bars, casino, dance club, library, show room, video game room
- Children's programs
- Dry-cleaning, laundry facilities, laundry service
- Internet terminal
- No-smoking cabins

3

HOLLAND AMERICA LINE

A brisk walk starts the day

STATENDAM-CLASS
Statendam, Maasdam, Ryndam, Veendam

CREW MEMBERS	580
ENTERED SERVICE	1993, 1993, 1994, 1996
GROSS TONS	55,819, 55,575, 55,819, 57,092
LENGTH	720 feet
NUMBER OF CABINS	630, 658, 630, 675
PASSENGER CAPACITY	1,260, 1,258, 1260, 1,350
WIDTH	101 feet

700 ft.
500 ft.
300 ft.

The sister ships included in the S- or Statendam-class retain the most classic and traditional characteristics of Holland America Line vessels. Routinely updated with innovative features, including Signature of Excellence upgrades, they combine all the advantages of intimate, midsize vessels with high-tech and stylish details.

At the heart of the ships, triple-deck atriums graced by suspended glass sculptures open onto three so-called promenade decks; the lowest contains staterooms encircled by a wide, teak outdoor deck furnished with padded steamer chairs, while interior, art-filled passageways flow past lounges and public rooms on the two decks above. Either reach the lower dining room floor via the aft elevator, or enter one deck above and make a grand entrance down the sweeping staircase.

Cabins

Layout: Staterooms are spacious and comfortable, although fewer of them have private balconies than on newer ships. Lanai cabins, with a door that directly accesses the promenade deck, were added to *Maasdam* and *Veendam* during the ships' latest upgrades. Every cabin has adequate closet and drawer/shelf storage, as well as bathroom shelves. Connecting cabins are featured in a range of categories.

Suites: Suites have duvets on beds, a fully stocked mini-bar, and personalized stationery. Penthouse Verandah and Deluxe Verandah suites have exclusive use of the private Neptune Lounge, personal concierge service, canapés before dinner on request, binoculars and umbrellas for use during the cruise, an invitation to a VIP party with the captain, and complimentary laundry, pressing, and dry-cleaning services.

Amenities: All staterooms and suites are now appointed with pillow-top mattresses, 250-thread-count cotton bed linens, magnifying lighted mirrors, hair dryers, a fruit basket, flat-panel TVs, and DVD players. Bathroom extras include Egyptian cotton towels, shampoo, body lotion, and bath gel, plus deluxe bathrobes to use during the cruise. Accommodations near the spa on *Ryndam, Statendam,* and *Veendam* offer extras such as a yoga mat and iPod docking station.

Accessibility: Nine cabins on each ship are modified with ramps although doors are standard width.

Top: Enjoy a Vegas-style show
Bottom: Deluxe veranda suite

Restaurants

The formal dining room offers open seating breakfast and lunch, as well as both assigned and open seating dinner. Pinnacle Grill (reservation, cover charge) serves lunch and dinner. A casual Lido restaurant serves buffet breakfast and lunch; at dinner the Lido offers waiter service; Italian fare is served in the adjacent Canaletto Restaurant (reservation, cover charge). Poolside lunch is served at the Terrace Grill; on *Veendam* the pizzeria is in the aft pool Retreat area. The extra-charge Explorations Café offers specialty coffees and pastries. Daily afternoon tea service is elevated to Royal Dutch High Tea once per cruise. Complimentary hors d'oeuvres are served by waiters during cocktail hour, hand-dipped chocolates are offered after dinner in the Explorer's Lounge, and a late-night buffet and chocolate extravaganza is served in the Lido restaurant during every cruise. Room service is available 24 hours.

Spas

Treatments in the Greenhouse Spa include a variety of massages, body wraps, and facials, as well as acupuncture services and tooth-whitening treatments. A thermal suite with heated ceramic loungers for relaxation as well as dry saunas and steam rooms can be used by anyone for a fee or is complimentary when a spa appointment is booked.

Bars and Entertainment

Popular before-dinner spots are the Ocean Club and Explorers Lounge, where servers pass through with appetizers. After dinner and a show, a movie, or concert, those bars are quiet spots for drinks and conversation. For livelier action, try Mix—where champagne, martinis, ales, and spirits are served near the piano. The late-night dance spot is still the Crow's Nest.

Pros and Cons

Pros: Statendam-class ships have some of the fleet's most trendy bars; the Ocean Bar hits the right balance for socializing with the after-dinner crowd; movie theaters double as culinary arts centers.

Cons: railings on the balcony level of the main show lounge obstruct the view of the stage; Club HAL can feel empty on some cruises; the addition of Explorations Café means no more free coffee bar.

Cabin Type	Size (sq. ft.)
Penthouse Suite	1,159
Deluxe Verandah Suite	556
Verandah Suite	292
Lanai	197
Ocean View	197
Inside	182

Dimensions include the square footage for balconies.

FAST FACTS

- 10 passenger decks
- Specialty restaurant, dining room, buffet, pizzeria
- Wi-Fi, safe, refrigerator, DVD
- 2 pools (1 indoor), 2 children's pools
- Fitness classes, gym, hot tubs, spa
- 9 bars, casino, dance club, library, show room, video game room
- Children's programs
- Dry-cleaning, laundry facilities, laundry service
- Internet terminal
- No-smoking cabins

3

HOLLAND AMERICA LINE

Share a sunset

VISTA-CLASS
Zuiderdam, Oosterdam, Westerdam, Noordam

ENTERED SERVICE	2002, 2003, 2004, 2006
PASSENGER CAPACITY	1,916, 1,916, 1,916, 1,924
CREW MEMBERS	817, 817, 817, 820
NUMBER OF CABINS	958, 958, 958, 959
GROSS TONS	82,305
LENGTH	936 feet
WIDTH	106 feet

700 ft.

500 ft.

300 ft.

Ships for the 21st century, Vista-class vessels integrate new, youthful, and family-friendly elements into Holland America Line's classic fleet. Exquisite Waterford-crystal sculptures adorn triple-deck atriums and reflect vivid, almost daring color schemes throughout. Although all the public rooms carry the traditional Holland America names (Ocean Bar, Explorer's Lounge, Crow's Nest) and aren't much different in atmosphere, their louder decor (toned down a bit since the introduction of the *Zuiderdam*) may make them unfamiliar to returning passengers.

Veterans of cruises on older Holland America ships will find the layout of public spaces somewhat different; still, everyone's favorite Crow's Nest lounges continue to offer those commanding views.

Cabins

Layout: Comfortable and roomy, 85% of all Vista-class accommodations have an ocean view, and almost 80% of those also have the luxury of a private balcony furnished with chairs, loungers, and tables. Every cabin has adequate closet and drawer/shelf storage, as well as bathroom shelves. Some suites have a whirlpool tub, powder room, and walk-in closet.

Suites: Suites include duvets on beds and a fully stocked minibar; some also have a whirlpool tub, powder room, and walk-in closet. Penthouse and Deluxe Verandah suites have exclusive use of the private Neptune Lounge, personal concierge service, canapés before dinner, and complimentary laundry, pressing, and dry-cleaning services.

Amenities: All staterooms and suites are appointed with pillow-top mattresses, 250-thread-count cotton bed linens, magnifying halogen-lighted makeup mirrors, hair dryers, a fruit basket, flat-panel TVs, and DVD players. Bathroom extras include Egyptian cotton towels, shampoo, body lotion, and bath gel, plus deluxe bathrobes to use during the cruise.

Accessibility: Twenty-eight staterooms are wheelchair accessible.

Top: Oosterdam hydropool
Bottom: Vista-class Ocean-
View stateroom

Restaurants

The formal dining room offers open seating breakfast and lunch, with a choice at dinner between two assigned seatings or open seating. The Pinnacle Grill (reservation, cover charge) serves lunch and dinner. A casual Lido restaurant serves buffet breakfast and lunch; at dinner the Lido offers table service with entrées from both the Lido and main dining room menus, and Italian fare is served in the adjacent Canaletto Restaurant (reservation, cover charge). Poolside lunch at the Terrace Grill includes nachos, hamburgers, and hot dogs with all the trimmings to sandwiches and gourmet sausages. The extra-charge Explorations Café offers specialty coffees and pastries. Daily afternoon tea service is elevated to Royal Dutch High Tea once per cruise. Complimentary hors d'oeuvres are served by waiters during cocktail hour, hand-dipped chocolates are offered after dinner in the Explorer's Lounge, and a late-night buffet and chocolate extravaganza is served in the Lido restaurant during every cruise. Room service is available 24 hours.

Spas

The Greenhouse Spa treatments include a variety of massages, body wraps, and facials, as well as acupuncture and tooth-whitening services. A hydrotherapy pool and thermal suite with heated ceramic lounges for relaxation and dry sauna and steam rooms are free to use when a spa appointment is booked and available for a fee to all other passengers.

Bars and Entertainment

Before dinner, the Ocean Club and Explorers Lounge are popular spots where servers pass through with appetizers. After dinner and a show or concert, those bars are quiet spots for drinks and conversation. For livelier action, there's the Sports Bar, a Piano Bar, or the Crow's Nest for late-night dancing.

Pros and Cons

Pros: next to the Crow's Nest, an outdoor seating area is a quiet hideaway; exterior panoramic elevators offer an elevated view of the seascape; you can borrow iPod shipboard art tours.

Cons: Vista-class ships do not have self-service laundry rooms; murals in Pinnacle Grill restaurants look out of place alongside priceless art found throughout the rest of the ships; some chairs in Pinnacle Grill are so heavy that they barely budge without effort.

Cabin Type	Size (sq. ft.)
Penthouse Suites	1,318
Deluxe Verandah Suite	510–700
Superior Verandah Suite	398
Deluxe Ocean View	254
Standard Ocean View	185
Inside	170–200

Dimensions include the square footage for balconies.

FAST FACTS

- 11 passenger decks
- Specialty restaurant, dining room, buffet, pizzeria
- Internet, Wi-Fi, safe, refrigerator, DVD
- 2 pools (1 indoor)
- Fitness classes, gym, hot tubs, spa
- 9 bars, casino, 2 dance clubs, library, show room, video game room
- Children's programs
- Dry-cleaning, laundry service
- Internet terminal
- No-smoking cabins

3

HOLLAND AMERICA LINE

Westerdam at sea

VOLENDAM, ZAANDAM

CREW MEMBERS	615
ENTERED SERVICE	1999, 2000
GROSS TONS	61,214, 61,396
LENGTH	781 feet
NUMBER OF CABINS	716
PASSENGER CAPACITY	1,432
WIDTH	106 feet

700 ft.

500 ft.

300 ft.

Similar in layout to Statendam-class vessels, these slightly larger sister ships introduced playful art and interior design theme elements to Holland America Line's classic vessels. Triple-deck atriums are distinguished by a fantastic—and fiber-optic-lighted—Murano-glass sculpture on *Volendam* and, in an attempt to be hip, an almost scary towering pipe organ on *Zaandam*.

The interior decor and much of the artwork found in each vessel has a predominant theme—*Volendam* centers on flowers and *Zaandam* around music. Look for *Zaandam*'s collection of guitars autographed by famous musicians such as the Rolling Stones and a saxophone signed by former President Bill Clinton. The extra space in these ships allows for a larger specialty restaurant and a roomier feel throughout.

Cabins

Layout: Staterooms are spacious and comfortable with a few more balconies than Statendam-class but still fewer than newer fleetmates. Every cabin has adequate closet and drawer/shelf storage, as well as bathroom shelves. As a nod to families, connecting cabins are featured in a range of categories. However, although the number of triple cabins is generous, there are not many that accommodate four.

Suites: Suite amenities include duvets on beds, a fully stocked minibar, and personalized stationery. Penthouse Verandah and Deluxe Verandah suites have exclusive use of the private Neptune Lounge, personal concierge service, canapés before dinner on request, binoculars and umbrellas for use during the cruise, an invitation to a VIP party with the captain, and complimentary laundry, pressing, and dry-cleaning services.

Amenities: All staterooms and suites are appointed with pillow-top mattresses, 250-thread-count cotton bed linens, magnifying halo-lighted mirrors, hair dryers, a fruit basket, flat-panel TVs, and DVD players. Bathrooms have Egyptian cotton towels, shampoo, body lotion, and bath gel, plus deluxe bathrobes to use during the cruise.

Accessibility: Twenty-two staterooms are designed for wheelchair accessibility.

Top: Celebrate a special occasion.
Bottom: Deluxe Verandah suite

Restaurants

The formal dining room offers open seating breakfast and lunch and a choice between two traditional assigned dinner seatings or open seating. The upscale Pinnacle Grill alternative restaurant serves lunch and dinner, requires reservations, and has a cover charge. A casual Lido restaurant serves buffet breakfast and lunch; at dinner the Lido offers waiter service featuring entrées from both the Lido and main dining room menus. Canaletto Restaurant, adjacent to the Lido restaurant dining area, serves classic Italian fare with tableside service for dinners only (reservation, cover charge). Poolside lunch at the Terrace Grill offers hamburgers, hot dogs, sandwiches, and gourmet sausages. The extra-charge Explorations Café offers specialty coffees and pastries. Daily afternoon tea service is elevated to Royal Dutch High Tea once per cruise. Complimentary hors d'oeuvres are served by waiters during cocktail hour, hand-dipped chocolates are offered after dinner in the Explorer's Lounge, and a late-night buffet and chocolate extravaganza is served in the Lido restaurant during every cruise. Room service is available 24 hours.

Spas

Treatments in the Greenhouse Spa include a variety of massages, body wraps, and facials, as well as acupuncture services and tooth-whitening treatment. A thermal suite with heated ceramic loungers for relaxation as well as dry sauna and steam rooms can be used by everyone for a fee or free whenever a spa appointment is booked. Changing rooms for men and women have free saunas.

Bars and Entertainment

Popular spots before dinner are the Ocean Club and Explorers Lounge, where servers pass through with appetizers. After dinner and a show or concert, those bars are quiet spots for drinks and conversation. For livelier action, there's a Piano Bar or the Crow's Nest for late night dancing.

Pros and Cons

Pros: ship theaters are also home to the Culinary Arts Institute; waiters serve made-to-order entrées in the Lido restaurant at dinner; an evening poolside barbecue buffet is usually scheduled during each cruise.

Cons: expanded spa facilities make the gym area somewhat tight; there are no longer complimentary men's and women's steam rooms; sandwiched between the Lido pool and Lido bar, the children's wading pool area can become quite boisterous.

Cabin Type	Size (sq. ft.)
Penthouse Suite	1,126
Deluxe Verandah Suite	563
Verandah Suite	284
Ocean View	197
Inside	182

Dimensions include the square footage for balconies.

FAST FACTS

- 10 passenger decks
- Specialty restaurant, dining room, buffet
- Wi-Fi, safe, refrigerator, DVD
- 2 pools (1 indoor), 2 children's pools
- Fitness classes, gym, hot tubs, sauna, spa
- 6 bars, casino, dance club, library, show room, video game room
- Children's programs
- Dry-cleaning, laundry facilities, laundry service
- Internet terminal
- No-smoking cabins

3

HOLLAND AMERICA LINE

Zaandam atrium organ

LINDBLAD EXPEDITIONS

Founded in 1979 as Special Expeditions by Sven-Olof Lindblad, the son of Lars-Eric Lindblad, the company changed its name in 1984 to Lindblad Expeditions. Every cruise is educational, focusing on soft adventure and environmentally conscientious travel. Since

National Geographic Sea Lion in Southeast Alaska

2004 the line has partnered with *National Geographic* to enhance the cruise experience by including experts and photographers on board to lead discussions and hold workshops and help balance "must-see" destinations and less-traveled spots.

☎ *212/765–7740 or 800/397–3348*
⊕ *www.expeditions. com*
☞ *Cruise Style: Small-ship.*

Beginning in 2008, National Geographic Expeditions began working exclusively with Lindblad Expeditions. The multifaceted strategic partnership that Lindblad Expeditions has with the National Geographic Society enables Lindblad travelers to participate in the world of natural and cultural history as engaged, active explorers who care about the planet.

The ships of Lindblad Expeditions spend time looking for wildlife, exploring out-of-the-way inlets, and making Zodiac landings at isolated beaches. Itineraries are flexible, so as to take maximum advantage of reported wildlife sightings and weather conditions. Each ship has a fleet of kayaks as well as a video-microphone: a hydrophone (underwater microphone) is combined with an underwater camera so passengers can listen to whale songs and watch live video of what's going on beneath the waves. In the evening the ship's naturalist recaps the day's sights and adventures over cocktails in the lounge. An "open bridge" policy provides passengers the opportunity to meet the captain and his officers and learn the intricacies of navigation or simply observe.

All activities and shore excursions, from guided walks and hikes to museum entrance fees to water activities like kayaking and snorkeling, are included in the cost of every Lindblad Expedition. Guests always have the freedom to pick and choose activities as the day unfolds. A video chronicler makes a DVD of the entire cruise that you may purchase.

Food

Appetizers are often served on deck as you sail from port, while regional specialties are served in the dining room. Lindblad prides itself on serving fresh Alaska seafood, including Dungeness crab, halibut, and Alaska king salmon, but there are also plenty of meat and vegetarian options. The "Seafood for Thought" program is meant to ensure that sustainable seafood is being served.

Entertainment

Lindblad clientele should not expect shuffleboard and glitzy Broadway shows or a casino, but it's more likely they prefer reflective moments gazing at constellations, speaking about maritime navigation with the ship's captain, or watching a video slide show about biodiversity anyway. Expect to have the most fun boarding a Zodiac for remote shore visits or snorkeling surrounded by spectacular marine wildlife.

Fitness and Recreation

Ships carry exercise equipment on deck and offer a holistic Tonic of Wellness program that might include activities such as kayaking and hiking, fitness activities like yoga and Pilates, or massage therapy and other body treatments. The fitness staff provides expertise in massage therapy and relaxation, water sports and aerobic hikes, stretching classes, and personalized guidance with the fitness equipment.

Your Shipmates

Lindblad attracts active, adventurous, well-traveled over-forties, and quite a few singles, as the line charges one of the industry's lowest single supplements. However, the line has made a successful push to be more family-friendly by adding cruises aimed specifically at families and children. To that end, staff members have undergone extensive training designed by several of Lindblad's family travel experts with years of experience in childhood and environmental education to tailor activities toward children. Some family expeditions are offered during the Alaska season, which follow the same itinerary as Lindblad's other trips but include a crew member dedicated to running educational programs for school-age kids. All Lindblad cruises offer substantial discounts for young people up to 21 traveling with their parents.

KNOWN FOR

■ Exotic Destinations: Expedition "soft adventure" cruising to destinations like Antarctica, the Arctic, Alaska, and other inaccessible areas of the world.

■ *National Geographic:* Partnered with *National Geographic*, cruises feature expedition experts, trained naturalists, and guest lecturers in various scientific fields depending on the destination.

■ Premium Pricing: Expensive all-inclusive fares include first-class travel accommodations and facilities.

■ Hands-on Family-Friendly Adventures: The educational emphasis of these cruises and customizable off-boat excursions are ideal for families with children.

■ Video Galore: Underwater and land videotaping to chronicle destinations and natural wildlife with regular topical presentations and discussions.

Enjoying the view from the top deck

3

LINDBLAD EXPEDITIONS

Top: Informal yet elegant dining
Bottom: Kayaking

Dress Code
Casual and comfortable attire is always appropriate. Recommendations are based on practicality and the likely weather conditions in the region you're exploring. Good walking shoes are essential.

Junior Cruisers
Although there are no dedicated children's facilities on board, families are welcome on all Lindblad itineraries. In fact, the number of families traveling with the company has grown substantially, so much so that the line will have dedicated staff on some designed "family" cruises that know how to inspire curiosity in young people of all ages. Lindblad emphasizes shared experiences, and while there are always some activities just for children or adults, most are done together.

Service
Service is friendly and helpful, if not overly polished.

Tipping
Although gratuities are at your discretion, tips of $12–$15 per person per day are suggested; these are pooled among the crew at journey's end. Tip the massage therapist individually following a treatment.

Ships of the Line
Lindblad Expeditions currently sails 10 vessels for adventure cruising to spectacular regions throughout the world. Ships are comfortable, outfitted with modern amenities, offer top-notch cuisine, and afford privileged travelers both quiet refuge and social interaction.

National Geographic Sea Bird & National Geographic Sea Lion. These identical triple-deck expedition ships each carry 62 guests in 31 outside cabins. Ideally suited for exploring Alaskan waters, the small, shallow-draft sister ships can tuck into nooks and crannies that bigger ships can't reach. Artwork on both includes a collection of photographs by expedition staff naturalists as well as whale and dolphin sculptures. An open-top sundeck, a forward observation lounge, and a viewing deck at the bow offer plenty of room to take in the scenery. The ships are also equipped with bowcams (underwater cameras that monitor activity), and you

CHOOSE THIS LINE IF ...

You want to be an ecologically responsible traveler.

You consider travel a learning experience.

What you see from the ship and landings are more important than the vessel itself.

can navigate the camera using a joystick to observe sea life. Additional expedition equipment includes a hydrophone for eavesdropping on marine mammals, an underwater video "splash" camera to record the passing undersea scenery, and a video microscope for use during naturalists' lectures. The ship's Internet kiosk provides email access. Fitness equipment is set up on the bridge deck, and the LEXspa Wellness room offers massages, body treatments, and a morning stretching program on deck.

All meals are served open seating during scheduled times in a single dining room. Breakfast is buffet-style, although you may order eggs and omelets from the kitchen, and lunch is served family-style. Afternoon tea includes sandwiches and sweets; hors d'oeuvres are served during the nightly cocktail hour. The open seating dinner typically consists of two entrées—meat or fish—as well as several always-available items such as steak and chicken. Special dietary restrictions can be accommodated with advance notice. Room service is restricted to ill passengers confined to cabins.

These ships are comfortable, but cabins are proportionately small and basic in decor (there are no TVs, for example). All staterooms are outside, and upper-category cabins have picture windows that open; the lowest-category cabins on main deck have portholes that admit light, but do not open or afford much of a view. Most cabins have single beds that can convert to a double, and a few on the upper deck have pull-out beds to accommodate a third person. No accommodations are designated accessible and the ships have no elevators.

HELPFUL HINTS

- Although fares are rather expensive, wine and cocktails are not included; nonalcoholic beverages are.

- All shore excursions except flightseeing are included, as are transfers to and from airports.

- Extensive pre-trip information, including recommended reading, photography guidelines, and what to pack, will arrive with your documents.

- There is no elevator on board, nor are there accessible features for the mobility impaired.

- Don't expect round-the-clock availability of food; room service is only available if you are sick and confined to your cabin.

DON'T CHOOSE THIS LINE IF ...

You are mobility-impaired; the ships are not accessible, and Zodiacs are used to reach shore for certain explorations.

Your happiness depends on being entertained; other than enrichment programs, there is no formal entertainment.

You consider TV essential; there are none in the staterooms.

NORWEGIAN CRUISE LINE

Norwegian Cruise Line (originally known as Norwegian Caribbean Line) set sail in 1966 with an entirely new concept: regularly scheduled Caribbean cruises from the then-obscure port of Miami. Good food and friendly service combined with value fares estab-

Norwegian's buffets are beautifully presented

lished Norwegian as a winner for active adults and families. With the introduction of the now-retired SS *Norway* in 1979, Norwegian ushered in the era of cruises on megasize ships. Innovative and forward-looking, Norwegian has been a cruise-industry leader for four decades, and is as much at home in Europe as it is in the Caribbean.

☎ *305/436–4000 or 800/327–7030*
⊕ *www.ncl.com*
☞ *Cruise Style: Mainstream.*

Noted for top-quality, high-energy entertainment and emphasis on fitness facilities and programs, Norwegian combines action, activities, and a variety of dining options in a casual, free-flowing atmosphere. Freestyle cruising signaled an end to rigid dining schedules and dress codes. Norwegian ships now offer a host of flexible dining options that allow passengers to eat in the main dining rooms or any of a number of à la carte and specialty restaurants at any time and with whom they please. Now co-owned by Genting Hong Kong Limited and Apollo Management, a private equity company, Norwegian continues to be an industry innovator.

From a distance, most cruise ships look so similar that it's often difficult to tell them apart, but Norwegian's largest, modern ships stand out with their distinctive use of hull art. Each new ship is distinguished by murals extending from bow to midship.

Food

Main dining rooms serve what is traditionally deemed Continental fare, although it's about what you would expect at a really good hotel banquet. Health-conscious menu selections are nicely prepared, and vegetarian choices are always available. Where Norwegian really shines is the specialty restaurants, especially the French-Mediterranean Le Bistro (on all ships), the pan-Asian restaurants, and steak houses (on the newer ships). As a rule of thumb, the newer the ship, the wider the variety, because new ships were purpose-built with as many as 10 or more places to eat. You may find Spanish tapas, an Italian trattoria, a steak house, a pub, and a pan-Asian restaurant complete with a sushi and sashimi bar and teppanyaki room. Most carry a cover charge or are priced à la carte and require reservations. A Norwegian staple, the late-night Chocoholic Buffet continues to be a favorite event.

Entertainment

More high jinks than highbrow, entertainment after dark features extravagant Las Vegas–style revues presented in main show lounges by lavishly costumed singers and dancers. Other performers might include comedians, magicians, jugglers, and acrobats. Passengers can get into the act by taking part in talent shows or step up to the karaoke microphone. Live bands play for dancing and listening in smaller lounges, and each ship has a lively dance club. Some ships include shows by Chicago's world-famous Second City improvisational comedy company. With the launch of *Norwegian Epic* in 2010, the Blue Man Group and Cirque Productions (a U.S.-based company somewhat similar in style to Cirque du Soleil) joined Norwegian's talent lineup.

Casinos, bingo sessions, and art auctions are well attended. Adult games, particularly the competitive ones, are fun to participate in and provide laughs for audience members. Goofy pool games are a Norwegian staple, and the ships' bands crank up the volume during afternoon and evening deck parties.

Fitness and Recreation

Mandara Spa offers exotic spa treatments fleet-wide on Norwegian, although facilities vary widely. Spa treatments include a long menu of massages, body wraps, and facials, and current trends in hair and nail services are offered in the salons. The latest addition on board is a Medi-Spa physician, who can create individualized treatment plans using nonsurgical treatments such as Botox Cosmetic. State-of-the-art exercise equipment, jogging tracks, and basic fitness classes are available at no charge. There's a fee for personal training, body composition analysis, and specialized classes such as yoga and Pilates.

KNOWN FOR

■ **Casual Atmosphere:** With no dress code, Norwegian's ships have shed the "stuffy" reputation of cruises in the past.

■ **Dining Options:** Norwegian Cruise Line is an industry innovator in onboard dining, from open seating dining rooms to specialty restaurants.

■ **Entertainment:** Their partnership with widely recognized acts and shows has made Norwegian a leader in entertainment at sea.

■ **Family-Friendliness:** Numerous connecting staterooms and suites on Norwegian's ships can be combined to create multicabin accommodations ideal for families.

■ **Itineraries:** With some exceptions, Norwegian's sailings don't stray far from the tried-and-true one-week length.

3

NORWEGIAN CRUISE LINE

Grab a front row seat at a show

Top: Casino play
Middle: Windows in the dining areas mean you don't miss a minute of the scenery
Bottom: *Norwegian Dream* superior Ocean View stateroom

Your Shipmates

Norwegian's mostly American cruise passengers are active couples ranging from their mid-thirties to mid-fifties. Many families enjoy cruising on Norwegian ships during holidays and summer months. Longer cruises and more exotic itineraries attract passengers in the over-55 age group.

Dress Code

Resort casual attire is appropriate at all times; the option of one formal evening is available on all cruises of seven nights and longer. Most passengers actually raise the casual dress code a notch to what could be called casual chic attire.

Junior Cruisers

For children and teens, each Norwegian vessel offers a Splash Academy program of supervised entertainment for young cruisers ages 3 to 17. Younger children are split into three groups, ages 3 to 5, 6 to 9, and 10 to 12; activities range from storytelling, games, and arts and crafts to dinner with counselors, pajama parties, and treasure hunts. The program now also offers activities for kids from six months to three years old. "Guppies" offers their parents the opportunity to engage in a variety of sensory-based programs with them, including baby art, storytelling, and a parent and baby mini-workout. Certain ships feature Nickelodeon programming, and the presence of favorite characters is a highlight for junior cruisers.

Group Port Play is available in the children's area to accommodate parents booked on shore excursions. Evening babysitting services are available for a fee. Parents whose children are not toilet trained are issued a beeper to alert them when diaper changing is necessary. Reduced fares are charged for third and fourth guests in the same stateroom, including all children. Infants under six months of age cannot travel on Norwegian ships.

For teens ages 13 to 17, options in the Entourage program include sports, pool parties, teen disco, movies, and video games. Some ships have their own cool clubs where teens hang out in adult-free zones.

CHOOSE THIS LINE IF ...

Doing your own thing is your idea of a real vacation. You could almost remove your watch and just go with the flow.

You want to leave your formal dress-up wardrobe at home.

You're competitive. There's always a pickup game in progress on the sports courts.

Service

Somewhat inconsistent, service is nonetheless congenial. Although crew members tended to be outgoing Caribbean islanders in the past; they have largely been replaced by Asians and Eastern Europeans who are well trained yet are inclined to be more reserved.

Tipping

A fixed service charge of $12 per person per day for passengers three years of age and older is added to shipboard accounts. An automatic 15% gratuity is added to bar tabs. Staff members may also accept cash gratuities. Passengers in suites who have access to concierge and butler services are asked to offer a cash gratuity at their own discretion.

Past Passengers

On completion of your first Norwegian cruise you're automatically enrolled in Latitudes, the club for repeat passengers. Membership benefits accrue based on the number of cruise nights sailed: Bronze (1 through 19), Silver (20 through 47), Gold (48 through 75), and Platinum (75 or more). Everyone receives *Latitudes*, Norwegian's e-magazine, Latitudes pricing, Latitudes check-in at the pier, a ship pin, access to a special customer service desk and liaison on board, and a members-only cocktail party. Higher tiers receive a welcome basket, an invitation to the captain's cocktail party, dinner in Le Bistro, and priority for check-in, tender tickets, and disembarkation. Milestone gifts are awarded at the 250, 500, 700, and 1,000 point levels.

HELPFUL HINTS

■ Norwegian's Signature Trio dining package saves you 15% if you book three dinners before sailing.

■ Popular Nickelodeon characters make regular appearances for photo opportunities on certain Norwegian ships and you don't have to pay for pictures if you use your own camera.

■ Although Norwegian has one of the newest fleets at sea, the oldest ships just don't have quite the panache or as many Freestyle dining venues as are found on the newer ships.

■ Children 3 years old and younger dine free in specialty restaurants, and children ages 4 to 12 can eat from the complimentary kids menu or a specialty kids menu for a reduced cover charge.

■ While the ships are family-friendly, the line has removed all its self-service laundries to add more inside staterooms.

3

NORWEGIAN CRUISE LINE

DON'T CHOOSE THIS LINE IF ...

You don't like to pay extra for food on a ship. All the best specialty restaurants have extra charges.

You don't want to stand in line. There are lines for nearly everything.

You don't want to hear announcements. They're frequent on these ships—and loud.

JEWEL-CLASS
Norwegian Jewel, Norwegian Jade, Norwegian Pearl, Norwegian Gem

CREW MEMBERS	1,081, 1,075, 1,084, 1,092
ENTERED SERVICE	2005, 2006, 2006, 2007
GROSS TONS	93,502, 93,558, 93,530, 93,530
LENGTH	965 feet
NUMBER OF CABINS	1,188, 1,201, 1,197, 1,197
PASSENGER CAPACITY	2,376, 2,402, 2,394, 2,394
WIDTH	105 feet

700 ft.
500 ft.
300 ft.

Jewel-class ships are the next step in the continuing evolution of Freestyle ship design: the interior location of some public rooms and restaurants has been tweaked since the introduction of Freestyle cruising vessels, and new categories of deluxe accommodations have been added.

These ships have more than a dozen dining alternatives, a variety of entertainment options, and expansive areas reserved for children and teens. Pools have waterslides and a plethora of lounge chairs, although when your ship is full, it can be difficult to find one in a prime location. *Norwegian Pearl* and *Norwegian Gem* introduced the line's first rock-climbing walls, as well as Bliss Lounge, which has trendy South Beach decor, and the first full-size 10-pin bowling alleys on modern cruise ships.

Cabins

Layout: Norwegian ships are not noted for large staterooms, but all have a small sitting area with sofa, chair, and table. Every cabin has adequate closet and drawer/shelf storage, as well as limited bathroom storage. Suites have walk-in closets. Some staterooms interconnect in most categories.

Garden and Courtyard Villas: Garden Villas, with three bedrooms, a living-dining room, and private deck garden with a spa tub, are among the largest suites at sea. Courtyard Villas—not as large as Garden Villas—have an exclusive concierge lounge and a shared private courtyard with pool, hot tub, sundeck, and small gym.

Amenities: A small refrigerator, tea/coffeemaker, personal safe, broadband Internet connection, duvets on beds, a wall-mounted hair dryer, and bathrobes are standard. Bathrooms have a shampoo/bath-gel dispenser on the shower wall and a magnifying mirror. Suites have a whirlpool tub, an entertainment center with a CD/DVD player, and concierge and butler service.

Accessibility: Twenty-seven staterooms are wheelchair accessible.

Top: *Norwegian Jewel's* Azura restaurant
Bottom: Hydropool in the spa

Restaurants

Two main complimentary dining rooms serve open seating breakfast, lunch, and dinner. Specialty restaurants, including Norwegian's signature French restaurant Le Bistro, Cagney's Steakhouse, an Asian restaurant, sushi bar, teppanyaki room, tapas and salsa eatery, and an Italian trattoria–style restaurant carry varying cover charges and require reservations. Screens located throughout the ship illustrate the status (full, moderately busy, empty) and waiting time you can expect for each restaurant on board. Casual choices are the Lido buffet for breakfast, lunch, and dinner; Blue Lagoon for soup, sandwiches, and snacks around the clock; and the poolside grill for lunch. Java Café serves specialty coffees and pastries for an additional charge. Although the 24-hour room-service menu is somewhat limited, suite occupants may order from any restaurant on the ship.

Spas

The Mandara Spa's treatments include a long menu of massages, body wraps, and facials and include the services of a Medi-Spa physician. Spa facilities include an enormous thermal suite with hydrotherapy pool, heated lounges, steam rooms, and saunas for which there is a charge.

Bars and Entertainment

Your evening might start with a high-energy production show, Second City comedy performance, or a show by a featured entertainer, then continue in the bar complex that includes a beer and whiskey bar, martini bar, and a champagne bar. You'll find music for dancing, signature Norwegian parties, and even a cigar lounge. The perfect spot to end the night is the Star Bar with its pianist and views of the pool deck and the sea.

Pros and Cons

Pros: there are both main-stage and nightclub performances by Second City; the ship's tranquil library offers a quiet escape with a sea view; Courtyard Villa accommodations are like a ship within a ship and have a private pool area.

Cons: there is a fee for use of the thermal suites in the spa; Freestyle dining doesn't mean you can get to eat precisely when you want to; for such a large ship, the Internet center is tiny.

Cabin Type	Size (sq. ft.)
Garden Villa	4,390
Courtyard Villa	574
Owner's Suites	823
Deluxe Owner's Suites*	928*
Penthouse Suite	575
Minisuite	284
Ocean View with Balcony	205–243
Ocean View	161
Inside	143

*Deluxe Owner's Suites on *Norwegian Pearl* and *Norwegian Gem* only.

FAST FACTS

- 15 passenger decks
- 7 restaurants, 2 dining rooms, buffet, ice cream parlor, pizzeria
- Internet, Wi-Fi, safe, refrigerator, DVD (some)
- 2 pools, children's pool
- Fitness classes, gym, hot tubs, spa
- 9 bars, casino, dance club, library, show room, video game room
- Children's programs
- Dry-cleaning, laundry service
- Internet terminal
- No-smoking cabins

The sports deck

3

NORWEGIAN CRUISE LINE

NORWEGIAN SKY, NORWEGIAN SUN

CREW MEMBERS	917,916
ENTERED SERVICE	1999, 2001
GROSS TONS	77,104, 78,309
LENGTH	853 feet
NUMBER OF CABINS	1,002, 968
PASSENGER CAPACITY	2,004, 1,936
WIDTH	105 feet

700 ft.

500 ft.

300 ft.

Norwegian Cruise Line hadn't introduced many new ships in awhile at the time *Norwegian Sky* was launched and *Norwegian Sun* was on the drawing board, but it didn't take long before they got the hang of it. With Freestyle cruising growing in popularity, the vessels moved into the forefront of the fleet with multiple restaurant choices, expansive casino, trendy spas, and more family- and kid-friendly facilities.

Rich wood tones and fabric colors prevail throughout. The Observation Lounge is a subdued spot for afternoon tea in a light, tropical setting with nothing to distract attention from the expansive views beyond the floor-to-ceiling windows.

The Internet café is large, and the nearby coffee bar is a delight. Sunshine pours into the atrium through an overhead skylight by day; at night it's the ship's glamorous hub of activity.

Cabins

Layout: Staterooms are a bit more generous in size than on the previous vessels in the Norwegian fleet and contain adequate closet and drawer space for a one-week cruise. More than two-thirds have an ocean view, and nearly two-thirds of those have a private balcony. All have a sitting area with sofa, chair, and table. Clever use of primary colors and strategically placed mirrors achieves an open feeling. Connecting staterooms are available in several categories, including those with balconies. Oddly sandwiched in between decks 6 and 7 forward is deck 6A, which has no direct elevator access.

Suites: Suites have walk-in closets as well as whirlpool tubs and entertainment centers. Butlers and a concierge are at the service of suite occupants.

Amenities: Light-wood cabinetry, mirrored accents, a small refrigerator, a tea/coffeemaker, a personal safe, broadband Internet connections, duvets on beds, a wall-mounted hair dryer over the dressing table, and bathrobes for use during the cruise are typical standard amenities. Bathrooms have shampoo and bath gel in shower-mounted dispensers, as well as limited storage.

Accessibility: Sixteen cabins are wheelchair accessible.

Top: Las Ramblas Tapas Bar & Restaurant
Bottom: *Norwegian Sun* at sea

Restaurants

Two complimentary dining rooms serve open seating breakfast, lunch, and dinner. Specialty restaurants on both ships that carry varying cover charges and require reservations include Norwegian's signature French restaurant Le Bistro, steak houses, and Italian eateries; *Norwegian Sun* also has an extra-charge Japanese restaurant, sushi bar, and teppanyaki room, and complimentary tapas bar. Screens located throughout the ship illustrate the status (full to empty) and waiting time you can expect for each restaurant. Casual choices are the Lido buffet for breakfast, lunch, and dinner; the poolside grill for lunch; a pizzeria; and an ice cream bar. A coffee bar serves specialty coffees and pastries priced by item. Room service is available 24 hours from a somewhat limited menu.

Spas

Although the facilities aren't as extensive as on newer ships, Mandara Spa offers a lengthy menu of massages, body wraps, and facials. A Medi-Spa physician is on hand to create individualized therapies. Each ship has saunas and steam rooms that are available to all at no extra charge.

Bars and Entertainment

You'll find a nice selection of bars and lounges where musicians or DJs provide dance tunes; the entertainment staff hosts Norwegian's signature late-night parties after performances by the production company; other nights, comedians or other entertainers perform in the main theater. Each ship has a top-deck lounge ideal for an intimate nightcap (*Norwegian Sky*) or complimentary tapas (*Norwegian Sun*).

Pros and Cons

Pros: many of the elements found in newer fleetmates have been added to these older ships; there is a hot tub exclusively for kids; *Norwegian Sun* has separate steam rooms and saunas for men and women.

Cons: the main restaurant is not on a direct route from the main atrium; these are sister ships but not twins, and dining facilities vary; standard accommodations are somewhat tight for more than two people.

Cabin Type	Size (sq. ft.)
Owner's Suite	828
Penthouse and Romance Suite	504
Minisuite	332
Ocean View with Balcony	221
Ocean View	145
Deluxe Interior	172
Interior	145

FAST FACTS

- 11 passenger decks
- 4 specialty restaurants, 2 dining rooms, buffet, ice cream parlor, pizzeria
- Wi-Fi, safe, refrigerator (some), DVD (some)
- 2 pools, children's pool
- Fitness classes, gym, hot tubs, sauna, spa, steam room
- 8 bars, casino, dance club, library, show room, video game room
- Children's programs
- Dry-cleaning, laundry service
- Internet terminal
- No-smoking cabins

3

NORWEGIAN CRUISE LINE

Balcony stateroom

OCEANIA CRUISES

This distinctive cruise line was founded by Frank Del Rio and Joe Watters, cruise-industry veterans with the know-how to satisfy the wants of inquisitive passengers. By offering itineraries to interesting ports of call and upscale touches— all for fares much lower than you

Oceania's *Regatta*

would expect—they are succeeding quite nicely. Oceania Cruises set sail in 2003 to carve a unique, almost boutique niche in the cruise industry by obtaining midsize R-class ships that formerly made up the popular Renaissance Cruises fleet. The line is now owned by Prestige Cruise Holdings.

☎ *305/514–2300 or 800/531–5658*
⊕ *www.oceania cruises.com*
☞ *Cruise Style: Premium.*

Intimate and cozy public spaces reflect the importance of socializing on Oceania ships. Indoor lounges feature numerous conversation areas, and even the pool deck is a social center. The Patio is a shaded slice of deck adjacent to the pool and hot tubs. Defined by billowing drapes and carpeting underfoot, it is furnished with plush sofas and chairs ideal for relaxation.

Thickly padded single and double loungers are arranged around the pool, but if more privacy appeals to you, private cabanas are available for rent. Each one has a double chaise longue with a view of the sea; overhead drapery can be drawn back for sunbathing, and the side panels can be left open or closed. Waiters are on standby to offer chilled towels or serve occupants with beverages or snacks. In addition, you can request a spa service in your cabana.

Varied, destination-rich itineraries are an important characteristic of Oceania Cruises, and most sailings are in the 10- to 12-night range.

Food
Several top cruise-industry chefs were lured away from other cruise lines to ensure that the artistry of world-renowned master chef Jacques Pépin, who crafted

five-star menus for Oceania, is properly carried out. The results are sure to please the most discriminating palate. Oceania simply serves some of the best food at sea, particularly impressive for a cruise line that charges far less than luxury rates. The main restaurant offers trendy, French-Continental cuisine with an always-on-the-menu steak, seafood, or poultry choice and a vegetarian option.

Intimate specialty restaurants require reservations, but there's no additional charge for Toscana, the Italian restaurant, or Polo Grill, the steak house. On *Marina* and *Riviera,* passengers have those and more restaurants from which to choose—Jacques, the first restaurant to bear Jacques Pépin's name, serves French cuisine; Red Ginger features contemporary interpretations of Asian classics; Privée hosts private, seven-course menu degustation dinners for a single party of up to 10; and La Reserve serves exclusive wine and food pairings.

A casual dinner option is alfresco dining at the Terrace Café (the daytime Lido deck buffet). Although service is from the buffet, outdoor seating on the aft deck is transformed into a charming Mediterranean courtyard with candleholders and starched linens.

The Terrace Café also serves breakfast and lunch buffet-style, and has a small pizzeria window that operates during the day. At an outdoor poolside grill you can order up burgers, hot dogs, and sandwiches for lunch and then take a seat; waiters are at hand to serve you either at a nearby table or your lounge chair by the pool. Afternoon tea is a decadent spread of finger foods and includes a rolling dessert cart, which has to be seen to be believed.

Entertainment

Culinary demonstrations by guest presenters and Oceania's own executive chefs are extremely popular. Lectures on varied topics, computer courses, hands-on arts and crafts classes, and wine or champagne seminars round out the popular enrichment series on board. Before arrival in ports of call, lectures are presented on the historical background, culture, and traditions of the destinations.

Evening entertainment leans toward light cabaret, solo artists, music for dancing, and conversation with fellow passengers; however, you'll find lively karaoke sessions on the schedule as well. The sophisticated, adult atmosphere on days at sea is enhanced by a combo performing jazz or easy-listening melodies poolside. Enrichment programs feature guest lecturers who are experts in such topics as wine appreciation, culinary arts, history, and world events.

KNOWN FOR

■ **Cuisine:** Oceania Cruises' chefs are serious about food and serve noteworthy cuisine in all restaurants on board.

■ **Great Destinations:** Oceania itineraries are destination-oriented and offer overnights in many top ports.

■ **Midsize Ships:** Oceania's deluxe ships are quite manageable in size: three have fewer than 850 passengers, the largest fewer than 1,300 passengers.

■ **No Smoking:** Oceania ships are almost entirely smoke-free, with small, designated areas set aside for smokers.

■ **Surprisingly Affordable:** Cruises on Oceania approach true luxury in style, but not when it comes to fares—they are quite affordable.

Top: Penthouse suite
Bottom: Toscana Restaurant

Top: Cocktails before dinner
Middle: Veranda stateroom
Bottom: Martini bar

Fitness and Recreation

The Canyon Ranch SpaClub spas and salons and well-equipped fitness centers are adequate for the number of passengers on board. In addition to individual body-toning machines and complimentary exercise classes, there's a walking-jogging track circling the top of the ship. A personal trainer is available for individual instruction for an additional charge.

Your Shipmates

Oceania Cruises appeal to singles and couples from their late-thirties to well-traveled retirees who have the time for and prefer longer cruises. Most are American couples attracted to the casually sophisticated atmosphere, creative cuisine, and high level of service. Many are past passengers of the now-defunct Renaissance Cruises who are loyal to their favorite ships, which now offer a variety of in-depth destination-rich itineraries.

Dress Code

Leave the formal wear at home—attire on Oceania ships is country-club casual every evening, although some guests can't help dressing up to dine in the beautifully appointed restaurants. A jacket and tie are never required for dinner, but many men wear sport jackets, as they would to dine in an upscale restaurant ashore. Jeans, shorts, T-shirts, and tennis shoes are discouraged after 6 pm in public rooms.

Junior Cruisers

Oceania Cruises are adult-oriented and not a good choice for families, particularly those traveling with infants and toddlers. No dedicated children's facilities are available, and parents are completely responsible for their behavior and entertainment. Teenagers with sophisticated tastes (and who don't mind the absence of a video arcade) might enjoy the intriguing ports of call.

Service

Highly personalized service by a mostly European staff is crisp and efficient without being intrusive. Butlers are on hand to fulfill the requests of suite guests and will even assist with packing and unpacking when asked.

CHOOSE THIS LINE IF ...

Socializing plays a more important role in your lifestyle than boogying the night away.

You love to read. These ships have extensive libraries that are ideal for curling up with a good book.

You have a bad back. You're sure to love the Tranquility Beds.

Tipping

Gratuities of $15 per person per day are added to shipboard accounts for distribution to stewards and waitstaff; an additional $7 per person per day is added for occupants of suites with butler service. Passengers may adjust the amount based on the level of service experienced. An automatic 18% gratuity is added to all bar tabs for bartenders and drink servers and to all bills for salon and spa services.

Past Passengers

After you take one Oceania cruise, you'll receive several benefits along with a free subscription to the *Oceania Club Journal.* Shipboard Club parties hosted by the captain and senior officers; complimentary amenities or exclusive privileges on select sailings; an Oceania Club membership recognition pin after 5, 10, 15, and 20 cruises; and special pricing and mailings about upcoming promotions are some of the benefits. Members further qualify for elite-level status based on the number of sailings aboard Oceania Cruises. Starting with your fifth cruise, you begin to accrue credit on every cruise you take, beginning with a $200 shipboard credit per stateroom on cruises five through nine. On your 10th cruise, you receive a $400 shipboard credit per stateroom plus complimentary gratuities on cruises 10 through 14. On your 15th cruise, you receive a $500 shipboard credit per stateroom, plus two complimentary spa treatments and complimentary gratuities on cruises 15 through 19. Once you take your 20th cruise, you get a free cruise as well as complimentary spa treatments, a shore excursion, and gratuities on all future cruises.

HELPFUL HINTS

■ Many Oceania voyages include airfare in the fare pricing.

■ Pre- or postcruise Hotel Collection Packages are available and include private group transfers.

■ There is never a dining charge on Oceania ships, but cocktail and wine prices are relatively high.

■ You may bring up to three bottles of wine per stateroom on board from ports of call, but there's a corkage fee of $25 per bottle if you bring wine to the dining room.

■ Oceania Cruises offers two shore excursion collections that must be reserved prior to sailing and can save a lot of money.

■ Oceania was the first cruise line to upgrade their bedding to the highest standard, so you can count on a good night's sleep on these ships.

DON'T CHOOSE THIS LINE IF ...

You like the action in a huge casino. Oceania casinos are small, and seats at a poker table can be difficult to get.

You want to bring your children. Most passengers book with Oceania anticipating a kid-free atmosphere.

Glitzy production shows are your thing. Oceania's show rooms are decidedly low-key.

INSIGNIA, REGATTA, NAUTICA

CREW MEMBERS	
400	
ENTERED SERVICE	
1998, 1998, 2000	
GROSS TONS	
30,277	
LENGTH	
594 feet	
NUMBER OF CABINS	
342	
PASSENGER CAPACITY	
684 (824 max)	
WIDTH	
84 feet	

700 ft.

500 ft.

300 ft.

Carefully furnished to impart the atmosphere of a private English country manor, these midsize ships are casual yet elegant, with sweeping central staircases and abundant flower arrangements. Brocade and toile fabrics window coverings, overstuffed sofas, and wing chairs create a warm and intimate feeling throughout. The entire effect is that of a weekend retreat in the English countryside.

Authentic-looking faux fireplaces are adjacent to cozy seating areas in the Grand Bar, near the martini bar's grand piano, and in the beautiful libraries—some of the best at sea, with an enormous selection of best sellers, nonfiction, and travel books. The casinos are quite small and can feel cramped, and smoking is prohibited. Though there may be a wait for a seat at a poker table, there are enough slot machines to go around.

Other than decorative trompe-l'oeil paintings in several public areas, the artwork is unremarkable.

Cabins

Layout: Private balconies outfitted with chairs and tables add additional living space to nearly 75% of all outside accommodations. All cabins have a vanity-desk and a seating area with sofa, chair, and table. Every cabin has generous closet and drawer/shelf storage and bathroom shelves. Owner's and Vista suites have a separate living-dining room, as well as a separate powder room. Concierge-level accommodations and above include an iPad for use during the cruise. Several cabins accommodate third and fourth passengers, but few have connecting doors.

Suites: Owner's and Vista suites have an entertainment center with a DVD and CD player, a small refrigerator, and a second TV in the bedroom; the main bathroom has a combination shower-whirlpool tub. Penthouse suites also have refrigerators and bathtubs. Butlers are on hand to coordinate reservations and serve evening canapés and dinner ordered from any of the ship's restaurants.

Amenities: Dark-wood cabinetry, soothing blue decor, mirrored accents, a safe, Tranquility Beds, 350-thread-count linens, goose-down pillows, and silk-cut duvets are typical stateroom features. Bathrooms have a hair dryer, shampoo, lotion, and bath gel, plus robes.

Accessibility: Three staterooms are designed for wheelchair accessibility.

Top: Teatime in Horizons
Bottom: Breakfast in bed

Restaurants

Oceania passengers enjoy the flexibility of four open seating restaurants. The Grand Dining Room, open for breakfast, lunch, and dinner, serves Continental cuisine. Alternative, reservations-required dinner options are Toscana, which serves gourmet Italian dishes, and Polo Grill, the steak house. Terraces, the buffet restaurant, serves breakfast, lunch, and dinner and is transformed into Tapas on the Terrace after dark for a relaxed atmosphere and alfresco dining. All dining venues have nearby bars, and there's no additional cover charge for dining. In addition, a poolside grill serves hamburgers and a variety of sandwiches and salads at lunchtime, and there is a pizzeria in the buffet area. Afternoon tea is an elaborate affair served in Horizons, the observation lounge. Room service is available 24 hours.

Spas

The Canyon Ranch SpaClub offers a long menu of body wraps, massages, conditioning body scrubs, skin care and tanning treatments, and acupuncture. Thermal suites include complimentary single-sex aromatic steam rooms. A highlight of the tranquil open-air Spa Terrace is a therapy whirlpool, to which all Concierge-level and suite guests have unlimited complimentary access; all other guests must purchase passes.

Bars and Entertainment

Bars and lounges have an intimate quality, from the martini bar, where piano music is played, to the show lounge that offers small-scale cabaret-style entertainment ranging from headline acts and concerts to comedians and magicians. The observation lounge is a late-night hot spot with music for dancing and even karaoke led by the entertainment staff.

Pros and Cons

Pros: a relaxed, social atmosphere pervades all areas on board; the lobby staircase is a must-see—it's practically identical to the one in the movie *Titanic*; on board, you'll find some of the most lavish afternoon teas at sea.

Cons: shipboard charges can add up fast, because drink prices and even Internet services are on the high side; there is only one self-serve laundry room; the absence of a sauna in the spa is an unfortunate oversight.

Cabin Type	Size (sq. ft.)
Owner's	962
Vista Suite	786
Penthouse Suite	322
Concierge/Ocean View with Balcony	216
Deluxe Ocean View	165
Standard Ocean View	150–165
Inside	160

FAST FACTS

- 9 passenger decks
- 2 specialty restaurants, dining room, buffet, pizzeria
- Wi-Fi, safe, refrigerator, DVD (some)
- 1 pool
- Fitness classes, gym, hot tubs, spa, steam room
- 4 bars, casino, dance club, library, show room
- Dry-cleaning, laundry facilities, laundry service
- Internet terminal
- No-smoking cabins

3

OCEANIA CRUISES

Regatta at sea

PRINCESS CRUISES

Princess Cruises may be best known for introducing cruise travel to millions of viewers, when its flagship became the setting for *The Love Boat* television series in 1977. Since that heady time of small-screen stardom, the Princess fleet has grown both in the

Watch iceburgs float by from your balcony

number and size of ships. Although most are large in scale, Princess vessels manage to create the illusion of intimacy through the use of color and decor in understated yet lovely public rooms graced by multimillion-dollar art collections.

☎ *661/753–0000 or 800/774–6237*
🌐 *www.princess.com*
☞ *Cruise Style: Premium.*

Princess has also become more flexible; Personal Choice Cruising offers alternatives for open seating dining (when you wish and with whom you please) and entertainment options as diverse as those found in resorts ashore.

Lovely chapels or the wide-open decks are equally romantic settings for weddings at sea with the captain officiating.

Food

Personal choices regarding where and what to eat abound, but because of the number of passengers, unless you opt for traditional assigned seating, you might have to wait for a table in one of the open seating dining rooms. Menus are varied and extensive in the main dining rooms, and the results are good to excellent, considering how much work is going on in the galleys. Vegetarian and healthy lifestyle options are always on the menu, as well as steak, fish, or chicken. A separate menu is designed especially for children.

Alternative restaurants are a staple throughout the fleet but vary by ship class. Grand-class ships have upscale steak houses and Sabatini's, an Italian restaurant; both require reservations and carry an extra cover charge.

Sun-class ships offer complimentary sit-down dining in the pizzeria and a similar steak-house option, although it's in a sectioned-off area of the buffet restaurant. On *Caribbean, Crown, Emerald,* and *Ruby Princess,* a casual evening alternative to the dining rooms and usual buffet is Café Caribe—adjacent to the Lido buffet restaurant, it serves cuisine with a Caribbean flair. With a few breaks in service, Lido buffets on all ships are almost always open, and a pizzeria and grill offer casual daytime snack choices. The fleet's patisseries and ice cream bars charge for specialty coffee, some pastries, and premium ice cream. A daily British-style pub lunch served in the ships' Wheelhouse Bar has been introduced fleet-wide, with the exception of the Sun-class and smaller ships.

Ultimate Balcony Dining—either a champagne breakfast or full-course dinner—is a full-service meal served on your cabin's balcony. The Chef's Table allows guests (for a fee) to dine on a special menu with wine pairings. After a meeting with the executive chef in the galley (and some champagne and appetizers), guests sit at a special table in the dining room. The chef joins them for dessert.

Entertainment

The roster of adult activities still includes standbys like bingo and art auctions, but you'll also find guest lecturers, cooking classes, wine-tasting seminars, pottery workshops, and computer and digital photography classes. Nighttime production shows tend toward Broadway-style revues presented in the main show lounge, and performers might include comedians, magicians, jugglers, and acrobats. Live bands play a wide range of musical styles for dancing and listening, and each ship has a dance club. The cruise director's staff leads lively evenings of fun with passenger participation. At the conclusion of the second formal night, champagne trickles down over a champagne waterfall, painstakingly created by the arrangement of champagne glasses in a pyramid shape. Ladies are invited to join the maître d' to assist in the pouring for a great photo op.

Fitness and Recreation

Spa rituals include a variety of massages, body wraps, and facials; numerous hair and nail services are offered in the salons. Both the salons and spa are operated by Steiner Leisure, and the menu of spa services includes special pampering treatments designed specifically for men and teens as well as couples. For a half-day

KNOWN FOR

■ **Accessibility:** Princess is a top choice for travelers with disabilities because the ships and even shore excursions offer more choices for them.

■ **Movies Under the Stars:** An innovative feature copied by other cruise lines, Princess was the first line to offer movies and other programming on giant poolside LED screens.

■ **Relaxation:** Ships in the Princess fleet feature another cruise industry first—the Sanctuary, where adults can get away from it all, has become a signature element, imitated by many other lines.

■ **Sophistication:** Princess Cruises' ships range from midsize to megaship, but all have a sophisticated ambience.

■ **Weddings:** Noted as the "Love Boats," Princess ships were the first at sea to offer captain-officiated weddings, and unlike most cruise lines they still do.

Top: Place a bet in the casino

Top: Sunset at sea
Middle: Morning stretch
Bottom: Freshwater Jacuzzi

fee, escape to the Sanctuary—the adults-only haven—which offers a relaxing outdoor spa-inspired setting with signature beverages, light meals, massages, attentive service, and relaxing personal entertainment.

Modern exercise equipment, a jogging track, and basic fitness classes are available at no charge. There's a fee for personal training, body composition analysis, and specialized classes such as yoga and Pilates. Grand-class ships have a resistance pool so you can get your laps in effortlessly.

Your Shipmates

Princess Cruises attract mostly American passengers, ranging from their mid-thirties to mid-fifties. Families enjoy cruising together on the Princess fleet, particularly during holiday seasons and in summer months, when many children are on board. Longer cruises appeal to well-traveled retirees and couples who have the time.

Dress Code

Two formal nights are standard on seven-night cruises; an additional formal night may be scheduled on longer sailings. Men are encouraged to wear tuxedos, but dark suits are appropriate. All other evenings are casual, although jeans are discouraged, and it's requested that no shorts be worn in public areas after 6 pm.

Junior Cruisers

For young passengers ages 3 to 17, each Princess vessel (except *Ocean Princess* and *Pacific Princess*) has a playroom, teen center, and programs of supervised activities designed for different age groups: ages 3 to 7, 8 to 12, and 13 to 17. Activities to engage youngsters include arts and crafts, pool games, scavenger hunts, deck parties, backstage and galley tours, games, and videos. Events such as dance parties in their own disco, theme parties, athletic contests, karaoke, pizza parties, and movie fests occupy teenage passengers. With a nod toward science and educational entertainment, children also participate in learning programs focused on the environment and wildlife in areas where the ships sail.

CHOOSE THIS LINE IF ...

You're a traveler with a disability. Princess ships are some of the most accessible at sea.

You like to gamble but hate a smoke-filled casino. Princess casinos are well ventilated and spacious.

You want a balcony. Princess ships feature them in abundance at affordable rates.

To allow parents independent time ashore, youth centers operate as usual during port days, including lunch with counselors. For an additional charge, group babysitting is available nightly from 10 pm until 1 am. Family-friendly conveniences include self-service laundry facilities. Infants under six months are not permitted; private in-cabin baby-sitting is not available on any Princess vessel. Children under age three are welcome in the playrooms if supervised by a parent.

Service
Professional service by an international staff is efficient and friendly. It's not uncommon to be greeted in passageways by smiling stewards who know your name.

Tipping
A gratuity of $11.50 per person per day ($12 for passengers in suites and minisuites) is added to shipboard accounts for distribution to stewards and waitstaff. Passengers may adjust the amount based on the level of service experienced. An automatic 15% is added to all bar tabs for bartenders and drink servers; gratuities to other staff members may be extended at passengers' discretion.

Past Passengers
Membership in the Captain's Circle is automatic following your first Princess cruise. All members receive a free subscription to *Captain's Circle News*, a quarterly newsletter, as well as discounts on selected cruises.

Perks are determined by the number of cruises completed: Gold (2 through 3), Medallion (4 and 5), Platinum (6 through 15), and Elite (16 and above). Although Gold members receive only the magazine, an invitation to an onboard event, and the services of the Circle Host on the ship, benefits really begin to accrue once you've completed five cruises. Platinum members receive upgraded insurance (when purchasing the standard policy), expedited check-in, a debarkation lounge to wait in on the ship, and, best of all, limited free Internet access during the cruise. Elite benefits are even more lavish, with many complimentary services.

HELPFUL HINTS

■ Princess Cruises pioneered the concept of affordable balcony accommodations and continues to lead the industry in that regard.

■ If you're unsure, select Traditional dining when you reserve your cruise; it can be impossible to change from Anytime Dining to Traditional on board, but it's easy to go the other way.

■ Princess Cruises is the only contemporary cruise line that offers deluxe Ultimate Balcony Dining—either an intimate breakfast or romantic dinner served by your own dedicated waiters on your stateroom balcony.

■ A Princess cruise can be enhanced by adding a Cruisetour, a five- to eight-day in-depth land tour, to your voyage to create a land and sea vacation.

DON'T CHOOSE THIS LINE IF ...

You have a poor sense of direction. Most ships, especially the Grand-class ships, are very large.

You think Princess is still as depicted in *The Love Boat*. That was just a TV show, and it was more than three decades ago.

You're too impatient to stand in line or wait. Debarkation from the large ships can be lengthy.

CARIBBEAN, CROWN, EMERALD, RUBY PRINCESS

CREW MEMBERS	
1,200, 1,200, 1,200, 1,225	
ENTERED SERVICE	
2004, 2006, 2007, 2008	
GROSS TONS	700 ft.
113,000	
LENGTH	
951 feet	
NUMBER OF CABINS	500 ft.
1,557, 1,538, 1,532, 1540	
PASSENGER CAPACITY	
3,080, 3,080, 3,080, 3,080	
WIDTH	300 ft.
118 feet	

With dramatic atriums and Skywalker's Nightclub (the spoiler hovering 150 feet above the stern), *Caribbean Princess* is a supersize version of the older Grand-class vessels with an extra deck of passenger accommodations. Not quite identical to *Caribbean Princess*, the younger ships in the class, *Crown*, *Emerald*, and *Ruby Princess* have introduced more dining options. Several signature public spaces have been redesigned or relocated on these ships as well—the atrium on *Crown*, *Emerald*, and *Ruby Princess* resembles an open piazza and sidewalk café; Sabatini's Italian Trattoria is found on a top deck with views on three sides and alfresco dining; and Skywalker's Disco is forward near the funnel (where it's topped with a sports court). Inside spaces on all three vessels are quietly neutral, with touches of glamour in the sweeping staircases and marble-floor atriums. Surprising intimacy is achieved by the number of public rooms and restaurants that swallow up passengers.

Cabins

Layout: On these ships 80% of the outside staterooms have balconies. The typical stateroom has a seating area with a chair and table; all have ample storage. Minisuites have a separate seating area, a walk-in closet, a combination shower-tub, and a balcony, as well as two TVs. Larger deluxe suites have separate sitting rooms and walk-in closets, some with sofa beds. Two family suites have interconnecting staterooms with a balcony and sleep up to eight (D105/D101 and D106/D102). Some staterooms can accommodate three and four, and some adjacent cabins can be connected through interior doors or balcony dividers.

Amenities: Decorated in attractive pastel hues, all cabins have a refrigerator, a hair dryer, a safe, and bathrobes to use during the cruise. Bathrooms have shampoo, lotion, and bath gel.

Accessibility: Twenty-five staterooms are wheelchair accessible on *Caribbean* and *Crown Princess*; *Emerald* and *Ruby Princess* have 31.

Top: Movies Under the Stars
Bottom: Broadway-style revue

Restaurants

Passengers choose between two assigned dinner seatings or open seating; breakfast and lunch are always open seating. Dinner options include reservations-only Sabatini's and Crown Grill (both with cover) and the complimentary Café Caribe, a casual Caribbean buffet with linen-dressed tables and limited waiter service. Lido buffets on all ships are almost always open. A pub lunch is served in the Wheelhouse Bar, and a pizzeria and grill offer casual daytime snack choices. The wine bars, patisseries, and ice cream bars charge for artisan cheeses, specialty coffee, some pastries, and premium ice cream. Ultimate Balcony Dining and Chef's Table options are available, as are afternoon tea and 24-hour room service.

Spas

Spas operated by Steiner Leisure offer the standard treatments, including a variety of massages, body wraps, and facials, as well as some designed specifically for men, teens, and couples. Medi-Spa treatments are also available. The spas' thermal suites have relaxing aromatic wet and dry saunas and heated loungers that are complimentary for those in suites, but a fee is charged for everyone else. Complimentary to all are saunas and steam rooms adjacent to men's and women's changing rooms.

Bars and Entertainment

Nighttime production shows tend toward Broadway-style revues presented in the main show lounge, and performers might include comedians, magicians, jugglers, and acrobats. Live bands play a wide range of musical styles for dancing and listening in the lounges and each ship has a dance club. The cruise director's staff leads lively evenings of fun with passenger participation. Movies Under the Stars with popcorn and other movie fare are a popular option.

Pros and Cons

Pros: Movies Under the Stars on the huge poolside screen have proven to be a big hit; the Wheelhouse Bar serves complimentary pub lunch at noon; the adults-only Sanctuary is a private deck with posh loungers for a fee.

Cons: priority dining reservations are extended only to Elite Captain's Circle members; the terrace overlooking the aft pool is a quiet spot after dark, but the nearest bar often closes early; opt for Anytime dining and you may encounter a wait for a table.

Cabin Type	Size (sq. ft)
Grand Suite	1,279
Other Suites	461–689
Family Suite	607
Minisuite	324
Ocean View with Balcony	233–285
Ocean View	158–182
Inside	163

All dimensions include the square footage for balconies.

FAST FACTS

- 15 passenger decks
- 2 specialty restaurants, 3 dining rooms, buffet, ice cream parlor, pizzeria
- Wi-Fi, safe, refrigerator, DVD (some)
- 4 pools (1 indoor), children's pool
- Fitness classes, gym, hot tubs, sauna, spa, steam room
- 9 bars, casino, 2 dance clubs, library, 2 show rooms, video game room
- Children's programs
- Dry-cleaning, laundry facilities, laundry service
- Internet terminal
- No kids under 6 months, no-smoking cabins

Sailing at sunset

CORAL-CLASS
Coral Princess, Island Princess

CREW MEMBERS	900
ENTERED SERVICE	2003, 2003
GROSS TONS	92,000
LENGTH	964
NUMBER OF CABINS	987
PASSENGER CAPACITY	1,970
WIDTH	106 feet

700 ft.
500 ft.
300 ft.

Princess includes *Coral Princess* and *Island Princess* in their Sun-class category; however, they are larger ships (albeit with a similar capacity to *Sun Princess* and her two sisters), which means much more space per passenger; we feel this necessitates a separate category. All the Personal Choice features attributed to the larger Grand-class ships were incorporated into this design as well as a few unique additions, such as a demonstration kitchen and ceramics lab complete with kiln where ScholarShip@ Sea programs are presented. The four-story atrium is similar to that on Sun-class ships, but public rooms are mainly spread fore and aft on two lower decks.

Although signature rooms such as the Wheelhouse Bar are more traditional, the casinos have subtle London- or Paris-like atmospheres with themed slot machines; Crooner's Bar is a retro 1960s Vegas-style martini and piano bar. In addition to the stately Princess Theater show room, the Universe Lounge has three stages for shows and flexible seating on two levels, making it a multipurpose space.

Cabins

Layout: Stepped out in wedding-cake fashion, more than 83% of ocean-view staterooms include Princess Cruises' trademark private balconies. Even the least expensive inside categories have plentiful storage and a small seating area with a chair and table. Suites have two TVs, a seating area, a wet bar, a large walk-in closet, and a separate bathtub and shower. Minisuites have a separate seating area, two TVs, a walk-in closet, and a combination bathtub/shower.

Suites: Occupants of 16 suites receive complimentary Internet access, dry cleaning, and shoe polishing, afternoon tea and evening canapés delivered to their suites, and priority embarkation, disembarkation, and tendering privileges. An extended room service menu is also available for them, as are priority reservations for dining and shore excursions.

Amenities: Decorated in pastels and light-wood tones, typical staterooms have a safe, hair dryer, refrigerator, and bathrobes for use during the cruise. Bathrooms have shampoo, lotion, and bath gel.

Accessibility: Twenty staterooms are designed for wheelchair accessibility and range in size from 217 to 374 square feet, depending on category.

Top: Fast-paced shows
Bottom: Plenty of locations on the ship to enjoy spectacular views

Restaurants

Passengers may choose between traditional dinner seating times in one assigned dining room or open seating in the other formal dining room; breakfast and lunch are open seating. Alternative dinner options include reservations-only Sabatini's Italian trattoria and Bayou Café & Steakhouse (both with an extra charge). With a few breaks in service, Lido buffets are almost always open. A pub lunch is served in the Wheelhouse Bar, and a pizzeria and grill offer casual daytime snack choices. The patisseries and ice cream bars charge for specialty coffee, some pastries, and premium ice cream. Ultimate Balcony Dining and Chef's Table options are available, as is afternoon tea, and 24-hour room service.

Spas

The spa, which is operated by Steiner Leisure, offers a menu of massages, body wraps, and facials, including treatments specifically designed for men, teens, and couples. Acupuncture is also available. Thermal suites have relaxing aromatic wet and dry saunas and heated loungers and are complimentary for those in suites, but there is a fee for everyone else. Adults can escape to the Sanctuary, a relaxing outdoor spa-inspired setting for which there is also a fee. Complimentary to all are saunas adjacent to men's and women's changing rooms.

Bars and Entertainment

Nighttime production shows tend toward Broadway-style revues presented in the main show lounge; other performers might include comedians, magicians, jugglers, and acrobats. Live bands play a wide range of musical styles for dancing and listening in the lounges and each ship has a dance club. The cruise director's staff leads lively evenings of fun with passenger participation. Movies Under the Stars with popcorn and other movie fare are a popular option.

Pros and Cons

Pros: as many as 20 courses in the ScholarShip@Sea program are offered on each cruise; cabins that sleep third and fourth passengers are numerous; the Fine Art Gallery is a dedicated area, so displays don't clutter other public spaces.

Cons: the library and card room often become noisy passageways; there are only 16 suites on each ship; engine pods on the funnel give the ships a futuristic space-age appearance but are mainly decorative.

Cabin Type	Size (sq. ft.)
Suite	470
Minisuite	285–302
Ocean View Balcony	217–232
Ocean View Stand	162
Deluxe	212
Inside	156–166

All dimensions include the square footage for balconies.

FAST FACTS

- 11 passenger decks
- 2 specialty restaurants, 2 dining rooms, buffet, ice cream parlor, pizzeria
- Wi-Fi, safe, refrigerator, DVD (some)
- 3 pools (1 indoor), children's pool
- Fitness classes, gym, hot tubs, sauna, spa
- 7 bars, casino, 2 dance clubs, library, 2 show rooms, video game room
- Children's programs
- Dry-cleaning, laundry facilities, laundry service
- Internet terminal
- No kids under 6 months, no-smoking cabins

Lavish buffets in Horizon Court

3

PRINCESS CRUISES

GRAND-CLASS
Grand Princess, Golden Princess, Star Princess

CREW MEMBERS	1,100, 1,100, 1,200
ENTERED SERVICE	1998, 2001, 2002
GROSS TONS	109,000
LENGTH	951 feet
NUMBER OF CABINS	1,300
PASSENGER CAPACITY	2,590
WIDTH	118 feet

700 ft.

500 ft.

300 ft.

When *Grand Princess* was introduced as the world's largest cruise ship in 1998, futuristic Skywalker's Disco hovered approximately 150 feet above the waterline, but in a dramatic—and fuel-saving—transformation, it was removed from *Grand Princess* in 2011 and replaced with a more conventional nightclub in the heart of the ship. Subsequent ships did not have the same design problem, so there are no plans on the drawing board to remove Skywalker's.

All Grand-class vessels have more than 700 staterooms that include private balconies. Like their predecessors, the interiors of Grand-class ships have splashy glamour in the sweeping staircases and marble-floor atriums. Surprisingly intimate for such large ships, human scale in public lounges is achieved by judicious placement of furniture as unobtrusive room dividers. The 300-square-foot Times Square–style LED screens that hover over the pools show up to seven movies or events daily.

Cabins
Layout: On these ships, 80% of the outside staterooms have balconies. The typical stateroom has a seating area with a chair and table; even the cheapest categories have ample storage. Minisuites have a separate seating area, a walk-in closet, a combination shower-tub, and a balcony, as well as two TVs. More deluxe suites have even more room, some with sofa beds. Two family suites have interconnecting staterooms with a balcony that can sleep up to eight people (D105/D101 and D106/D102). Staterooms in a variety of categories will accommodate three and four people, and some adjacent cabins can be interconnected through interior doors or by unlocking doors in the balcony dividers.

Amenities: Decorated in attractive pastel hues, all cabins have a refrigerator, hair dryer, safe, and bathrobes to use during the cruise. Bathrooms have shampoo, lotion, and bath gel.

Accessibility: Twenty-eight staterooms are wheelchair accessible.

Top: *Star Princess* at sea
Bottom: *Golden Princess*
grand plaza atrium

Restaurants

Passengers choose between two assigned dinner seatings or open seating; breakfast and lunch are open seating. Alternative dinner options include the reservations-only Crown Grill and Sabatini's Italian restaurants (both with cover). Lido buffets on all ships are open around the clock. A pub lunch is served in the Wheelhouse Bar, and a pizzeria and grill offer casual daytime snack choices. The patisseries and ice cream bars charge for specialty coffee, some pastries, and premium ice cream. A wine bar serves extra-charge evening snacks and artisan cheeses. Ultimate Balcony Dining and Chef's Table options are available, as is afternoon tea and 24-hour room service.

Spas

Spas operated by Steiner Leisure offer a menu of massages, body wraps, and facials, as well as treatments specifically designed for men, teens, and couples. Acupuncture is also available. Only *Star Princess* has a thermal suite (complimentary for those in suites but open to others for a fee), but saunas and steam rooms adjacent to men's and women's changing rooms are complimentary on all three ships. Adults can escape to the Sanctuary, a relaxing outdoor spa-inspired setting for which there is a fee.

Bars and Entertainment

Nighttime production shows presented in the main show lounge lean toward Broadway-style revues; guest performers might include comedians, magicians, jugglers, and acrobats. Live bands play a wide range of musical styles for dancing and listening in the lounges, and each ship has a dance club. The cruise director's staff leads lively evenings of fun with passenger participation. Movies Under the Stars, where popcorn is free, is a popular evening option.

Pros and Cons

Pros: Skywalker's Nightclub on *Golden Princess* and *Star Princess* is virtually deserted during the day, when it's the ideal quiet spot to watch the sea; self-service passenger laundry rooms have ironing stations; the nautical Wheelhouse Bar is a Princess tradition for predinner cocktails and dancing.

Cons: sports bars get jam-packed—and stuffy—when big games are on; accommodations aft and above the Vista lounge are noisy when bands crank up the volume; minisuites don't include the perks offered to full suites.

Cabin Type	Size (sq. ft.)
Grand Suite	730/ 1,314*
Other Suites	468–591
Family Suite	607
Minisuite	323
Ocean View Balcony	232–274
Standard	168
Inside	160

All dimensions include the square footage for balconies. *Grand Princess* dimensions followed by *Golden* and *Star Princess*.

FAST FACTS

- 14 passenger decks
- 2 specialty restaurants, 3 dining rooms, buffet, ice cream parlor, pizzeria
- Wi-Fi, safe, refrigerator
- 4 pools (1 indoor), children's pool
- Fitness classes, gym, hot tubs, sauna, spa, steam room
- 9 bars, casino, 2 dance clubs, library, 2 show rooms, video game room
- Children's programs
- Dry-cleaning, laundry facilities, laundry service
- Internet terminal
- No kids under 6 months, no-smoking cabins

Grand-class balcony stateroom

PACIFIC, OCEAN PRINCESS

CREW MEMBERS	373
ENTERED SERVICE	1999
GROSS TONS	30,277
LENGTH	592 feet
NUMBER OF CABINS	334
PASSENGER CAPACITY	670
WIDTH	84 feet

700 ft.

500 ft.

300 ft.

At 30,277 tons, these ships appear positively tiny beside their megaship fleetmates. In reality, they are medium-size ships that entered service for the now-defunct Renaissance Cruises. With their entry into the Princess lineup, real choice is available to Princess passengers—a true alternative for those who prefer the clubby atmosphere of a smaller boutique-style ship but with big-ship features galore.

These sister ships have cozy public spaces, a stunning observation lounge—where the view is visible through floor-to-ceiling windows on three sides—and some of the loveliest libraries at sea, with their domed trompe-l'oeil–painted ceilings, faux fireplaces, comfortable seating areas, and (most important) well-stocked bookshelves. Although the main show room isn't particularly suited for glitzy production-company performances, it is ideal for cabaret shows.

Cabins

Layout: Designed for longer cruises, all staterooms have ample closet and storage space, although bathrooms in lower-priced categories are somewhat tight. Dark-wood cabinetry adds warmth to the pastel decor. In keeping with the rest of the fleet, 73% of all outside cabins and suites have a balcony, and interiors are similar in size to those you'll find on other Princess ships.

Suites: Full suites are particularly nice, with living/dining rooms, entertainment centers, separate bedrooms, whirlpool bathtubs, a guest powder room, and large balconies overlooking the bow or stern.

Amenities: Amenities in standard cabins are a bit spartan compared to other Princess ships, yet all have at least a small seating area. Bath toiletries, a hair dryer, a safe, and robes for use during the cruise are all included, but you must move up to a minisuite or suite to have a real bathtub.

Accessibility: Five staterooms are wheelchair accessible on *Pacific Princess* and four on *Ocean Princess*.

Ocean Princess at sea

Restaurants

The only disappointment in this ship class is the lack of a Personal Choice dining room. Although open seating breakfast and lunch are served in the main dining room, the only dinner option is in one of two assigned seatings. Sabatini's Italian Trattoria and Sterling Steakhouse specialty restaurants are reservations-required and extra-charge dinner alternatives. With a few breaks in service, Lido buffets on all ships are almost always open. There's a pizzeria window in the buffet area and a separate poolside grill for casual lunch and snacks. Ultimate Balcony Dining is available, as is afternoon tea, and 24-hour room service.

Spas

Spa treatments offered by Steiner Leisure include a variety of massages, body wraps, and facials, including some designed especially for men. All the way forward is a relaxing outdoor spa-inspired setting with loungers and a therapy pool, for which there is a fee for everyone except those in suites. Complimentary to all are steam rooms in men's and women's changing facilities.

Bars and Entertainment

Nighttime shows in the main lounge, which is on the small side, tend to be cabaret style; guest performers often include comedians and magicians. Live bands play a wide range of musical styles for dancing and listening in the lounges. The entertainment staff leads lively evenings of fun with passenger participation.

Pros and Cons

Pros: decks 6 and 7 have two aft-facing standard cabins with balconies larger than other similar cabins; the pianist in the Casino Bar drowns out the clanging of slot machines; many of Princess Cruises' trademark features are present even though these ships were built to another cruise line's specifications.

Cons: show rooms are all on one level and have low ceilings; there are no dedicated children's facilities; the solitary main dining room offers only assigned seating for dinner.

Cabin Type	Size (sq. ft.)
Suites	786–962
Minisuite	322
Ocean View Balcony	216
Ocean View	165
Inside	158

FAST FACTS

- 9 passenger decks
- 2 specialty restaurants, dining room, buffet, pizzeria
- Wi-Fi, safe, refrigerator (some), DVD (some)
- 1 pool
- Fitness classes, gym, hot tubs, spa, steam room
- 8 bars, casino, dance club, library, show room
- Children's programs
- Dry-cleaning, laundry facilities, laundry service
- Internet terminal
- No kids under 6 months, no-smoking cabins

3

PRINCESS CRUISES

Pacific Princess Grand Lobby

REGENT SEVEN SEAS

The 1994 merger of Radisson Diamond Cruises and Seven Seas Cruise Line launched Radisson Seven Seas Cruises with an eclectic fleet of vessels that offers a nearly all-inclusive cruise experience in sumptuous, contemporary surroundings. The line was

The end of a perfect day

rebranded as Regent Seven Seas Cruises in 2006, and ownership passed to Prestige Cruise Holdings (which also owns Oceania Cruises) in 2008.

☎ *877/505–5370*
⊕ *www.rssc.com*
☞ *Cruise Style:*
Luxury.

Even more inclusive than in the past, the line has maintained its traditional tried-and-true formula—delightful ships offering exquisite service, generous staterooms with abundant amenities, a variety of dining options, and superior lecture and enrichment programs. Guests are greeted with champagne on boarding and find an all-inclusive beverage policy that offers not only soft drinks and bottled water, but also cocktails and select wines at all bars and restaurants throughout the ships. Round-trip air, ground transfers, and shore excursions in every port are included in the cruise fare.

On board, casinos are more akin to Monaco than Las Vegas. All ships display tasteful and varied art collections, including pieces that are for sale.

Food
Menus may appear to include the usual beef Wellington and Maine lobster, but in the hands of Regent Seven Seas chefs the results are some of the most outstanding meals at sea. Specialty dining varies within the fleet, but *Seven Seas Voyager* and *Seven Seas Mariner,* have the edge with the sophisticated Signatures, featuring the most authentic French cuisine to be found outside of Paris. Prime 7, on all three ships,

is a contemporary adaptation of the classic American steak house offering fresh, distinctive decor and an innovative menu of the finest prime-aged steak and chops, along with fresh seafood and poultry specialties. In addition, Mediterranean-influenced bistro dinners that need no reservations are served in Sette Mari at La Veranda, the venue that is the daytime casual Lido buffet restaurant.

Wine Connoisseurs Dinners are offered occasionally on longer cruises to bring together people with an interest in wine and food. Each course on the degustation menu is complemented by a wine pairing. The cost varies according to the special vintage wines that are included.

Room-service menus are fairly extensive, and you can also order directly from the restaurant menus during regular serving hours.

Although special dietary requirements should be relayed to the cruise line before sailing, general considerations such as vegetarian, low-salt, or low-cholesterol food requests can be satisfied on board the ships simply by speaking with the dining room staff. Wines chosen to complement dinner menus are freely poured each evening.

Entertainment

Most sailings host guest lecturers, including historians, anthropologists, naturalists, and diplomats, and there are often discussions and workshops. Spotlight cruises center around popular pastimes and themes, such as food and wine, photography, history, archaeology, literature, performing arts, design and cultures, active exploration and wellness, antiques, jewelry and shopping, the environment, and marine life. All passengers have access to these unique experiences on board and on shore.

Activities and entertainment are tailored for each of the line's distinctive ships with the tastes of sophisticated passengers in mind. Don't expect napkin-folding demonstrations or nonstop action. Production revues, cabaret acts, concert-style piano performances, solo performers, and comedians may be featured in show lounges, with combos playing for listening and dancing in lounges and bars throughout the ships.

KNOWN FOR

■ All-Inclusive: Regent Seven Seas Cruises offers the longest list of inclusive features for the money.

■ Destination Focused: Regent even includes select shore excursions in the fare—a real bonus when the ships reach ports of call.

■ Fine Cuisine: Ships in the Regent fleet have some of the finest specialty restaurants afloat and there is no charge for dining in them.

■ Great Service: Exemplary service is a signature feature of Regent's voyages.

■ Luxurious but Informal: Socializing is easygoing on Regent's less formal ships.

Top: Sunrise jog
Bottom: *Seven Seas Navigator*

Fitness and Recreation

Although gyms and exercise areas are well equipped, these are not large ships, so the facilities also tend to be limited in size. Each ship has a jogging track, and the larger ones feature a variety of sports courts. The spas and salons aboard Regent Seven Seas ships are operated by Canyon Ranch SpaClub, which offers an array of customizable treatments and services.

Your Shipmates

Regent Seven Seas Cruises are inviting to active, affluent, well-traveled couples ranging from their late-thirties to retirees who enjoy the ship's chic ambience and destination-rich itineraries. Longer cruises attract veteran passengers in the over-sixty age group.

Dress Code

Elegant casual is the dress code for most nights; formal and semiformal attire is optional on sailings of 16 nights or longer, but it's no longer required. It's requested that dress codes be observed in public areas after 6 pm.

Junior Cruisers

Regent Seven Seas' vessels are adult-oriented and do not have dedicated children's facilities. However, a Club Mariner youth program for children ages 5 to 8, 9 to 12, and 13 to 17 is offered on select sailings, both during summer months and during school holiday periods. Supervised by counselors, the organized, educational activities focus on nature and the heritage of the ship's destinations. Activities, including games, craft projects, movies, and food fun, are organized to ensure that every child has a memorable experience. Teens are encouraged to help counselors select the activities they prefer. Only infants that are one year of age before the first day of the cruise may sail.

Service

The efforts of a polished, unobtrusive staff go almost unnoticed, yet special requests are handled with ease. Butlers provide an additional layer of personal service to guests in the top-category suites.

Top: Fitness center
Middle: Pool decks are never crowded
Bottom: Pampering in the Carita of Paris spa

CHOOSE THIS LINE IF ...

You want to learn the secrets of cooking like a Cordon Bleu chef (for a charge, of course).

You don't want the hassle of signing bar tabs or extra expense of shore excursions.

A really high-end spa experience is on your agenda.

Tipping

Gratuities are included in the fare, and none are expected. To show their appreciation, passengers may elect to make a contribution to a crew welfare fund that benefits the ship's staff.

Past Passengers

Membership in the Seven Seas Society is automatic on completion of a Regent Seven Seas cruise. Members receive discounted cruise fare savings on select sailings, exclusive shipboard and shore-side special events on select sailings, a Seven Seas Society recognition cocktail party on every sailing, and *Inspirations* newsletter highlighting special events, sailings, and destination- and travel-related information. The tiered program offers rewards based on the number of nights you have sailed with RSSC. The more you sail, the more you accrue. Bronze benefits are offered to members with 4 to 20 nights. From 21 through 74 nights, Silver members also receive complimentary Internet access on board, free pressing, and an hour of free phone time. From 75 through 199 nights, Gold members are awarded priority disembarkation at some ports, an additional two hours of complimentary phone time, more complimentary pressing, an exclusive Gold & Platinum activity aboard or ashore on every sailing, and priority reservations at restaurants and spas. From 200 through 399, Platinum members can add complimentary air deviation services (one time per sailing), nine hours of complimentary phone use, and unlimited free pressing and laundry services. Titanium members who have sailed 400 or more nights also get free dry-cleaning and free transfers.

HELPFUL HINTS

■ Other luxury lines don't always include round-trip air, ground transfers, and unlimited shore excursions in every port of call.

■ Regent Seven Seas ships offer all-suite accommodations.

■ Regent Choice Shore Excursions carry a supplement, but they delve much deeper into a region's culture and history.

■ Multinight pre- and postcruise land programs are available to extend your cruise vacation.

■ Regent Seven Seas ships are luxurious but not stuffy, and there's a "block party" on every cruise where passengers are invited to meet their neighbors in adjacent suites.

REGENT SEVEN SEAS

3

DON'T CHOOSE THIS LINE IF ...

Connecting cabins are a must. Very few are available, and only the priciest cabins connect.

You can't imagine a cruise without the hoopla of games in the pool; these ships are much more discreet.

You don't want to dress up for dinner. Most passengers still dress more formally than on other lines.

SEVEN SEAS NAVIGATOR

CREW MEMBERS	340
ENTERED SERVICE	1999
GROSS TONS	33,000
LENGTH	560 feet
NUMBER OF CABINS	245
PASSENGER CAPACITY	490
WIDTH	81 feet

700 ft.

500 ft.

300 ft.

The first ship outfitted uniquely to Regent Seven Seas' specifications, the *Seven Seas Navigator* is a particular favorite of returning passengers for its small-ship intimacy, big-ship features, and comfortable, well-designed accommodations, which are all considered suites.

The generous use of wood and the addition of deep-tone accents to the predominantly blue color palette give even the larger lounges an inviting feel. Artwork and elaborate flower arrangements add a bit of sparkle and interest to the somewhat angular modern decor.

Due to the aft location of the two-deck-high main show room, the only lounges that afford sweeping seascapes are Galileo's—typically the most popular public space, with nightly entertainment—and the Vista Lounge. Although views from the Vista Lounge are spectacular, there's no permanent bar, and it's primarily a quiet spot for reading when there are no lectures or activities scheduled there.

Cabins

Layout: Attractive textured fabrics and honeyed wood finishes add a touch of coziness to the larger-than-usual suites in all categories, 90% of which have balconies. All have a vanity-desk, walk-in closet, and seating area with a sofa, chairs, and table. Marble bathrooms have a separate tub and shower. Master suites have a separate sitting–dining room, a separate bedroom, and a powder room; only Grand suites also have a powder room. Master suites have a second TV in the bedroom, butler service, and whirlpool tub in the master bathroom. Grand and Navigator suites are similarly outfitted. The top three suite categories feature Bose music systems, an iPad, and an iPod docking station. Penthouse suites, which include butler service, are only distinguished from Deluxe suites by location and do not have a whirlpool bathtub. Few suites have the capacity to accommodate three people, and only 10 far-forward suites adjoin with those adjacent to them.

Amenities: Every suite has an entertainment center with CD/DVD player, stocked refrigerator, stocked bar, safe, hair dryer, and beds dressed with fine linens and duvets. Bath toiletries include shampoo, lotion, and bath gel. Passengers in Concierge suites and higher receive 15

Top: Casino
Bottom: *Navigator suite*

minutes of free ship-to-shore phone time and 60 minutes of free Internet access.

Accessibility: Four suites are wheelchair accessible.

Restaurants

Compass Rose restaurant, the main dining room, functions on an open seating basis for breakfast, lunch, and dinner, so there are no set dining assignments. La Veranda, the daytime buffet, which serves breakfast and lunch, is transformed into an evening bistro serving Mediterranean cuisine. Prime 7, the specialty steak house, requires reservations for dinner, but there is no charge. At least once during each cruise, dinner is served alfresco on the pool deck. In addition to the buffet, a choice for casual lunch and snacks is the poolside grill. Afternoon tea is served daily, and room service is available 24 hours a day. Dinner can be ordered from the main dining room menu during restaurant hours and served en suite, course by course.

Spas

Canyon Ranch SpaClub offers an array of treatments, such as massages, facials, and body wraps utilizing organic and natural materials that can be individually customized. Guests can also enjoy complimentary aromatic steam rooms infused with pure plant essences or Finnish-style saunas.

Bars and Entertainment

Socializing over dinner is a major evening pursuit, and there's music for dancing before and after dining, including deck parties when the weather permits. Dance hosts are on hand to partner unaccompanied ladies on the dance floor. The main show lounge features small-scale production shows, and guest entertainers range from classical to modern vocalists and musicians.

Pros and Cons

Pros: library is excellent and includes a wide selection of both books and DVDs; fellow passengers might be as wealthy as Midas, but most are unpretentious; when nothing on the menu appeals to you, just ask for what you'd really like to have.

Cons: computer room is next to the library and can cause noise and congestion when Internet use is heavy; if you book a suite in the far-aft section of the ship, be prepared for an annoying vibration; unless you pre-book tables in specialty restaurants online, you could find them unavailable after boarding.

Cabin Type	Size (sq. ft.)
Master Suite	1,067
Grand Suite	539
Navigator Suite	448
Penthouse/Balcony Suite	301
Window Suite	301*

*Except for Suite 600, which easures 516 square feet.

FAST FACTS

- 8 passenger decks
- Specialty restaurant, dining room, buffet
- Wi-Fi, safe, refrigerator, DVD
- Pool
- Fitness classes, gym, hot tub, sauna, spa, steam room
- 4 bars, casino, dance club, show room
- Children's programs
- Dry-cleaning, laundry facilities, laundry service
- Internet terminal
- No-smoking cabins

3

REGENT SEVEN SEAS

Casual poolside dining

ROYAL CARIBBEAN INTL.

Big, bigger, biggest! In the early 1990s, Royal Caribbean launched Sovereign-class ships, the first of the modern megacruise liners, which continue to be the all-around favorite of passengers who enjoy traditional cruising ambience with a touch of daring

Adventure of the Seas solarium

and whimsy. Plunging into the 21st century, each ship in the current fleet carries more passengers than the entire Royal Caribbean fleet of the 1970s, and has amenities—such as new surfing pools—that were unheard of in the past.

☎ *305/539–6000 or 800/327–6700*
⊕ *www.royal caribbean.com*
☞ *Cruise Style: Mainstream.*

All Royal Caribbean ships are topped by the company's signature Viking Crown Lounge, a place to watch the seascape by day and dance at night. Expansive multideck atriums and promenades, as well as the generous use of brass and floor-to-ceiling glass windows, give each vessel a sense of spaciousness and style. The action is nonstop in casinos and dance clubs after dark, while daytime hours are filled with poolside games and traditional cruise activities. Port talks tend to lean heavily on shopping recommendations and the sale of shore excursions.

Food

Dining is an international experience, with nightly changing themes and cuisines from around the world. Passenger preference for casual attire and a resortlike atmosphere has prompted the cruise line to add laidback alternatives to the formal dining rooms: the Windjammer Café and, on certain ships, Johnny Rockets Diner; Seaview Café evokes the ambience of an island beachside stand. Royal Caribbean offers you the choice of early or late dinner seating and has introduced an open seating program fleet-wide.

Room service is available 24 hours, but for orders between midnight and 5 am there's a $3.95 service charge. There's a limited menu.

Royal Caribbean doesn't place emphasis on celebrity chefs or specialty alternative restaurants, although they have introduced a more upscale and intimate dinner experience in the form of an Italian specialty restaurant and/or a steak house on all ships.

Entertainment

A variety of lounges and high-energy stage shows draw passengers of all ages out to mingle and dance the night away. Production extravaganzas showcase singers and dancers in lavish costumes. Comedians, acrobats, magicians, jugglers, and solo entertainers fill show lounges on nights when the ships' companies aren't performing. Professional ice shows are a highlight of cruises on Voyager-, Freedom-, and Oasis-class ships—the only ships at sea with ice-skating rinks.

Fitness and Recreation

Royal Caribbean has pioneered such new and previously unheard of features as rock-climbing walls, ice-skating rinks, bungee trampolines, and even the first self-leveling pool tables on a cruise ship. Interactive water parks, boxing rings, surfing simulators, and cantilevered whirlpools suspended 112 feet above the ocean made their debuts on the Freedom-class ships.

Facilities vary by ship class, but all Royal Caribbean ships have state-of-the-art exercise equipment, jogging tracks, and rock-climbing walls; passengers can work out independently or in classes guaranteed to sweat off extra calories. Most exercise classes are included in the fare, but there's a fee for specialized spin, yoga, and Pilates classes, as well as the services of a personal trainer. Spas and salons are top-notch, with full menus of day spa–style treatments and services for pampering and relaxation for adults and teens.

Your Shipmates

Royal Caribbean cruises have a broad appeal for active couples and singles, mostly in their thirties to fifties. Families are partial to the newer vessels that have larger staterooms, huge facilities for children and teens, and seemingly endless choices of activities and dining options.

KNOWN FOR

■ **A Step Above:** Offering the same value as other mainstream lines, Royal Caribbean's ships are more sophisticated than its competitors'.

■ **Big Ships:** The Royal Caribbean fleet boasts the world's largest cruise ships.

■ **Extra Charges:** You will have to break out your wallet quite often once on board, as the cruise fare is far from inclusive.

■ **Recreation:** Gym rats and sports and fitness buffs find multiple facilities available to satisfy their active lifestyles while at sea.

■ **Something for Everyone:** With activities that appeal to a broad demographic, Royal Caribbean is a top choice for multigenerational cruise vacations.

Top: Adventure Beach for kids
Bottom: Voyager-class interior stateroom

3

ROYAL CARIBBEAN INTERNATIONAL

Top: Miniature golf
Middle: *Adventure of the Seas*
Bottom: *Serenade of the Seas*
rock-climbing wall

Dress Code

Two formal nights are standard on seven-night cruises; one formal night is the norm on shorter sailings. Men are encouraged to wear tuxedos, but dark suits or sport coats and ties are more prevalent. All other evenings are casual, although jeans are discouraged in restaurants. It's requested that no shorts be worn in public areas after 6 pm, although there are passengers who can't wait to change into them after dinner.

Junior Cruisers

Supervised age-appropriate activities are designed for children ages 3 through 17; babysitting services are available as well. Children are assigned to the Adventure Ocean youth program by age. They must be at least three years old and toilet trained to participate (children who are in diapers and pull-ups or who are not toilet trained are not allowed in swimming pools or whirlpools; however, they may use the Baby Splash Zone designated for them on the *Freedom, Liberty, Independence, Oasis,* and *Allure of the Seas*). Youngsters who wish to join a different age group must participate in one daytime and one night activity session with their proper age group first; the manager will then make the decision based on their maturity level.

In partnership with toymaker Fisher-Price, Royal Caribbean offers interactive 45-minute Aqua Babies and Aqua Tots play sessions for children ages 6 months to 36 months. The playgroup classes, which are hosted by youth staff members, were designed by early childhood development experts for parents and their babies and toddlers, and teach life skills through playtime activities. Nurseries have been added for babies 6 to 36 months old, with drop-off options during the day and evening—and if parents supply diapers, attendants will change them. There is an hourly fee, and only eight babies and toddlers can be accommodated at a time.

A teen center with a disco is an adult-free gathering spot that will satisfy even the pickiest teenagers.

CHOOSE THIS LINE IF ...

You want to see the sea from atop a rock wall—it's one of the few activities on these ships that's free.

You're active and adventurous. Even if your traveling companion isn't, there's an energetic staff on board to cheer you on.

You want your space. There's plenty of room to roam; quiet nooks and crannies are there if you look.

Service

Service on Royal Caribbean ships is friendly but inconsistent. Assigned meal seatings assure that most passengers get to know the waiters and their assistants, who in turn get to know the passengers' likes and dislikes; however, that can lead to a level of familiarity that is uncomfortable for some people. Most ships have a concierge lounge for the use of suite occupants and top-level past passengers.

Tipping

Tips that are not prepaid when the cruise is booked are automatically added to shipboard accounts in the amount of $12 per person, per day ($14.25 for suites), to be shared by dining and housekeeping staff. A 15% gratuity is automatically added to all bar tabs and spa and salon services.

Past Passengers

After one cruise, you can enroll in the Crown & Anchor Society. Tiered membership levels are achieved according to a point system. All members receive the *Crown & Anchor* magazine and have access to the member section on the Royal Caribbean website. All members receive an Ultimate Value Booklet and an invitation to a welcome-back party. Platinum members also have the use of a private departure lounge and receive priority check-in (where available), the onboard use of robes during the cruise, an invitation to an exclusive onboard event, and complimentary custom air arrangements. As points are added to your status, the benefits increase to Emerald, Diamond, Diamond Plus, and Pinnacle Club. For instance, Diamond and above receive such perks as access to a private lounge, behind-the-scenes tours, and priority seating for certain events.

HELPFUL HINTS

■ Reservations can be made online precruise for specialty restaurants, shore excursions, and spa treatments on all ships, as well as the shows on *Oasis of the Seas, Allure of the Seas, Freedom of the Seas,* and *Liberty of the Seas.*

■ The signature Viking Crown Lounge found on every Royal Caribbean ship is a daytime observation lounge and a nightclub after dark.

■ Popular with children of all ages, the DreamWorks Experience on certain ships offers character meals, meet-and-greet gatherings, and photo ops.

■ With a multibottle package you can save up to 25% off regular list prices on wine.

■ A complimentary Coca-Cola souvenir cup is included with the fountain soft drink package.

■ Bottled water and bottled juice packages of varying quantities can be delivered to your stateroom and will save you up to 25%.

3

ROYAL CARIBBEAN INTERNATIONAL

DON'T CHOOSE THIS LINE IF ...

Patience is not one of your virtues. Lines are not uncommon.

You want to do your own laundry. There are no self-service facilities on any Royal Caribbean ships.

You don't want to hear announcements. There are a lot on Royal Caribbean ships.

RADIANCE-CLASS
Radiance, Brilliance, Serenade, Jewel of the Seas

CREW MEMBERS	857
ENTERED SERVICE	2001, 2002, 2003, 2004
GROSS TONS	90,090
LENGTH	962 feet
NUMBER OF CABINS	1,056
PASSENGER CAPACITY	2,112 (2,501 max)
WIDTH	106 feet

700 ft.

500 ft.

300 ft.

Considered by many people to be the most beautiful vessels in the Royal Caribbean fleet, Radiance-class ships are large but sleek and swift, with sun-filled interiors and panoramic elevators that span 10 decks along the ships' exteriors.

High-energy and glamorous spaces are abundant throughout these sister ships. From the rock-climbing wall, children's pool with waterslide, and golf area to the columned dining room, sweeping staircases, and the tropical garden of the solarium, these ships hold appeal for a wide cross section of interests and tastes.

The ships are packed with multiple dining venues, including the casual Windjammer, with its indoor and outdoor seating, and the Latte-Tudes patisserie, offering specialty coffees, pastries, and ice cream treats.

Cabins

Layout: With the line's highest percentage of outside cabins, standard staterooms are bright and cheery as well as roomy. Nearly three-quarters of the outside cabins have private balconies. Every cabin has adequate closet and drawer/shelf storage, as well as bathroom shelves.

Suites: All full suites and family suites have private balconies and include concierge service. Top-category suites have wet bars, separate living–dining areas, multiple bathrooms, entertainment centers with flat-screen TVs, DVD players, and stereos. Some bathrooms have twin sinks, steam showers, and whirlpool tubs. Junior suites have a seating area, vanity area, and bathroom with a tub.

Amenities: Light-wood cabinetry, a small refrigerator-minibar, broadband Internet connection, a vanity-desk, a TV, a safe, a hair dryer, and a seating area with sofa, chair, and table are typical Radiance-class features in all categories. Bathroom extras include shampoo and bath gel.

Accessibility: Fifteen staterooms are designed for wheelchair accessibility on *Radiance* and *Brilliance*; 19 on *Serenade* and *Jewel*.

Top: Pool deck
Bottom: Shared moments on your personal balcony

Restaurants

The double-deck-high formal dining room serves open seating breakfast and lunch; dinner is served in two assigned seatings, but open seating is an option. For a more upscale dinner, each ship has an Italian restaurant and a steak house. In addition, *Radiance of the Seas* has a Brazilian-style steak house. All but *Jewel* have an Asian restaurant; *Brilliance*, *Serenade*, and *Radiance* have Mexican restaurants. There is a supplement charged for specialty dining, and reservations are required. The casual Lido buffet serves nearly around the clock for breakfast, lunch, dinner, and snacks. Seaview Café is open for quick lunches and dinners on *Jewel of the Seas*. A pizzeria in *Serenade*'s Solarium serves slices; the other ships have Park Café for casual fare in that space, and *Radiance* also serves custom hot dogs at Boardwalk Doghouse. The coffee bar features specialty coffees and pastries, for which there is a charge. Room service is available 24 hours; however there is a charge after midnight.

Spas

The full-service spa operated by Steiner Leisure offers an extensive treatment menu including facials, teeth whitening, body wraps and scrubs. Spa rituals also include treatments designed especially for men and teens. There are thermal suites for a fee as well as complimentary saunas, and steam rooms are located in men's and women's changing rooms.

Bars and Entertainment

Nightlife options range from Broadway-style productions in the main show lounge to movies in the cinema or on the outdoor screen overlooking the pool. Bars and lounges include a piano bar and wine bar, and most have music for dancing or listening. There's also a pub or sports bar and a lounge for billiards. Look high above for aerial performances in the central atriums on *Serenade*, *Brilliance*, and *Jewel of the Seas*.

Pros and Cons

Pros: aft on deck 6, four distinct lounges and a billiard room form a clubby adult entertainment center; spacious family ocean-view cabins sleep up to six people; ships offer a wide range of family-friendly activities and games.

Cons: upgraded features of the fleet are not consistent throughout this ship class, so check before booking; dining options that charge have replaced some that were previously complimentary; libraries are tiny and poorly stocked for ships this size.

Cabin Type	Size (sq. ft.)
Royal Suite	1,001
Owner's Suite	512
Grand Suite	358–384
Royal Family Suite	533–586
Junior Suites	293
Superior Ocean View	204
Deluxe Ocean View	179
Large Ocean View	170
Family Ocean View	319
Interior	165

FAST FACTS

- 12 passenger decks
- 2 specialty restaurants on *Jewel*; 4 on *Serenade* and *Brilliance*; 5 on *Radiance*, dining room, buffet, pizzeria
- Internet, Wi-Fi, safe, refrigerator, DVD (some)
- 2 pools (1 indoor), children's pool
- Fitness classes, gym, hot tubs, sauna, spa, steam room
- 11 bars, casino, dance club, library, show room, video game room
- Children's programs
- Dry-cleaning, laundry service
- Internet terminal
- No-smoking cabins

Sports courts

3

ROYAL CARIBBEAN INTERNATIONAL

VISION-CLASS
Legend, Splendour, Grandeur, Rhapsody, Vision of the Seas

CREW MEMBERS	
726, 762, 760, 765, 742	
ENTERED SERVICE	
1995, 1996, 1996, 1997, 1998	
700 ft. **GROSS TONS**	
69,130–78,491	
LENGTH	
867, 867, 916, 915, 915 feet	
500 ft. **NUMBER OF CABINS**	
902, 915, 996, 1,020, 999	
PASSENGER CAPACITY	
1,800–2,000 (2,076–2,435 max)	
300 ft. **WIDTH**	
106 feet	

The first Royal Caribbean ships to offer balconies in a number of categories, these Vision-class vessels, named for sister ship *Vision of the Seas,* have acres of glass skylights that allow sunlight to flood in and windows that offer wide sea vistas. The soaring central atrium at the heart of each ship is anchored by a chic bar that fills with music after dark and is the ideal spot for watching the daring aerial performances overhead.

Built in pairs, the ships follow the same general layout but are different in overall size and the total number of passengers on board. Cabin sizes also vary somewhat; as the total size of the ships increased from *Legend* and *Splendour* at 69,130 tons (1,800 passengers) to *Grandeur* at 74,140 tons (1,992 passengers), and finally, *Rhapsody* and *Vision* at 78,491 tons (2,000 passengers), so did the size of the accommodations. In some categories, it's only a matter of a few feet, so don't look for huge—or even noticeable—differences.

Cabins

Layout: Cabins are airy and comfortable, but the smaller categories are a tight squeeze for more than two adults. Every cabin has adequate closet and drawer/shelf storage.

Suites: All full suites and family suites have private balconies and a small minibar; full suites also include concierge service. Royal suites have a living room; wet bar; separate dining area; entertainment center with TV, stereo, and DVD player; separate bedroom; bathroom (twin sinks, whirlpool tub, separate steam shower, bidet); and separate powder room. Owner's suites have a separate living area; minibar; entertainment center with TV, stereo, and DVD player; dinette area; and one bathroom (twin sinks, bathtub, separate shower, bidet). Grand suites have similar amenities on a smaller scale.

Amenities: A vanity-desk, a TV, a safe, a hair dryer, and a seating area with sofa, chair, and table are typical Vision-class features in all categories. Bathrooms have shampoo and bath gel.

Accessibility: On *Legend* and *Splendour,* 17 cabins are wheelchair accessible; on *Grandeur, Vision,* and *Rhapsody,* 14 cabins are wheelchair accessible.

Top: Vision-class Owner's suite
Bottom: *Splendour of the Seas*

Restaurants

The two-deck formal dining room serves evening meals in two assigned seatings or an open seating; breakfast and lunch in the dining room are always open seating. Windjammer, the casual Lido buffet, serves three meals a day, including a laid-back dinner. As was the norm when these ships were built, dining selections on board are pretty basic; however, specialty-dining options have been added. All ships now have restaurants serving Asian cuisine and a steak house, while *Rhapsody* and *Grandeur* also have Italian restaurants. Depending on the ship, Park Café or Solarium Café serves light fare and snacks in the solarium. *Splendour* also has Boardwalk Doghouse serving custom hot dogs. A coffee bar and ice cream bar offer specialty coffees and frozen treats for an additional fee. Room service is available 24 hours a day; however, there is a delivery charge after midnight.

Spas

The full-service spa operated by Steiner Leisure offers an extensive treatment menu including facials, teeth whitening, body wraps and scrubs, massages, and acupuncture. Spa rituals also include treatments designed especially for men and teens. Although there is no thermal suite, complimentary saunas and steam rooms are in men's and women's changing rooms.

Bars and Entertainment

Enjoy a Broadway-style production show, performances by guest entertainers, or a movie on the outdoor screen overlooking the pool, but don't forget to look high above the central atrium for dazzling aerial performances. You'll find lounges with music for listening and dancing when the entertainment staff ramps up the fun with themed parties. The Viking Crown Lounge is a great spot for late-night dancing or a nightcap.

Pros and Cons

Pros: open, light-filled public areas offer sea views from almost every angle; each vessel now offers numerous dining options, both free and for a fee; daring aerialists offer a new wow-factor high above the central atrium.

Cons: some lounges serve as a thoroughfare and suffer from continuous traffic flow; except for premium suites, accommodations lean toward the small side; there are no self-service laundry rooms.

Cabin Type	Size (sq. ft.)
Royal Suite	1,074
Owner's Suite	523
Grand Suite	355
Royal Family Suite	512
Junior Suite	240
Superior Ocean View	193
Large Ocean View*	154
Interior	135–174

All cabin sizes are averages of the five ships since cabins vary somewhat in size among the Vision-class ships (all *Legend* and *Splendour* cabins are the same size). *Rhapsody* has family Ocean View cabins at 237 sq. ft.

FAST FACTS

- 11 passenger decks
- 2 specialty restaurants (3 on *Grandeur* and *Rhapsody*), dining room, buffet, ice cream parlor, pizzeria
- Wi-Fi, safe, refrigerator (some), DVD (some)
- 2 pools (1 indoor)
- Fitness classes, gym, hot tubs, sauna, spa, steam room
- 6 bars, casino, dance club, library, show room, video game room
- Children's programs
- Dry-cleaning, laundry service
- Internet terminal

Viking Crown lounge overlooks the pool deck.

3

ROYAL CARIBBEAN INTERNATIONAL

SILVERSEA CRUISES

Silversea Cruises was launched in 1994 by the former owners of Sitmar Cruises, the Lefebvre family of Rome, whose concept for the new cruise line was to build and sail the highest-quality luxury ships at sea. Intimate ships, paired with exclusive amenities and unparal-

The most captivating view on board

leled hospitality, are the hallmarks of Silversea cruises. All-inclusive air-and-sea fares can be customized to include not just round-trip airfare but all transfers, porterage, and deluxe precruise accommodations as well.

☎ *954/522–2299 or 877/276–6816*
⊕ *www.silversea.com*
☞ *Cruise Style: Luxury.*

Personalization is a Silversea maxim. Their ships offer more activities than other comparably sized luxury vessels. Take part in those that interest you, or opt instead for a good book and any number of quiet spots to read or snooze in the shade. Silversea's third generation of ships introduced even more luxurious features when the 36,000-ton *Silver Spirit* launched late in 2009. Silversea's *Silver Explorer* is the top choice for luxurious soft adventure expedition cruising, and in 2013 Silversea added a second exploration ship, *Silver Galapagos*, that will sail exclusively in the Galápagos Islands.

Food
Dishes from the galleys of Silversea's master chefs are complemented by those of La Collection du Monde, created by Silversea's culinary partner, the world-class chefs of Relais & Châteaux. Menus include hot and cold appetizers, at least four entrée selections, a vegetarian alternative, and Cruiselite cuisine (low in cholesterol, sodium, and fat). Special off-menu orders are prepared whenever possible, provided that the ingredients are available on board. In the event that they aren't, you may find after a day in port that a trip to the market was made in order to fulfill your request.

Chef Marco Betti, the owner of Antica Pasta restaurants in Florence, Italy, and Atlanta, Georgia, has designed a new menu for La Terrazza that focuses on one of the most luxurious food trends: the Slow Food movement. The goal of the movement is to preserve the gastronomic traditions of Italy through the use of fresh, traditional foods, and it has spread throughout the world. At La Terrazza (by day, a casual buffet) the menu showcases the finest in Italian cooking, from classic favorites to Tuscan fare. The restaurant carries no surcharge. Seating is limited, so reservations are a must to ensure a table—it's one reservation you'll be glad you took the time to book.

An intimate dining experience aboard each vessel is the wine restaurant by Relais & Châteaux—Le Champagne. Adding a dimension to dining, the exquisite cuisine is designed to celebrate the wines served—a different celebrated vintage is served with each course. Menus and wines are chosen by Relais & Châteaux sommeliers to reflect regions of the world noted for their rich wine heritage.

An evening poolside barbecue is a weekly dinner event, weather permitting. A highlight of every cruise is the Galley Brunch, when passengers are invited into the galley to select from a feast decorated with imaginative ice and vegetable sculptures. Even when meals are served buffet style in La Terrazza, you will seldom have to carry your own plate, as waiters are at hand to assist you to your table. Wines are chosen to complement each day's luncheon and dinner menus.

Grilled foods, sandwiches, and an array of fruits and salads are served daily for lunch at the Poolside Grill. After dark, the venue is transformed into the Grill featuring "hot rock" dining under the stars. Always available are extensive selections from the room-service menu. The full restaurant menu may be ordered from room service and can be served course by course in your suite during regular dining hours.

Entertainment

Guest lecturers are featured on nearly every cruise; language, dance, and culinary lessons and excellent wine-appreciation sessions are always on the schedule of events. Silversea also schedules culinary arts cruises and a series of wine-focused voyages that feature award-winning authors, international wine experts, winemakers, and acclaimed chefs from the world's top restaurants. During afternoon tea the ranks of highly competitive trivia teams increase every successive day.

KNOWN FOR

■ **All Suites:** All accommodations on Silversea ships are suites and all come with the service of butlers.

■ **Friendly Crowd:** Unlike on some luxury lines, the well-traveled and well-heeled, sophisticated Silversea passengers are anything but stodgy.

■ **International Clientele:** An international mix of passengers are often found on the luxury line's voyages.

■ **Luxury Chic:** The style of Silversea ships is chic, but not stuffy.

■ **Varied Destinations:** Silversea's destination-intensive fleet roams the globe, seldom repeating ports from one voyage to the next.

Top: Stylish entertainment
Bottom: La Terrazza alfresco dining

Top: Table tennis
Middle: Caring personal service
Bottom: Verandah Suite

After dark, the Bar is a predinner gathering spot and the late-night place for dancing to a live band. A multitiered show lounge is the setting for talented singers and musicians, classical concerts, magic shows, big-screen movies, and folkloric entertainers from ashore. A small casino offers slot machines and gaming tables.

Fitness and Recreation

The rather small gyms are equipped with cardiovascular and weight-training equipment, and fitness classes on *Silver Whisper* and *Silver Shadow* are held in the mirror-lined, but somewhat confining, exercise room. *Silver Spirit* introduced an expansive 8,300-square-foot spa and more spacious fitness center.

South Pacific–inspired Mandara Spa offers numerous treatments including exotic-sounding massages, facials, and body wraps. Hair and nail services are available in the busy salon. A plus is that appointments for spa and beauty salon treatments can be made online from 60 days until 48 hours prior to sailing.

Golfers can sign up with the pro on board for individual lessons utilizing a high-tech swing analyzer and attend complimentary golf clinics or participate in a putting contest.

Your Shipmates

Silversea Cruises appeal to sophisticated, affluent couples who enjoy the country-club-like atmosphere, exquisite cuisine, and polished service on board, not to mention the exotic ports and unique experiences ashore.

Dress Code

Two formal nights are standard on seven-night cruises and three to four nights, depending on the itinerary, on longer sailings. Men are required to wear tuxedos or dark suits after 6 pm. All other evenings are either informal, when a jacket is called for (a tie is optional, but most men wear them), or casual, when slacks with a jacket over an open-collar shirt for men and sporty dresses or skirts or pants with a sweater or blouse for women are suggested.

CHOOSE THIS LINE IF ...

Your taste leans toward learning and exploration.

You enjoy socializing as well as the option of live entertainment, just not too much of it.

You like to plan ahead. You can reserve shore tours, salon services, and spa treatments online.

Junior Cruisers

Silversea Cruises is adult-oriented, does not accommodate children less than six months of age, and the cruise line limits the number of children under the age of three on board. The availability of suites for a third passenger is capacity controlled. A youth program staffed by counselors is available on holiday and select sailings. No dedicated children's facilities are available, so parents are responsible for the behavior and entertainment of their children.

Service

Personalized service is exacting and hospitable yet discreet. The staff strives for perfection and often achieves it. The attitude is decidedly European and begins with a welcome-aboard flute of champagne, then continues throughout as personal preferences are remembered and satisfied. The word *no* doesn't seem to be in the staff vocabulary in any language. Guests in all suites are pampered by butlers.

Tipping

Tipping is neither required nor expected.

Past Passengers

Membership in the Venetian Society is automatic on completion of one Silversea cruise, and members begin accruing benefits: Venetian Society cruise days and eligibility for discounts on select voyages, onboard recognition and private parties, milestone rewards; exclusive gifts, the *Venetian Society Newsletter*, ship visitation privileges, and complimentary early embarkation or late debarkation at certain milestones. After reaching the 500-day milestone, the Venetian Society member will receive a complimentary seven-day voyage for each additional 150 days sailed.

HELPFUL HINTS

■ Every Silversea voyage includes an exclusive Silversea Experience—a complimentary shoreside event, such as private access to museums after hours.

■ Silversea offers a customized collection of pre- and post-cruise land programs linking some of Relais & Châteaux's worldwide properties together with Silversea's global itineraries.

■ For a fee, Silversea will pick up your bags at home and deliver them to the ship, or vice versa.

■ If adults travel with minors under the age of 18 who are not their children, a signed parental consent guardianship form is required.

■ Requests must be made in writing no later than 14 days prior to departure if you want to arrange a Bon Voyage Party or have visitors board the ship at your embarkation port.

3

SILVERSEA CRUISES

DON'T CHOOSE THIS LINE IF ...

You want to dress informally at all times on your cruise. Passengers on these cruises tend to dress up.

You need highly structured activities and have to be reminded of them.

You prefer the glitter and stimulation of Las Vegas to the understated glamour of Monte Carlo.

SILVER SHADOW, SILVER WHISPER

CREW MEMBERS	295
ENTERED SERVICE	2000, 2001
GROSS TONS	28,258
LENGTH	610 feet
NUMBER OF CABINS	191
PASSENGER CAPACITY	382
WIDTH	82 feet

700 ft.
500 ft.
300 ft.

The logical layout of these sister ships, with suites in the forward two-thirds of the ship and public rooms aft, makes orientation simple. The clean, modern decor that defines public areas and lounges might seem almost stark, but it places the main emphasis on large expanses of glass for sunshine and sea views as well as passenger comfort.

Silversea ships boast unbeatable libraries stocked with best sellers, travel books, classics, and movies for en suite viewing. Extremely wide passageways in public areas are lined with glass-front display cabinets full of interesting and unusual artifacts from the places the ships visit. The Connoisseur's Corner is a clubby cigar smoking room with overstuffed leather seating and a ventilation system that makes it possible for even non-smokers to appreciate.

Cabins

Layout: Every suite has an ocean view, and more than 80% have a private teak-floor balcony. Standard suites have a seating area that can be curtained off from the bed. Marble bathrooms have double sinks and a separate glass-enclosed shower as well as a tub. All suites have generous walk-in closets.

Top Suites: In addition to much more space, top-category suites have all the standard amenities plus dining areas, separate bedrooms, and CD players. Silver suites and above have whirlpool tubs. The top three categories have espresso makers and separate powder rooms. All are served by butlers.

Amenities: Standard suites have a TV and DVD, personalized stationery, cocktail cabinet, safe, and stocked refrigerator. A hair dryer is provided at a vanity table, and you can request a magnifying mirror. Beds are dressed with high-quality linens and your choice of synthetic or down pillows. Bathrooms have huge towels and terry robes for use during the cruise as well as designer shampoo, soaps, and lotion.

Accessibility: Two suites are designed for wheelchair accessibility.

Top: The casino
Bottom: Silver Shadow at sea

Restaurants

The Restaurant offers open seating breakfast, lunch, and dinner. Le Champagne (reservation, cover charge) offers a gourmet meal and wine pairings; La Terrazza serves Italian cuisine. For casual meals, La Terrazza has indoor and outdoor seating for buffet-style breakfast and lunch. The outdoor Grill offers a laid-back lunch option with poolside table service. The do-it-yourself Black Rock Grill allows you to cook meats and seafood to your liking on preheated volcanic stones table-side. Elaborate afternoon tea is served daily. An evening poolside barbecue is a weekly dinner event as a galley brunch. Room service is available anytime and arrives with crystal, china, and a linen tablecloth; if desired, service can be course by course.

Spas

South Pacific–inspired Mandara Spa, a division of Steiner Leisure, offers treatments including exotic-sounding massages, facials, and body wraps, teeth whitening, acupuncture, and Medi-Spa cosmetic treatments. There is no thermal suite, but complimentary saunas and steam rooms are in the men's and ladies' locker rooms.

Bars and Entertainment

The show lounge is the setting for singers and musicians, classical concerts, magic shows, big-screen movies, and folkloric entertainers from ashore. The Bar is the most popular predinner gathering spot and a late-night place for dancing to a live band. A pianist or other entertainers perform in the Panorama Lounge for listening and dancing. Concerts or movies are presented on deck, weather permitting.

Pros and Cons

Pros: champagne flows freely throughout your cruise; sailing on a Silversea ship is like spending time as a guest at a home in the Hamptons where everything is at your fingertips; Silversea is so all-inclusive that you'll seldom use your room card for anything but opening your suite door.

Cons: lines can form to use a washing machine in the smallish (yet totally free) laundry rooms; in an odd contrast to the contents of display cases and lovely flower arrangements, artwork on the walls is fairly ho-hum; the spa's complimentary saunas and steam rooms are quite small.

Cabin Type	Size (sq. ft.)
Grand Suite	1,286–1,435
Royal Suite	1,312–1,352
Owner's Suite	1,208
Silver Suite	701
Medallion Suite	521
Verandah Suite	345
Terrace Suite	287
Vista Suite	287

FAST FACTS

- 7 passenger decks
- 2 specialty restaurants, dining room, buffet
- Wi-Fi, safe, refrigerator, DVD
- Pool
- Fitness classes, gym, hot tubs, sauna, spa, steam room
- 3 bars, casino, dance club, library, show room
- Dry-cleaning, laundry facilities, laundry service
- Internet terminal
- No-smoking cabins

3

SILVERSEA CRUISES

The Poolside Grill serves lunch and light snacks.

UN-CRUISE ADVENTURES

Small-ship line American Safari Cruises pioneered yacht cruising in Alaska in 1997; its sister line InnerSea Discoveries enjoyed an inaugural season of expedition-style active exploration of Alaska's Inside Passage in 2011. The parent company merged the two lines in January 2013 and changed the name of the combined line to Un-Cruise Adventures.

Wilderness Discoverer at sea

☎ *206/284–0300 or 888/862–8881*
⊕ *www.un-cruise.com*
☞ *Cruise Style: Small-ship.*

Under the Un-Cruise Adventures brand, the line offers several small-ship cruising styles from which to choose—Active Adventures, Luxury Adventures, and Heritage Adventures—each designed to provide a unique experience. Active Adventures are expedition-style cruises offering more active adventures and delivering them aboard expedition vessels at an economical price point. Luxury Adventures are offered aboard more upscale, yachtlike ships that are loaded with extra amenities; soft-adventure activities are emphasized, and fares range from moderate to high. Heritage Adventures focus on history, both on the ship and ashore. Living History programs are offered aboard a replica Victorian-style steamship for a moderate to high price. All the line's ships are also available for charter by private groups.

All cruises, regardless of the style, include guided tours ashore, but more included excursions are offered on Luxury Adventures. Heritage Adventures offer more port calls with shore visits to museums and historical sites. Kayaks and paddleboards are available at no charge on Active and Luxury Adventures, but there is a nominal daily use charge for snorkeling gear and wet suits on Active Adventures. Limited quantities of hiking poles, binoculars, mud boots, and rain gear are available on board for use during your cruise.

Food

Chefs serve a choice of nicely presented dinner entrées, featuring fresh local ingredients and plenty of seafood. Both Luxury and Heritage cruises are nearly all-inclusive, so premium wines and liquors are available at every meal, and guests are welcome to help themselves to the well-provisioned bar as well as snack options set up between meals. Meals on Active cruises are simpler and often served buffet-style, and on these cruises there is a separate charge for alcoholic beverages. Espresso, coffee, and tea are available 24 hours a day on all ships.

Entertainment

Expert naturalists give informative presentations on board and are available throughout the trip as a resource for assistance and information. Libraries are stocked with books and DVDs. The Victorian-style steamship SS *Legacy* has a dance floor for evenings on board for its Heritage cruises.

Fitness and Recreation

Exercise equipment, hot tubs, a sauna, and yoga sessions are featured on board. Kayaking and nature hikes are offered for a more adventurous workout.

Your Shipmates

Typical passengers tend to be inquisitive couples from mid-thirties to retirees. Children are welcome, but there are no facilities specifically designed for them.

Dress Code

Dress is always comfortably casual, so guests can feel free to pack any clothing they like. Although there are a limited number of rain slickers, rain pants, and mud boots on board for passenger use, guests may also bring their own to ensure the best fit. Evening attire tends to be more upscale casual on Luxury and Heritage Adventures.

Junior Cruisers

With the exception of the smaller yachts, children are welcome on any sailing. Families with children age 12 and under might prefer one of the limited "Kids in Nature" departures, which are geared toward entertaining and educating kids of all ages.

KNOWN FOR

- Flexible Itineraries: Itineraries are flexible to take advantage of wildlife sightings.

- Wilderness Access: Maneuverability of the small vessels offers unique access to wilderness areas for viewing wildlife and exploration by skiff.

- Intimate Tours: Small groups that do not overwhelm the areas visited allow more up-close discoveries ashore on excursions led by trained leaders and guides.

- Personal Encounters: Insightful cultural encounters ashore are a highlight of off-the-beaten path explorations.

- Eco-Friendly: The line follows a "Leave No Trace" policy to protect the environment.

- By supporting and promoting local culture, the line makes a positive impact on communities.

Kayaking

Top: Comfortable deck on
Wilderness Adventurer
Middle: Scenic views from
Wilderness Discoverer
Bottom: Enjoying the outdoors

Service
Crew members tend to passenger needs discreetly, yet in a personal way—they know your name and preferences and your needs will be satisfied in an attentive manner.

Tipping
Tips are discretionary, but a generous 10% of the fare is suggested. A lump sum is pooled and shared among the crew after the cruise.

Ships of the Line
Un-Cruise Adventures currently sails eight vessels for soft adventure cruising to regions throughout Alaska, the Columbia and Snake rivers, coastal Washington state and British Columbia, the Hawaiian Islands, and Mexico's Sea of Cortés. Vessels are comfortable and feature modern amenities, although these vary by ship.

Wilderness Adventurer, Wilderness Discoverer, Wilderness Explorer. The Active Adventure ships with capacities of 60, 76, and 76 respectively provide maximum comfort and upgraded amenities that are often unexpected on expedition ships this size. Casual and inviting public areas decorated in contemporary colors impart the feeling of a 1940s-era National Park Service Lodge crossed with a neighborhood pub that features a bar top made from salvaged wood. On deck you'll find plenty of space to view the passing scenery, either at the rail, from a deck chair, or in a strategically placed hot tub. The top decks have covered areas where exercise equipment and saunas—with a view—are located. The ships also feature kayak launching platforms for convenience and safety. They are not, however, very accessible to passengers with disabilities.

Safari Endeavour, Safari Explorer, Safari Quest. The line's Luxury Adventure ships have capacities of 86, 36, and 22 respectively. *Safari Endeavour* is exquisitely appointed with features such as an intimate Wine Bar and spa area including two hot tubs, sauna, fitness equipment, yoga classes, and massage suite (with a complimentary massage.) *Safari Explorer*'s three public decks offer comfort amid casually elegant appointments. The library and cozy salons for dining and socializing are nicely balanced, with a large open

CHOOSE THIS LINE IF ...

You consider yourself more an adventurer than a tourist.	Your idea of a fun evening includes board games and quiet conversation.	You want to get up close to glaciers, waterfalls, whales, and other wildlife.

viewing deck highlighted by a hot tub and nearby sauna. *Safari Quest* has warm wood trim throughout and plenty of outer deck space for spotting wildlife and taking in the scenery. A top deck lounge is a pleasant hideaway from which to enjoy the views. Hydrophones for listening to below-surface sounds are found on all three ships. There is no Internet access on board, and cell-phone service is only available when the ships are near shore and within range of a cell tower. Smoking is limited to designated outside deck areas. No cabins are wheelchair-accessible.

SS Legacy. Refurbished before entering service in 2013 as the Heritage Adventures vessel, the 88-passenger SS Legacy emulates the old-world ambience and charm of an early turn-of-the-20th-century coastal steamer. Appointed with period decor, the vessel features carved wooden appointments. The Grand Salon, complete with a full bar and dance floor, and the Pesky Barnacle Saloon each have an adjacent outdoor viewing area. Two hot tubs, a sauna, fitness equipment, yoga classes, and a massage suite are features accessible to all guests. The ship's four decks provide ample outside viewing spaces and public areas for gathering with fellow passengers. Elevator access is available to three of the public decks. Smoking is limited to designated areas on outside decks away from doors and windows. There are no wheelchair-accessible cabins.

HELPFUL HINTS

■ Pick a ship to suit your personal style of adventure—either active on an expedition vessel, luxurious on an upscale yacht, or with an emphasis on history aboard a coastal steamer.

■ With the exception of the smaller yachts, children are welcome on any departure, and the "Kids in Nature" program on certain sailings is geared toward entertaining and educating kids of all ages.

■ Children 12 years and under save 25% on select departures.

■ Guest hosts on theme cruises might include winery owners and winemakers, whale experts, photographers, or authorities in marine biology and ornithology.

■ A complimentary massage is an included amenity aboard the *SS Legacy, Safari Endeavour, Safari Explorer,* and *Safari Voyager.* Massages are available aboard all the expedition vessels at an additional charge.

DON'T CHOOSE THIS LINE IF ...

You can't entertain yourself; except for dancing on Heritage cruises, there is no organized entertainment at night.

You have to ask the price—except for Active cruises, these are primarily expensive trips.

You would rather play a slot machine than attend an evening lecture.

DID YOU KNOW?

Experience Music Project's interactive space has 12 mini-studios, where you can learn simple licks or jam with friends on real or MIDI-compatible instruments. You can also record a CD of your playing or singing in the Jam Studio.

PORTS OF EMBARKATION

Many northbound cruises begin in Vancouver, British Columbia, but Seattle became an important port as well, with the opening of the Smith Cove Cruise Terminal at Terminal 91 in 2009. Small-ship cruise lines usually begin and end their itineraries in Alaska, offering sailings from such ports as Juneau, Petersburg, and Sitka, Alaska.

Anchorage is the primary starting point for cruise passengers heading south, but most ships don't actually dock there. Instead, travelers fly into and may overnight in Anchorage before being transported by bus or train to the ports of Seward or Whittier for southbound departures.

Cruise travelers frequently opt for combination packages that include a one-way north- or southbound Inside Passage cruise plus a tour by bus or train through interior Alaska (and sometimes the Yukon). Denali National Park, too far inland to be included on round-trip Inside Passage cruises, is a particular focus of these "CruiseTour" trips *(see ⇨ Chapter 6, "Inland Cruise Tour Destinations," for more information).*

Before or after the cruise, travelers with a more independent streak may want to rent a car and strike out on their own to places not often visited by cruise ships, such as Homer or Valdez *(see ⇨ Chapter 5, "Ports of Call," for more information on these cities).*

PORT ESSENTIALS

CAR RENTALS

If you plan on lingering before or after your cruise, rental cars are available in most Alaska ports of embarkation, as well as in Seattle and Vancouver. In Anchorage and other major destinations, expect to pay at least $55 to $75 a day or $300 (and up) a week for an economy or compact car with automatic transmission and unlimited mileage. Some locally owned companies offer lower rates for older cars. Also, be sure to ask in advance about discounts if you have a AAA or Costco card, or are over age 50.

Major Agencies **Alamo** ☎ *877/222–9075* ⊕ *www.alamo.com.*
Avis ☎ *800/331–1212* ⊕ *www.avis.com.* **Budget** ☎ *800/527–0700*
⊕ *www.budget.com.* **Hertz** ☎ *800/654–3131* ⊕ *www.hertz.com.*
National Car Rental ☎ *877/222–9058* ⊕ *www.nationalcar.com.*

DINING

Given the seaside location of the embarkation towns, it's no surprise that fresh fish and other seafood are especially popular. Fresh halibut and salmon are available throughout the summer, along with specialties such as shrimp, oysters, and crab.

Seafood meals can be simply prepared fast food, like beer-battered fish-and-chips, or more-elaborate dinners of halibut baked in a macadamia-nut crust with fresh mango chutney. If seafood isn't your first choice, rest assured that all the staples—including restaurants serving steaks, burgers, pizza, or Mexican or Chinese food—can also be found.

HOTEL AND RESTAURANT PRICES

Prices in the restaurant reviews are the average cost of a main course at dinner or, if dinner is not served, at lunch. Prices in the hotel reviews are the lowest cost of a standard double room in high season, excluding taxes.

LODGING

Whether you're driving or flying into your port of embarkation, it's often more convenient to arrive the day before or to stay for a day (or longer) after your cruise. Cruise travelers often stay in one of the larger downtown hotels booked by the cruise lines to be closer to the ports, but you might like to make your own arrangements for a pre- or post-cruise sojourn. Therefore, we offer lodging suggestions for each port.

The hotels we list are convenient to the cruise port and the cream of the crop in each price category. Properties are assigned price categories based on the range between their least and most expensive standard double room in high season (excluding holidays).

Assume that hotels do not include meals unless they are specified in the review.

ANCHORAGE

By Sarah
Henning

By far Alaska's largest and most sophisticated city, Anchorage is in a truly spectacular location. The permanently snow-covered peaks and volca-noes of the Alaska Range lie to the west of the city, part of the craggy Chugach Range is actually within the eastern edge of the municipality, and the Talkeetna and Kenai ranges are visible to the north and south. On clear days Mt. McKinley looms on the northern horizon, and two arms of Cook Inlet embrace the town's western and southern borders.

Anchorage is Alaska's medical, financial, and banking center, and home to the executive offices of most of the Native corporations. The city has a population of roughly 290,000, approximately 40% of the people in the state. The relative affluence of this white-collar city—with a sprin-kling of olive drab from nearby military bases—fosters fine restaurants and pricey shops, first-rate entertainment, and sporting events.

Boom and bust periods followed major events: an influx of military bases during World War II; a massive buildup of Arctic missile-warning stations during the Cold War; reconstruction after the devastating Good Friday earthquake of 1964; and in the late 1960s the biggest jackpot of all—the discovery of oil at Prudhoe Bay and the construction of the Trans-Alaska Pipeline. Not surprisingly, Anchorage positioned itself as the perfect home for the pipeline administrators and support industries, and it continues to attract a large share of the state's oil-tax dollars.

ESSENTIALS

HOURS

During the summer cruise season, most attractions are open daily. Stores are generally open from 10 to 7 or 8, but government offices and banks may have earlier closing times.

VISITOR INFORMATION

Contacts **Visit Anchorage.** Housed in a rustic log cabin, the center's sod roof is festooned with huge hanging baskets of flowers, and a giant jade boulder stands outside. After a stop in the cabin, step out the back door to the more spacious visitor center stocked with brochures. Ask advice from the friendly and incredibly erudite volunteers: if they don't know something, it's not worth knowing. There are also two visitor information centers in Ted Stevens Anchorage International Airport, one in the north terminal and one in the south terminal in the C Concourse baggage claim area. ⊠ *524 W. 4th Ave., Downtown* ☎ *907/276–4118, 800/478–1255 to order visitor guides* ⊕ *www.anchorage.net.*

THE CRUISE PORT

Anchorage is the starting (or ending) point for many Alaskan cruises, but few ships call here directly. However, if your cruise originates in or ends in Alaska, it's very likely you'll be flying into or out of the Anchorage airport, and some passengers choose to spend time before or after a cruise in Anchorage.

Cruises board or disembark either in Seward (125 miles south on Resurrection Bay) or in Whittier (59 miles southwest of Anchorage), on the western shore of Prince William Sound.

Access between Anchorage and these ports is by bus or train. Transfers are offered by the cruise lines, either as an add-on to your fare or, in the case of some luxury cruise lines or small-ship cruise lines, included in the price of your cruise. Cruise-line representatives meet airport arrivals to make the process as effortless as possible. You spend virtually no shore time in either Seward or Whittier before you embark or after disembarkation—buses and the train also offer dock-to-airport service in both places; however, it is possible to spend time in Seward or Whittier and make your own transportation arrangements. The few ships that do dock at Anchorage proper dock just north of downtown. There's an information booth on the pier. It's only a 15- or 20-minute walk from the town to the dock, but this is through an industrial area with heavy traffic, so it's best to take a taxi.

The Glenn Highway enters Anchorage from the north and becomes 5th Avenue near Merrill Field; this route leads directly into downtown. Gambell Street leads out of town to the south, becoming New Seward Highway at about 20th Avenue. South of town, it becomes the Seward Highway.

Ted Stevens Anchorage International Airport is 6 miles from downtown. Taxis queue up outside baggage claim. A ride downtown runs about $20, not including tip.

Airport Information Ted Stevens Anchorage International Airport (*ANC*). ☎ *907/266–2525* ⊕ *dot.alaska.gov/anc/.*

RENTAL CARS

Anchorage is the ideal place to rent a car for exploring sites farther afield before or after your cruise. National Car Rental has a downtown office. All the major companies (and several local operators) have airport desks and free shuttle service to the airport to pick up cars.

Local Agencies Arctic Rent-A-Car ☎ *888/714–4690, 907/561–2990 Anchorage, 800/478–8696, 907/479–8044 Fairbanks* ⊕ *www.arcticrentacar.com.* **Denali Car Rental** ☎ *907/276–1230, 800/757–1230 in Anchorage* ⊕ *akdenalicarrental.com.*

TAXIS

Downtown Anchorage is easy to navigate on foot. If you want to see some of the outlying attractions, such as Lake Hood, you'll need to hire a taxi. Taxis are on a meter system; rates start at $2 to $3 for pickup and $2.50 for each mile. Most people call for a cab, although it's possible to hail one. Alaska Yellow Cab has taxis with wheelchair lifts. In the snow-free months a network of paved trails provides good avenues for in-city travel for bicyclists and walkers.

Contact Alaska Yellow Cab ☎ *907/222–2222* ⊕ *www.akyellowcab.com.*

EXPLORING ANCHORAGE

DOWNTOWN ANCHORAGE

Alaska Center for the Performing Arts. The distinctive stone-and-glass building overlooks an expansive park filled with brilliant flowers all summer. Look inside for upcoming events, or relax amid the blossoms on a sunny afternoon. The center—which has four theaters—is home to 10 resident performing arts companies, including Alaska Dance Theatre, Anchorage Opera, and the Anchorage Symphony Orchestra. ✉ *621 W. 6th Ave., at G St., Downtown* ☎ *907/263–2787, 877/278–7849 tickets* ⊕ *www.myalaskacenter.com* ✆ *Tours by appointment only.*

FAMILY **Alaska Public Lands Information Center.** Stop here for information on all of Alaska's public lands, including national and state parks, national forests, and wildlife refuges. You can plan a hiking, sea-kayaking, bear-viewing, or fishing trip; find out about public-use cabins; learn about Alaska's plants and animals; or head to the theater for films highlighting different parts of the state. The bookstore sells maps and nature books. Guided walks to historic downtown sights detail the role Captain James Cook played in Alaska's history. Tours depart

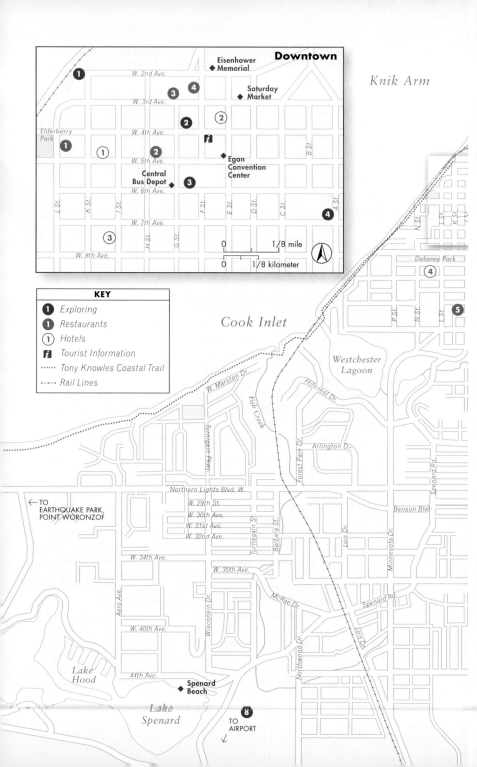

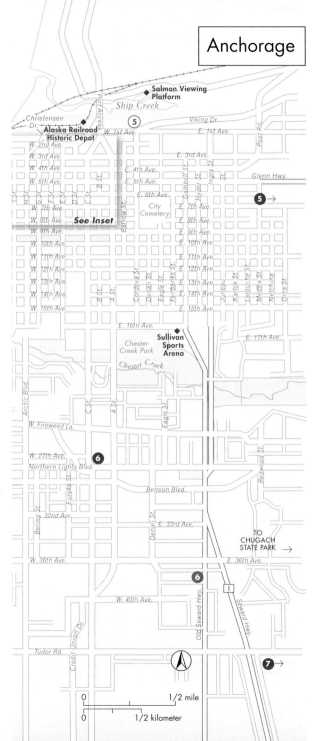

Anchorage

daily throughout the summer at 11 am and 2:30 pm. ✉ *605 W. 4th Ave., Suite 105, at F St., Downtown* ☎ *907/644–3661* ⊕ *www. alaskacenters.gov* ⊙ *Memorial Day–Labor Day, daily 9–5; mid-Sept.– mid-May, weekdays 10–5.*

FAMILY **Anchorage Museum.** This is no just-in-case-of-a-rainy-day attraction.
Fodor's Choice An extensive renovation in 2010 made the Anchorage Museum an
★ essential stop for visitors. There's no better way to deepen your under-standing of the state's history, people, and, thanks to an impressive collection of paintings and photographs, beauty. The post-renovation star of the museum is the Smithsonian Arctic Studies Center, featuring more than 600 objects from Alaska Native cultures, short films that teach visitors about modern-day Native life, and much more. If you have a strong interest in history, art, or culture, leave extra time for the center—though it's just one large room, you might end up staying for hours. A good follow-up: wander the galleries filled with paintings and other art that showcases Alaska landscape and history through the talents of painters and other artists. The Alaska History Gallery's dioramas and other traditional museum exhibits focus on the state's history. Cap the visit in the Imaginarium Discovery Center. Kids and their parents—and, okay, adults without kids, too—won't want to leave the museum once they step into the 9,000-square-foot center loaded with hands-on science exhibits. There's also a planetarium. Muse restaurant, a bright and modern spot operated by local favorite the Marx Bros. Café, serves delicious lunches, dinners, and cocktails. The gift shop is one of Anchorage's best places to buy Alaska Native art and other souvenirs. Book lovers beware (or you may spend your vacation budget all at once): the shop's book department runs the gamut from Alaska fiction to history, cookbooks, and beyond. ✉ *625 C St., Downtown* ☎ *907/929–9201, 907/929–9200 recorded information* ⊕ *www.anchoragemuseum.org* 🎟 *$15* ⊙ *May–Sept., daily 9–6; Oct.–Apr., Tues.–Sat. 10–6, Sun. noon–6.*

Fodor's Choice **Tony Knowles Coastal Trail.** Strollers, runners, bikers, dog walkers, and
★ in-line skaters cram this recreation trail on sunny summer evenings, particularly around Westchester Lagoon. In winter, cross-country skiers take to it by storm. The trail begins off 2nd Avenue, west of Christensen Drive, and curls along Cook Inlet for approximately 11 miles to Kincaid Park, beyond the airport. In summer you might spot beluga whales offshore in Cook Inlet. Access points are on the waterfront at the ends of 2nd, 5th, and 9th avenues and at Westchester Lagoon.

MIDTOWN

Alaska Heritage Museum at Wells Fargo. More than 900 Alaska Native artifacts are the main draw in the quiet, unassuming lobby of a large midtown bank—it's reputed to be one of the largest private collections of Native artworks in the country. Also here are paintings by Alaskan artists, a library of rare books, and a 46-troy-ounce gold nugget. ✉ *Wells Fargo Bank, 301 W. Northern Lights Blvd., at C St., Midtown* ☎ *907/265–2834* ⊕ *www.wellsfargohistory.com/museums* 🎟 *Free* ⊙ *Late May–early Sept., weekdays noon–5; early Sept.–late May, weekdays noon–4.*

EAST ANCHORAGE

FAMILY **Alaska Botanical Garden.** The garden showcases perennials hardy enough to make it in South Central Alaska in several large display gardens, a pergola-enclosed herb garden, and a rock garden amid 110 acres of mixed boreal forest. There's a 1-mile nature trail loop to Campbell Creek, with views of the Chugach Range and a wildflower trail between the display gardens. Interpretive signs guide visitors and identify plants along the trail. Children can explore the garden with an activity-filled duffel bag. Docent tours are available at 1 pm daily June through August; in addition, you can schedule your own tour by appointment between June 1 and September 15. The gift shop and retail nursery are open Tuesday through Sunday late May to mid-September. ✉ *4601 Campbell Airstrip Rd., off Tudor Rd. (park at Benny Benson School), East Anchorage* ☎ *907/770–3692* ⊕ *www.alaskabg.org* ✉ *$7* ☼ *Daily during daylight hrs.*

FAMILY **Alaska Native Heritage Center.** On a 26-acre site facing the Chugach
Fodor's Choice Mountains, this facility provides an introduction to Alaska's Native
★ peoples. The spacious Welcome House has interpretive displays, artifacts, photographs, demonstrations, Native dances, storytelling, and films, along with a café and a gift shop selling museum-quality crafts and artwork. Step outside for a stroll around the adjacent lake, where seven village exhibits represent 11 Native cultural groups through traditional structures and exhibitions. As you enter the homes in these villages, you can visit with the culture hosts, hear their stories, and experiment with some of the tools, games, and utensils used in the past. **■TIP➡ There's a free shuttle to the Heritage Center from the downtown Log Cabin and Visitor Information Center that runs several times a day in the summer.** You can also hop a bus at the downtown transit center; Route 4 (Glenn Highway) will take you to the Heritage Center's front door. A Culture Pass Joint Ticket for $28.95 provides admission here and to the Anchorage Museum downtown; it's available at either location. ✉ *8800 Heritage Center Dr.(Glenn Hwy. at Muldoon Rd.), East Anchorage* ☎ *907/330–8000, 800/315–6608* ⊕ *www.alaskanative.net* ✉ *$24.95, $9.95 Alaska residents* ☼ *Mid-May (Mother's Day)–Sept., daily 9–5.*

WEST ANCHORAGE

FAMILY **Alaska Aviation Museum.** The state's unique aviation history is presented with more than 25 vintage aircraft, a flight simulator, a theater, and an observation deck along **Lake Hood,** the world's busiest seaplane base. Highlights include a Stearman C2B, the first plane to land on Mt. McKinley back in the early 1930s. Volunteers recently restored a 1931 Fairchild Pilgrim aircraft and are eager to talk about their bush pilot experiences. **■TIP➡ A free shuttle to and from Anchorage Airport is available, as is luggage storage.** ✉ *4721 Aircraft Dr., West Anchorage* ☎ *907/248–5325* ⊕ *www.alaskaairmuseum.org* ✉ *$10* ☼ *May 15–Sept. 15, daily 9–5; Sept. 16–May 14, Wed.–Sat. 9–5, Sun. noon–5.*

Learn about Alaska's art, history, and landscapes at the Anchorage Museum.

SHOPPING

Stock up for your travels around Alaska in Anchorage, where there's no sales tax. The weekend markets are packed with Alaskan-made products of all types, and you're likely to meet local artisans.

BOOKS

Title Wave Books. Easily the largest independent bookstore in Alaska, Title Wave Books fills a 30,000-square-foot space at the other end of the Northern Lights Center, a strip mall that also houses REI. The shelves are filled with nearly half a million used books, CDs, records, and DVDs across more than 1,600 categories, including a large section of Alaska-focused books; the staff is very knowledgeable. Anyone can bring in used books and trade them for store credit. ⌧ *1360 W. Northern Lights Blvd., Midtown* ☎ *907/278–9283, 888/598–9283* ⊕ *www.wavebooks.com.*

NEED A BREAK?

Kaladi Brothers Coffee. Kaladi Brothers Coffee, between Title Wave Books and REI, will caffeinate you and provide free Wi-Fi access to boot. ⌧ *1340 W. Northern Lights Blvd., Suite 409, Midtown* ☎ *907/277–5127* ⊕ *www.kaladi.com.*

MARKETS

Fodor's Choice ★ **Anchorage Market and Festival.** On weekends throughout the summer the Anchorage Market and Festival opens for business (and loads of fun) in the parking lot at 3rd Avenue and E Street. Dozens of vendors offer Alaskan-made crafts, ethnic imports, and deliciously fattening food. Stock up on birch candy and salmon jerky to snack on while traveling or as perfect made-in-Alaska gifts for friends back home. The open-air market runs from mid-May to mid-September on weekends from 10 to 6. ⊠ *3rd Ave. between E and C Sts.* ☎ *907/272–5634* ⊕ *www. anchoragemarkets.com/main.html.*

NATIVE CRAFTS

Alaska Native Heritage Center. Find Native art and crafts at the Alaska Native Heritage Center gift shop. ⊠ *8800 Heritage Center Dr., Glenn Hwy. at Muldoon Rd., East Anchorage* ☎ *907/330–8000, 800/315–6608* ⊕ *www.alaskanative.net.*

Alaska Native Medical Center. Several downtown shops sell quality Alaska Native artwork, but the best buys can be found in the gift shop at the Alaska Native Medical Center, which is open weekdays 10–2 and 11–2 on the first and third Saturday of the month. It doesn't take credit cards. ⊠ *4315 Diplomacy Dr., at Tudor and Bragaw Rds., East Anchorage* ☎ *907/729–1122* ⊕ *www.anmc.org.*

Oomingmak. The Native-owned cooperative Oomingmak sells items made of qiviut, the warm undercoat of musk ox. Scarves, shawls, hats, and tunics are knitted in traditional patterns. ⊠ *604 H St., Downtown* ☎ *907/272–9225, 888/360–9665* ⊕ *www.qiviut.com.*

NIGHTLIFE

Anchorage does not shut down when it gets dark. Bars here—and throughout Alaska—open early (in the morning) and close as late as 3 am on weekends. There's a ban on smoking in bars and bingo parlors, as well as in restaurants. The listings in the *Anchorage Daily News* entertainment section, published on Friday, and in the free weekly *Anchorage Press* (⊕ *www.anchoragepress.com*) range from concerts and theater performances to movies and a roundup of nightspots featuring live music.

Fodor's Choice
★ **Chilkoot Charlie's.** Chilkoot Charlie's, a rambling timber building with sawdust floors, multiple bars, three dance floors, loud music (rock bands and DJs) nightly, two DJs every Thursday, Friday, and Saturday, and rowdy customers, is where young Alaskans go to get crazy. This legendary bar has many unusual nooks and crannies, including a room filled with Russian artifacts where vodka is the drink of choice, plus a reconstructed version of Alaska's infamous Birdhouse Bar. If you haven't been to Koots, you haven't seen Anchorage nightlife at its wildest. ⊠ *2435 Spenard Rd., Spenard* ☎ *907/272–1010* ⊕ *www.koots.com.*

Club Paris. Lots of old-timers favor the dark bar of Club Paris. The Paris mural and French street lamps hanging behind the bar have lost some luster, but there's still a faithful clientele. This is your spot if you like a stiff, no-nonsense drink. ⊠ *417 W. 5th Ave., Downtown* ☎ *907/277–6332* ⊕ *www.clubparisrestaurant.com.*

Simon & Seafort's Saloon & Grill. A trendy place for the dressy "in" crowd, the bar at Simon & Seafort's Saloon & Grill has stunning views of Cook Inlet, a special single-malt Scotch menu, and tempting cocktails. The lavender martini is particularly a palate pleaser. ⊠ *420 L St., Downtown* ☎ *907/274–3502* ⊕ *www.simonandseaforts.com.*

Snow Goose Restaurant and Sleeping Lady Brewing Company. With comedy improv and live acoustic music (check the website for the schedule), Snow Goose is a good place to unwind with a beer inside or on the airy outside deck overlooking Cook Inlet. ☒ *717 W. 3rd Ave., Downtown* ☎ *907/277–7727* ⊕ *www.alaskabeers.com.*

WHERE TO EAT

Smoking is banned in all Anchorage restaurants. Most local restaurants are open daily in summer, with reduced hours in winter. Only a few places require reservations, but it's always best to call ahead, especially for dinner.

$$
AMERICAN
✕ **Glacier BrewHouse.** The scent of hops permeates the cavernous, wood-beam BrewHouse, where a dozen or so ales, stouts, lagers, and pilsners are brewed on the premises. Locals mingle with visitors in this noisy, always-busy heart-of-town restaurant, where dinner selections range from thin-crust, 10-inch pizzas to chipotle shrimp cocktail and from barbecue pork ribs to fettuccine jambalaya and fresh seafood (in season). The bacon-laced seafood chowder is a must on cooler days. For dessert, don't miss the wood-oven-roasted apple-and-currant bread pudding (though, really, you can't go wrong with the peanut-butter pie either). You can watch the hardworking chefs in the open kitchen. The brewery sits behind a glass wall, and the same owners operate the equally popular Orso, next door. ▥ **TIP→** Several large tour companies have this restaurant on their itinerary, so in summer make reservations, even for lunch. ⑤ *Average main: $28* ☒ *737 W. 5th Ave., Downtown* ☎ *907/274–2739* ⊕ *www.glacierbrewhouse.com.*

$$$$
EUROPEAN
Fodor'sChoice
★
✕ **Marx Bros. Cafe.** Inside a little frame house built in 1916, this nationally recognized 14-table café opened in 1979 and is still going strong. The menu changes frequently, and the wine list encompasses more than 700 international choices. For an appetizer, try the Neapolitan seafood mousse or the fresh Kachemak Bay oysters with pepper vodka and pickled ginger sorbet. The outstanding made-at-your-table Caesar salad is a superb opener for the baked halibut with a macadamia-nut crust served with coconut-curry sauce and fresh mango chutney. And if the homemade Alaska birch syrup butter pecan ice cream is on the menu, get it! ⑤ *Average main: $36* ☒ *627 W. 3rd Ave., Downtown* ☎ *907/278–2133* ⊕ *www.marxcafe.com* ⌦ *Reservations essential* ☾ *Closed Sun. and Mon. No lunch.*

$
ECLECTIC
✕ **New Sagaya's City Market.** Stop at either the downtown or midtown New Sagaya's for quick lunches, healthy to-go food, and Kaladi Brothers espresso. The in-house bakery, L'Aroma, makes specialty breads and a wide range of snack-worthy pastries, and the international deli and grocery serves California-style pizzas, Chinese food, lasagna, rotisserie chicken, salads, and even stuffed cabbage. At the downtown location, you can eat inside on the sheltered patio or grab an outside table on a summer afternoon. New Sagaya's has one of the best seafood counters in town, and will even box and ship your fish. The employee-owned grocery stores carry an extensive selection of Asian foodstuffs, and the produce and meat selections are excellent.

$ *Average main: $8* ✉ *900 W. 13th Ave., Downtown* ☎ *907/274–6173* ⊕ *www.newsagaya.com* $ *Average main: $8* ✉ *3700 Old Seward Hwy., Midtown* ☎ *907/561–5173.*

$ | **ECLECTIC** | **Fodor's Choice** | ★ — ✗ **Snow City Cafe.** On summer days, Snow City attracts some serious crowds—and for good reason. This modern but unassuming café, convenient to many of the downtown hotels, serves one of Anchorage's best (and reasonably priced) breakfasts. Oh, lunch, too. Service is fast in the chipper and family-friendly restaurant. The breakfast menu, served all day, features inventive spins on eggs Benedict, including one topped with king crab cakes; omelets; pancakes; and more. Snow City's lunch menu consists of hot or cold sandwiches, fresh soups, and salads, and has lots of vegetarian options. Meat eaters need look no further than the excellent meatloaf sandwich; since Snow City offers a refrigerator case filled with to-go sandwiches, the meatloaf is also a perfect picnic or hiking companion. If you're not an early riser, be prepared to wait—or make a reservation. ■**TIP→** Snow City now accepts reservations via phone and Web. $ *Average main: $12* ✉ *1034 W. 4th Ave., Downtown* ☎ *907/272–2489* ⊕ *www.snowcitycafe.com* ☾ *No dinner.*

$$ | **AMERICAN** — ✗ **Snow Goose Restaurant and Sleeping Lady Brewing Company.** Although you can dine indoors at this comfortable edge-of-downtown eatery, the real attraction in summer is alfresco dining on the back deck or hoisting a Hefeweizen on the rooftop. On clear days you can see Mt. McKinley on the northern horizon, the Chugach Mountains to the east, and the brewery's namesake Sleeping Lady mountain across Cook Inlet. The menu emphasizes Alaskan takes on classic pub fare, including smoked salmon corn chowder and caribou burgers, but the award-winning beer and the view are the best reasons to visit. To sample the specialty beers, gather around oak tables in the upstairs pub for a brewed-on-the-premises ale, oatmeal stout, barley wine, or porter. Several of the beers, including the Portage Porter and 49er, an amber ale, pay homage to Alaska. The restaurant also hosts a range of events in its theater, including improv comedy nights and live music. $ *Average main: $16* ✉ *717 W. 3rd Ave., Downtown* ☎ *907/277–7727* ⊕ *www.alaskabeers.com.*

WHERE TO STAY

Lodging for most cruise-ship travelers is typically included in package tours set up through a travel agency, an online site, or directly from the cruise line. If you prefer to pick your own hotel or bed-and-breakfast, make your reservations well ahead of time, since many central hotels fill up months in advance for the peak summer season. Rooms are generally available, though you may be staying in midtown, 2 miles from downtown.

$$$$ | **HOTEL** — 🛏 **Anchorage Marriott Downtown.** One of Anchorage's biggest lodgings, the brightly decorated Marriott appeals to business travelers, tourists, and corporate clients. **Pros:** one of the newest hotels in town; modern, up-to-date facilities. **Cons:** no free Wi-Fi; pricey valet parking; cruise-ship crowds at times in summer. $ *Rooms from: $309* ✉ *820 W. 7th Ave., Downtown* ☎ *907/279–8000, 800/228–9290* ⊕ *www.marriott.com* ⤷ *390 rooms, 3 suites* ⦿❘*No meals.*

$$ ⊡ **Comfort Inn Ship Creek.** Try catching salmon in the namesake Ship
HOTEL Creek gurgling past this popular family hotel, which is a short walk
FAMILY northeast of the Alaska Railroad Historic Depot and practically on top
of the Tony Knowles Coastal Trail. **Pros:** pet-friendly; pool; free Wi-Fi.
Cons: the walk into the downtown area is an uphill climb; rooms are a
bit noisy at times. ⑤ *Rooms from: $189* ⊠ *111 Ship Creek Ave., Down-
town* ☎ *907/277–6887, 800/424–6423* ⊕ *www.choicehotels.com/hotel/
ak006* ⤳ *88 rooms, 12 suites* ⊙⏐ *Multiple meal plans.*

$$$ ⊡ **Historic Anchorage Hotel.** The little building has been around since
HOTEL 1916, and experienced travelers call it the only hotel in Anchorage with
charm: the original sinks and tubs have been restored, and upstairs hall-
ways are lined with Old Anchorage photos. **Pros:** excellent staff; new
flat-screen TVs; free Wi-Fi, convenient downtown location. **Cons:** rooms
are small; no airport shuttle. ⑤ *Rooms from: $219* ⊠ *330 E St., Down-
town* ☎ *907/272–4553, 800/544–0988* ⊕ *www.historicanchoragehotel.
com* ⤳ *16 rooms, 10 junior suites* ⊙⏐ *Breakfast.*

$$$$ ⊡ **Hotel Captain Cook.** Recalling Captain Cook's voyages to Alaska
HOTEL and the South Pacific, dark teak paneling lines the hotel's interior, and
a nautical theme continues into the guest rooms. **Pros:** staff is very
well trained and accommodating; excellent lobby bar. **Cons:** 24-hour
parking passes cost $20. ⑤ *Rooms from: $280* ⊠ *939 W. 5th Ave.,
Downtown* ☎ *907/276–6000, 800/843–1950* ⊕ *www.captaincook.com*
⤳ *547 rooms, 96 suites* ⊙⏐ *No meals.*

$ ⊡ **Oscar Gill House.** Originally built by Gill in the settlement of Knik
B&B/INN (north of Anchorage) in 1913, this historic home has been transformed
into a comfortable B&B in a quiet neighborhood along Delaney Park
Strip, with downtown attractions a short walk away. **Pros:** great breakfast; very hospitable owners in a bit of Old Anchorage history. **Cons:**
shared bath in two of the rooms; no king-size beds. ⑤ *Rooms from:
$115* ⊠ *1344 W. 10th Ave., Downtown* ☎ *907/279–1344* ⊕ *www.
oscargill.com* ⤳ *3 rooms, 1 with bath* ⊙⏐ *Breakfast.*

SEATTLE

By Cedar
Burnett

Seattle has much to offer: a gorgeous setting, lively arts and entertainment, innovative restaurants, friendly residents, green spaces galore,
and Pike Place Market, which provides a wonderfully earthy focal point
for downtown Seattle, with views of the ferries crossing Elliott Bay.
Visitors to the city will almost certainly wish they had set aside more
time to take in Seattle's charms.

Seattle, like Rome, is said to be built on seven hills. As a visitor, you're
likely to spend much of your time on only two of them (Capitol Hill
and Queen Anne Hill), but the city's hills are indeed the most definitive
element of the city's natural and spiritual landscape. Years of largely
thoughtful building practices have kept tall buildings from obscuring
the lines of sight, maintaining vistas in most directions and around
almost every turn. The hills are lofty, privileged perches from which
residents are constantly reminded of the beauty of the forests, mountains, and waters surrounding the city—that is, when it stops raining
long enough for you to enjoy those amazing views.

Seattle is a city of many hills—and many spectacular views.

In the heart of downtown Seattle's bustling retail core, the Seattle Convention and Visitors Bureau offers ticket sales, reservation and concierge services, dining suggestions, and a handy visitor information packet and coupon book that can be emailed to you.

ESSENTIALS

HOURS

Most attractions are open from 10 to 6 (some with extended hours during the summer), but some museums may close on Monday. Businesses are usually open from 10 to 6 (or later).

VISITOR INFORMATION

Contacts **Seattle Convention and Visitors Bureau** ☎ 866/732–2695 *visitor information, 206/461–5800 main office* ⊕ *www.visitseattle.org.*

THE CRUISE PORT

Ships from Norwegian Cruise Line and Celebrity Cruises dock at the Bell Street Pier Cruise Terminal at Pier 66. Pier 66 is within walking distance of downtown attractions, and a city bus wrapped in the Waterfront Streetcar logo (the real 1927 Waterfront Streetcars are out of commission until they can be upgraded) provides trolley service along the shoreline to the cruise terminal.

Holland America Line, Princess Cruises, Carnival Cruise Lines, and Royal Caribbean dock at the new Smith Cove Cruise Terminal at Pier 91, at the north end of the downtown waterfront. It is best accessed by cruise-line motor-coach transfer, taxi, or shuttle service.

Many cruise passengers drive themselves to the port via I–90 west. The Port of Seattle website has clear maps and directions to each pier. Amtrak provides train service north to Vancouver; south to Portland, Oakland, and Los Angeles; and east to Spokane, Chicago, and other cities. Amtrak's King Street Station is just south of downtown at 3rd Avenue South and South King Street.

Cruise-Port Information Bell Street Pier Cruise Terminal at Pier 66 ⊠ *2225 Alaskan Way, Seattle* ☎ *206/615–3900* ⊕ *www.portseattle.org/seaport/cruise/.* **Smith Cove Cruise Terminal at Terminal 91** ⊠ *2001 W. Garfield St., Seattle* ☎ *206/615–3900* ⊕ *www.portseattle.org/seaport/cruise/.*

Train Information Amtrak ☎ *800/872–7245* ⊕ *www.amtrak.com.*

AIRPORT TRANSFERS

The major gateway is Seattle–Tacoma International Airport (Sea-Tac). Sea-Tac is about 15 miles south of downtown on Interstate 5 (I–5). It takes 25–40 minutes to ride between the airport and downtown, depending on traffic. Metered cabs make the trip for $30–$40. Shuttle Express Downtown Airporter has the only 24-hour door-to-door service, a flat $15 per person ($25 round-trip) from the airport to downtown. You can make arrangements at the Downtown Airporter counter upon arrival at Sea-Tac or online. If you're traveling directly to Pier 91 from the airport ($36 per person, one-way), contact Shuttle Express.

Transfers to the piers between Sea-Tac Airport and designated hotels are offered by the cruise lines, either as an add-on to your fare or, in the case of some luxury cruise lines or small-ship cruise lines, included in the price of your cruise. Cruise-line representatives meet airport arrivals and are present at hotel transfer points to make the process virtually seamless.

Airport Information Seattle–Tacoma International Airport ☎ *206/787–5388* ⊕ *www.portseattle.org/seatac.*

Airport Transfer Shuttle Express ☎ *425/981–7000* ⊕ *www.shuttleexpress.com.*

PARKING

Note that parking at both piers fills up fast, and both parking lots discussed here offer handicapped parking spaces. If you're driving to Pier 66, you can reserve a parking space at Bell Street Pier Garage (directly across from the pier) at a discount online with Republic Parking. Fares are $20 per day (discounted if prepaid online). Note that there are no facilities for oversize vehicles such as RVs.

If you're sailing from Pier 91 (Smith Cove Terminal), you can also reserve a spot ahead of time with Republic Parking. Fares are $25 per day. RV and overheight vehicles for those sailing from Pier 66 can also park here at $28 plus tax per day. For those parking here but departing from Pier 66, a taxi voucher is available.

Contacts Republic Parking ☎ *206/783–4144, Ext. 1113* ⊕ *www.rpnw.com.* **Port of Seattle** ⊕ *www.portseattle.org/seaport/cruise.*

PUBLIC TRANSPORTATION

The bus system, Metro Bus, will get you anywhere you need to go, although some routes farther afield require a time commitment and several transfers. Within the downtown core, however, the bus is efficient—and, most of the time, it won't cost you a dime, thanks to the Ride-Free Area. The Trip Planner is a useful resource.

Sound Transit's Central Link Light Rail connects downtown and other areas of Seattle to Sea-Tac Airport. The train runs every 10 to 15 minutes from 5 am to 1 am weekdays and Saturday, and every 15 minutes from 6 am to midnight on Sunday. The downtown terminus is Westlake Station, which is convenient to many hotels—or at least a much quicker and cheaper cab ride away. The Sound Transit Central Link fare is $2.50 one-way, and the ride is very comfortable.

Built for the 1962 World's Fair, the monorail is the shortest transportation system in the city. It runs from Westlake Center (at 5th and Pine) to Seattle Center. But it is a great option for visitors who plan to spend a day at the Space Needle and the Seattle Center's museums. A single ride is $2.

The Seattle Streetcar, the second-shortest system in the city, was built to connect downtown to the up-and-coming neighborhood of South Lake Union (which is directly east of Seattle Center). It runs from Westlake and Olive to the southern shore of Lake Union. A single ride is $2.25.

Contacts Metro Transit ☎ 206/553–3000 *for customer service, schedules, and information,* 206/263–3582 *for bus-pass and ticket sales* ⊕ *metro. kingcounty.gov for information;* buypass.kingcounty.gov *for online pass sales.* **Seattle Center Monorail** ☎ 206/905–2620 ⊕ www.seattlemonorail.com. **Seattle Streetcar** ☎ 866/205–5001, 206/553–3000 ⊕ www.seattlestreetcar.org. **Sound Transit** ☎ 888/889–6368, 206/398–5000 ⊕ www.soundtransit.org.

TAXIS

Seattle's taxi fleet is small, but you can sometimes hail a cab on the street, especially downtown. Most of the time you must call for one. Except on Friday and Saturday nights, you rarely have to wait more than a few minutes for pickup. Cab rides can be pricey but useful, especially late at night when buses run infrequently. Two major cab companies are Farwest and Yellow Cab.

Contacts Farwest Taxi ☎ 206/622–1717 *Seattle Metro Area,* 425/454–5055 *Eastside* ⊕ www.farwesttaxi.net. **Yellow Cab** ☎ 206/622–6500 ⊕ www.yellowtaxi.net.

EXPLORING SEATTLE

The Elliott Bay waterfront is one of Seattle's most fascinating features, and Pike Place Market, the Seattle Aquarium, and the Seattle Art Museum (SAM) are all within close walking distance. Just south of downtown is the historic Pioneer Square area, and a short distance north of Pike Place Market lies the Olympic Sculpture Park, a magnificent waterfront urban playground filled with gigantic works of art. North of the sculpture park is Seattle Center, a civic gathering place that's home to the Space Needle, the Experience Music Project and Science Fiction Museum (EMP/SFM), the Children's Museum, and the Pacific Science Center.

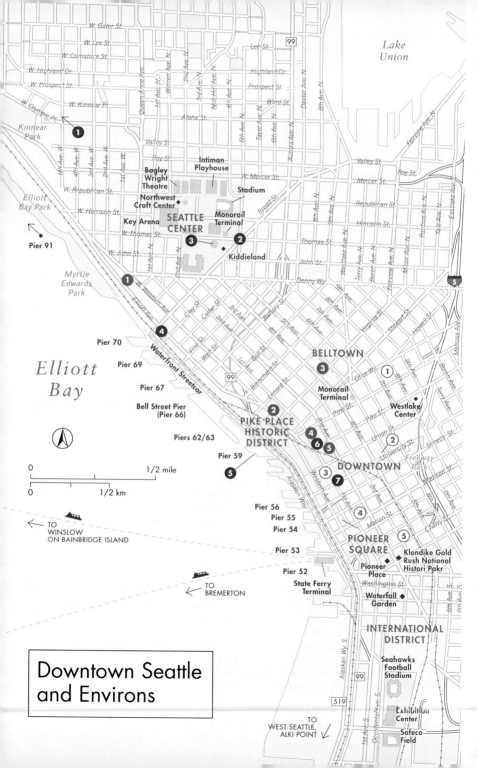

Downtown Seattle and Environs

Lake Union

Elliott Bay Park

Pier 91

Kinnear Park

Myrtle Edwards Park

Elliott Bay

SEATTLE CENTER

Bagley Wright Theatre
Intiman Playhouse
Stadium
Northwest Craft Center
Key Arena
Monorail Terminal
Kiddieland

Pier 70
Pier 69
Pier 67
Bell Street Pier (Pier 66)
Piers 62/63
Pier 59

Waterfront Streetcar

BELLTOWN

Monorail Terminal
Westlake Center

PIKE PLACE HISTORIC DISTRICT

DOWNTOWN

Freeway Park

Pier 56
Pier 55
Pier 54
Pier 53
Pier 52

PIONEER SQUARE

Pioneer Place
Klondike Gold Rush National Histori Pakr
State Ferry Terminal
Waterfall Garden

INTERNATIONAL DISTRICT

Seahawks Football Stadium

Exhibition Center

Safeco Field

TO WINSLOW ON BAINBRIDGE ISLAND

TO BREMERTON

TO WEST SEATTLE, ALKI POINT

0 — 1/2 mile
0 — 1/2 km

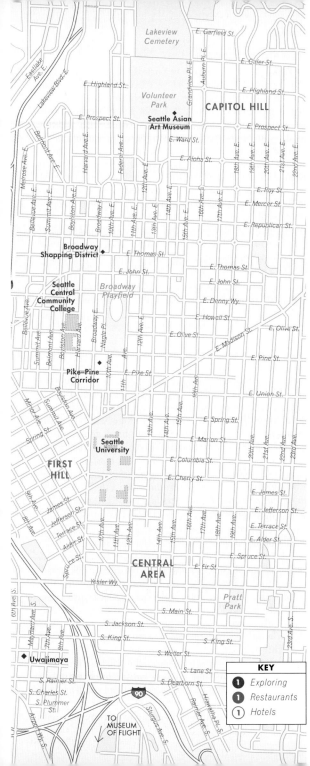

DOWNTOWN AND BELLTOWN

Fodor'sChoice ★   **Olympic Sculpture Park.** This 9-acre open-air park is the spectacular outdoor branch of the Seattle Art Museum. The Sculpture Park is a favorite destination for picnics, strolls, and quiet contemplation. Nestled at the edge of Belltown with views of Elliott Bay, this gently sloping green space is planted with native plants and is crisscrossed with walking paths. On sunny days, the park flaunts an astounding panorama of the Olympic Mountain Range, but even the grayest afternoon casts a favorable light on the site's sculptures. The grounds are home to works by such artists as Richard Serra, Roy McMakin, Louise Bourgeois, Mark di Suvero, and Alexander Calder, whose bright-red steel "Eagle" sculpture is a local favorite—indeed, you may even see a real bald eagle passing by overhead. The PACCAR Pavilion has a gift shop, café, and more information about the park. ⊠ *2901 Western Ave., between Broad and Bay Sts., Belltown* ☎ *206/654–3100* ⊕ *www.seattleartmuseum.org/visit/osp* ⌨ *Free* ⊙ *Park daily sunrise–sunset. PACCAR Pavilion May–Labor Day, Tues.–Sun. 10–5; Sept.–Apr., Tues.–Sun. 10–4.*

FAMILY Fodor'sChoice ★   **Pike Place Market.** One of the nation's largest and oldest public markets, Pike Place Market dates from 1907, when the city issued permits allowing farmers to sell produce from wagons parked at Pike Place. At one time the market was a madhouse of vendors hawking their produce and haggling with customers over prices; now you might find fishmongers engaging in frenzied banter and hilarious antics, but chances are you won't get them to waver on prices. There are many restaurants, bakeries, coffee shops (including the flagship Starbucks), lunch counters, and ethnic eateries. Go to the Market hungry and you won't be disappointed. The flower market is also a must-see—gigantic fresh arrangements can be had for as little as $5. Strap on some walking shoes and enjoy the Market's many corridors: Specialty-food items, quirky gift shops, tea, honey, jams, comic books, beads, eclectic crafts and cookware—you'll find it all here. ⊠ *Pike Pl. at Pike St., west of 1st Ave., Downtown* ☎ *206/682–7453* ⊕ *www.pikeplacemarket.org* ⊙ *Market opens daily for breakfast at 6 am; fresh produce and fish 7 am–6 pm; merchants 0 am–6 pm; restaurants and bars last call, 1:30 am.*

FAMILY Fodor'sChoice ★   **Seattle Aquarium.** Located right at the water's edge, the Seattle Aquarium is one of the nation's premier aquariums. Among its most engaging residents are the sea otters—kids, especially, seem able to spend hours watching the delightful antics of these creatures and their river cousins. In the Puget Sound Great Hall, "Window on Washington Waters," a slice of Neah Bay life, is presented in a 20-foot-tall tank holding 120,000 gallons of water. The aquarium's darkened rooms and large, lighted tanks brilliantly display Pacific Northwest marine life. The "Life on the Edge" tide pools re-create Washington's rocky coast and sandy beaches. Huge glass windows provide underwater views of the renovated harbor seal exhibit; go up top to watch them play in their pools. Kids love the Discovery Lab, where they can touch starfish, sea urchins, and sponges. ■TIP➔ If you're visiting in fall or winter, dress warmly— the Marine Mammal area is outside on the waterfront and catches all of those chilly Puget Sound breezes. The café serves Ivar's chowder and kid-friendly food like burgers and chicken fingers; the balcony has views of Elliott Bay. ✉ *1483 Alaskan Way, Pier 59, Downtown* ☎ *206/386–4300* ⊕ *www.seattleaquarium.org* ✉ *$19.95; children 4–12, $13.95* ⊙ *Daily 9:30–6 (last entry at 5 pm)*.

Seattle Art Museum. Long the pride of the city's art scene, SAM is better than ever after a massive expansion connected the iconic old building on University Street (where sculptor Jonathan Borofsky's several-stories-high *Hammering Man* still pounds away) to a sleek, light-filled high-rise adjacent space, on 1st Avenue and Union Street. Wander two floors of free public space. The first floor includes the museum's fantastic shop, a café that focuses on local ingredients, and drop-in workshops where the whole family can get creative. The second floor features free exhibitions, including awesome large-scale installations.

SAM's permanent collection surveys American, Asian, Native American, African, Oceanic, and pre-Columbian art. Collections of African dance masks and Native American carvings are particularly strong. Kanye Quaye's *Mercedes Benz Coffin* installation and the Italian Room, a reproduction of typical Lombard Renaissance–era room, are also favorites.

You can download SAM Audio—podcasts about the museum's collection—to your iPod or smart phone. ✉ *1300 1st Ave., Downtown* ☎ *206/654–3100* ⊕ *www.seattleartmuseum.org* ✉ *$17* ⊙ *Wed. and weekends 10–5, Thurs. and Fri. 10–9; closed Mon. and Tues. Free on 1st Thurs.*

SEATTLE CENTER AND QUEEN ANNE

A few blocks north of downtown, at the base of Queen Anne Hill, Seattle Center is a legacy of the 1962 World's Fair. Today the 74-acre site is home to a multitude of attractions that encompass a children's museum, an opera hall, a skate park, a fantastic science museum, the Monorail, a basketball arena, and much more. We cover only a handful of highlights here; for more information, call ☎ 206/684–7200 or check out ⊕ *www.seattlecenter.com*. Definitely farther afield but worth the transportation effort, Discovery Park is in the Magnolia neighborhood, northwest of Queen Anne.

OFF THE BEATEN PATH

Discovery Park. You won't find more spectacular views of Puget Sound, the Cascades, and the Olympics. Discovery Park, located on Magnolia Bluff, northwest of downtown, is Seattle's largest park at 534 acres, and it has an amazing variety of terrain: shaded, secluded forest trails lead to meadows, saltwater beaches, sand dunes, a lighthouse, and 2 miles of protected beaches. The North Beach Trail, which takes you along the shore to the lighthouse, is a must-see. Head to the South Bluff Trail to get a view of Mt. Rainier. The park has several entrances—if you want to stop at the visitor center to pick up a trail map before exploring, use the main entrance at Government Way. The North Parking Lot is much closer to the North Beach Trail and to Ballard and Fremont, if you're coming from that direction. ◼ TIP➔ Note that the park is easily reached from Ballard and Fremont. It's easier to combine a park day with an exploration of those neighborhoods than with a busy downtown itinerary. ✉ *3801 W. Government Way, Magnolia* ✛ *From downtown, take Elliot Ave. W (which turns into 15th Ave. W), and get off at the Emerson St. exit and turn left onto W. Emerson. Make a right onto*

Lighthouse, Discovery Park

Gilman Ave. W (which eventually becomes W. Government Way). As you enter the park, the road becomes Washington Ave.; turn left on Utah Ave. ☎ *206/386–4236* ⊕ *seattle.gov/parks/environment/discovery. htm* ✉ *Free* ☉ *Park daily 6 am–11 pm, visitor center Tues.–Sun. 8:30–5.*

FAMILY
Fodor's Choice
★

EMP Museum. Seattle's most controversial architectural statement is the 140,000-square-foot complex designed by architect Frank Gehry, who drew inspiration from electric guitars to achieve the building's curvy metallic design. It's a fitting backdrop for rock memorabilia from the likes of Bob Dylan and the grunge-scene heavies.

Two permanent exhibits provide a primer on the evolution of Seattle's music scene. "Nirvana: Taking Punk to the Masses" features rare and unseen artifacts and photography from the band, their crews and families. "Jimi Hendrix: An Evolution of Sound" illustrates Hendrix's rise from his early days in Seattle, including sound effects and mixing interactives, showing Hendrix as an innovator and forefather of modern recording technology.

What was once a separate wing at EMP—the Science Fiction Museum and Hall of Fame—is now a permanent exhibit. Here you'll find iconic artifacts from sci-fi literature, film, television, and art, including an Imperial Dalek from *Doctor Who*, the command chair from the classic television series *Star Trek*, and Neo's coat from *The Matrix Reloaded*. ✉ *325 5th Ave. N, between Broad and Thomas Sts., Seattle Center* ☎ *206/770–2700* ⊕ *www.empsfm.org* ✉ *$20* ☉ *Daily 10–5.*

FAMILY
Space Needle. Over 50 years old, Seattle's most iconic building is as quirky and beloved as ever. The distinctive, towering structure of the 605-foot-high Space Needle is visible throughout much of Seattle—but

the view from the inside out is even better. A less-than-one-minute ride up to the observation deck yields 360-degree vistas of Downtown Seattle, the Olympic Mountains, Elliott Bay, Queen Anne Hill, Lake Union, and the Cascade Range. Built for the 1962 World's Fair, the Needle has educational kiosks, interactive trivia game stations for kids, and the glass-enclosed Space-Base store and Pavilion spiraling around the base of the tower. The top-floor SkyCity restaurant is "revolutionary" (literally—watch the skyline evolve as you dine) and the elevator trip and observation deck are complimentary with your reservation. ■TIP➜ If the forecast says you may have a sunny day during your visit, schedule the Needle for that day! If you can't decide whether you want the daytime or nighttime view, for $26 you can buy a ticket that allows you to visit twice in one day. ⊠ *400 Broad St., Seattle Center* ☎ *206/905–2100* ⊕ *www.spaceneedle.com* ✉ *$19* ⊙ *Daily 9 am–midnight.*

> ### SEATTLE CITYPASS
>
> If you're in Seattle for several days before or after your cruise, look into the CityPASS, which gives admission to six different attractions for just $74 ($49 for kids 12 and under)—nearly half off what admission for all six would be without a discount. The pass covers admission to the Space Needle, the Seattle Aquarium, a Seattle harbor tour, the Pacific Science Center, Woodland Park Zoo, and either the Museum of Flight or the Experience Music Project/Science Fiction Museum. See ⊕ www.citypass.com/seattle for more information.

SHOPPING

Seattle's retail core might feel business-crisp by day, but it's casual and arts-centered by night, and the shopping scene reflects both these moods. Within a few square blocks—between 1st Avenue to the west and Boren Avenue to the east, and from University Street to Olive Way—you can find department-store flagships, several glossy vertical malls, dozens of upper-echelon boutiques, and retail chains. One block closer to Elliott Bay, on Western Avenue, high-end home-furnishings showrooms make up an informal "Furniture Row." The Waterfront, with its small, kitschy stores and open-air restaurants, is a great place to dawdle. ■TIP➜ Seattle's best shopping is found in the small neighborhood made up of 4th, 5th, and 6th avenues between Pine and Spring streets, and 1st Avenue between Virginia and Madison streets.

Fodor's Choice **Peter Miller Architectural & Design Books and Supplies.** Aesthetes and archi-
★ tects haunt this shop, which is stocked floor to ceiling with all things design. Rare, international architecture, art, and design books mingle with high-end products from Alessi and Iittala; sleek notebooks, bags, portfolios, and drawing tools round out the collection. This is a great shop for quirky, unforgettable gifts, like a Black Dot sketchbook, an Arne Jacobsen wall clock, or an aerodynamic umbrella. ⊠ *1930 1st Ave., Downtown* ☎ *206/441–4114* ⊕ *www.petermiller.com.*

Fodor'sChoice **REI.** The enormous flagship for Recreational Equipment, Inc. (REI)
★ has an incredible selection of outdoor gear—polar-fleece jackets, wool
socks, down vests, hiking boots, rain gear, and much more—as well as
its own 65-foot climbing wall. The staff is extremely knowledgeable;
there always seems to be enough help on hand, even when the store is
busy. You can test things out on the mountain-bike test trail or in the
simulated rain booth. REI also rents gear such as tents, sleeping bags,
skis, snowshoes, and backpacks. ⊠ *222 Yale Ave. N, South Lake Union*
☎ *206/223–1944* ⊕ *www.rei.com.*

FAMILY **Schmancy.** Weird and wonderful, this toy store is more surreal art fun-
Fodor'sChoice house than FAO Schwarz. Pick up a crocheted zombie (with a cute little
★ bow), a felted Ishmael's whale, your very own Hugh Hefner figurine—
or how about a pork-chop pillow? With collectibles from cult favorites
Plush You!, Kidrobot, and Lovemongers, this quirky shop is full of sur-
prises. Warning: Sense of humor required. ⊠ *1932 2nd Ave., Downtown*
☎ *206/728–8008* ⊕ *www.schmancytoys.com.*

NIGHTLIFE

The grunge-rock legacy of Nirvana, Soundgarden, and Pearl Jam still
reverberates in local music venues, which showcase up-and-coming
pop, punk, heavy metal, and alternative bands, along with healthy
doses of other genres.

Two free papers, the *Stranger* and *Seattle Weekly* (see ⊕ *www.
thestranger.com* or ⊕ *www.seattleweekly.com*), provide detailed music,
art, and nightlife listings. Friday editions of the *Seattle Times* have pull-
out sections detailing weekend events.

Bars and clubs stay open until 2 am. Cabs are easy to find, and some
buses run until the early morning hours (see ⊕ *metro.kingcounty.gov*).
After the witching hour, cabs are the best option for those not willing to hoof it. Pioneer Square—home to a plethora of rock, jazz, and
electronic music clubs—features a joint cover charge of $10 that covers
admission to six bars; simply pay the cover at the first club you visit,
get a hand stamp, and roam at will.

BARS AND CLUBS

Black Bottle. Sleek and sexy, Black Bottle makes the northern reaches
of Belltown look good. The interior of this gastro-tavern is simple but
stylish, with black chairs and tables and shiny wood floors. It gets
crowded on nights and weekends with a laid-back but often dressed-
up clientele. A small selection of beers on tap and a solid wine list
(with Washington, Oregon, California, and beyond well represented)
will help you wash down the sustainably sourced pub snacks, including house-smoked wild boar ribs, pork belly with kimchi, and oysters
on the half shell. ⊠ *2600 1st Ave., Belltown* ☎ *206/441–1500* ⊕ *www.
blackbottleseattle.com.*

Fodor'sChoice **The Crocodile.** The heart and soul of Seattle's music scene since 1991,
★ the Crocodile has hosted the likes of Nirvana, Pearl Jam, and Mud-
honey, along with countless other bands. Seattleites mourned when
it closed in 2007, and rejoiced even harder when it reopened, with

DID YOU KNOW?

The colorful and dramatic Chihuly Bridge of Glass, at the Museum of Glass in Tacoma, is a 500-foot-long pedestrian bridge that connects downtown Tacoma to the waterfront; it was completed in 2002.

much improved sightlines, in 2009. Nightly shows are complemented by cheap beer on tap and pizza right next door at Via Tribunali. All hail the Croc! ⊠ *2200 2nd Ave., Belltown* ☎ *206/441–7416* ⊕ *www.thecrocodile.com.*

Fodor's Choice ★ **Zig Zag Café.** When it comes to pouring perfect martinis, Zig Zag Café gives Oliver's a run for its money—and it's much more eclectic and relaxed here. A mixed crowd of mostly locals hunts out this unique spot at Pike Place Market's Street Hill Climb (a nearly hidden stairwell leading down to the piers). Several memorable cocktails include the Don't Give Up the Ship (gin, Dubonnet, Grand Marnier, and Fernet Branca), the One-Legged Duck (rye whiskey, Dubonnet, Mandarine Napoleon, and Fernet Branca), and Satan's Soulpatch (bourbon, sweet and dry vermouth, Grand Marnier, orange, and orange bitters). A very simple, ho-hum food menu includes cheese and meat plates, bruschetta, soup, salad, olives, and nuts. A small patio is the place to be on a summery happy-hour evening. Zig Zag is friendly—retro without being obnoxiously ironic—and very Seattle, with the occasional live music show to boot. ⊠ *1501 Western Ave., Downtown* ☎ *206/625–1146* ⊕ *zigzagseattle.com.*

WHERE TO EAT

Downtown is a good area for lunch; come evening, its action centers on hotel restaurants and a handful of watering holes. Belltown, on the other hand, comes alive nightly with chic restaurants and bars, plus music and other entertainment. Pioneer Square is a bit more rough around the edges at night and features bars and restaurants that cater to baseball fans.

DOWNTOWN

$$$
PACIFIC
NORTHWEST
Fodor's Choice ★

✕ **Matt's in the Market.** Your first dinner at Matt's is like a first date you hope will never end. One of the most beloved of Pike Place Market's restaurants, Matt's is now owned by Dan Bugge, who continues to value intimate dining, fresh ingredients, and superb service. An expansion nearly doubled the number of seats, and some tables are now held for walk-ins. You can perch at the bar for pints and a delicious pulled pork or hot grilled-tuna sandwich or a cup of gumbo, or be seated at a table—complete with vases filled with flowers from the market—for a seasonal menu that synthesizes the best picks from the restaurant's produce vendors and an excellent wine list. Dinner entrées always include at least one catch of the day—perhaps a whole fish in saffron broth or Alaskan halibut with pea vines. ■TIP➔ Looking for the original Matt, former owner Matt Janke? He's pleasing diners at his new joint, Lecosho, a few blocks down at 89 University St. ⑤ *Average main: $32* ⊠ *94 Pike St., Suite 32, Downtown* ☎ *206/467–7909* ⊕ *www.mattsinthemarket.com* ⊘ *Closed Sun.*

$$$
MODERN
AMERICAN

✕ **Place Pigalle.** Large windows look out on Elliott Bay in this cozy spot tucked behind a meat vendor in Pike Place Market's main arcade. In nice weather, open windows let in the fresh salt breeze. Flowers brighten each table, and the staff is warm and welcoming. Despite its name, this restaurant has only a few French flourishes on an otherwise American/

Pacific Northwest menu. Go for the rich oyster stew, the sea scallops with rosé champagne beurre blanc, Dungeness crab (in season), poussin with barley risotto, or the fish of the day. Local microbrews are on tap, and the wine list is thoughtfully compact, but if you want to feel more like you're in France, sip a pastis as you gaze out the window. ⑤ *Average main: $28* ⊠ *81 Pike St., Downtown* ☎ *206/624–1756* ⊕ *www. placepigalle-seattle.com.*

$$$ ✕ **Steelhead Diner.** Think New Jersey diner meets Seattle seafood flair—
AMERICAN with an amazing Washington wine menu, to boot. You can depend on finding expertly prepared fresh fish, and salmon might come from Bristol Bay in Alaska or from Washington's Quinault River, depending on season, but there's much more on the menu, and the fried chicken can't be beat. Other fine favorites include "jumbo lump" crab cakes and a decadent Theo Chocolate pecan pie. Beware of blaring music, odd lighting, touristy crowds, and steep prices, but that goes with the location, smack in the heart of Pike Place Market. ⑤ *Average main: $25* ⊠ *95 Pine St., Downtown* ☎ *206/625–0129* ⊕ *www. steelheaddiner.com.*

BELLTOWN

$ ✕ **Boat Street Café & Kitchen.** Tables at this French bistro–meets–Nan-
MODERN tucket bistro often fill up with couples at night, but the lunchtime
AMERICAN scene runs the gamut from downtown office workers to tourists. Food
Fodor'sChoice is understated, fresh, and simply divine: start with raw oysters and a
★ crisp glass of white wine. Next up, sautéed Medjool dates sprinkled with *fleur de sel* and olive oil, a radish salad with pine nuts, or a plate of the famous house-made pickles. Entrées, too, take advantage of whatever is in season, so expect anything from Oregon hanger steak with olive tapenade to Alaskan halibut with cauliflower. Though it's on the ground floor of an odd office building (just north of the Olympic Sculpture Park), Boat Street positively blooms in the quirky space. Monday through Sunday, brunch and lunch are served 10:30–2:30. ⑤ *Average main: $16* ⊠ *3131 Western Ave., Belltown* ☎ *206/632–4602* ⊕ *www.boatstreetcafe.com* ⊗ *No dinner Sun. and Mon.*

$$$ ✕ **Lola.** Tom Douglas dishes out his signature Northwest style, spiked
MEDITERRANEAN with Greek and Mediterranean touches here—another huge suc-
Fodor'sChoice cess for the local celebrity chef. Try a glorious tagine of goat meat
★ with mustard and rosemary; grape leaf–wrapped trout; lamb burgers with chickpea fries; and scrumptious spreads including hummus, tzatziki, and *harissa* (a red-pepper concoction). Booths are usually full at this bustling, dimly lighted restaurant, which anchors the Hotel Ändra. The fabulous weekend brunches are inventive: try Tom's Big Breakfast—octopus, mustard greens, cumin-spiced yogurt, bacon, and an egg. If you still have room, there are made-to-order doughnuts, too. ⑤ *Average main: $25* ⊠ *2000 4th Ave., Belltown* ☎ *206/441–1430* ⊕ *www.tomdouglas.com/index.php?page=lola.*

WHERE TO STAY

$$$
HOTEL
Fodor's Choice
★

⌂ **The Arctic Club Seattle—a DoubleTree by Hilton Hotel.** From the Alaskan-marble-sheathed foyer and the antique walrus heads on the third floor, to the Northern Lights Dome room with its leaded glass ceiling and rococo touches, the Arctic Club pays homage to an era of gold rush opulence. **Pros:** cool, unique property; great staff; light rail and bus lines just outside the door. **Cons:** not in the heart of downtown; rooms are a bit dark; style may be off-putting for travelers who like modern hotels; charge for Wi-Fi. ⑤ *Rooms from: $289* ⊠ *700 3rd Ave., Downtown* ☎ *206/340–0340, 800/445–8667* ⊕ *www.arcticclubhotel.com* ↪ *118 rooms, 2 suites* ⎢◯⎢ *No meals.*

$$$$
HOTEL
FAMILY
Fodor's Choice
★

⌂ **The Fairmont Olympic Hotel.** Grand and stately, the Fairmont Olympic transports travelers to another time: with marble floors, brocade chairs, massive chandeliers, and sweeping staircases, this old-world hotel personifies class and elegance. **Pros:** great location; excellent service; fabulous on-site dining and amenities. **Cons:** not much in the way of views; may be a little too old-school for trendy travelers; remodel in 2013 means some rooms may be unavailable. ⑤ *Rooms from: $409* ⊠ *411 University St., Downtown* ☎ *206/621–1700, 888/363–5022* ⊕ *www. fairmont.com/seattle* ↪ *232 rooms, 218 suites* ⎢◯⎢ *No meals.*

$$$$
HOTEL
FAMILY
Fodor's Choice
★

⌂ **Four Seasons Hotel Seattle.** Just south of the Pike Place Market and steps from the Seattle Art Museum, this downtown gem is polished and elegant, with Eastern accents and plush furnishings set against a modern-Northwest backdrop in which materials, such as stone and fine hardwoods, take center stage. **Pros:** fantastic location with amazing views of Elliott Bay; large rooms with luxurious bathrooms; lovely spa. **Cons:** Four Seasons regulars might not click with this modern take on the brand; street-side rooms not entirely soundproofed; some room views are partially obscured by industrial sites. ⑤ *Rooms from: $405* ⊠ *99 Union St., Downtown* ☎ *206/749–7000, 800/332–3442* ⊕ *www. fourseasons.com/seattle* ↪ *134 rooms, 13 suites* ⎢◯⎢ *No meals.*

$$
HOTEL
FAMILY
Fodor's Choice
★

⌂ **Hotel 1000.** Chic and modern yet warm and inviting, the Hotel 1000 is luxe, with a distinctly Pacific Northwest feel, without being campy. **Pros:** useful high-tech gadgets; guests feel pampered; hotel is hip without being alienating. **Cons:** rooms can be dark; rooms without views look out on a cement wall; small gym. ⑤ *Rooms from: $239* ⊠ *1000 1st Ave., Downtown* ☎ *206/957–1000, 877/315–1088* ⊕ *www.hotel1000seattle. com* ↪ *101 rooms, 19 suites* ⎢◯⎢ *No meals.*

$$
HOTEL
Fodor's Choice
★

⌂ **Hyatt at Olive 8.** In a city known for environmental responsibility, being the greenest hotel in Seattle is no small feat—and green is rarely this chic. **Pros:** central location; superb amenities; environmental responsibility; wonderful spa. **Cons:** standard rooms have showers only; guests complain of hallway and traffic noise; translucent glass bathroom doors offer little privacy; fee for Wi-Fi. ⑤ *Rooms from: $219* ⊠ *1635 8th Ave., Downtown* ☎ *206/695–1234, 800/233–1234* ⊕ *www.olive8. hyatt.com* ↪ *331 rooms, 15 suites* ⎢◯⎢ *No meals.*

SEWARD

By Teeka A.
Ballas

It seems hard to believe that such beauty exists as in Seward. Surrounded on all sides by Kenai Fjords National Park, Chugach National Forest, and Resurrection Bay, Seward offers all the quaint realities of a small railroad town with the bonus of jaw-dropping scenery. This little town of fewer than 3,000 citizens was founded in 1903, when survey crews arrived at the ice-free port and began planning a railroad to the Interior. Since its inception, Seward has relied heavily on tourism and commercial fishing. It is also the launching point for excursions into Kenai Fjords National Park, where it is quite common to see marine life and calving glaciers.

Seward is an important embarkation and disembarkation port for cruise-ship travelers. Many large cruise ships terminate (or start) their seven-day Alaskan voyages

SEWARD BEST BETS

■ **Get your sea legs.** Seward's main claims to fame and most notable draws are Resurrection Bay and Kenai Fjords National Park.

■ **Landlubber?** Visit the park at Exit Glacier north of town, hike any of the numerous trails in the area, or shop at one of the stores near the small-boat harbor or in the downtown business district.

■ **Rainy day?** The SeaLife Center is not to be missed. It's a combination aquarium, rescue facility for marine animals, and research center. If the seas are too rough or the rain is too bothersome, there's interesting stuff here for all ages.

in Seward. Although many cruise ships stop here, travelers are often shunted off to Anchorage on waiting buses or train cars, with no time to explore this lovely town.

ESSENTIALS

TOURS

Kenai Fjords Tours. Kenai Fjords Tours, part of the Native-owned Alaska Heritage Tours, is the oldest and largest company running tours through the park. Visitors can take a four-hour gray whale-watch tour from the end of March through mid-May. From March through mid-September tour options include 3½- to 9-hour Resurrection Bay wildlife tours, priced from $64 to $214. Cruise options include exclusive visits to Fox Island, interpretive programs by National Park Service rangers, cruise and kayak combinations, glacier viewing, and opportunities to see whales, puffins, otters, and Steller sea lions. The fleet includes catamarans, which are less susceptible to the rolling motion that can cause seasickness. Lunch or dinner on Fox Island is included in tours. To feast on king crab for dinner, be sure to order in advance (additional $12 per person). Transportation and overnight options are also available. ☎ 907/276–6249, 877/777–4051 ⊕ www.kenaifjords.com.

Major Marine Tours. Major Marine Tours conducts half-day and full-day cruises of Resurrection Bay and Kenai Fjords National Park. Park cruises are narrated by a National Park Service ranger, and meals of salmon, prime rib, or vegetarian chile are an option. A custom-built

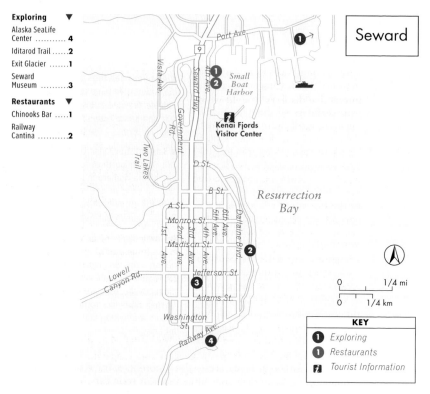

Seward

Port Ave.

Small
Boat
Harbor

Kenai Fjords
Visitor Center

Resurrection
Bay

D St.

B St.

A St.

Monroe St.

Madison St.

Jefferson St.

Adams St.

Washington
St.

Railway Ave.

Vista Ave.

Seward Hwy.

4th Ave.

Government Rd.

Two Lakes Trail

1st Ave.

2nd Ave.

3rd Ave.

4th Ave.

5th Ave.

6th Ave.

Dairlaine Blvd.

Lowell Canyon Rd.

0   1/4 mi

0   1/4 km

KEY
❶ Exploring
❶ Restaurants
🅹 Tourist Information

catamaran runs daily from March through September. Summer cruises
include a three-hour whale-watching tour and a six-hour Kenai Fjords
trip, featuring narration by a national park ranger. Major Marine
Tours can arrange transportation between Anchorage and Seward.
☎ *907/274–7300, 800/764–7300* ⊕ *www.majormarine.com.*

VISITOR INFORMATION

The **Seward Chamber of Commerce** has a visitor information center at the
cruise-ship dock that is staffed when ships are in port.

Contacts Seward Visitors Bureau ✉ *Mile 2, Seward Hwy.* ☎ *907/224–8051*
⊕ *www.sewardchamber.org.*

THE CRUISE PORT

Most cruises that begin in Alaska actually start or end in Seward, but
transportation from (or to) Anchorage is either included in your cruise
fare or available as an add-on. Check with your cruise line for tours to
the SeaLife Center that can be added on to an airport transfer. Cruise
ships dock approximately ½ mile from downtown.

EXPLORING

FAMILY
Fodor's Choice
★

Alaska SeaLife Center. Spend an afternoon at the Alaska SeaLife Center, with massive cold-water tanks and outdoor viewing decks as well as interactive displays of cold-water fish, seabirds, and marine mammals, including harbor seals and a 2,000-pound sea lion. A research center as well as visitor center, it also rehabilitates injured marine wildlife and provides educational experiences for the general public. Appropriately, the center was partially funded with reparations money from the *Exxon Valdez* oil spill. Films, hands-on activities, a gift shop, and behind-the-scenes tours ($12 and up) complete the offerings. ⊠ *301 Railway Ave.* ☎ *907/224–6300, 888/378–2525* ⊕ *www.alaskasealife.org* ⊇ *$20* ⊗ *Mid-May–mid-Sept., Mon.–Thurs. 9–6:30, Fri.–Sun. 8–6:30; mid-Sept.–mid-May, daily 10–5.*

MARITIME EXPLORATIONS

The protected waters of the bay provide the perfect environment for sailing, fishing, sea kayaking, and marine wildlife–watching. There are numerous tours to choose from—just check out the boardwalk area adjacent to the docks. Half-day tours include Resurrection Bay, and all-day tours also allow you to view parts of spectacular Kenai Fjords National Park. The more adventurous trips venture out of the bay and into the Gulf of Alaska when the notoriously fickle weather permits visits to the more distant glaciers and attractions.

Exit Glacier. A short walk from the parking lot along a paved path will bring you face to face with Exit Glacier, just outside Seward. Look for the marked turnoff at Mile 3.7 as you enter town or ask locals for directions. There's a small walk-in campground here, a ranger station, and access to the glacier. Exit Glacier is the most accessible part of the **Harding Icefield.** This mass of ice caps the Kenai Mountains, covering more than 1,100 square miles, and it oozes more than 40 glaciers from its edges and down the mountainsides. Reach it from Mile 3.7. The hike to the ice field from the parking lot is a 9-mile round-trip that gains 3,000 feet in elevation, so it's not for the timid or out of shape. But if you're feeling up to the task, the hike and views are breathtaking. Local wildlife includes mountain goats and bears both black and brown, so keep a sharp eye out for them. Once you reach the ice, don't travel across it unless you have the gear and experience with glacier travel. Glacier ice is notoriously deceptive—the surface can look solid and unbroken, while underneath a thin crust of snow crevasses lie in wait for the unwary.

Iditarod Trail. The first mile of the historic original Iditarod Trail runs along the beach and makes for a nice, easy stroll. There is also a great walking tour designed by the city—maps are available at the visitor bureau, the converted railcar at the corner of 3rd Avenue and Jefferson Street, or the Seward Chamber of Commerce Visitor Center at Mile 2 on the Seward Highway.

Seward Museum. The Seward Museum displays photographs of the 1964 quake's damage, model rooms and artifacts from the early pioneers, and historical and current information on the Seward area. ✉ *336 3rd Ave., at Jefferson St.* ☎ *907/224–3902* 🖼 *Free, donation suggested* ⊙ *Mid-May–Labor Day, Wed.–Sun., 1–5 pm.*

SPORTS AND THE OUTDOORS

FISHING

The Fish House. Operating out of Seward since 1974, this booking agency represents dozens of Resurrection Bay and Kenai Peninsula fishing charters, specializing in silver salmon and halibut fishing, and can hook you up for half-day or full-day charters (full-day only for halibut fishing). ✉ *Small-boat harbor* ☎ *907/224–3674, 800/257–7760* ⊕ *www.thefishhouse.net.*

HIKING

For a comprehensive listing of all the trails, cabins, and campgrounds in the Seward Ranger District of Chugach National Forest, check the website of the U.S. Forest Service.

Mt. Marathon Race. One of the biggest events of the year in Seward, the Mt. Marathon Race—run on July 4 since 1915—attracts runners from near and far, and the entire town comes out to celebrate. It doesn't take the winners very long—44 minutes or so—but the route is straight up the mountain (3,022 feet) and back down to the center of town. Ambitious hikers can hit the Runner's Trail behind Providence Medical Center on Jefferson, while those who prefer a more leisurely (though still steep) climb can take the Hiker's Trail from 1st Avenue. ⚠ You don't want to attempt to break personal records in Alaska; fatigue can cause serious injuries or cause runners to lose the trail and get lost in the wilderness.

Seward Chamber of Commerce. For more information, contact the Seward Chamber of Commerce. ☎ *907/224–8051* ⊕ *www.sewardak.org.*

SHOPPING

FAMILY **Ranting Raven.** The Ranting Raven is a combination gift shop, bakery, and lunch spot, adorned with raven murals on the side of the building. You can indulge in fresh-baked goods, espresso drinks, and daily lunch specials such as quiche, focaccia, and homemade soups while perusing the packed shelves of local artwork, Native crafts, and jewelry. ✉ *238 4th Ave.* ☎ *907/224–2228.*

Resurrect Art Coffeehouse. Resurrect Art Coffeehouse is a darling coffeehouse and gallery-gift shop. It is housed in a 1932 church, and the ambience and views from the old choir loft are reason enough to stop by. Local art is showcased, and it's a good place to find Alaskan gifts that aren't mass-produced. ✉ *320 3rd Ave.* ☎ *907/224–7161* ⊕ *www.resurrectart.com.*

Fishing is an important industry and popular recreational activity in Seward.

WHERE TO EAT

$$$ ✕ **Chinooks Bar.** On the waterfront in the small-boat harbor, this year-
SEAFOOD round restaurant offers a dazzling selection of fresh seafood dishes,
beers on tap, a great wine selection, and a stunning view from the
upstairs window seats. The award-winning chef serves only Alaskan
sustainable seafood. Be sure to try the smoked-scallop mac and cheese.
⑤ *Average main: $25* ✉ *1404 4th Ave.* ☎ *907/224–2207* ⊕ *www.
chinooksbar.com* ⊙ *Closed mid-Oct.–May.*

$ ✕ **Railway Cantina.** This little hole-in-the-wall in the harbor area is a
MEXICAN local favorite. A wide selection of burritos, quesadillas, and great
halibut and rockfish tacos incorporates local seafood and is supple-
mented by an array of hot sauces, many contributed by customers
who brought them from their travels. ⑤ *Average main: $10* ✉ *1401
4th Ave.* ☎ *907/224–8226.*

VANCOUVER, BRITISH COLUMBIA

By Chris
McBeath

Cosmopolitan Vancouver has a spectacular setting. Tall fir trees stand practically downtown, the Coast Mountains tower close by, the ocean laps at the doorstep, and people from every corner of Earth create a youthful and vibrant atmosphere.

Vancouver is a young city, even by North American standards. It was not yet a town in 1871, when British Columbia became part of the Canadian confederation. The city's history, such as it is, remains visible to the naked eye: eras are stacked east to west along the waterfront like some century-old archaeological dig—from cobblestone, late-Victorian Gastown to shiny postmodern glass cathedrals of commerce grazing the sunset.

Long a port city in a resource-based province, Vancouver is relatively new to tourism and, for that matter, to its now-famous laid-back West Coast lifestyle. Most locals mark Expo '86, when the city cleaned up old industrial sites and generated new tourism infrastructure, as the turning point. Little did they know that was a mere dress rehearsal for what was to come: the 2010 Winter Games not only brought Vancouver to the forefront of the world's attention, but was the major impetus to expand the convention center, upgrade many sports and community venues, build a rapid-transit connection between the airport and downtown, and develop the last of Vancouver's former industrial areas. Some land development projects were left struggling after the Games ended. The most controversial of these is the former Athlete's Village, which is only now finding new life as the fashionable hub of a sustainable, upscale, and mixed-housing neighborhood. There is much to see and do in Vancouver, but when time is limited (as it usually is for cruise-ship passengers), the most popular options are a stroll through Gastown and Chinatown, a visit to Granville Island, or a driving or biking tour of Stanley Park. If you have more time, head to the Museum of Anthropology, on the University of British Columbia campus; it's worth a trip.

ESSENTIALS

HOURS

Most stores are open from 10 am to 6 pm, with extended hours on Thursday and Friday until 9 pm. Sunday hours are likely to be from noon to 6 pm. Although many banks are open on Saturday, services may be limited to over-the-counter transactions.

TOURS

Stanley Park Shuttle. The Vancouver Trolley Company runs the hop-on/hop-off Stanley Park Shuttle, a narrated tour within the park that provides frequent (every 15 minutes) transportation to 15 major park sights. Pick it up on Pipeline Road, near the Georgia Street park entrance. Hop-on/hop-off tours around Vancouver operate year-round. ⊠ *Stanley Park, Pipeline Rd., near Georgia St.* ☎ *604/801–5515* ⊕ *www.vancouvertrolley.com* ▱ *C$10 Stanley Park; C$40 full Vancouver circuit.*

VISITOR INFORMATION

For maps and information, stop at the Vancouver Visitors Centre. It's across the street from Canada Place, next door to the Fairmont Waterfront Hotel. Tourism Victoria also offers information on Vancouver accommodation listings, attractions, and guides on its website.

Contacts Vancouver Visitors Centre ⊠ *200 Burrard St.* ☎ *604/683–2000* ⊕ *www.tourismvancouver.com.*

THE CRUISE PORT

Embarkation or disembarkation in Vancouver makes a scenic start or finish to an Alaska cruise. Sailing through Burrard Inlet, ships pass the forested shores of Stanley Park and sail beneath the graceful sweep of the Lions Gate Bridge. Most ships calling at Vancouver dock at the Canada Place cruise-ship terminal on the downtown waterfront, a few minutes' walk from the city center. Its rooftop of dramatic white sails makes it instantly recognizable.

A few vessels depart from the Ballantyne cruise-ship terminal, which is a 10- to 15-minute, C$15 cab ride from downtown.

Transfers between the airport and the piers are offered by the cruise lines, either as a fare add-on or, in the case of some luxury cruise lines or small-ship cruise lines, included in the price of your cruise. Cruise-line representatives meet airport arrivals or are present at hotel transfer points to make the process stress-free.

From the south, I–5 from Seattle becomes Highway 99 at the U.S.–Canada border. Vancouver is a three-hour drive (226 km [140 miles]) from Seattle. It's best to avoid border crossings during peak times such as holidays and weekends. Highway 1, the Trans-Canada Highway, enters Vancouver from the east. To avoid traffic, arrive after rush hour (8:30 am).

Vancouver's evening rush-hour traffic starts early—about 3 pm on weekdays. The worst bottlenecks outside the city center are the North Shore bridges, the George Massey Tunnel on Highway 99 south of Vancouver, and Highway 1 through Coquitlam and Surrey. The BC Ministry of Transportation (☎ *800/550–4997* ⊕ *www.drivebc.ca*) has updates.

Port Information Ballantyne Cruise Ship Terminal ⊠ *655 Centennial Rd., Vancouver* ☎ *604/665–9000, 866/284–4271* ⊕ *www.portvancouver.com.* **Canada Place Cruise Ship Terminal** ⊠ *999 Canada Place Way, Vancouver* ☎ *604/665–9000, 866/284-4271* ⊕ *www.portvancouver.com.*

AIRPORT TRANSFERS

Vancouver International Airport is 16 km (10 miles) south of downtown in the suburb of Richmond. It takes 30 to 45 minutes to get downtown from the airport.

Taxi stands are in front of the terminal building; the fare from the airport to downtown is about C$35 (about C$40 to Ballantyne Pier). Local cab companies include Black Top Cabs and Yellow Cabs, both of which serve the whole Vancouver area. Limousine service from AeroCar costs about C$50 one-way. There is no shared shuttle service between the airport and downtown Vancouver.

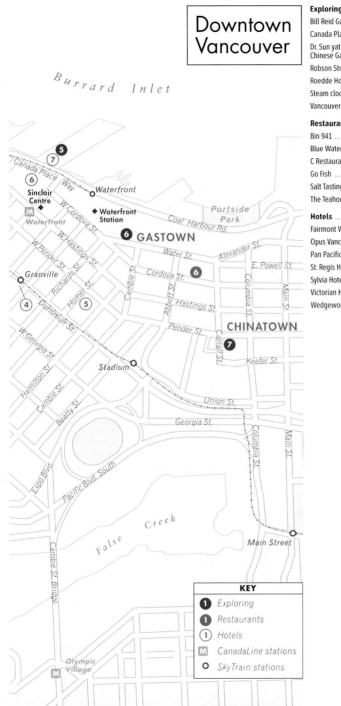

Downtown Vancouver

KEY

① Exploring

① Restaurants

① Hotels

Ⓜ CanadaLine stations

○ SkyTrain stations

The Canada Line, part of Vancouver's rapid transit system, runs passengers directly from Vancouver International Airport to the Canada Place cruise-ship terminal (and stops en route) in just 25 minutes. The station is inside the airport, on Level 4 between the domestic and international terminals. The trains, which are fully wheelchair accessible and allow plenty of room for luggage, begin running before 5 am and leave every four to six minutes during peak hours, and every 10 minutes from 11 pm until end of service (between 12:30 and 1:15 am). Fares are C$5 plus the cost of a fare for the time of day you're traveling (C$2.75–C$4). Passes such as DayPasses or FareSavers are exempt from the extra C$5 charge. Visit TransLink's website for more fare details.

Airport Information Vancouver International Airport (YVR) ☎ *604/207-7077* ⊕ *www.yvr.ca.*

Airport Transfers AeroCar ☎ *604/298-1000, 888/821-0021* ⊕ *www.aerocar.ca.* **Airport Link Shuttle** ☎ *604/594-3333* ⊕ *www.airportlinkshuttle.com.* **Black Top and Checker Cabs** ☎ *604/731-1111* ⊕ *www.btccabs.ca.* **TransLink** ☎ *604/953-3333* ⊕ *www.translink.ca.* **Yellow Cab** ☎ *604/681-1111* ⊕ *www.yellowcabonline.com.*

PARKING

Vinci Park offers secure underground parking in a two-level garage at Canada Place. Rates are C$23 per day for cruise passengers if reserved in advance. The entrance is at the foot of Howe Street.

Contacts Vinci Park ✉ *999 Canada Place Way, Vancouver* ☎ *604/684-2251, 866/856-8080* ⊕ *www.vinciparkcanadaplace.ca.*

EXPLORING VANCOUVER

Vancouver is easy to navigate. The heart of the city—which includes the downtown area, the Canada Place cruise-ship terminal, Gastown, Chinatown, Stanley Park, and the West End high-rise residential neighborhood—sits on a peninsula hemmed in by English Bay and the Pacific Ocean to the west; by False Creek, the inlet home to Granville Island, to the south; and by Burrard Inlet, the working port of the city, to the north, past which loom the North Shore mountains. Indeed, they become your compass point if ever you feel that you're getting lost.

DOWNTOWN AND THE WEST END

Fodor's Choice **Bill Reid Gallery.** Named after one of British Columbia's preeminent
★ artists, Bill Reid (1920–98), this small aboriginal gallery is as much a legacy of his works as it is a showcase of current First Nations artists. Displays include wood carvings, jewelry, print, and sculpture, and programs often include artist talks and themed exhibitions such as basket weaving. Reid is best known for his bronze statue *The Spirit of Haida Gwaii, The Jade Canoe*—measuring 12 feet by 20 feet; the original is an iconic meeting place at the Vancouver International Airport, and its image is on the back of the Canadian $20 bill. More Bill Reid pieces are at the Museum of Anthropology. ✉ *639 Hornby St., Downtown* ☎ *604/682–3455* ⊕ *www.billreidgallery.ca* 🎫 *C$10* ⏱ *Wed.–Sun. 11–5.*

Beaches might not be the first thing you think of in Vancouver, but in summer, the shores of Kits Beach, Second Beach in Stanley Park, and English Bay in the West End are quite the hot spots.

Canada Place. Extending four city blocks (about a mile and a half) north into Burrard Inlet, this complex mimics the style and size of a luxury ocean liner, complete with exterior esplanades and a landmark roofline that resembles five sails—actually made with NASA-invented material, a Teflon-coated fiberglass once used in astronaut space suits. Home to Vancouver's main cruise-ship terminal, Canada Place can accommodate up to four liners at once. The **Canadian Trail** on the west side of the building features displays about the country's provinces and territories; use your smartphone or tablet to access multimedia content along the way: there's free Wi-Fi. Also check out the **War of 1812 Experience,** which commemorates the bicentennial of this conflict. Canada Place is also home to the posh **Pan Pacific Hotel,** and both buildings make up the **Vancouver Convention Centre** (☎ *604/689–8232*). A waterfront promenades winds all the way to (and around) Stanley Park, presenting spectacular vantage points from which to view Burrard Inlet and the North Shore Mountains; plaques posted at intervals offer historical information about the city and its waterfront. ✉ *999 Canada Place Way, Downtown* ☎ *604/775–7200* ⊕ *www.canadaplace.ca.*

Robson Street. Running from the Terry Fox Plaza outside BC Place Stadium down to the West End, Robson is Vancouver's busiest shopping street, where fashionistas hang out at see-and-be-seen sidewalk cafés, chain stores, and high-end boutiques. Most of the designer action takes place between Jervis and Burrard streets and stays that way into the evening with buskers and entertainers. ⊕ *www.robsonstreet.ca.*

OFF THE
BEATEN
PATH
Roedde House Museum. Two blocks south of Robson Street, on a pretty residential street, the Roedde (pronounced *roh*-dee) House Museum is an 1893 house in the Queen Anne Revival style, set among Victoriana gardens. Tours of the restored, antiques-furnished interior take about an hour. On Sunday, tours are followed by tea and cookies. The gardens (free) can be visited anytime. ⊠ *1415 Barclay St., between Broughton and Nicola Sts., West End* ☎ *604/684–7040* ⊕ *www.roeddehouse.org* ✉ *C$5; Sun. C$8, including tea* ☉ *Tues.–Sun. 1–4.*

Vancouver Art Gallery. Painter Emily Carr's haunting evocations of the British Columbian hinterland are among the attractions at western Canada's largest art gallery. Carr (1871–1945), a grocer's daughter from Victoria, fell in love with the wilderness around her and shocked middle-class Victorian society by running off to paint it. Her work accentuates the mysticism and the danger of B.C.'s wilderness, and records the diminishing presence of Native cultures during that era (there's something of a renaissance now). The gallery, which also hosts touring historical and contemporary exhibitions, is housed in a 1911 courthouse that Canadian architect Arthur Erickson redesigned in the early 1980s as part of the Robson Square redevelopment. Stone lions guard the steps to the parklike Georgia Street side; the main entrance is accessed from Robson Square or Hornby Street. ⊠ *750 Hornby St., Downtown* ☎ *604/662–4719* ⊕ *www.vanartgallery.bc.ca* ✉ *C$21; higher for some exhibits; by donation Tues. 5–9* ☉ *Wed.–Mon. 10–5, Tues. 10–9.*

GASTOWN AND CHINATOWN

Despite the city's rapid gentrification, you might come across one or two seedy corners: it's all pretty safe by day, but you might prefer to cab it at night.

Dr. Sun Yat-Sen Chinese Garden. The first authentic Ming Dynasty–style garden outside China, this small garden was built in 1986 by 52 Chinese artisans from Suzhou. It incorporates design elements and traditional materials from several of Suzhou's centuries-old private gardens. No power tools, screws, or nails were used in the construction. Guided tours (45 minutes long), included in the ticket price, are conducted on the hour between mid-June and the end of August (call ahead or check the website for off-season tour times); tours are valuable for understanding the philosophy and symbolism that are central to the garden's design. A concert series, including classical, Asian, world, jazz, and sacred music, plays on Friday evenings in July, August, and early September. The free public park next door is also designed as a traditional Chinese garden. ■ **TIP→ Covered walkways make this a good rainy-day choice.** ⊠ *578 Carrall St., Chinatown* ☎ *604/662–3207* ⊕ *www.vancouverchinesegarden.com* ✉ *C$14* ☉ *May–mid-June and Sept., daily 10–6; mid-June–Aug., daily 9:30–7; Oct., daily 10–4:30; Nov.–Apr., Tues.–Sun. 10–4:30.*

Steam Clock. An underground steam system, which also heats many local buildings, supplies the world's first steam clock—possibly Vancouver's most-photographed attraction. On the quarter hour a steam whistle rings out the Westminster chimes, and on the hour a huge cloud of steam spews from the apparatus. The ingenious design, based on an 1875 mechanism, was built in 1977 by Ray Saunders of Landmark Clocks to commemorate the community effort that saved Gastown from demolition. ⊠ *Water St. at Cambie St., Gastown.*

STANLEY PARK

Fodor's Choice ★ A 1,000-acre wilderness park, only blocks from the downtown section of a major city, is a rare treasure. Vancouverites use it, protect it, and love it with such zeal that when it was proposed that the 120-year-old Hollow Tree be axed

> **NIGHT MARKET**
>
> If you're in the area in summer on a Friday, Saturday, or Sunday, check out Chinatown's small and bustling Night Market for food and tchotchkes: the 200 block of East Pender and Keefer are closed to traffic from 6:30 to 11 pm (until midnight on Saturday). Or hop aboard the SkyTrain for a 20-minute ride to Bridgeport, and one of the two much larger night markets in Richmond.

because of safety concerns, citizens rallied, raised funds, and literally engineered its salvation.

Stanley Park is, perhaps, the single most prized possession of Vancouverites, who make use of it fervently to cycle, walk, jog, Rollerblade, play cricket and tennis, and enjoy outdoor art shows and theater performances alongside attractions such as the renowned aquarium.

When a storm swept across the park's shores in December 2006, it destroyed close to 10,000 trees as well as parts of the perimeter seawall. Locals contributed thousands of dollars to the cleanup and replanting effort in addition to the monies set aside by local authorities. The storm's silver lining was that it cleared some deadwood areas, making room for the reintroduction of many of the park's original species of trees.

GETTING THERE AND AROUND

To get to the park by public transit, take Stanley Park Bus 19 from the corner of Pender and Howe, downtown. It's possible to see the park by car, entering at the foot of Georgia Street and driving counterclockwise around the one-way Stanley Park Drive.

Prospect Point. At 211 feet, Prospect Point is the highest point in the park and provides striking views of the Lions Gate Bridge (watch for cruise ships passing below), the North Shore, and Burrard Inlet. There's also a year-round souvenir shop, a snack bar with terrific ice cream, and a restaurant. From the seawall, you can see where cormorants build their seaweed nests along the cliff ledges.

Fodor's Choice ★ **Seawall.** The seawall path, a 9-km (5½-mile) paved shoreline route popular with walkers, cyclists, and in-line skaters, is one of several car-free zones within the park. If you have the time (about a half day) and the energy, strolling the entire seawall is an exhilarating experience. It extends an additional mile east past the marinas, cafés, and waterfront condominiums of Coal Harbour to Canada Place downtown, so you could start your walk or ride from there. From the south side of the park, the seawall continues for another 28 km (17 miles) along Vancouver's waterfront, to the University of British Columbia, allowing for a

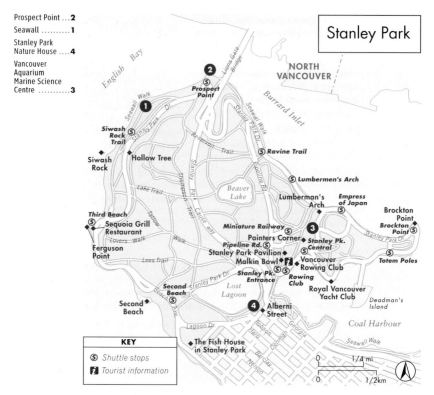

Stanley Park

KEY

⑤ Shuttle stops

🛈 Tourist information

pleasant, if ambitious, day's bike ride. Along the seawall, cyclists must wear helmets and stay on their side of the path. Within Stanley Park, cyclists must ride in a counterclockwise direction.

The seawall can get crowded on summer weekends, but inside the park is a 28-km (17-mile) network of peaceful walking and cycling paths through old- and second-growth forest. The wheelchair-accessible Beaver Lake Interpretive Trail is a good choice if you're interested in park ecology. Take a map—they're available at the park-information booth and many of the concession stands—and don't go into the woods alone or after dusk.

Stanley Park Nature House. Vancouver's only ecology center is a treasure trove of information and showcases Stanley Park's true natural beauty with a host of programs and guided walks. The Nature House is on the south shore of Lost Lagoon, at the foot of Alberni Street. ✉ *Stanley Park, Alberni St., north end, under the viewing platform* ☎ *604/257–8544* ⊕ *www.stanleyparkecology.ca* ⊗ *July and Aug., Tues.–Sun. 10–5; Sept.–June, weekends 10–4.*

FAMILY **Vancouver Aquarium Marine Science Centre.** Massive floor-to-ceiling windows let you come face-to-face with beluga whales, sea otters, sea lions, dolphins, and harbor seals at this award-winning research and educational facility. In the Amazon Gallery you walk through a rain-forest jungle populated with piranhas, caimans, and tropical birds in the Amazon Gallery; in summer, hundreds of free-flying butterflies add to the mix. The Tropic Zone is home to exotic freshwater and saltwater life, including clown fish, moray eels, and black-tip reef sharks. Other displays, many with hands-on features for kids, show the underwater life of coastal British Columbia and the Canadian Arctic. Beluga whale, sea lion, and dolphin shows, as well as dive shows (where divers swim with aquatic life, including sharks) are held daily. Be sure to check out the "4-D" film experience; it's a multisensory show that puts mist, smell, and wind into the 3-D equation. For an extra fee, you can help the trainers feed and train otters, belugas, and sea lions. There's also a café and a gift shop. Be prepared for lines on weekends and school holidays. ■TIP→ In summer, the quietest time to visit is before 11 am or after 4 pm; in other seasons, the crowds are smaller before noon or after 2 pm. ⊠ *845 Avison Way, Stanley Park* ☎ *604/659–3474* ⊕ *www. vanaqua.org* ✉ *C$30* ⏱ *July–Labor Day, daily 9:30–6; Labor Day– June, daily 9:30–5:30.*

Fodor's Choice **GRANVILLE ISLAND**
★ This 35-acre peninsula in False Creek, just south of downtown Vancouver, is home to one of North America's most successful urban-redevelopment schemes. Once a derelict industrial site, Granville Island is now a vibrant urban park, with a bustling public market, several theaters, galleries, crafts shops, and artisans' studios.

GETTING THERE AND AROUND
The mini Aquabus ferries are a favorite way to get to Granville Island (it's about a two-minute ride); they depart from the south end of Hornby Street, a 15-minute walk from downtown Vancouver. The Aquabus delivers passengers across False Creek to the Granville Island Public Market. The slightly larger False Creek ferries leave every five minutes for Granville Island from a dock behind the Vancouver Aquatic Centre, on Beach Avenue. The latter offers shuttle service to Vanier Park (home to a summer-long Shakespeare festival, Bard on the Beach), and is the drop-off point for Kits Beach. Still another option is to take a 20-minute ride on a TransLink bus: from Waterfront Station or stops on Granville Street, take False Creek South Bus 50 to the edge of the island. Buses 4 UBC and 7 Dunbar will also take you within a few minutes' walk of the island. The market is a short walk from the bus, ferry, or tram stop. If you drive, know that finding a parking space can be difficult, especially if you're looking for one of the few spaces that are free for up to three hours. Paid parking, either outside or in one of the five garages on the island, is C$3.50 per hour to a maximum of C$15. If your schedule is tight, you can tour Granville Island in two to three hours. If you like to shop, you could spend a full day.

TOP ATTRACTIONS
Fodor's Choice **Granville Island Public Market.** Dozens of stalls in this 50,000-square-
★ foot building sell locally grown fruits and vegetables direct from the farm and other produce from farther afield; others stock crafts, chocolates, artisan cheeses and pastas, fish, meat, flowers, and exotic foods. On Thursday in summer, farmers sell fruit and vegetables from trucks outside. At the north end of the market, you can pick up a snack,

DID YOU KNOW?

The view from Stanley Park out over the marina and Coal Harbour shows just how close this fabulous 1,000-plus-acre park is to downtown.

lunch, or coffee from one of the many prepared-food vendors. The Market Courtyard, on the waterside, not only offers some great shots of the city from a different perspective, but it's a good place to catch street entertainers—be prepared to get roped into the action, if only to check the padlocks of an escape artist's gear. Weekends can get madly busy. ☒ *1689 Johnston St., Granville Island* ☎ *604/666–6655* ⊕ *www. granvilleisland.com* ☉ *Daily 9–7.*

THE WEST SIDE AND KITSILANO

Fodor's Choice **Museum of Anthropology.** Part of the University of British Columbia, the
★ MOA has one of the world's leading collections of Northwest Coast First Nations art. The Great Hall displays dramatic cedar poles, bentwood boxes, and canoes adorned with traditional Northwest Coast–painted designs. On clear days, the gallery's 50-foot-tall windows reveal a striking backdrop of mountains and sea. Another highlight is the work of the late Bill Reid, one of Canada's most respected Haida artists. In *The Raven and the First Men* (1980), carved in yellow cedar, he tells a Haida story of creation. Reid's gold-and-silver jewelry work is also on display, as are exquisite carvings of gold, silver, and argillite (a black shale found on Haida Gwaii, also known as the Queen Charlotte Islands) by other First Nations artists. The museum's visible storage section displays, in drawers and cases, contain thousands of examples of tools, textiles, masks, and other artifacts from around the world. The Koerner Ceramics Gallery contains 600 pieces from 15th- to 19th-century Europe. Behind the museum are two Haida houses, set on the cliff over the water. Free guided tours—given several times daily (call for confirm times)—are immensely informative. For an extra C$5 you can rent a VUEguide, an electronic device which senses where you are in the museum and shows relevant artist interviews, archival footage, and photographs of the artifacts in their original contexts, on a handheld screen. Arthur Erickson designed the cliff-top museum which also has an excellent book and fine-art shop and a café. To reach the museum by transit, take any UBC-bound bus from Granville Street downtown to the university bus loop, a 10-minute walk from the museum. ■ TIP→ Pay parking is available in the Rose Garden parking lot, across Marine Drive from the museum. ☒ *University of British Columbia, 6393 N.W. Marine Dr., Point Grey* ☎ *604/822–5087* ⊕ *www.moa.ubc.ca* ☒ *C$16.75, Tues. 5–9 C$9* ☉ *Late May–mid-Oct., Tues. 10–9, Wed.–Mon. 10–5; mid-Oct.–late May, Tues. 10–9, Wed.–Sun. 10–5.*

SHOPPING

Unlike many cities where suburban malls have taken over, Vancouver is full of individual boutiques and specialty shops. Ethnic markets, art galleries, gourmet-food shops, and high-fashion outlets abound, and both Asian and First Nations influences in crafts, home furnishings, and foods are quite prevalent.

Stretching from Burrard to Bute, **Robson Street** is the city's main fashion-shopping and people-watching artery. The Gap and Banana Republic have their flagship stores here, as do Canadian fashion outlets

Take a walk and explore the outdoor totem poles at Vancouver's Museum of Anthropology.

Club Monaco and Roots. Souvenir shops and cafés fill the gaps. One block north of Robson, **Alberni Street** is geared to the higher-income visitor, and is where you'll find duty-free shopping. At the stores in and around Alberni, and around Burrard, you'll find names such as Tiffany & Co., Louis Vuitton, Gucci, Coach, Hermés, and Betsey Johnson. Treasure hunters like the 300 block of **West Cordova Street** in **Gastown**, where offbeat shops sell curios, vintage clothing, and locally designed clothes. Bustling **Chinatown**—centered on Pender and Main streets—is full of Chinese bakeries, restaurants, herbalists, tea merchants, and import shops. Frequently described as Vancouver's SoHo, **Yaletown** on the north bank of False Creek is home to boutiques and restaurants—many in converted warehouses—that cater to a trendy, moneyed crowd. On the south side of False Creek, **Granville Island** has a lively food market and a wealth of galleries, crafts shops, and artisans' studios.

NATIVE CRAFTS

Fodor'sChoice
★
Hill's Native Art. This highly respected store has Vancouver's largest selection of First Nations art. The main floor is crammed with souvenirs, keepsakes, and high-quality pieces, including carvings, masks, and drums. If you think that's impressive, head upstairs for collector one-of-a-kind pieces and limited editions. ⊠ *165 Water St., Gastown* ☎ *604/685–4249* ⊕ *www.hills.ca.*

NIGHTLIFE

For information on events, pick up a free copy of the *Georgia Straight*, available at cafés and bookstores around town, or look in the entertainment section of the *Vancouver Sun* (Thursday's paper has listings). Tickets for many venues can be booked via Ticketmaster either by phone or online. Tickets Tonight sells half-price day-of-the-event tickets and full-price advance tickets to the theater, concerts, festivals, and other performing arts events around the city. It's at the Vancouver Tourist Info Centre.

Ticketmaster ☎ *855/985–5000* ⊕ *www.ticketmaster.ca.* **Tickets Tonight** ✉ *200 Burrard St., Downtown* ☎ *604/684–2787* ⊕ *www.ticketstonight.ca.*

Fodor'sChoice ★ **The Diamond.** At the top of a narrow staircase above Maple Tree Square, the Diamond occupies one of the city's oldest buildings. A bartending school by day, cool hangout and cocktail lounge by night, the venue's official name is the Diamond Preparatory School For All Things Drinks. Standing at the bar, co-owner Josh Pape is like a conductor at the symphony. You can choose among "boozy," "proper," or "delicate" options on the drinks menu. Many are one-of-a-kind concoctions: a Colin's Lawn puts sake and mint together; the Buck Buck Mule is a refreshing mix of gin, sherry, cucumber juice, cilantro, lime juice, and ginger beer; and the Tequila Martinez features tequila, vermouth, Lillet, peach bitters, and an orange twist. ✉ *6 Powell St., at Carrall St., Gastown* ☎ *604/568–8272* ⊕ *www.di6mond.com.*

Fodor'sChoice ★ **Pourhouse Vancouver.** The brick-and-beam 1910 architecture combines antiques, a 38-foot bar, and a menu of classic cocktails. Most are inspired from the 1862 bartending bible *How to Mix Drinks* by Jerry Thomas, the first bartending manual ever to put oral traditions to print with recipes for mint juleps, sloe gin fizzes, and more. Test the bartender's skill by asking for a Pick-Me-Up, a Chain-Lightning, or a Corpse Reviver. Parties of six or more can book family-style dinners: everything is set in the center of the kitchen table, and it's a help-yourself affair, just like at home. ✉ *162 Water St., Gastown* ☎ *604/568–7022* ⊕ *www.pourhousevancouver.com.*

Yaletown Brewing Company. In a renovated warehouse with a glassed-in brewery turning out several tasty beers, this always-crowded gastropub and patio has a lively singles' scene. Despite its popularity it still feels like a neighborhood place. ✉ *1111 Mainland St., Yaletown* ☎ *604/681–2739* ⊕ *www.markjamesgroup.com/yaletown.html.*

WHERE TO EAT

A diverse gastronomic experience awaits you in cosmopolitan Vancouver. A wave of Asian immigration and tourism has brought a proliferation of upscale Asian eateries. Cutting-edge restaurants currently perfecting and defining Pacific Northwest fare—including homegrown regional favorites such as salmon and oysters, accompanied by British Columbia wines—have become some of the city's leading attractions.

You're also spoiled for choice when it comes to casual and budget dining. Good choices include Asian cafés or any of the pubs listed in the Nightlife section; many have both an adults-only pub and a separate restaurant section where kids are welcome. A bylaw bans smoking indoors in all Vancouver restaurants, bars, and pubs.

Vancouver dining is fairly informal. Casual but neat dress is appropriate everywhere. A 15% tip is expected. A 5% sales tax (GST) is added to the bill.

DOWNTOWN AND THE WEST END

$$ ✕ **Bin 941.** Part tapas restaurant, part up-tempo bar, this bustling, often
ECLECTIC noisy hole-in-the-wall claims to have launched Vancouver's small-plates trend. Adventurous snack-size dishes change frequently and might include smoked black cod paired with a cauliflower-and-goat-cheese purée, Kobe meat balls, crab cakes topped with burnt-orange chipotle sauce, or braised lamb shank with a spicy pomegranate-date glaze. Snack on one or two, or order a bunch and have a feast. The Bin is open until 2 am most nights. $ *Average main: C$16* ✉ *941 Davie St., Downtown* ☎ *604/683–1246* ⊕ *www.bin941.com* ⌖ *Reservations not accepted* ☽ *No lunch.*

$$$$ ✕ **C Restaurant.** This is a well-deserved splurge for fish fans. Dishes such
SEAFOOD as seared scallops paired with pork belly, apple beignets, and foie gras
Fodor's Choice in a burnt apple sauce; trout served with crispy squid and a chorizo-
★ lemon risotto; and lingcod with braised kale and smoked and pureed artichoke have established C as Vancouver's most innovative seafood restaurant. If you've the time and inclination, the elaborate eight-course tasting menu (C$95) with optional wine pairings is stunning in taste, presentation, and flawless service. Both the ultramodern interior and the waterside patio overlook False Creek, but dine before dark to enjoy the view. $ *Average main: C$33* ✉ *2–1600 Howe St., Downtown* ☎ *604/681–1164* ⊕ *www.crestaurant.com.*

GASTOWN AND CHINATOWN

$$ ✕ **Salt Tasting Room.** If your idea of a perfect lunch or light supper
ECLECTIC revolves around fine cured meats, artisanal cheeses, and a glass of wine from a wide-ranging list, find your way to this sleek space in a decidedly unsleek Gastown location. The restaurant has no kitchen and simply assembles its first-quality provisions that change daily—perhaps smoked beef tenderloin or British Columbian–made Camembert, with accompanying condiments—into artfully composed grazers' delight. The whole shebang is more like an upscale picnic than a full meal. There's no sign out front, so look for the saltshaker flag in Blood Alley, off Abbott Street. $ *Average main: C$16* ✉ *45 Blood Alley, Gastown* ☎ *604/633–1912* ⊕ *www.salttastingroom.com.*

YALETOWN AND FALSE CREEK

$$$$ ✕ **Blue Water Cafe & Raw Bar.** Executive chef Frank Pabst features both
SEAFOOD popular and lesser-known local seafood (including frequently over-
Fodor's Choice looked varieties like mackerel or herring) at this fashionable fish res-
★ taurant. You might start with Gulf Island scallops baked with tomatoes, olives, and capers; Dungeness crab and white asparagus *panna cotta*; or a seafood tower, ideal for sharing. Main dishes are seafood-centric, too—perhaps white sturgeon with beets, or arctic char with trout caviar and pearl couscous. Ask the staff to recommend wine pairings from the B.C.–focused list. You can dine in the warmly lighted interior or outside

Coming nose-to-nose with a beluga whale—these underwater views are star attractions at the Vancouver Aquarium.

on the former loading dock that's now a lovely terrace. ■TIP→ The sushi chef turns out both classic and new creations—they're pricey but rank among the city's best. $ *Average main: C$34* ✉ *1095 Hamilton St., Yaletown* ☎ *604/688–8078* ⊕ *www.bluewatercafe.net* ⊗ *No lunch.*

STANLEY PARK

$$$
MODERN
CANADIAN

✗ **The Teahouse in Stanley Park.** The former officers' mess at Ferguson Point in Stanley Park is a prime location for water views by day, and for watching sunsets at dusk. The Pacific Northwest menu is not especially innovative, but its broad appeal will please those looking for Haida Gwaii halibut, rack of lamb, steaks, and a host of other options, including gluten-free pasta. Lunch menus include popular (and somewhat gourmet) burgers, soups, and sandwiches. Various tasting boards—charcuterie, cheese, seafood, and vegetarian options—make for good grazing in the afternoon. In summer you can dine on the patio. $ *Average main: C$25* ✉ *7501 Stanley Park Dr., Stanley Park* ☎ *604/669–3281* ⊕ *www.vancouverdine.com.*

GRANVILLE ISLAND

$
SEAFOOD
Fodor'sChoice
★

✗ **Go Fish.** If the weather's fine, head for this seafood stand on the seawall overlooking the docks beside Granville Island. The menu is short—highlights include fish-and-chips, grilled salmon or tuna sandwiches, and fish tacos—but the quality is first-rate. It's hugely popular, and on sunny summer days the waits can be maddening, so try to avoid the busiest times: noon to 2 pm and 5 pm to closing (which is at dusk). Since there are just a few outdoor tables, be prepared to take your food to go. $ *Average main: C$10* ✉ *Fisherman's Wharf, 1505 W. 1st Ave., Kitsilano* ☎ *604/730–5040* ⊕ *www.bin941.com* ⊗ *Closed Mon. No dinner.*

WHERE TO STAY

Accommodations in Vancouver range from luxurious waterfront hotels to neighborhood B&Bs and basic European-style pensions. Many of the best choices are in the downtown core, either in the central business district or in the West End near Stanley Park. From mid-October through May, rates throughout the city can drop as much as 50%. Most Vancouver hotels are completely nonsmoking in both rooms and public areas.

For expanded hotel reviews, visit Fodors.com.

DOWNTOWN AND THE WEST END

$$$$
HOTEL

Fairmont Waterfront. This luxuriously modern 23-story hotel sits across the street from the cruise-ship terminal and the convention center, but it's the floor-to-ceiling windows with ocean, park, and mountain views that really make this hotel special. **Pros:** harbor views; proximity to the waterfront; terraced pool. **Cons:** long elevator queues; busy lobby lounge. $ *Rooms from: C$379* ⊠ *900 Canada Place Way, Downtown* ☎ *604/540–4509* ⊕ *www.fairmont.com* ⤳ *489 rooms, 29 suites* ⊚ *No meals.*

$$$$
HOTEL

Pan Pacific Vancouver. Located in the waterfront Canada Place complex, the sophisticated Pan Pacific has easy access to the city's convention center and the main cruise-ship terminal. **Pros:** lovely harbor views; staff has a "go the extra mile" attitude. **Cons:** atrium is open to the convention center, so it's often full of business executives talking shop. $ *Rooms from: C$369* ⊠ *999 Canada Pl., Downtown* ☎ *604/662–8111, 800/663–1515 in Canada, 800/937–1515 in U.S.* ⊕ *www.panpacificvancouver.com* ⤳ *465 rooms, 39 suites.*

$$$
HOTEL

St. Regis Hotel. While its renovations are clearly inspired by New York, this 1916 boutique hotel retains a distinctly Canadian feel. **Pros:** hot location; in-room wine delivery service; full breakfast and other perks. **Cons:** no views; slow elevator sometimes make the stairs a faster option (you can view original artwork at every turn in the stairwell). $ *Rooms from: C$239* ⊠ *602 Dunsmuir St., Downtown* ☎ *604/681–1135, 800/770–7929* ⊕ *www.stregishotel.com* ⤳ *50 rooms, 15 suites* ⊚ *Breakfast.*

$$
HOTEL
Fodor's Choice
★

Sylvia Hotel. This Virginia-creeper-covered 1912 heritage building is popular because of its affordable rates and its near-perfect location: a stone's throw from the beach on scenic English Bay, two blocks from Stanley Park, and a 20-minute walk from Robson Street. **Pros:** beachfront location; close to restaurants; a good place to mingle with the locals. **Cons:** older building; parking can be difficult; walk to downtown is slightly uphill. $ *Rooms from: C$189* ⊠ *1154 Gilford St., West End* ☎ *604/681–9321* ⊕ *www.sylviahotel.com* ⤳ *97 rooms, 22 suites* ⊚ *No meals.*

$$
B&B/INN

Victorian Hotel. Budget hotels can be handsome, as in the gleaming hardwood floors, high ceilings, and chandeliers at this prettily restored 1898 European-style pension. **Pros:** Gastown location; complimentary breakfast; historical vibe. **Cons:** the neighborhood is relatively safe, but you'll probably want to take a cab after midnight. $ *Rooms from: C$179* ⊠ *514 Homer St., Downtown* ☎ *604/681–6369, 877/681–6369* ⊕ *www.victorianhotel.ca* ⤳ *39 rooms, 18 with bath* ⊚ *Breakfast.*

$$$$
HOTEL
Fodor's Choice
★

⌂ Wedgewood Hotel and Spa. A member of the exclusive Relais & Châteaux Group, the lavish Wedgewood is owned by a woman who cares fervently about her guests. **Pros:** personalized service; great location close to shops; destination restaurant and lounge. **Cons:** small size means it books up quickly. ⑤ *Rooms from: C$320* ⊠ *845 Hornby St., Downtown* ☎ *604/689–7777, 800/663–0666* ⊕ *www.wedgewoodhotel. com* ⟿ *41 rooms, 43 suites.*

YALETOWN AND FALSE CREEK

$$$
HOTEL
Fodor's Choice
★

⌂ Opus Vancouver Hotel. The design team had a ball with this boutique hotel, creating fictitious characters and decorating rooms for each. **Pros:** great Yaletown location, right by rapid transit; funky and hip vibe; the lobby bar is a fashionable meeting spot. **Cons:** surrounding neighborhood is mostly high-rises; trendy nightspots nearby can be noisy at night. ⑤ *Rooms from: C$279* ⊠ *322 Davie St., Yaletown* ☎ *604/642–6787, 866/642–6787* ⊕ *www.opushotel.com* ⟿ *85 rooms, 11 suites* ⧖ *No meals.*

WHITTIER

By Teeka A. Ballas

The entryway to Whittier is unlike any other: a 2½-mile drive atop railroad tracks through the Anton Anderson Memorial Tunnel, cut through the Chugach Mountain Range. Once on the other side of the tunnel, you enter the mysterious world of Whittier, the remnants of a military town developed in World War II. The only way to get to Whittier was by boat or train until the tunnel opened to traffic in 2000.

This hamlet, sitting at the base of snow-covered peaks at the head of Passage Canal on the Kenai Peninsula, has an intriguing history. During World War II the U.S. Army constructed a port in Whittier and built the Hodge and Buckner buildings to house soldiers. These enormous monoliths are eerily reminiscent of Soviet-era communal apartment buildings. The Hodge Building (now called Begich Towers) houses almost all of Whittier's 180 year-round residents. The town averages 30 feet of snow in the winter, and in summer gets a considerable amount of rainfall. Whittier's draw is primarily fishing, but there are a number of activities to be had on Prince William Sound, including kayaking and glacier tours with some of the best glacier viewing in South Central Alaska.

Whittier is very small, and there is not much to look at in town, but the location is unbeatable. Surrounding peaks cradle alpine glaciers, and when the summer weather melts the huge winter snow load, you can catch glimpses of the brilliant blue ice underneath. Sheer cliffs drop into Passage Canal and provide nesting places for flocks of black-legged kittiwakes, sea otters and harbor seals cavort in the small-boat harbor, and salmon return to spawn in nearby streams. A short boat ride out into the sound reveals tidewater glaciers, and an alert wildlife watcher can catch sight of mountain goats clinging to the mountainsides and black bears patrolling the beaches and hillsides in their constant search for food.

ESSENTIALS
HOURS
Seasonal shops and restaurants will be open when a ship is in port.

Continued on page 213

KEEPERS OF THE DEEP:
A LOOK AT ALASKA'S WHALES

It's unforgettable: a massive, barnacle-encrusted humpback breaches skyward from the placid waters of an Alaskan inlet, shattering the silence with a thundering display of grace, power, and beauty. Welcome to Alaska's coastline.

Alaska's cold, nutrient-rich waters offer a bounty of marine life that's matched by few regions on earth. Eight species of whales frequent the state's near-shore waters, some migrating thousands of miles each year to partake of Alaska's marine buffet. The state's most famous cetaceans (the scientific classification of marine mammals that includes whales, dolphins, and porpoises) are the humpback whale, the gray whale, and the orca (a.k.a. the killer whale).

(top) A breaching humpback (left) An orca whale

BEST REGIONS TO VIEW WHALES

Whales can be viewed throughout the world; after all, they are migratory animals. But thanks to its pristine environment, diversity of cetacean species, and jaw-dropping beauty, Alaska is perhaps the planet's best whale-watching locale.

From April through October, humpbacks visit many of Alaska's coastal regions, including the Bering Sea, the Aleutian Islands, and Prince William Sound. The **Inside Passage,** though, is the best place to see them: it's home to a migratory population of up to 600 humpbacks. Good bets for whale-viewing include taking a trip on the **Alaska Marine Highway,** spending time in **Glacier Bay National Park,** or taking a day cruise out of any of Southeast's main towns. While most humpbacks return to

Mutually curious!

Hawaiian waters in the winter, some spend the whole year in Southeast Alaska.

Gray whales favor the coastal waters of the Pacific, which terminate in the Bering Sea. Their healthy population—some studies estimate that 30,000 gray whales populate the west coast of North America—make

THE HUMPBACK: Musical, Breaching Giant

Humpbacks' flukes allow them to breach so effectively that they can propel two-thirds of their massive bodies out of the water.

Known for their spectacular breaching and unique whale songs, humpbacks are captivating. Most spend their winters in the balmy waters off the Hawaiian Islands, where females, or sows, give birth. Come springtime, humpbacks set off on a 3,000-mile swim to their Alaskan feeding grounds.

Southeast Alaska is home to one of the world's only groups of bubble-net feeding humpbacks. Bubble-netting is a cooperative hunting technique in which one humpback circles below a school of baitfish while exhaling a "net" of bubbles, causing the fish to gather. Other humpbacks then feed at will from the deliciously dense group of fish.

The Song of the Humpback

All whale species communicate sonically, but the humpback is the most musical. During mating season, males emit haunting, songlike calls that can last for up to 30 minutes at a time. Most scientists attribute the songs to flirtatious, territorial, or competitive behaviors.

QUICK FACTS:

Scientific name: *Megaptera novaeangliae*

Length: Up to 50 ft.

Weight: Up to 90,000 pounds (45 tons)

Coloring: Dark blue to black, with barnacles and knobby, lighter-colored flippers

Life span: 30 to 40 years

Reproduction: One calf every 2 to 3 years; calves are generally 12 feet long at birth, weighing up to 2,000 pounds (1 ton)

them relatively easy to spot in the spring and early summer months, especially around **Sitka** and **Kodiak Island** and south of the **Kenai Peninsula**, where numerous whale-watching cruises depart from Seward into **Resurrection Bay.**

Orcas populate nearly all of Alaska's coastal regions. They're most commonly viewed in the **Inside Passage** and **Prince William Sound**, where they reside year-round. A jaunt on the Alaska Marine Highway is one option, but so is a kayaking or day-cruising trip out of **Whittier** to Prince William Sound.

When embarking on a whale-watching excursion, don't forget rain gear, a camera, and binoculars!

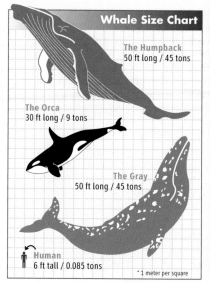

Whale Size Chart

The Humpback
50 ft long / 45 tons

The Orca
30 ft long / 9 tons

The Gray
50 ft long / 45 tons

Human
6 ft tall / 0.085 tons

* 1 meter per square

4

THE GRAY WHALE: Migrating Leviathan

Though the average lifespan of a gray whale is 50 years, one individual was reported to reach 77 years of age—a real old-timer.

While frequenting Alaska during the long days of summer, gray whales tend to stay close to the coastline. They endure the longest migration of any mammal on earth—some travel 14,000 mi each way between Alaska's Bering Sea and their mating grounds in sunny Baja California.

Gray whales are bottom-feeders that stir up sediment on the sea floor, then use their baleen—a comblike collection of long, stiff hairs inside their mouths—to filter out sediment and trap small crustaceans and tube worms.

Their predilection for near-shore regions, coupled with their easygoing demeanor—some "friendly" gray whales have even been known to approach small tour boats—cements their spot on the short list of Alaska's favorite cetacean celebrities. (Gray whales aren't always in such amicable spirits: whalers dubbed mother gray whales "devilfish" for the fierce manner in which they protected their young.)

QUICK FACTS:

Scientific name:
Eschrichtius robustus

Length: Up to 50 ft.

Weight: Up to 90,000 pounds (45 tons)

Coloring: Gray and white, usually splotched with lighter growths and barnacles

Life span: 50 years

Reproduction: One calf every 2 years; calves are generally 15 feet long at birth, weighing up to 1,500 pounds (3/4 ton)

AN AGE-OLD CONNECTION

Nearly every major Native group in Alaska has relied on whales for some portion of its diet. The Inupiaq and Yup'ik counted on whales for blubber, oil, meat, and intestines to survive. Aleuts used whale bones to build their semisubterranean homes. Even the Tlingit, for whom food was perennially abundant, considered a beached whale a bounty.

Subsistence whaling lives on in Alaska: although gray-whale hunting was banned in 1996, the Eskimo Whaling Commission permits the state's Native populations to harvest 50 bowhead whales every year.

Other Alaskan whale species:
Bowhead, northern right, minke, fin, and beluga whales also inhabit Alaskan waters.

barnacles

BARNACLES These ragged squatters of the sea live on several species of whales, including humpbacks and gray whales. They're conspicuously absent from smaller marine mammals, such as orcas, dolphins, and porpoises. The reason? Speed. Scientists theorize that barnacles are only able to colonize the slowest-swimming cetacean species, leaving the faster swimmers free from their unwanted drag.

THE ORCA: Conspicuous, Curious Cetacean

Orcas are smaller than grays and humpbacks, and their 17-month gestation period is the longest of any cetacean. They are identified by their white-and-black markings, as well as by the knifelike shape of their dorsal fins, which, in the case of mature males, can reach 6 feet in height.

Pods generally adhere to one of three common classifications: **residents,** which occupy inshore waters and feed primarily on fish; **transients,** which occupy larger ranges and hunt sea lions, squid, sharks, fish, and whales; and **offshores,** about which little is known.

Why the name killer whale? Perhaps for this animal's skilled and fearsome hunting techniques, which are sometimes used on other, often larger, cetaceans.

Perhaps the most recognizable of all the region's marine mammals, orcas (also called killer whales) are playful, inquisitive, and intelligent whales that reside in Alaskan waters year-round. Orcas travel in multigenerational family groups known as pods, which practice cooperative hunting techniques.

QUICK FACTS:

Scientific name:
Orcinus orca

Length: Up to 30 ft.

Weight: Up to 18,000 pounds (9 tons)

Coloring: Smooth, shiny black skin with white eye patches and chin and white belly markings

Life span: 30 to 50 years

Reproduction: One calf every 3 to 5 years; calves are generally 6 feet long at birth, weighing up to 400 pounds (0.2 ton)

THE CRUISE PORT

Ships dock in Whittier, and there is a small cruise terminal. Within easy walking distance of the dock are other seasonal shops and casual restaurants. There are also a couple of lodging options, but most people will prefer Anchorage, which has many more choices. Whittier is reached by rail or road, though both trains and road traffic pass through the same tunnel.

SPORTS AND THE OUTDOORS

BOATING AND WILDLIFE-VIEWING

Alaska Sea Kayakers. Alaska Sea Kayakers supply sea kayaks and gear for exploring Prince William Sound and conduct guided day trips, multiday tours, instruction, and boat-assisted and boat live-aboard kayaking trips. The company practices a leave-no-trace camping ethos, and is very conscientious about avoiding bear problems. All guides are experienced Alaskan paddlers, and group sizes are kept small. Trips are May through mid-September. ☎ 907/472–2534 ⊕ *www.alaskaseakayakers.com.*

Lazy Otter Charters. The small fleet of boats at Lazy Otter Charters is available for private charter, sightseeing, and sea-kayak drop-offs. Groups of up to 22 people can join trips throughout Prince William Sound; you can also get transport to Cordova and Valdez. Customized sightseeing trips run from four or five hours to eight or nine hours. Day trips include lunch from Lazy Otter Cafe. ☎ 800/587–6887 ⊕ *www. lazyotter.com.*

Major Marine Tours. Major Marine Tours runs a five-hour cruise from Whittier that visits two tidewater glaciers. The waters of Prince William Sound are well protected and relatively calm, making this a good option if you tend to get queasy. Seabirds, waterfowl, and bald eagles are always present, and the chance to get close to the enormous walls of glacier ice is not to be missed. A number of different cruises are available from mid-March to mid-September, ranging from $70 to $150 per person. For an additional $19 (+ tax) every cruise features a freshly prepared all-you-can-eat salmon, prime rib, or vegetarian chili meal and reserved table seating for every guest inside a heated cabin. ☎ 800/764–7300 ⊕ *www.majormarine.com.*

26 Glacier Cruise. Phillips' Cruises & Tours has been running the 26 Glacier Cruise through Prince William Sound for many years. The high-speed catamaran covers 135 miles of territory in 4½ hours, leaving Whittier and visiting Port Wells, Barry Arm, and College and Harriman fjords. The boat is a very stable platform, and even visitors prone to seasickness can take this cruise with no ill effects. The heated cabin has large windows, upholstered booths, and wide aisles, and all seats are pre-reserved. There's a snack bar and a saloon on board, and wildlife encounters are commonplace. You can drive to Whittier and catch the boat at the dock, or you can arrange with the company to travel from Anchorage by rail or bus. The trip is $139 per person, plus tax, and includes a hot lunch of cod or chicken; tours are given May through September. ☎ 907/276–8023, 800/544–0529 ⊕ *www.26glaciers.com.*

WHERE TO EAT

$$ ✕ **China Sea.** The menu is filled with the standard Chinese fare, but you'll
CHINESE also find a significant number of fresh, local seafood dishes that make
this place a stand-out choice. Try the excellent grilled halibut (or, for
non–fish lovers, the Mongolian beef). $ *Average main: $15* ✉ *Harbor*
☎ *907/472–3663* ☉ *Closed mid-Sept.– mid-May.*

$ ✕ **Lazy Otter Café & Gifts.** Amid the summer shops and docks this little
AMERICAN café offers warm drinks, an array of soups, sandwiches, and fresh-baked
pastries, along with an Alaskan favorite: soft-serve ice cream. The busy
shop only offers a couple of indoor seats, but there's outdoor seating
that overlooks the harbor and is pleasant on sunny days. $ *Average
main: $9* ✉ *Lot 2, Whittier Harbor* ☎ *907/472–6887.*

$ ✕ **Varly's Ice Cream & Pizza.** Even though ice cream hardly seems like the
PIZZA thing you'd seek when in Alaska, hot days (and even not-so-hot days)
beg for Varly's. If the weather's cold and rainy, pizza is the alternative
fare. If you're not sure which way to lean, we wouldn't blame you if
you opted for a little of each. The owners (of Varly's Swiftwater Sea-
food Café fame) take great pride in what they do, and it shows: the
delicious pizza is homemade and something to write home about. It
might sound frightening, but trust us when we say the Kraut—a pizza
topped with sauerkraut and pepperoni (no kidding!)—is the best.
$ *Average main: $9* ✉ *Lot 1A Triangle Lease Area* ☎ *907/472–2547*
☉ *Closed Oct.–Apr.*

$$ ✕ **Varly's Swiftwater Seafood Café.** This is a great place to get the feel
SEAFOOD of Whittier. Place your order at the window and then grab a seat at
the counter and wait for your food. There's outdoor seating that
overlooks the small-boat harbor. Menu items include homemade
chowders, hand-battered seafood, peel-and-eat shrimp, burgers, and
chicken. $ *Average main: $20* ✉ *Harbor Loop* ☎ *907/472–2550*
☉ *Closed mid-Sept.–May.*

WHERE TO STAY

$$$ ⚏ **Inn at Whittier.** Set among shanties and harbor boats, this three-story
HOTEL luxury hotel sits right on the water overlooking the harbor. **Pros:** every
Fodor'sChoice room has a great view. **Cons:** no kitchen amenities. $ *Rooms from:*
★ *$175* ✉ *5a Harbor Rd.* ☎ *907/472–3200* ⊕ *www.innatwhittier.com*
⤴ *25 rooms* ☉ *Closed Oct. –Mar.* ⦿*Breakfast.*

$$ ⚏ **June's Whittier Condo Suites.** June's rents out 10 condominiums in the
HOTEL Begich Towers building, half with bay views, half with mountain views.
Pros: private condos in Penthouse area of Begich Towers; lovely view.
Cons: old building is a little rough outside. $ *Rooms from: $155* ✉ *Be-
gich Towers, Kenai St.* ☎ *888/472–6001* ⊕ *www.whittiersuitesonline.
com* ⤴ *10 rooms.*

5

PORTS OF CALL

Updated by
Teeka Ballas,
Linda Coff-
man, Lisa
Hupp, Sue
Kernaghan,
Edward
Readicker-Hen-
derson, and
Jenna Schnuer

There's never a dull day on an Alaskan cruise, and whether your ship is scheduled to make a port call, cruise by glaciers, or glide through majestic fjords, you'll have constant opportunities to explore the culture, wildlife, history, and amazing scenery that make Alaska so unique. Most port cities are small and easily explored on foot, but if you prefer to be shown the sights, your ship will offer organized shore excursions at each stop along the way.

Popular activities include city tours, flightseeing, charter fishing, whale-watching, river rafting, and visits to Native communities. You can also, for the sake of shorter trips or more active excursions, readily organize your own tour through a local vendor.

GOING ASHORE

The ports visited on an Alaska cruise and the amount of time spent in each vary depending on the cruise line and itinerary, but most ships stop in Ketchikan, Juneau, and Skagway—the three big draws in Southeast Alaska. Some ports, such as Homer and Wrangell, are visited by only a couple of the small-ship cruise lines, whereas other adventure ships head out to explore the wild places in the Bering Sea.

Each town has its highlights. For example, Ketchikan has a wealth of Native artifacts, Skagway has lots of gold-rush history, Sitka has a rich Russian and Native heritage, and Juneau has glacier trips. There are also ample shopping opportunities in most ports, but beware of tacky tourist traps. Nearly all Southeast towns, but especially Haines, Sitka, and Ketchikan, have great art galleries.

To help you plan your trip, we've compiled a list of the most worthwhile excursions available in each port of call. Also look out for "Best Bets" boxes; these highlight a port's top experiences so you don't shell out for a flightseeing trip in one place, for example, when the experience would be better elsewhere.

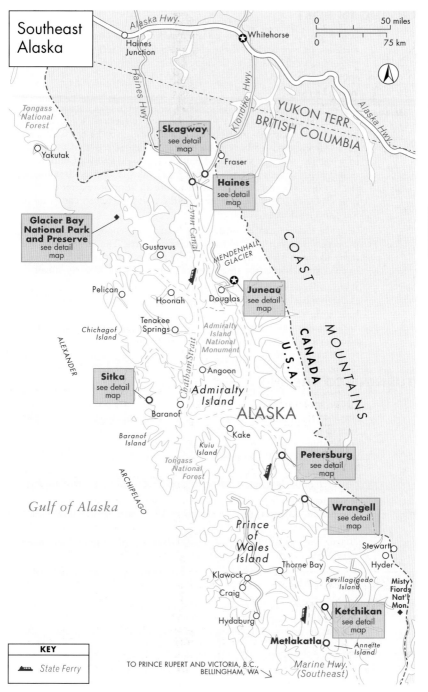

Southeast Alaska

Skagway
see detail map

Haines
see detail map

Glacier Bay National Park and Preserve
see detail map

Juneau
see detail map

Sitka
see detail map

Petersburg
see detail map

Wrangell
see detail map

Ketchikan
see detail map

Metlakatla

Alaska Hwy.

Whitehorse

Haines Junction

YUKON TERR.

BRITISH COLUMBIA

Klondike Hwy.

Haines Hwy.

Fraser

Alaska Hwy.

Tongass National Forest

Yakutat

Gustavus

MENDENHALL GLACIER

COAST

Lynn Canal

Pelican

Hoonah

Douglas

ALEXANDER

Chichagof Island

Tenakee Springs

Admiralty Island National Monument

CANADA

U.S.A.

MOUNTAINS

Angoon

Admiralty Island

ALASKA

Sitka

Baranof

Baranof Island

Kake

Chatham Strait

Kuiu Island

Tongass National Forest

Gulf of Alaska

ARCHIPELAGO

Prince of Wales Island

Thorne Bay

Stewart

Hyder

Klawock

Craig

Revillagigedo Island

Misty Fiords Nat'l Mon.

Hydaburg

Annette Island

Marine Hwy. (Southeast)

TO PRINCE RUPERT AND VICTORIA, B.C.,
BELLINGHAM, WA

50 miles

75 km

KEY

State Ferry

ARRIVING IN PORT

When your ship arrives in a port, it will tie up alongside a dock or anchor out in a harbor. If the ship is docked, passengers walk down the gangway to go ashore. Docking makes it easy to move between the shore and the ship.

TENDERING

If your ship anchors in the harbor, you will have to take a small boat—called a launch or tender—to get ashore. Tendering is a nuisance; however, participants in shore excursions are given priority. Passengers wishing to disembark independently may be required to gather in a public room, get sequenced tendering passes, and wait until their numbers are called. The ride to shore may take as long as 20 minutes. If you don't like waiting, plan to go ashore an hour or so after the ship drops its anchor. On a very large ship, the wait for a tender can be quite long and frustrating.

Because tenders can be difficult to board, passengers with mobility problems may not be able to visit certain ports. The larger ships are more likely to use tenders. It is usually possible to learn before booking a cruise whether the ship will dock or anchor at its ports of call.

Before anyone is allowed to walk down the gangway or board a tender, the ship must be cleared for landing. Immigration and customs officials board the vessel to examine the ship's manifest or possibly passports and sort through red tape. It may be more than an hour before you're allowed ashore. You will be issued a boarding pass, which you'll need to get back on board.

RETURNING TO THE SHIP

Cruise lines are strict about sailing times, which are posted at the gangway and elsewhere and announced in the daily schedule of activities. Be sure to be back on board (not on the dock waiting to get a tender back to the ship) at least an hour before the announced sailing time or you may be stranded. If you are on a shore excursion that was sold by the cruise line, however, the captain will wait for your group before casting off. That is one reason many passengers prefer ship-packaged tours.

If you're not on one of the ship's tours and the ship sails without you, immediately contact the cruise line's port representative, whose phone number is often listed on the daily schedule of activities. You may be able to hitch a ride on a pilot boat, although that is unlikely. Passengers who miss the boat must pay their own way to the next port.

ALASKA ESSENTIALS

CURRENCY

Alaska cruises may call in ports in either the United States or Canada (Canadian ports are much more likely on itineraries that focus on the Inside Passage). In such cases, you may need to change some currency into Canadian dollars, though U.S. dollars are accepted in some places.

KEEPING IN TOUCH

Internet cafés are less common than they used to be, but you'll sometimes find Internet access in the cruise-ship terminal itself, or perhaps in an attached or nearby shopping center. Such access is often Wi-Fi. If you want to call home, most cruise-ship terminal facilities have phones that accept credit cards or phone cards (local phone cards are almost always the cheapest option). But mobile phones work in almost all these ports, though you will likely have to pay a roaming charge if you make a call in Canada, depending on your cell phone calling plan.

WHERE TO EAT

Not surprisingly, seafood dominates most menus. In summer, salmon, halibut, crab, cod, and prawns are usually fresh. Restaurants are informal and casual clothes are the norm; you'll never be sent away for wearing jeans in an Alaskan restaurant. However, prices are typically higher than in the continental United States.

OUTDOOR ACTIVITIES

There are hikes and walks in or near every Alaska port town. Well-maintained trails are easily accessible from even the largest cities; lush forests and wilderness areas, port and glacier views, and mountaintop panoramas are often within a few hours' walk of downtown areas. More adventurous travelers will enjoy paddling sea kayaks in the protected waters of Southeast and South Central Alaska; companies in most ports rent kayaks and give lessons and tours. Fishing enthusiasts from all over the world come to Alaska for a chance to land a trophy salmon or halibut. Cycling, glacier hikes, flightseeing, or bear-viewing shore excursions in some ports also offer cruise passengers an opportunity to engage with Alaska's endless landscape.

SHOPPING

Alaskan Native handicrafts range from Tlingit totem poles—a few inches high to more than 30 feet tall—to Athabascan beaded slippers and fur garments. Traditional pieces of art (or imitations thereof) are found in gift shops up and down the coast: Inupiat spirit masks, Yupik dolls and dance fans, Tlingit button blankets and silver jewelry, and Aleut grass baskets and carved wooden items. Salmon, halibut, crab, and other frozen fish are very popular souvenirs (shipped home to meet you, of course) and make great gifts. Although Ketchikan is probably your best bet, with several outlets, most towns have at least one local company that packs and ships fresh, smoked, or frozen seafood.

To ensure authenticity, buy items tagged with the state-approved "authentic Native handcraft from Alaska" "Silverhand" label, or look for the polar-bear symbol indicating products made in Alaska. Although these symbols are designed to ensure authentic Alaskan and Native-made products, not all items lacking them are inauthentic. Better prices tend to be found in the more remote villages, in museum shops, or in crafts fairs such as Anchorage's downtown Saturday Market. ⇨ *For more on buying Native crafts, see Made in Alaska in this chapter.*

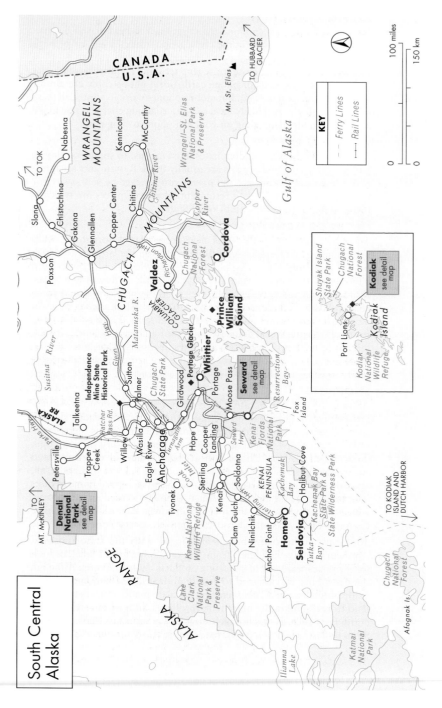

South Central Alaska

SHORE EXCURSIONS

Shore excursions arranged by the cruise line are a convenient way to see the sights, but you'll pay extra for this convenience. Before your cruise, you'll receive a booklet or be directed to a Web page describing the shore excursions your cruise line offers. Most cruise lines let you book excursions in advance online, where you'll find descriptions and pricing; all sell them on board during the cruise. If you cancel your excursion, you may incur penalties, the amount varying with the number of days remaining until the tour. Because these trips are specialized, many have limited capacity and are sold on a first-come, first-served basis.

GLACIER BAY NATIONAL PARK AND PRESERVE

Your cruise experience in Glacier Bay will depend partly on the size of your ship. Large cruise ships tend to stay midchannel, while small yachtlike ships spend more time closer to shore. Smaller ships give you a better view of the calving ice and wildlife, but on a big ship you can get a loftier perspective. Both come within ¼ mile of the glaciers themselves.

Fodor's Choice ★ **Glacier Bay National Park and Preserve.** Near the northern end of the Inside Passage, Glacier Bay National Park and Preserve is one of America's most magnificent national parks. Visiting Glacier Bay is like stepping back into the Little Ice Age—it's one of the few places in the world where you can approach such a variety of massive tidewater glaciers. Sounding like cannon fire, bergs the size of 10-story office buildings come crashing from the "snout" of a glacier, each cannon blast signifying another step in the glacier's steady retreat. The calving iceberg sends tons of water and spray skyward, propelling mini–tidal waves outward from the point of impact. **Johns Hopkins Glacier** calves so often and with such volume that large cruise ships can seldom come within 2 miles of its face.

Glacier Bay is a still-forming body of water fed by the runoff of the ice fields, glaciers, and mountains that surround it. In the mid-18th century, ice floes so covered the bay that Captain James Cook and then Captain George Vancouver sailed by and didn't even know it. At the time of Vancouver's sailing in 1794, the bay was still hidden behind and beneath a vast glacial wall of ice, which was more than 20 miles across and in places more than 4,000 feet in depth. It extended more than 100 miles north to its origins in the St. Elias Mountain Range, the world's tallest coastal mountains. Since then, the face of the glacial ice has melted and retreated with amazing speed, exposing 65 miles of fjords, islands, and inlets.

In 1879, about a century after Vancouver's sail-by, one of the earliest white visitors to what is now Glacier Bay National Park and Preserve came calling. The ever-curious naturalist John Muir, who would become one of the region's earliest proponents, was drawn by the flora and fauna that had followed in the wake of glacial withdrawals; he was also fascinated by the vast ice rivers that descended from the mountains

Don your jacket and head to the outside deck for spectacular views of Glacier Bay.

to tidewater. Today the naturalist's namesake glacier, like others in the park, continues to retreat dramatically: the Muir Glacier's terminus is now scores of miles farther up the bay from the small cabin he built at its face during his time there.

Glacier Bay is a marvelous laboratory for naturalists of all persuasions. Glaciologists, of course, can have a field day. Animal lovers can hope to see the rare glacial "blue" bears of the area, a variation of the black bear, which is here along with the brown bear; whales feasting on krill; mountain goats in late spring and early summer; and seals on floating icebergs. Birders can look for the more than 200 species that have already been spotted in the park, and if you're lucky, you may witness bald eagles engaging in aerobatics.

A remarkable panorama of plants unfolds from the head of the bay, which is just emerging from the ice, to the mouth, which has been ice-free for more than 200 years. In between, the primitive plants—algae, lichens, and mosses—that are the first to take hold of the bare, wet ground give way to more-complex species: flowering plants such as the magenta dwarf fireweed and the creamy dryas, which in turn merge with willows, alders, and cottonwood. As the living plants mature and die, they enrich the soil and prepare it for new species to follow. The climax of the plant community is the lush spruce-and-hemlock rain forest, rich in life and blanketing the land around **Bartlett Cove**. ✉ *Gustavus* ☎ *907/697–2230, 907/697–2627 boating information* ⊕ *www.nps.gov/glba.*

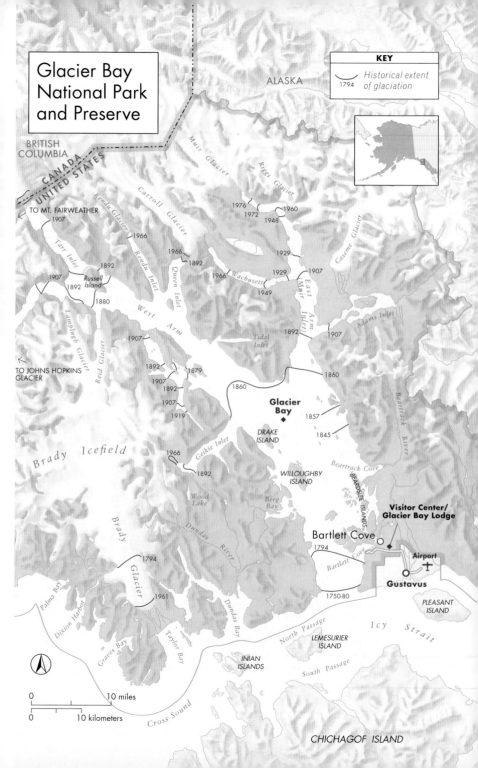

Glacier Bay National Park and Preserve

KEY

1794 ⌣ *Historical extent of glaciation*

ALASKA

BRITISH COLUMBIA

CANADA
UNITED STATES

TO MT. FAIRWEATHER
1907

Muir Glacier

Riggs Glacier

Carroll Glacier

Caseme Glacier

Rendu Glacier

1966

Tarr Inlet

1892

Russell Island

1907

1892

1880

Rendu Inlet

West Arm

Queen Inlet

1966

1892

1966

Wachusett

1976
1972

1960
1948

1929

1929
1949

1907

East Arm Muir Inlet

Adams Inlet

1892

1907

TO JOHNS HOPKINS GLACIER

Lamplugh Glacier

Reid Glacier

1907

1892

1879

1907

1892

1907

1919

Tidal Inlet

1860

1860

Beartrack River

Brady Icefield

Geikie Inlet

1966

1892

Wood Lake

Glacier Bay

DRAKE ISLAND

1857

1845

WILLOUGHBY ISLAND

Berg Bay

Beartrack Cove

BEARDSLEE ISLANDS

Visitor Center/ Glacier Bay Lodge

Brady Glacier

1794

1961

Dundas River

Bartlett Cove
1794

Bartlett Cove

Bartlett Cove

Airport

Gustavus

1750-80

PLEASANT ISLAND

Palma Bay

Dixion Harbor

Graves Bay

Taylor Bay

Dundas Bay

North Passage

LEMESURIER ISLAND

Icy Strait

INIAN ISLANDS

South Passage

0 —— 10 miles

0 —— 10 kilometers

Cross Sound

CHICHAGOF ISLAND

GLACIER RUNDOWN

The most frequently viewed glaciers are in the west arm of Glacier Bay. Ships linger in front of five glaciers, giving you ample time to admire their stunning and ever-changing faces. First, most ships stop briefly at Reid Glacier, which flows down from the Brady Icefield, before continuing on to Lamplugh Glacier—one of the bluest in the park—at the mouth of Johns Hopkins Inlet. Next, at the end of the inlet, is the massive Johns Hopkins Glacier, where you're likely to see a continuous shower of calving ice. (Sometimes there are so many icebergs in the inlet that ships must avoid the area. And access isn't allowed early in the season because it's where sea lions give birth to their babies.) Farther north, near the end of the western arm, is Margerie Glacier, which is also quite active. Adjacent is Grand Pacific Glacier, the largest glacier in the park.

Competition for entry permits into Glacier Bay is fierce. To protect the humpback whale, which feeds here in summer, the Park Service limits the number of ships that can call. Check your cruise brochure to make sure Glacier Bay is included in your sailing. Most ships that do visit spend at least one full day exploring the park. There are no shore excursions or landings in the bay—the steep-sided and heavily forested fjords aren't conducive to pedestrian exploration—but a Park Service naturalist boards every cruise ship to offer a running commentary throughout the day.

GUSTAVUS

By Amy
Fletcher

Gustavus is the gateway to Glacier Bay National Park and Preserve. The long, paved jet airport, built as a refueling strip during World War II, is one of the best and longest in Southeast Alaska, all the more impressive because of its limited facilities at the field.

COMING ASHORE

Large cruise ships do not dock anywhere in Glacier Bay, and only a few small cruise lines stop in nearby Gustavus, 9 miles down the road. Small ships that dock here use the same dock as the ferries of the Alaska Marine Highway

EXPLORING GUSTAVUS

Before you get too excited about visiting this remote outpost, be forewarned: Gustavus has no downtown. In fact, Gustavus is not really a town at all. Instead, it's a scattering of homes, farmsteads, a craft studio, fishing and guiding charters, an art gallery, and other tiny enterprises peopled by hospitable individualists. Visitors enjoy the unstructured outdoor activities in the area, including beach and trail hiking in the Nature Conservancy's Forelands Preserve.

SPORTS AND THE OUTDOORS

Glacier Bay is best experienced from the water, whether from the deck of a cruise ship, on a tour boat, or from the level of a sea kayak. National Park Service naturalists often come aboard to explain the great glaciers and to help spot bears, mountain goats, whales, porpoises, and birds. Those ships lucky enough to land in Gustavus will have other opportunities to see Glacier Bay.

BOAT TOURS

Huna Totem Corporation/Aramark. Daily summertime boat tours leave from the dock at Bartlett Cove, near Glacier Bay Lodge. These eight-hour trips into Glacier Bay have a Park Service naturalist aboard a high-speed 155-passenger catamaran. A light lunch is included. Campers and sea kayakers heading up the bay ride the same boat. ⊠ *179 Bartlett Cove* ☎ *907/264–4600, 888/229–8687* ⊕ *www.visitglacierbay.com.*

GUSTAVUS BEST BETS

■ **Glacier Bay Boat Tours.** Whether you are on a simple boat tour or a whale-watching trip, the best way to see Glacier Bay up close and personal is aboard a smaller boat.

■ **Flightseeing.** Alaska Seaplanes, based at the Gustavus airport, offers flights over the glaciers.

■ **Hiking.** The Gustavus Forelands Preserve, set aside by the Nature Conservancy, stretches along the beach and into the surrounding wetlands, providing plentiful opportunities for hiking and wildlife-viewing.

FLIGHTSEEING

Alaska Seaplanes. Besides daily scheduled air service year-round to Gustavus/Glacier Bay, Elfin Cove, Tenakee Springs, Hoonah, Angoon, Haines, Kake, and Skagway, Alaska Seaplanes also offers flightseeing tours and charters to other destinations in Southeast Alaska. ⊠ *1873 Shell Simmons Dr., Juneau* ☎ *907/789–3331* ⊕ *www.flyalaskaseaplanes.com.*

HIKING

Glacier Bay's steep and heavily forested slopes aren't the most conducive to hiking, but there are several short hikes that begin at the Glacier Bay Lodge. Among the most popular is the **Forest Loop Trail,** a pleasant 1-mile jaunt that begins in a forest of spruce and hemlock and finishes on the beach. Also beginning at the lodge is the **Bartlett River Trail**—a 5-mile round-trip hike that borders an intertidal lagoon, culminating at the Bartlett River estuary. The **Bartlett Lake Trail,** part of a 6-mile walk that meanders through rain forest, ends at the quiet lakeshore. The entire Gustavus beachfront was set aside by the Nature Conservancy, enabling visitors to hike the shoreline for miles without getting lost. The beachfront is part of the **Alaska Coastal Wildlife Viewing Trail** (⊕ *wildlife. alaska.gov*). The spring and fall bird migrations are exceptional on Gustavus estuaries, including Dude Creek Critical Habitat Area, which provides a stopover before crossing the ice fields for sandhill cranes. Maps and wildlife-viewing information are available from the **Alaska Division of Wildlife Conservation** (⊕ *wildlife.alaska.gov*).

QUAKE HAPPY IN GLACIER BAY

Glacier Bay's impressive landscape is the result of plate tectonics. The region sits directly above a chaotic intersection of fault lines—credited for creating the region's stunning topography as well as wreaking some havoc more recently. On September 10, 1899, the area was rocked by a massive temblor registering 8.4 on the Richter scale. The quake, which had its epicenter in Yakutat Bay, rattled Glacier Bay so much that the entire bay was choked with icebergs.

On July 9, 1958, a tremendous earthquake—a 7.9 on the Richter scale—triggered a landslide of epic proportions in nearby Lituya Bay: 40 million cubic yards of rock tumbled into the bay, and created a tidal wave that reached 1,720 feet.

SEA KAYAKING

The most adventurous way to explore Glacier Bay is by paddling your own kayak through the bay's icy waters and inlets. But unless you're an expert, you're better off signing on with the guided tours.

Alaska Mountain Guides. Take day kayaking trips for whale-watching at Point Adolphus, a premier humpback gathering spot, as well as multiday sea-kayaking expeditions next to tidewater glaciers in Glacier Bay National Park, with Alaska Mountain Guides. ☎ 907/766–3366, 800/766–3396 ⊕ www.alaskamountainguides.com.

Glacier Bay Sea Kayaks. Kayak rentals for Glacier Bay exploring and camping can be arranged through Glacier Bay Sea Kayaks. You will be given instructions on handling the craft plus camping and routing suggestions for unescorted trips. Guided day trips are available in Bartlett Cove. The company is an official NPS concession for guided day kayak trips. ⊠ Bartlett Cove ☎ 907/697–2257 ⊕ www.glacierbayseakayaks.com.

Spirit Walker Expeditions. Take one- to seven-day sea-kayaking trips from Gustavus to various parts of Icy Strait with Spirit Walker Expeditions. Trips to Glacier Bay and other remote areas of Southeast Alaska, including Ford's Terror and West Chichagof, are also offered on a limited basis. ☎ 907/697–2266, 800/529–2537 ⊕ www.seakayakalaska.com.

WHALE-WATCHING

M/V TAZ. Step aboard the M/V *TAZ* and check out Icy Strait and Point Adolphus, near the entrance to Glacier Bay, for awesome views of humpback whales and many other marine mammals. All tours out of Gustavus include binoculars, snacks, and hot beverages. Half-day tours and custom charters accommodating up to 28 passengers are offered, as well as "Weddings with the Whales," where you can get married while surrounded by humpbacks. ☎ 907/321–2302, 888/698–2726 ⊕ www.taz.gustavus.com.

HAINES

Haines encompasses an area that has been occupied by Tlingit peoples for centuries on the collar of the Chilkat Peninsula, a narrow strip of land that divides the Chilkat and Chilkoot inlets. Missionary S. Hall Young and famed naturalist John Muir were intent on establishing a Presbyterian mission in the area, and, with the blessing of local chiefs, they chose the site that later became Haines. It's hard to imagine a more beautiful setting—a heavily wooded peninsula with magnificent views of Portage Cove and the snowy Coast Range.

The downtown area feels as small as a postage stamp, and the town exudes a down-home friendliness. Haines's popularity as a stop for cruise ships both large and small is growing, especially as travelers look for an alternative to the crowds in Skagway. Visitors should be prepared for a relative lack of souvenir and T-shirt shops compared to other ports. Local weather is drier than in much of Southeast Alaska.

HAINES BEST BETS

■ **Float the Chilkat River.** Running through one of Alaska's most stunning mountain ranges, the mellow Chilkat caters more to sightseers than to thrill-seekers.

■ **Pound the pavement.** Haines has a delightfully funky vibe welcoming to visitors; Mountain Market, Sheldon Bookstore, and the public library are favorite local hangouts.

■ **Hit the road.** The Haines Highway is one of the nation's most beautiful roads. Whether you enlist a local tour operator or rent a car, a drive up this highway is an unforgettable experience.

COMING ASHORE

Cruise ships and catamaran ferries dock in front of Ft. Seward, and downtown Haines is just a short walk away (about ½ mile). Complimentary shuttle service is provided to downtown and the Ft. Seward area.

TOURS

Jilkat Kwaan Cultural Tours. Built near Klukwan, a Native village 23 miles up the road from Haines, this site offers visitors the chance to learn about the Tlingit, including their arts, language, and traditions. Visit the site's Long House, built using traditional methods; find out about traditional Native crafts, including wood carving, beading, and the distinctive Chilkat blanket; see the process for smoking salmon; and much more. A small but well-stocked gift shop sells crafts made by Klukwan locals. ⊠ *Klukwan* ☎ *907/767–5797* ⊕ *www.visitklukwan.com.*

VISITOR INFORMATION

Haines Convention and Visitors Bureau. At this helpful tourist office you can pick up hiking- and walking-tour brochures, learn about lodging and attractions, and check out menus from local restaurants. ⊠ *122 2nd Ave. S, Box 530* ☎ *907/766–2234, 800/458–3579* ⊕ *www.haines.ak.us* ⊙ *Mid-May–mid-Sept., weekdays 8–5, weekends 9–4; mid-Sept.–mid-May, weekdays 8–5.*

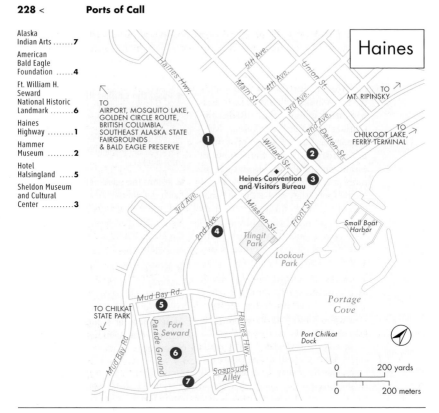

EXPLORING

FAMILY **Alaska Indian Arts.** Dedicated to the revival of Tlingit art, this nonprofit organization is housed in the former fort hospital, on the south side of the parade ground. You can watch artisans doing everything from carving totem poles to creating delicate silver jewelry. ⊠ *Ft. Seward* ☏ *907/766–2160* ⊕ *www.alaskaindianarts.com* ✆ *Free* ⊙ *Weekdays 9–5.*

FAMILY **American Bald Eagle Foundation.** The main focuses here are bald eagles and associated fauna of the Chilkat Preserve, explored in lectures, displays, and videos. A taxidermy-heavy diorama also shows examples of local animals. Opened in summer of 2010, a raptor center features live presentations and an aviary displaying live eagles. The gift shop sells natural-history items. ⊠ *113 Haines Hwy., Box 49* ☏ *907/766–3094* ⊕ *www. baldeagles.org* ✆ *$3–$10* ⊙ *Summer, daily 9–5; winter, daily 10–2.*

Ft. William H. Seward National Historic Landmark. Circle the sloping parade grounds of Alaska's first U.S. army post, where stately clapboard homes stand against a mountain backdrop. ■TIP➜ **The Haines Convention and Visitors Bureau provides a walking-tour brochure of the fort.** ⊠ *Ft. Seward* ⊕ *www.haines.ak.us/history.*

Haines Highway. The breathtaking Haines Highway, a National Scenic Byway, starts at Mile 0 in Haines and continues 152 miles to Haines Junction. You don't have to drive the entire length to experience its beauty, as worthwhile stops are all along the route. At about Mile 6 a delightful picnic spot is near the Chilkat River. At Mile 9.5 the view of Cathedral Peaks, part of the Chilkat Range, is magnificent. Though at Mile 9 the Alaska Chilkat Bald Eagle Preserve begins; the best viewing is between Mile 19 and Mile 21. At Mile 33 is a roadside restaurant called, aptly, **33-Mile Roadhouse**, where you fill your tank and coffee mug and grab a burger and, most importantly, a piece of pie—do not leave without trying the pie. The United States–Canada border lies at Mile 42; stop at Canadian customs and set your clock ahead one hour. ⊠ *Haines Hwy.* ☏ *907/767–5510 Mile 33 Roadhouse, 907/766–2234 HCVB* ⊕ *www.haines.ak.us/highway.*

Alaska Chilkat Bald Eagle Preserve. In winter, the Alaska Chilkat Bald Eagle Preserve, on Mile 19–Mile 21 of the Haines Highway, harbors the largest concentration of bald eagles in the world. In November and December, more eagles gather outside of Haines than live in the continental United States. Thousands come to feast on the late run of salmon in the clear, ice-free waters of the Chilkat River, which is heated by underground warm springs. ⊠ *Haines Hwy.* ☏ *907/766–2292* ⊕ *www. dnr.alaska.gov/parks/units/eagleprv.htm.*

Hammer Museum. The owner started his collection decades ago and founded the Hammer Museum—the world's first—in 2001. Among his impressive collection of 1,800 hammers are a Roman battle hammer and 6-foot-long posting hammers used to secure advertisements to local outside walls. ⊠ *108 Main St.* ☏ *907/766–2374* ⊕ *www. hammermuseum.org* ▨ *$3* ⊗ *May–Sept., weekdays 10–5.*

Hotel Halsingland. In Ft. Seward, wander past the huge, gallant, white-columned former commanding officers' home, now a part of the hotel on Officers' Row. ⊠ *Ft. Seward* ⊕ *www.hotelhalsingland.com.*

Sheldon Museum and Cultural Center. Steve Sheldon began assembling Native artifacts, items from historic Ft. Seward, and gold-rush memorabilia, such as Jack Dalton's sawed-off shotgun, in the 1880s, and started an exhibit of his finds in 1925. Today his collection is the core of the museum's impressive array of artifacts, including Chilkat blankets, a model of a Tlingit tribal house, and the original lens from the Eldred Rock lighthouse just south of Haines on the Lynn Canal. Repatriated Bear Clan items such as an 18th-century carved ceremonial Murrelet hat are are on display, thanks to loans to the museum. ⊠ *11 Main St.* ☏ *907/766–2366* ⊕ *www.sheldonmuseum.org* ▨ *$5* ⊗ *Mid-May–mid-Sept., weekdays 10–5, weekends 1–4; mid-Sept.–mid-May, Mon.–Sat. 1–4.*

SPORTS AND THE OUTDOORS

BOATING AND FISHING

Alaska Fjordlines. Alaska Fjordlines operates a high-speed catamaran from Skagway and Haines to Juneau and back throughout the summer, stopping along the way to watch sea lions, humpbacks, and other marine mammals. One-way service is also available. ☏ *907/766–3395, 800/320–0146* ⊕ *www.alaskafjordlines.com.*

River Adventures. The jet-boat tours offered by River Adventures are a great way to experience the bald eagle preserve in majestic Chilkat River valley. ☎ *907/766–2050, 800/478–9827* ⊕ *www.jetboatalaska.com.*

HIKING

Battery Point Trail. This is a fairly level path that hugs the shoreline for 1.2 miles, providing fine views across Lynn Canal. The trail begins a mile east of town, and a campsite can be found at Kelgaya Point near the end. For other hikes, pick up a copy of "Haines Is for Hikers" at the Haines Convention and Visitors Bureau. ⊠ *End of Beach Rd.* ⊕ *www. seatrails.org/com_haines/trl-battery.htm.*

NATURE TOURS

Fodor'sChoice **Alaska Nature Tours.** Alaska Nature Tours conducts bird-watching and
★ natural-history tours through the Alaska Chilkat Bald Eagle Preserve, operates brown bear–watching excursions in July and August, and leads hiking treks in summer and ski tours in winter. ⊠ *109 2nd Ave.* ☎ *907/766–2876* ⊕ *www.alaskanaturetours.net.*

SHOPPING

A surprising number of artists live in the Haines area and sell their works in local galleries.

Birch Boy Products. Birch Boy Products produces tart and tasty birch syrup; it's sold in local gift shops. ☎ *907/767–5660* ⊕ *www.birchboy.com.*

Sea Wolf Gallery. Tresham Gregg's Sea Wolf Gallery sells wood carvings, silver jewelry, prints, and T-shirts with his Native-inspired designs. ⊠ *Ft. Seward* ☎ *907/766–2540* ⊕ *www.tresham.com.*

Wild Iris Gallery. Haines's most charming gallery, the Wild Iris Gallery, displays attractive jewelry, prints, and fashion wear created by owner Fred Shields and his daughter Melina. Other local artists are also represented. It's just up from the cruise-ship dock, and its summer gardens alone are worth the visit. ⊠ *Portage St.* ☎ *907/766–2300* ⊕ *www. haines.ak.us/artists.*

WHERE TO EAT

$$ ✕ **Bamboo Room.** Pop culture meets greasy spoon in this unassuming
AMERICAN coffee shop with red-vinyl booths, which has been in the same family for more than 50 years. The menu doesn't cater to light appetites—it includes sandwiches, burgers, fried chicken, chili, and halibut fish-and-chips, but the place really is at its best for an all-American breakfast (available until 3 pm). The adjacent bar has pool, darts, a big-screen TV, and a jukebox. ⑤ *Average main: $10* ⊠ *2nd Ave. near Main St.* ☎ *907/766–2800* ⊕ *www.bamboopioneer.net.*

$$ ✕ **Mosey's.** The fare at this Mexican restaurant just one block up from
MEXICAN the cruise-ship dock is on the spicy side—owner Martha Stewart (yes, that's her real name) travels to New Mexico each year and brings back bushels of roasted green chilies, the signature ingredient. If your taste buds can handle the kick, you'll be rewarded: the food is bursting with fresh flavors, and the atmosphere is a cheery south-of-the-border alternative to the rest of Haines's more mainstream offerings. Order lunch

at the counter or sit down for table service in the evening. ⑤ *Average main: $10* ✉ *Soap Suds Alley, Ft. Seward* ☎ *907/766–2320* ⊕ *www. moseyscantina.com* ☾ *Closed Tues. No lunch weekends.*

$ ✕ **Mountain Market.** Meet the locals

AMERICAN over espresso, brewed from fresh-roasted beans, and a fresh-baked pastry at this busy corner natural-foods store, deli, café, wine-and-spirits shop, de facto meeting hall, and hitching post. Mountain Market is great for lunchtime sandwiches, wraps, soups, and salads. Friday is pizza day, but come early, since it's often gone by early afternoon. ⑤ *Average main: $8* ✉ *3rd Ave. and Haines Hwy.* ☎ *907/766–3340* ⊕ *www.mountain-market.com.*

HOMER BEST BETS

■ **Charter a fishing boat.** Nothing beats wrestling a monster halibut out of the icy depths.

■ **People-watch on the Spit.** Homer is home to a thriving arts community, and makes for an interesting cultural mix.

■ **Cruise to a waterfront gallery.** Crossing the bay to Halibut Cove for gallery hopping is another favorite experience.

5

HOMER

It's a shame that of the hundreds of thousands of cruise passengers who visit Alaska each year only a very few get to see Homer. Its scenic setting on Kachemak Bay, surrounded by mountains, spruce forest, and glaciers, makes Homer unique even in Alaska.

Founded in the late 1800s as a gold-prospecting camp, this community was later used as coal-mining headquarters. Chunks of coal are still common along local beaches; they wash into the bay from nearby slopes where the coal seams are exposed. Today the town of Homer is an eclectic community with most of the tacky tourist paraphernalia relegated to the Spit (though do note the Spit has plenty else to recommend it, not the least of which is the 360-degree view of the surrounding mountains); the rest of the town is full of local merchants and artisans. The community is an interesting mix of fishermen, actors, artists, and writers. Much of the commercial fishing centers on halibut, and the popular Homer Jackpot Halibut Derby is often won by enormous fish weighing more than 300 pounds. The local architecture includes everything from dwellings that are little more than assemblages of driftwood to steel commercial buildings and magnificent homes on the hillside overlooking the surrounding bay, mountains, forests, and glaciers.

COMING ASHORE

Ships and Alaska Marine Highway ferries dock at the end of the Homer Spit, where you can find charters, restaurants, and shops. The routine for cruise lines calling in Homer is to provide a shuttle from the Spit to downtown. Since Homer isn't a common port and the town itself offers so much to explore, shore-excursion offerings aren't as predictable here as in other ports of call. Your ship may offer boat charters to Gull Island (a nearby island chock-full of cacophonous seagulls and other seabirds) or Seldovia (a small, scenic town with quality art galleries across Katchemak Bay). Halibut fishing is also huge here, and if you take one fishing-charter excursion during your trip this would be the place to do it.

VISITOR INFORMATION

Visitor Information Center. Start your visit with a stop at the Homer Chamber of Commerce's Visitor Information Center, where racks are filled with brochures from local businesses and attractions. ⊠ *201 Sterling Hwy.* ☎ *907/235–7740* ⊕ *www.homeralaska.org* ☉ *Memorial Day–Labor Day, weekdays 9–7, weekends 10–6; early Sept.–late May, weekdays 9–5.*

EXPLORING

Halibut Cove. Directly across from the end of Homer Spit is Halibut Cove, a small artists' community. Spend a relaxing afternoon or evening meandering along the boardwalk and visiting galleries. The cove is lovely, especially during salmon runs, when fish leap and splash in the clear water. Several lodges are on this side of the bay, on pristine coves away from summer crowds. The *Danny J* ferries people across from Homer Spit, with a stop at the rookery at Gull Island and two or three hours to walk around Halibut Cove. The ferry makes two trips daily: the first ($57.50) leaves Homer at noon and returns at 5 pm, and the second ($34.50) leaves at 5 pm and returns at 10 pm. Central Charters handles all bookings. (⇨ *Fishing, in Sports and the Outdoors, below.*) ☎ *907/399–2683* ⊕ *www.halibut-cove-alaska.com/ferry.htm.*

FAMILY
Fodor's Choice
★
Homer Spit. Protruding into Kachemak Bay, Homer Spit provides a sandy focal point for visitors and locals. A paved path stretches most of the 4 miles and is great for biking or walking. A commercial-fishing-boat harbor at the end of the path has restaurants, hotels, charter-fishing businesses, sea-kayaking outfitters, art galleries, and on-the-beach camping spots. Fly a kite, walk the beaches, drop a line in the Fishing Hole, or just wander through the shops looking for something interesting; this is one of Alaska's favorite summertime destinations.

FAMILY
Islands and Ocean Center. Islands and Ocean Center provides a wonderful introduction to the Alaska Maritime National Wildlife Refuge. The refuge covers some 3.5 million acres spread across some 2,500 Alaskan islands, from Prince of Wales Island in the south to Barrow in the north. Opened in 2003, this 37,000-square-foot facility with towering windows facing Kachemak Bay is a must-see for anyone interested in wild places—and it's free! A film takes visitors along on a voyage of the Fish and Wildlife Service's research ship, the MV *Tiglax.* Interactive exhibits detail the birds and marine mammals of the refuge (the largest seabird refuge in America), and one room even re-creates the noisy sounds and pungent smells of a bird rookery. In summer, guided bird-watching treks and beach walks are offered. ⊠ *95 Sterling Hwy.* ☎ *907/235–6961* ⊕ *www.islandsandocean.org* ⊠ *Free* ☉ *May 24–Sept. 1, daily 9–5; Sept.–Apr., Tues.–Sat. noon–5; May 1–May 23, Mon. – Sat. 10–5.*

Continued on page 238

NATIVE HANDICRAFTS

Intricate Aleut baskets, Athabascan birch-bark wonders, Inupiaq ivory carvings, and towering Tlingit totems are just some of the eye-opening crafts you'll encounter as you explore the 49th state. Alaska's native peoples—who live across 570,000 square miles of tundra, boreal forest, arctic plains, and coastal rain forest—are undeniably hardy, and their unique artistic traditions are just as resilient and enduring.

TIPS ON CHOOSING AN AUTHENTIC ITEM

1 The Federal Trade Commission has enacted strict regulations to combat the sale of falsely marketed goods; it's illegal for anything made by non-native Alaskans to be labeled as "Indian," "Native American," or "Alaska Native."

2 Some authentic goods are marked by a silver hand symbol or are labeled as an "Authentic Native Handicraft from Alaska."

3 The "Made in Alaska" label, often accompanied by an image of a polar bear with cub, denotes that the handicraft was made in the state.

4 Be sure to ask for written proof of authenticity with your purchase, as well as the artist's name. You can also request the artist's permit number, which may be available.

5 The Alaska State Council on the Arts, in Anchorage, is a great resource if you have additional questions or want to confirm a permit number. Call 907/269–6610 or 888/278–7424 in Alaska.

6 Materials must be legal. For example, only some feathers, such as ptarmigan and pheasant feathers, comply with the Migratory Bird Act. Only Native artisans are permitted to carve new walrus ivory. The seller should be able to answer your questions about material and technique.

THE NATIVE PEOPLE OF ALASKA

There are many opportunities to see the making of traditional crafts in native environments, including the Southeast Alaska Indian Cultural Center in Sitka and Anchorage's Alaska Native Heritage Center.

After chatting with the artisans, pop into the gift shops to peruse the handmade items. Also check out prominent galleries and museum shops.

RUSSIA

Inupiaq

Athabascan

CANADA

Yup'ik, Cup'ik

Eyak, Tlingit, Haida, Tsimshian

Aleut, Alutiiq

NORTHWEST COAST INDIANS: TLINGIT, HAIDA & TSIMSHIAN

Scattered throughout Southeast Alaska's rain forests, these highly social tribes traditionally benefited from the region's mild climate and abundant salmon, which afforded them a rare luxury: leisure time. They put this time to good use by cultivating highly detailed crafts, including ceremonial masks, elaborate woven robes, and, most famously, totem poles.

(left) A wagging tongue at the Juneau-Douglas City Museum
(right) A Tlingit totem reaches for the skies in Ketchikan

TOWERING TOTEM POLES

Throughout the Inside Passage's braided channels and forested islands, Native peoples use the wood of the abundant cedar trees to carve totem poles, which illustrate history, pay reverence, commemorate

a potlatch, or cast shame on a misbehaving person.

Every totem pole tells a story with a series of animal and human figures arranged vertically. Traditionally the totem poles of this area feature ravens, eagles, killer whales, wolves, bears, frogs, the mythic thunderbird, and the likenesses of ancestors.

K'alyaan Totem Pole

Carved in 1999, the K'alyaan totem pole is a tribute to the Tlingits who lost their lives in the 1804 Battle of Sitka between invading Russians and Tlingit warriors. Tommy Joseph, a venerated Tlingit artist from Sitka, and an apprentice spent three months carving the pole from a 35-ft western red cedar. It now stands at the very site of the skirmish, in Sitka National Historical Park.

Woodworm: The woodworm—a Tlingit clan symbol—is a wood-boring beetle that leaves a distinctive mark on timber.

Beaver: Sporting a fearsome pair of front teeth, this beaver symbol cradles a child in its arms, signifying the strength of Tlingit family bonds.

Frog: This animal represents the Kik.sádi Clan, which was very instrumental in organizing the Tlingit's revolt against the Russian trespassers. Here, the frog holds a raven helmet—a tribute to the Kik.sádi warrior who wore a similar headpiece into battle.

Raven: Atop the pole sits the striking raven, the emblem of one of the two moieties (large multi-clan groups) of Tlingit culture.

Sockeye Salmon (above) and Dog/Chum Salmon (below): These two symbols signify the contributions of the Sockeye and Dog Salmon Clans to the 1804 battle. They also illustrate the symbolic connection to the tribe's traditional food sources.

Tools and Materials

As do most modern carvers, Joseph used a steel adz to carve the cedar. Prior to European contact—and the accompanying introduction of metal tools—Tlingit artists carved with jade adzes. Totem poles are traditionally decorated with paint made from salmon-liver oil, charcoal, and iron and copper oxides.

5

IN FOCUS NATIVE HANDICRAFTS

ALEUT & ALUTIIQ

The Aleut inhabit the Alaska Peninsula and the windswept Aleutian Islands. Historically they lived and died by the sea, surviving on a diet of seals, sea lions, whales, and walruses, which they hunted in the tumultuous waters of the Gulf of Alaska and the Bering Sea. Hunters pursued their prey in *Sugpiaq*, kayaklike boats made of seal skin stretched over a driftwood frame.

WATERPROOF *KAMLEIKAS*
The Aleut prize seal intestine for its remarkable waterproof properties; they use it to create sturdy cloaks, shelter walls, and boat hulls. To make their famous cloaks, called *kamleikas*, intestine is washed, soaked in salt water, and arduously scraped clean. It is then stretched and dried before being stitched into hooded, waterproof pullovers.

FINE BASKETRY
Owing to the region's profusion of wild rye grass, Aleutian women are some of the planet's most skilled weavers, capable of creating baskets with more than 2,500 fibers per square inch. They also create hats, socks, mittens, and multipurpose mats. A long, sharpened thumbnail is their only tool.

ATHABASCANS

Inhabiting Alaska's rugged interior for 8,000 to 20,000 years, Athabascans followed a seasonally nomadic hunter-gatherer lifestyle, subsisting off of caribou, moose, bear, and snowshoe hare. They populate areas from the Brooks Range to Cook Inlet, a vast expanse that encompasses five significant rivers: the Tanana, the Kuskwin, the Copper, the Susitna, and the Yukon.

BIRCH BARK: WATERPROOF WONDER
Aside from annual salmon runs, the Athabascans had no access to marine mammals—or to the intestines that made for such effective boat hulls and garments. They turned to the region's birch, the bark of which was used to create canoes. Also common were birch-bark baskets and baby carriers.

FUNCTIONAL & ORNAMENTED PIECES
Much like that of the neighboring Eskimos, Athabascan craftwork traditionally served functional purposes. But tools, weapons, and clothing were often highly decorated with colorful embroidery and shells. Athabascans are especially well known for ornamenting their caribou-skin clothing with porcupine quills and animal hair—both of which were later replaced by imported western beads.

INUPIAQ, YUP'IK & CUP'IK

Residing in Alaska's remote northern and northwestern regions, these groups are often collectively known as Eskimos or Inupiaq. They winter in coastal villages, relying on migrating marine mammals for sustenance, and spend summers at inland fish amps. Ongoing artistic traditions include ceremonial mask carving, ivory carving (not to be confused with scrimshaw), sewn skin garments, basket weaving, and soapstone carvings.

Thanks to the sheer volume of ivory art in Alaska's marketplace, you're bound to find a piece of ivory that fits your fancy—regardless of whether you prefer traditional ivory carvings, scrimshaw, or a piece that blends both artistic traditions.

IVORY CARVING

While in Alaska, you'll likely see carved ivory pieces, scrimshaw, and some fake ivory carvings (generally plastic). Ivory carving has been an Eskimo art form for thousands of years. After harvesting ivory from migrating walrus herds in the Bering Sea, artisans age tusks for up to one year before shaping it with adzes and bow drills.

KEEP IN MIND

The Marine Mammal Protection Act states that only native peoples are allowed to harvest fresh walrus ivory, which is legal to buy after it's been carved by a native person. How can you tell if a piece is real and made by a native artisan? Real ivory is likely to be pricey; be suspect of anything too cheaply priced. It should also be hard (plastic will be softer) and cool to the touch. Keep an eye out for mastery of carving technique, and be sure to ask questions when you've found a piece you're interested in buying.

WHAT IS SCRIMSHAW?

The invention of scrimshaw is attributed to 18th-century American whalers who etched the surfaces of whale bone and scrap ivory. The etchings were filled with ink, bringing the designs into stark relief.

More recently the line between traditional Eskimo ivory carving and scrimshaw has become somewhat blurred, with many native artisans incorporating both techniques.

TIPS

Ivory carving is a highly specialized native craft that is closely regulated. As it is a by-product of subsistence hunting, all meat and skin from a walrus hunt is used.

Ivory from extinct mammoths and mastodons (usually found buried underground or washed up on beaches) is also legal to buy in Alaska; many native groups keep large stores of it, as well as antique walrus tusk, for craft purposes. Many of the older pieces have a caramelized color.

5

IN FOCUS NATIVE HANDICRAFTS

Kachemak Bay. Kachemak Bay abounds with wildlife, including a large population of puffins and eagles. Tour operators take you past bird rookeries or across the bay to gravel beaches for clam digging. Most fishing charters include an opportunity to view whales, seals, porpoises, and birds close up. At the end of the day, walk along the docks on Homer Spit and watch commercial fishing boats and charter boats unload their catch.

Kachemak Bay State Park. Across Kachemak Bay from Homer Spit lies 400,000-acre Kachemak Bay State Park, one of the largest coastal parks in America. The park encompasses a line of snowcapped mountains and several large glaciers; the prominent one visible from the Spit is called Grewingk Glacier. One of the most popular trails leads 2 miles, ending at the lake in front of Grewingk Glacier. Several state park cabins can be rented for $50–$65 a night, and a number of luxurious private lodges occupy remote coves. ☎ 907/235–7024 ⊕ *www.alaskastateparks.org.*

Mako's Water Taxi. Park access is primarily by water taxi from the Spit; contact Mako's Water Taxi. ☎ 907/235–9055 ⊕ *www.makoswatertaxi.com.*

FAMILY **Pratt Museum.** The Pratt Museum is an art gallery and natural history museum rolled into one. In addition to a monthly showcase of an Alaskan artist, it has a saltwater aquarium, an exhibit on the 1989 *Exxon Valdez* oil spill, botanical gardens, nature trails, a gift shop, and pioneer, Russian, and Alaska Native displays. You can spy on wildlife with robotic video cameras set up on a seabird rookery and at the McNeil River Bear Sanctuary. A refurbished homestead cabin and outdoor summer exhibits are along the trail out back. ⊠ *Bartlett St. off Pioneer Ave.* ☎ 907/235–8635 ⊕ *www.prattmuseum.org* 🏷 *$8 adults, $6 seniors, $4 youth* ⊙ *Mid-May–mid-Sept., daily 10–6; mid-Sept.–mid-May, Tues.– Sun. noon–5* ⊙ *Closed Jan.*

SPORTS AND THE OUTDOORS

BEAR WATCHING

Emerald Air Service. Homer is a favorite departure point for viewing Alaska's famous brown bears in Katmai National Park. Emerald Air Service is one of several companies offering all-day and custom photography trips starting around $650 per person. ☎ 907/235–4160, 877/235–9600 ⊕ *www.emeraldairservice.com.*

Hallo Bay Wilderness. Hallo Bay Wilderness offers guided close-range viewing without the crowds. Day trips are offered, but it's the two- to seven-day stays at this comfortable coastal location that provide the ultimate in world-class bear- and wildlife-viewing. ☎ 907/235–2237, 888/535–2237 ⊕ *www.hallobay.com.*

FISHING

Homer is a major commercial fishing port (especially for halibut) and a popular destination for sport anglers in search of giant halibut or feisty king and silver salmon. Quite a few companies offer charter fishing in summer, from about $250 to $350 per person per day, including bait and tackle. The pricing is usually based on how many different types of fish you're fishing for.

Fishing Hole. Near the end of the Spit, Homer's famous Fishing Hole is a small bight stocked with king and silver salmon smolt (baby fish) by the Alaska Department of Fish and Game. The salmon then head out to sea, returning several years later to the Fishing Hole, where they are easy targets for wall-to-wall bank-side anglers throughout summer. The Fishing Hole isn't anything like casting for salmon along a remote stream, but your chances are good and you don't need to drop $800 for a flight into the wilderness. Fishing licenses and rental poles are available from fishing-supply stores on the Spit.

CHARTERS

Central Charters & Tours. Central Charters & Tours can arrange fishing trips in outer Kachemak Bay and Lower Cook Inlet—areas known for excellent halibut fishing. Boat sizes vary considerably; some have a six-person limit, whereas others can take up to 16 passengers. They can also arrange non-fishing tours. ⊠ *4241 Homer Spit Rd.* ☎ *907/235–7847* ⊕ *www.centralcharter.com.*

Homer Ocean Charters. Homer Ocean Charters on the Spit sets up fishing and sightseeing trips, as well as sea-kayaking and water-taxi services and remote-cabin rentals. Some of its most popular cruises go to the famous **Otter Cove Resort.** ☎ *800/426–6212* ⊕ *www.homerocean.com.*

Inlet Charters. Also try Inlet Charters for fishing charters, water-taxi services, sea-kayaking, and wildlife cruises. ☎ *800/770–6126* ⊕ *www. halibutcharters.com.*

Homer Jackpot Halibut Derby. Anyone heading out on a halibut charter is advised to buy a $10 ticket for the Homer Jackpot Halibut Derby; first prize for the largest halibut is more than $40,000. ☎ *907/235–7740* ⊕ *www.homerhalibutderby.com.*

SEA KAYAKING

Across the Bay Tent & Breakfast. For something more unusual, book an overnight trip to Kasitsna Bay through the beautiful Across the Bay Tent & Breakfast. Grounds are gorgeous, facilities are basic, and guests can take kayak tours, rent a mountain bike, or just hang out on the shore and participate in workshops on topics like fish-skin basketry, wildlife photography, and permaculture design. ☎ *907/235–3633, 907/345–2571 Sept.–May* ⊕ *www.tentandbreakfastalaska.com.*

True North Kayak Adventures. Several local companies offer guided sea-kayaking trips to protected coves within Kachemak Bay State Park and nearby islands. True North Kayak Adventures has a range of such adventures, including a three-day trip for $495 and an all-day boat and kayak trip to Yukon Island for $150 (both trips include round-trip water taxi to the island base camp, guide, all kayak equipment, and meals). ☎ *907/235–0708* ⊕ *www.truenorthkayak.com.*

SHOPPING

A variety of art by the town's residents can be found in the galleries on and around Pioneer Avenue.

Alaska Wild Berry Products. Alaska Wild Berry Products sells chocolate-covered candies, jams, jellies, sauces, and syrups made from wild berries handpicked on the Kenai Peninsula, as well as Alaska-theme gifts and clothing. Drop by for free samples of the chocolates. ✉ *528 E. Pioneer Ave.* ☎ *907/235–8858* ⊕ *www.alaskawildberryproducts.com.*

Bunnell Street Gallery. The Bunnell Street Gallery showcases and sells innovative contemporary art, all of it produced in Alaska. The gallery, which occupies the first floor of a historic trading post, also hosts workshops, lectures, musical performances, and other community events. ✉ *106 W. Bunnell St., on corner of Main St.* ☎ *907/235–2662* ⊕ *www. bunnellstreetgallery.org.*

Nomar. Nomar creates Polarfleece garments and other rugged Alaskan outerwear, plus duffels, rain gear, and children's clothing. The company manufactures equipment and clothing for commercial fishermen. ✉ *104 E. Pioneer Ave.* ☎ *907/235–8363, 800/478–8364* ⊕ *www. nomaralaska.com.*

Ptarmigan Arts. Ptarmigan Arts is a cooperative gallery with photographs, paintings, pottery, jewelry, woodworking, and other pieces by local artisans. ✉ *471 E. Pioneer Ave.* ☎ *907/235–5345* ⊕ *www. ptarmiganarts.com.*

WHERE TO EAT

$ ✕ **Fritz Creek General Store.** Directly across the road from the Homestead
ECLECTIC   Restaurant is this old-fashioned country store, gas station, liquor store, post office, video-rental shop, and deli. The latter is the primary reason for stopping at Fritz's. The food is amazingly good, from the hot and fattening turkey sandwiches to incredible freshly baked breads and pastries, pizza by the slice, veggie burritos, tamales, and ribs to go. Pull up a chair at a table crafted from an old cable spool and join the back-to-the-land crowd as they drink espresso, talk Alaskan politics, and pet the cats. $ *Average main: $6* ✉ *55770 E. End Rd.(Mile 8.2)* ☎ *907/235–6753.*

$ ✕ **Two Sisters Bakery.** This very popular café is a short walk from both
CAFÉ   Bishops Beach and the Islands and Ocean Center. In addition to fresh breads and pastries, Two Sisters specializes in deliciously healthful lunches, such as vegetarian focaccia sandwiches, homemade soups, quiche, and salads. Sit on the wraparound porch on a summer afternoon, or take your espresso and scone down to the beach to watch the waves roll in. ■TIP➔ **Upstairs are three comfortable guest rooms ($), all with private baths.** Your latte and Danish pastry breakfast is served in the café. $ *Average main: $5* ✉ *233 E. Bunnell Ave.* ☎ *907/235–2280* ⊕ *www.twosistersbakery.net.*

HUBBARD GLACIER

The 24-million-acre international wilderness that embraces Hubbard can only be described with superlatives. For example, the massive St. Elias and Fairweather ranges form the largest nonpolar glaciated mountain system in the world. British Columbia's only winter range for Dall sheep is here, and the region supports a population of both grizzlies and rare, silver-blue "glacier" bears.

This glacier is famous for "surging"—moving forward quickly. Most glaciers slide an inch or two a day. However, in 1986, the Hubbard Glacier made headlines around the world by advancing to the mouth of Russell Fjord, damming it, and creating a huge lake that lasted five months. By September it was advancing 30 meters a day. This was an event without precedent in recent geologic history, and it was mapped by the Landsat 5 satellite from 6 miles above Earth. Seals, sea lions, and porpoises were trapped behind the dam, and efforts were mounted to relocate them. "Russell Lake" eventually reached a level almost 90 feet higher than the level of Disenchantment Bay. When the dam broke on October 8, it produced an enormous rush of freshwater—something like a tidal wave in reverse.

The glacier surged again in summer 2002, creating another dam in the space of a month—by coincidence, just about the time glaciologists convened in Yakutat for an international symposium on fast glacier flow. Nervous Yakutat residents continue to lobby the government to build a channel to make sure the glacier cannot form "Russell Lake" again. They fear this would change river courses, endanger important fisheries, and inundate the Yakutat Airport, the chief transportation link with the rest of Alaska.

EXPLORING HUBBARD GLACIER

The Hubbard Glacier is an icy tongue with its root on Mt. Logan in Yukon Territory. The vast Hubbard ice field originates near 15,300-foot Mt. Hubbard and flows 76 miles to lick the sea at Yakutat and Disenchantment bays. With its 400-foot snout, Hubbard Glacier is also a prime pausing point for cruise ships. Hubbard calves great numbers of icebergs, making it difficult to get close. There are no roads to the glacier. Unless you are a seasoned mountaineer with ice experience, Hubbard Glacier is no shore excursion.

ICY STRAIT POINT

By Amy
Fletcher

In the late 1990s, Icy Strait Point was little more than a quiet grouping of defunct cannery buildings, in sporadic use as a maintenance facility for the fishing fleet of the nearby village of Hoonah. Beginning in 2004, after three years of preparation, it was reborn as Alaska's only private cruise destination, complete with restaurants, gifts shops, and guided excursions into the surrounding wilderness. Though an "artificial" port, set up specifically for the tourist trade, the site was carefully designed by locals to showcase the history, culture, and natural beauty of the area, and this emphasis on local expertise gives Icy Strait Point its authentically Alaskan appeal.

Owned by Huna Totem Corp., a Native corporation established in 1973 as part of the Alaska Native Claims Settlement Act, Icy Strait Point employs an 85% local Tlingit staff, so it's a particularly good place to find out more about Alaska Native culture and traditions.

GETTING HERE AND AROUND

Alaska Marine Lines operates ferry service two or three times a week in the summer from Juneau; the trip takes about three hours and costs $33. Two companies, Wings of Alaska and Alaska Seaplanes, make the 20-minute flight from Juneau for about $150.

Contacts Alaska Seaplanes ☎ *907/789–3331* ⊕ *www.flyalaskaseaplanes.com.* **Wings of Alaska** ☎ *907/789–0790, 800/789–9464* ⊕ *www.wingsofalaska.com.*

COMING ASHORE

Nearly all of the visitors to Icy Strait Point arrive via catamaran ferry from the cruise ships anchored just offshore, though Alaska Marine Lines also operates a ferry here, and it stops at the same dock. Upon disembarking, passengers will find a self-contained and tightly organized port within steps of the dock. Icy Strait Point became a hub for fish processing beginning in 1912, when Hoonah Packing Company built the salmon cannery, and it is in these same buildings that current tourist operations are based.

Hoonah, a mile and a half down the road, is Alaska's largest Tlingit village (pop. 747). This small, friendly town can be reached via shuttle bus on or foot—a pleasant walk along a paved shorefront sidewalk. It's a great place to have lunch and explore, but excursion and shopping options are best at Icy Strait.

Icy Strait Point is also open to independent travelers arriving by plane or ferry from Juneau. Be sure to check the cruise-ship schedule before planning your trip, as the facilities at Icy Strait Point are only open during scheduled cruise-ship stops

TOURS

Independent travelers or those whose ships don't call in Icy Strait Point can book a 20-minute flight from Juneau on one of two commuter airlines, Wings of Alaska or Alaska Seaplanes (formerly called Air Excursions) for about $150 round-trip.

VISITOR INFORMATION

You can read about everything the cruise port has to offer before your cruise at the port's website.

Contacts Icy Strait Point Cruise Port ✉ *108 Cannery Rd., Hoonah* ☎ *907/945–3141* ⊕ *www.icystraitpoint.com.*

EXPLORING ICY STRAIT POINT

Icy Strait Point's 21 excursions include whale-watching, a Native dance performance, and a 5,330-foot zipline. Cruise-ship passengers are strongly encouraged to book their excursions in advance through the cruise line. However, if there are unsold spots available on any excursions, they will be sold at the pier on a first-come first-served basis (at the same price as offered on the ship). Visitors can also explore the cannery buildings, adjacent beach, and forest trails independently, but the small size of this port makes booking an excursion a good idea.

In Alaska's Wildest Kitchen. Part culinary class, part tasting session, In Alaska's Wildest Kitchen offers visitors to Icy Strait Point a quick tutorial in preparing Alaska seafood. Led by Dodie Lunda, a retired commercial fisherwoman, this 90-minute, hands-on activity includes simple preparation techniques, recipe suggestions, and a filleting lesson. Participants gather around a horseshoe-shape counter for the prep portion and then assemble outside around a giant alder-fired grill to cook their own fillets of salmon or halibut. ⊠ *108 Cannery Rd., Hoonah* ⊕ *icystraitpoint.com.*

Tribal Dance and Cultural Legends. The appeal of this hour-long performance is twofold. It provides an introduction to some of the more formal elements of Tlingit culture, such as traditional dancing, regalia (ceremonial clothing), and storytelling, and at the same time offers the audience a vibrant and entertaining performance. The show also highlights the important fact that Tlingit culture is still thriving in Southeast Alaska, in part through the revitalization of traditions such as the ones on view in this theater. Performers share a story from Tlingit oral tradition, such as "How Raven Stole the Sun," and at the end, members of the audience are invited up on stage to try a few dance steps. ⊠ *108 Cannery Rd., Hoonah* ⊕ *icystraitpoint.com.*

SPORTS AND THE OUTDOORS

Icy Strait Point is a purpose-built cruise port and, as such, offers shore excursions only for the ship calling on that day. If there are unsold spots available on any excursions, they will be sold at the pier on a first-come first-served basis (at the same price as offered on the ship). So there's no benefit in waiting if there's an activity that interests you. Passengers have a choice of guided explorations of the area by kayak, bike, boat, plane, ATV, bus, and open-car tram, and other visitors can buy unused spots.

WILDLIFE-VIEWING

Wildlife Tours. Although wildlife-viewing is a possibility on any excursion, several tours are geared specifically toward this purpose, including the **Spasski River Valley Wildlife and Bear Search**, which entails a bus trip to a nearby meadow, and the **Whale and Marine Mammals Cruise** to Point Adolphus. Bears are sighted about 70% of the time, according to staff, and with whales, that figure climbs to 100% (if they don't spot any, you get a refund). Both excursions take about 2.5 hours. If you've got more time, the five-hour **Whales, Wildlife and Brown Bear Search** allows you to do both tours back-to-back. ⊠ *Icy Strait Point Cruise Port, 108 Cannery Rd., Hoonah* ⊕ *icystraitpoint.com.*

ZIPLINES

ZipRider. Icy Strait Point's ZipRider is a major draw, and there's really no good reason to skip this adventure while you're here. Apart from the bragging rights you'll have earned after riding the world's longest zipline—5,330 feet—the ride is an unforgettable minute and a half, and an experience that can't be recreated elsewhere. This adventure begins with an 8-mile bus ride through the village of Hoonah and up a series of bumpy logging roads to the zipline tower. There, groups of six riders are strapped into their harnesses and released into the air by Icy Strait Point staff. One advantage for the nervous: you can't see over the metal gate while you're being strapped in, so it's easy to forget how high up you are; the zipline has a vertical drop of 1,300 feet. Once in the air, nerves probably won't be an issue, as the spectacular scenery quickly commands attention. There are no age requirements, but riders must be between 90 and 270 pounds. ⊠ *Icy Strait Point Cruise Port, 108 Cannery Rd., Hoonah* ⊕ *icystraitpoint.com.*

> **ICY STRAIT POINT BEST BETS**
>
> ■ **Hoonah.** If you have time, walk in to quiet Hoonah, where you can grab a beer at The Office, voted one of the best bars in America by *Esquire* in 2006, or a salmon taco at Chipper Fish, a local favorite.
>
> ■ **Kayaking.** Experienced kayakers will appreciate the advanced-level kayak excursion, recently added to accommodate adventurers ready for a more challenging paddle.
>
> ■ **Ziplining.** The ZipRider at Icy Strait Point, billed as the world's largest zipline, is an experience you won't forget, an exhilarating ride in a spectacular setting.

SHOPPING

The cannery buildings at Icy Strait Point house about a dozen shops, all of which are Alaska-owned and -operated. Here you will find the usual range of site-specific T-shirts and baseball hats, but very few tacky souvenirs and no glitzy diamond stores—a refreshing break from the tourist zones.

Brenner's Fine Clothing and Gifts. Brenner's Fine Clothing and Gifts is another standout in the cruise port, offering an interesting and tasteful selection of women's clothing and accessories. Brenner's is an offshoot of a shop in Sitka that's been in business for 45 years. ⊠ *Icy Strait Point Cruise Port, 108 Cannery Rd., Hoonah* ☎ *907/945–3141 Cruise Port* ⊕ *www.icystraitpoint.com/Plan/Shopping* ⊗ *Open only when a ship is in port.*

Fishbone Gifts. If you're in downtown Hoonah, stop in to Fishbone Gifts. Right on the main road, this small, locally owned shop carries a nice selection of art prints, jewelry, cards, T-shirts, coffee mugs, and other Alaskan items. ⊠ *Front St., at Harbor Way, Hoonah* ⊕ *fishbonegiftshoonah.com.*

Hoonah Schools Book Shop. The bookstore at Icy Strait Point, Hoonah Schools Book Shop, is notable for its shopkeepers: they're all students from tiny Hoonah High School (the graduating class of 2013 had nine members). The students learn about running a business through their work at the store while raising money for the school activities program. ✉ *108 Cannery Rd., Hoonah* ☎ *907/945–3141* ⊕ *www.icystraitpoint. com/Plan/Shopping* ☉ *Open only when a ship is in port.*

Lisa's Art Store. If you're interested in Alaska Native artwork, don't miss this small gallery and gift shop in the cruise port, which offers a wide range of traditional and contemporary handcrafted items, from delicate dentalium shell earrings to woven red cedar baskets. This shop also stocks a line of herbal remedies called Tlingit Rx, which includes traditional salves and lotions made from cottonwood, devil's club, and other local flora. ✉ *Icy Strait Point Cruise Port, 108 Cannery Rd., Hoonah* ☎ *907/945–3141 Cruise Port* ⊕ *www.icystraitpoint.com/Plan/ Shopping* ☉ *Open only when a ship is in port.*

WHERE TO EAT

Icy Strait Point cruise port has four main eateries, as well as an espresso stand and a donut shop.

$$ ✕ **Chipper Fish.** This little roadside restaurant in Hoonah doesn't look
SEAFOOD like much from the outside, but it comes highly recommended by the locals. The salmon tacos garner particularly high praise. Hours can be variable, especially in the off-season. ⑤ *Average main: $12* ✉ *316 Front St., Hoonah* ☎ *907/945–3434* ☉ *Closed Mon.*

$$ ✕ **The Cookhouse Restaurant.** A short way down the waterfront board-
AMERICAN walk from the cruise port is the Cookhouse, a casual restaurant with indoor and outdoor seating. Heat lamps on the deck make the outdoor seating attractive even on cooler days, and with views like this, it makes sense to head outside. Menu items include burgers, reindeer slider sloppy joes, and (highly recommended) halibut-and-chips. ⑤ *Average main: $18* ✉ *Icy Strait Point Cruise Port, 108 Cannery Rd., Hoonah* ☎ *907/945–3141* ⊕ *www.icystraitpoint.com/Plan/Dining* ☉ *Closed when a cruise ship is not in port.*

$$ ✕ **The Crab Station.** King, Dungeness, and tanner (or snow) crabs are
SEAFOOD served in various forms when in season at the Crab Station, an outdoor stand with tables on the docks extending out over the water. During Dungeness season, crab are caught in the surrounding waters of Port Frederick and kept alive until your order is prepared. ⑤ *Average main: $22* ✉ *Icy Strait Point Cruise Port, 108 Cannery Rd., Hoonah* ☎ *907/945–3141* ⊕ *www.icystraitpoint.com/Plan/Dining* ☉ *Closed when a cruise ship is not in port.*

$$ ✕ **The Landing Zone Bar and Grill.** Down the boardwalk from the port
SEAFOOD you'll find the Landing Zone. Larger and a bit more upscale than the Cookhouse, the Landing gets its name from its location at the end of the ZipRider zipline; those who remained on the ground can watch their braver friends fly through the air on live-stream video monitors while sipping an Alaskan-brewed beer at the bar. The Landing's half-dozen menu items include salmon prepared at an outdoor grill, beef brisket, and reindeer sausage. ⑤ *Average main: $14* ✉ *Icy Strait Point Cruise Port, 108 Cannery Rd., Hoonah* ☎ *907/945–3141* ⊕ *www. icystraitpoint.com/Plan/Dining* ☉ *Closed when no ships are in port.*

5

JUNEAU

Juneau, Alaska's capital and third-largest city, is on the North American mainland but can't be reached by road. The city owes its origins to two colorful sourdoughs (Alaskan pioneers)—Joe Juneau and Richard Harris—and to a Tlingit chief named Kowee, who led the two men to rich reserves of gold at Snow Slide Gulch, the drainage of Gold Creek around which the town was eventually built. That was in 1880, and shortly thereafter a modest stampede resulted in the formation of a mining camp, which quickly grew to become the Alaska district government capital in 1906. The city may well have continued under its original appellation—Harrisburg, after Richard Harris—were it not for Joe Juneau's political jockeying at a miner's meeting in 1881.

For some 60 years after Juneau's founding, gold was the mainstay of the economy. In its heyday the AJ (for Alaska Juneau) Gold Mine was the biggest low-grade ore mine in the world. It was not until World War II, when the government decided it needed Juneau's manpower for the war effort, that the AJ and other mines in the area ceased operations. After the war, mining failed to start up again, and government became the city's principal employer. Juneau's mines leave a rich legacy, though; the AJ Gold Mine alone produced more than $80 million in gold.

Perhaps because of its colorful history, Juneau is full of contrasts. Its dramatic hillside location and historic downtown buildings provide a frontier feeling, but the city's cosmopolitan nature comes through in fine museums, noteworthy restaurants, and a literate and outdoorsy populace. Here you can enjoy the Mt. Roberts Tramway, plenty of densely forested wilderness areas, quiet bays for sea kayaking, and even the famous drive-up Mendenhall Glacier.

COMING ASHORE

Most cruise ships dock on the south edge of town between the **Marine Park** and the **A.J. Dock.** Several ships can tie up at once; others occasionally anchor in the harbor. Juneau's downtown shops are a pleasant walk from the docks. A shuttle bus ($2 all day) runs from the A.J. Dock to town whenever ships are in port.

TOURS

Alaska Coach Tours. Alaska Coach Tours operates the Historic Juneau Trolley, providing a 45-minute tour of Alaska's capital city. ☎ 907/586–7433 ⊕ www.alaskacoachtours.com.

Mighty Great Trips. The company leads guided bus tours that include a visit to Mendenhall Glacier as well as helicopter tours, river rafting, and whale-watching. ☎ 907/789–5460 ⊕ www.mightygreattrips.com.

VISITOR INFORMATION

Pick up maps, bus schedules, charter-fishing information, and tour brochures at the small kiosks on the pier at Marine Park and in the cruise-ship terminal on South Franklin Street. Both are staffed when ships are in port.

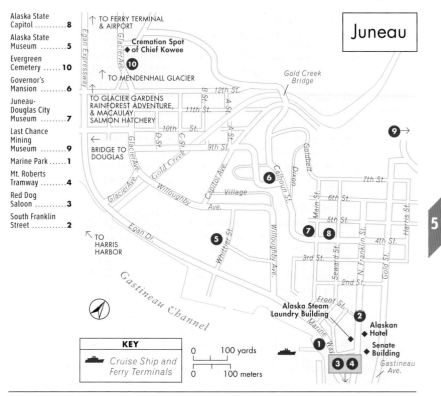

Juneau

TO FERRY TERMINAL
& AIRPORT

Cremation Spot
◆ of Chief Kowee

TO MENDENHALL GLACIER

Gold Creek
Bridge

TO GLACIER GARDENS
RAINFOREST ADVENTURE,
& MACAULAY
SALMON HATCHERY

BRIDGE TO
DOUGLAS

Village

TO
HARRIS
HARBOR

Gastineau Channel

KEY

Cruise Ship and
Ferry Terminals

0   100 yards
0   100 meters

Alaska Steam
Laundry Building

Alaskan
◆ Hotel

Senate
◆ Building

Gastineau
Ave.

EXPLORING

DOWNTOWN

Alaska State Capitol. Completed in 1931 and remodeled in 2006, this rather unassuming building houses the governor's office and hosts state legislature meetings in winter, placing it at the epicenter of Alaska's increasingly animated political discourse. Historical photos line the upstairs walls. Feel free to stroll right in. ▤ **TIP**➔ **You can pick up a self-guided tour brochure as you enter.** Complimentary guided tours are available daily mid-May through mid-September. ⊠ *Corner of Seward and 4th Sts.* ☎ *907/465–4648* ⊕ *w3.legis.state.ak.us/misc/capitol.php.*

FAMILY **Alaska State Museum.** This is one of Alaska's finest museums. Those interested in Native cultures will enjoy examining the 38-foot walrus-hide *umiak* (an open, skin-covered Inupiaq boat). Natural-history exhibits include preserved brown bears and a two-story-high eagle-nesting tree. Russian-American and gold-rush displays and contemporary art complete the collection. ▤**TIP**➔ **Be sure to visit the gift shop (run by the Friends of the Alaska State Museum) and its extraordinary selection of Native art, including baskets, carvings, and masks.** ⊠ *395 Whittier St.* ☎ *907/465–2901* ⊕ *www.museums.state.ak.us* ➥ *$7 mid-May–mid-Sept., $3 mid-Sept.–mid-May* ☉ *Mid-May–mid-Sept., daily 8:30–5:30; mid-Sept.–mid-May, Tues.–Sat. 10–4.*

Evergreen Cemetery. Many Juneau pioneers, including Joe Juneau and Richard Harris, are buried here. Juneau (1836–99), a Canadian by birth, died in Dawson City, Yukon, but his body was returned to the city that bears his name. Harris (1833–1907), whose name can be found on downtown's Harris Street, died here. A meandering gravel path leads through the graveyard, and at the end of it is the monument commemorating the cremation spot of Chief Kowee. ⌧ *Martin and Seater Sts.*

Governor's Mansion. Completed in 1912, this stately colonial-style home overlooks downtown Juneau. With 14,400 square feet, six bedrooms, and 10 bathrooms, it's no miner's cabin. Out front is a totem pole that tells three tales: the history of man, the cause of ocean tides, and the origin of Alaska's ubiquitous mosquitoes. Unfortunately, tours of the residence are not permitted. ⌧ *716 Calhoun Ave.*

> ### JUNEAU BEST BETS
>
> ■ **Walk South Franklin Street.** Juneau's historic downtown still retains much of its hardscrabble mining feel. While away hours in the saloons and shops of this charming district.
>
> ■ **Ride the Mt. Roberts Tram.** On Juneau's favorite attraction, enjoy panoramic views of the area's stunning scenery from 1,800 feet above town.
>
> ■ **Marvel at the Mendenhall Glacier.** With an otherworldly blue hue and a visitor center that answers all your glacier questions, Alaska's most accessible— and most popular—glacier is a must-see.

FAMILY **Juneau-Douglas City Museum.** Among the exhibits interpreting local mining and Tlingit history are an Assay Lab diorama, a reconstructed Tlingit fish trap and video of excavation, historic photos, and pioneer artifacts, including a century-old store and kitchen. Digital story kiosks highlight Alaska's government, civil rights in Alaska, Alaska's quest for statehood, and cultures of Juneau. Youngsters will appreciate the hands-on room, where they can try on clothes similar to ones worn by the miners or look at gold-rush stereoscopes. Guided historic walking tours are offered May through September. ⌧ *114 4th St.* ☎ *907/586–3572* ⊕ *www.juneau.org/parksrec/museum* ⌧ *$6 May–Sept., free Oct.–Apr.* ☉ *May and June, weekdays 9–6; July–Sept., weekdays 9–6, weekends 10–5; Oct.–Apr., Tues.–Sat. 10–4.*

OFF THE
BEATEN
PATH
Last Chance Mining Museum. A 1½-mile hike or taxi ride behind town, this small museum is housed in the former compressor building of Juneau's historic AJ Gold Mine. The collection includes old mining tools, railcars, minerals, and a 3-D map of the ore body. If you have time, and didn't arrive on foot, meander down **Basin Road** back toward town. Unlike most of Juneau, Basin Road is flat and relatively quiet. The surrounding country is steep and wooded, with trails leading in all directions, including one to the summit of Mt. Juneau. At the base of the Perseverance Trail, not far from the museum, you can see the boarded-up opening to an old mining tunnel; even from a safe distance you can feel a chilly breeze wafting through the cracks. ⌧ *1001 Basin Rd.* ☎ *907/586–5338* ⊕ *www.traveljuneau.com/cms/d/juneau_museums. php* ⌧ *$4* ☉ *Mid-May–mid-Sept., daily 9:30–12:30 and 3–6:30.*

CLOSE UP

Best Ports for Kids

Juneau: For a day of family togetherness, the Gold Creek Salmon Bake hits the spot. After an all-you-can-eat buffet lunch of barbecued fresh Alaska salmon (there are chicken and ribs for picky eaters), baked beans, corn bread, and blueberry cake, the kids can roast marshmallows over the open fire and explore the abandoned Wagner Mine. If you're lucky, you'll spot salmon spawning in the clear water beneath the Salmon Creek waterfall.

Ketchikan: One of the cheesiest, yet most kid-pleasing tastes of old-time woodsman skills is the Great Alaskan Lumberjack Show. All summer long this hour-long contest demonstrates such authentic "sports" as sawing, ax throwing, chopping, and a log-rolling duel. There's even a speed climb up a 50-foot tree. At 50 Main Street, all the fun's within walking distance of the cruise-ship pier.

Skagway: Spend the day in real Alaskan wilderness. Get a map at the Convention and Visitors Bureau and take the entire family on the inexpensive city bus to 23rd Avenue, where a 10-minute walk on a dirt road leads to the Gold Rush Cemetery. Let the kids discover where the town's villain Soapy Smith and its hero Frank Reid are buried, and then continue along the trail a quarter mile to Reid Falls.

Marine Park. On the dock where the cruise ships "tie up" is a little urban oasis with benches, shade trees, and shelter. It's a great place to enjoy an outdoor meal from one of Juneau's street vendors, and on Friday evenings in summer it features live performances by Juneau musicians. A visitor kiosk is staffed according to cruise-ship schedules. ⊠ *Marine Way* ⊕ *www.juneau.org/parkrec/facilities/downtown.php.*

FAMILY **Mt. Roberts Tramway.** One of Southeast Alaska's most popular tourist attractions, this tram whisks you from the cruise terminal 1,800 feet up the side of Mt. Roberts. After the six-minute ride you can take in a film on the history and legends of the Tlingits, visit the nature center, go for an alpine walk on hiking trails (including the 5-mile round-trip hike to Mt. Roberts's 3,819-foot summit), purchase Native crafts, or enjoy a meal while savoring mountain views. A local company leads guided wilderness hikes from the summit, and the bar serves locally brewed beers. ⊠ *490 S. Franklin St.* ☎ *907/463–3412, 888/461–8726* ⊕ *www. goldbelttours.com/mount-roberts-tramway* ⊠ *$31* ⊙ *May–Sept., daily 8 am–9 pm; hrs may vary depending on cruise-ship schedule.*

Red Dog Saloon. The frontierish quarters of the Red Dog have housed an infamous Juneau watering hole since 1890. Nearly every conceivable surface in this two-story bar is cluttered with graffiti, business cards, and memorabilia, including a pistol that reputedly belonged to Wyatt Earp, who failed to reclaim the piece after checking it in at the U.S. Marshall's office on June 27, 1900. The saloon's food menu includes halibut, reindeer sausage, potato skins, burgers, and locally brewed Alaskan beers. A little atmospheric sawdust covers the floor as well. Musicians pump out ragtime piano tunes when cruise ships are docked. ⊠ *278 S. Franklin St.* ☎ *907/463–3658* ⊕ *www.reddogsaloon.com.*

"We hiked to the tongue of the Mendenhall Glacier to find this roaring waterfall crashing into the bay. It gave us a perspective on man's insignificance next to mother nature." —Chris Marlow, Photo Contest Winner

South Franklin Street. The buildings on South Franklin Street (and neighboring Front Street), among the oldest and most inviting structures in the city, house curio and crafts shops, snack shops, and a salmon shop. Many reflect the architecture of the 1920s and '30s. When the small **Alaskan Hotel** opened in 1913, Juneau was home to 30 saloons; the Alaskan gives today's visitors the most authentic glimpse of the town's whiskey-rich history. The barroom's massive, mirrored oak back bar is accented by Tiffany lights and panels. Topped by a wood-shingled turret, the 1901 **Alaska Steam Laundry Building** now houses a coffeehouse and other stores. The **Senate Building,** another of South Franklin's treasured landmarks, is across the street. ✉ *S. Franklin St.*

OUTSIDE TOWN

DIPAC Macaulay Salmon Hatchery. Watch through an underwater window as salmon fight their way up a fish ladder from mid-June to mid-October. Inside the busy hatchery, which produces almost 125 million young salmon annually, you will learn about the environmental considerations of commercial fishermen and the lives of salmon. A retail shop sells gifts and salmon products. The salmon hatchery is part of a larger nonprofit, Douglas Island Pink & Chum, Inc., and is usually referred to locally by its acronym, DIPAC. ✉ *2697 Channel Dr.* ☎ *907/463–4810, 877/463–2486* ⊕ *dipac.net* ✉ *$3.25 including short tour* ☉ *May–Sept., weekdays 10–6, weekends 10–5; Oct.–May by appointment.*

Glacier Gardens Rainforest Adventure. Spread over 50 acres of rain forest, the family-owned Glacier Gardens has ponds, waterfalls, hiking paths, a large atrium, and gardens. The roots of fallen trees, turned upside down and buried in the ground, act as bowls to hold planters that overflow with begonias, fuchsias, and petunias. Guided tours in covered golf carts lead you along the 4 miles of paved paths, and a 580-foot-high overlook provides dramatic views of the Mendenhall wetlands wildlife refuge, Chilkat mountains, and downtown Juneau. A café and gift shop are here, and the conservatory is a popular wedding spot. Admission includes a guided tour. ■ TIP➔ The Juneau city bus, which departs from multiple locations in downtown Juneau, stops right in front of Glacier Gardens. ⊠ *7600 Glacier Hwy.* ☎ *907/790–3377* ⊕ *www.glaciergardens.com* ▣ *$24.95* ☉ *May–Sept., daily 9–6.*

FAMILY
Fodor'sChoice
★

Mendenhall Glacier. Alaska's most-visited drive-up glacier spans 12 miles and is fed by the massive Juneau Icefield. Like many other Alaska glaciers, it is retreating up the valley, losing more than 100 feet a year as massive chunks of ice calve into the small lake separating Mendenhall from the **Mendenhall Visitor Center.** The center has highly interactive exhibits on the glacier, a theater and bookstore, educational exhibits, and panoramic views. It's a great place for children to learn the basics of glacier dynamics. Nature trails lead along Mendenhall Lake and into the mountains overlooking Mendenhall Glacier; the trails are marked by posts and paint stripes delineating the historic location of the glacier, providing a sharp reminder of the Mendenhall's hasty retreat. An elevated viewing platform allows visitors to look for spawning sockeye and coho salmon—and the bears that eat them—at Steep Creek, ½ mile south of the visitor center along the Moraine Ecology Trail. Several companies lead bus tours to the glacier. A glacier express bus leaves from the cruise-ship terminal and heads right out to Mendenhall Glacier; ask at the visitor information center there. ⊠ *End of Glacier Spur Rd. off Mendenhall Loop Rd.* ☎ *907/789–0097* ⊕ *www.fs.usda.gov/detail/tongass/about-forest/offices* ▣ *Visitor center $3 May–Sept., free Oct.–Apr.* ☉ *May–Sept., daily 8–7:30; Oct.–Apr., Fri.–Sun. 10–4.*

SPORTS AND THE OUTDOORS

BIKING

Driftwood Lodge. Drop by the Juneau Convention & Visitors Bureau kiosk at Marine Park for details on local trails open to bikes. Nearby is Driftwood Lodge, which has basic bikes for rent. ⊠ *435 Willoughby Ave.* ☎ *907/586–2280* ⊕ *www.driftwoodalaska.com.*

BOATING, CANOEING, AND KAYAKING

Above & Beyond Alaska. In the Juneau area, Above & Beyond Alaska guides day and overnight camping, ice climbing, Mendenhall Glacier trips, and sea-kayaking trips. ⊠ *Auke Bay* ☎ *907/364–2333* ⊕ *www.beyondak.com.*

Adventure Bound Alaska. All-day trips to Sawyer Glacier within Tracy Arm in summer are available from Adventure Bound Alaska. ⊠ *76 Egan Dr.* ☎ *907/463–2509, 800/228–3875* ⊕ *www.adventureboundalaska.com.*

FLIGHTSEEING

Several local companies operate helicopter flightseeing trips to the spectacular glaciers flowing from Juneau Icefield. Most have booths along the downtown cruise-ship dock. All include a touchdown on a glacier, providing guests of almost all ages and abilities a chance to romp on these rivers of ice. Some also lead trips that include a dogsled ride on the glacier, an increasingly popular tourist pastime. Helicopter tours in Juneau have a controversial history due to noise complaints from residents. Note that although we recommend the best companies, even some of the most experienced pilots have had accidents; always ask a carrier about its recent safety record before booking a trip.

Temsco Helicopters. The self-proclaimed pioneers of Alaska glacier helicopter touring, Temsco Helicopters offers glacier tours, dogsled adventures, and year-round flightseeing. ⊠ *1650 Maplesden Way* ☎ *907/789–9501, 877/789–9501* ⊕ *www.temscoair.com.*

Ward Air. Take flightseeing trips to Glacier Bay, the Juneau Icefield, Tracy Arm, and Pack Creek with Ward Air. ⊠ *8991 Yandukin Dr.* ☎ *907/789–9150, 800/478–9150* ⊕ *www.wardair.com.*

Wings Airways and Taku Glacier Lodge. This Juneau-based company specializes in tours of the surrounding ice fields and the Taku Flight & Feast ride, on which a salmon feast awaits you at a classic Alaskan cabin, complete with glacier views—one of the best day trips out of the state capital. ⊠ *2 Marine Way, Suite 175* ☎ *907/586–6275* ⊕ *www.wingsairways.com.*

GOLD PANNING

FAMILY **Alaska Travel Adventures.** Gold panning is fun, especially for children, and Juneau is one of Southeast's best-known gold-panning towns. Sometimes you actually discover a few flecks of the precious metal in the bottom of your pan. You can buy a pan at almost any Alaska hardware or sporting-goods store. Alaska Travel Adventures has gold-panning tours near the famous Alaska-Juneau Mine. ☎ *800/323–5757, 907/789–0052* ⊕ *www.bestofalaskatravel.com.*

HIKING

Gastineau Guiding. This company leads a variety of hikes in the Juneau area. Especially popular are the walks from the top of the tram on Mt. Roberts. ⊠ *1330 Eastaugh Way, Suite 2* ☎ *907/586–8231* ⊕ *www.stepintoalaska.com.*

WHALE-WATCHING

Alaska Whale Watching. The company offers small-group excursions (up to 20 guests) aboard a luxury yacht with an onboard naturalist as well as a whale-watching–fishing combination tour, which is popular with multigenerational groups. ☎ *907/321–5859, 888/432–6722* ⊕ *www.akwhalewatching.com.*

Juneau Sportfishing & Sightseeing. Several companies lead whale-watching trips from Juneau. Juneau Sportfishing & Sightseeing has been around for many years, and its boats carry a maximum of six passengers, providing a personalized trip. ☎ *907/586–1887* ⊕ *www.juneausportfishing.com.*

Orca Enterprises (with Captain Larry). Take whale-watching tours via jet boats designed for comfort and speed with Orca Enterprises (with Captain Larry). The operator boasts a whale-sighting success rate of 99.9% between May 1 and October 15. ⊠ *495 S. Franklin St.* ☎ *907/789–6801, 888/733–6722* ⊕ *www.alaskawhalewatching.com.*

Fodor's Choice ★ **Weather Permitting Alaska.** Take small-boat luxury whale-watching trips that last four hours, including van travel, with Weather Permitting Alaska. Visitors get plenty of time to view whales and to look for other animals, including orcas, bears, sea lions, eagles, and porpoises, all while enjoying dramatic scenery. There are never more than 10 customers on a trip, making this one of the most flexible, intimate, and comprehensive whale-watches anywhere. The boat is stable and roomy. All trips include generous snacks featuring shrimp or salmon and homemade brownies along with nonalcoholic beverages. There is a money-back guarantee for whale viewing. The boat captain is a certified Wilderness First Aid Responder and is certified in swift water rescue and proficiency in survival craft. ⊠ *19400 Beardsley Way* ☎ *907/209–4221* ⊕ *www.weatherpermittingalaska.com.*

SHOPPING

Decker Gallery. In downtown Juneau, see Rie Muñoz's paintings and tapestries at Decker Gallery. ⊠ *233 S. Franklin St.* ☎ *907/463–5536, 800/463–5536.*

Hummingbird Hollow. A surprising exception to the cheesy-airport-gift-shop epidemic, Juneau's airport gift shop, Hummingbird Hollow, sells authentic Native art, including a diverse selection of jewelry, baskets, and Eskimo dolls. ⊠ *1873 Shell Simmons Dr.* ☎ *907/789–4672.*

Rie Muñoz Gallery. Rie Muñoz, of the Rie Muñoz Gallery, is one of Alaska's best-known artists. She's the creator of a stylized, simple, and colorful design technique that is much copied but rarely equaled. The gallery is located in Mendenhall Valley, a convenient 10-minute walk from the airport. ⊠ *2101 N. Jordan Ave.* ☎ *907/789–7449, 800/247–3151* ⊕ *www.riemunoz.com.*

Wm. Spear Design. Located upstairs through a separate entrance next to Heritage Coffee, Wm. Spear Design is an interesting store, where this lawyer-turned-artist produces a fun and colorful collection of enameled pins and zipper pulls. ⊠ *174 S. Franklin St.* ☎ *907/586–2209* ⊕ *www.wmspear.com.*

WHERE TO EAT

$$$$ SEAFOOD ✕ **Gold Creek Salmon Bake.** Trees, mountains, and the rushing water of Salmon Creek surround the comfortable, canopy-covered benches and tables at this authentic salmon bake. Fresh-caught salmon is cooked over an alder fire and served with a succulent sauce. For $44 there is all-you-can-eat salmon, pasta, and chicken along with baked beans, rice pilaf, salad bar, corn bread, and blueberry cake. Wine and beer are extra. After dinner you can pan for gold in the stream, wander up the hill to explore the remains of the Wagner gold mine, or roast marshmallows

over the fire. A round-trip bus ride from downtown is included; arrangements should be made in advance through Alaska Travel Adventures. ⑤ *Average main: $44* ✉ *1061 Salmon Lane Rd.* ☎ *907/789–0052, 800/323–5757* ⊕ *www.bestofalaskatravel.com/alaska_day_tours/pages/ j_gold_creek_salmon.htm* ☉ *Closed Oct.–Apr.*

$$
ECLECTIC

✗ **The Hangar on the Wharf.** Crowded with locals and travelers, the Hangar occupies the building where Alaska Airlines started business. Flight-theme puns dominate the menu (i.e., "Pre-flight Snacks" and the "Plane Caesar"), but the comfortably worn wood and vintage airplane photos create a casual dining experience that outweighs the kitsch. Every seat has views of the Gastineau Channel and Douglas Island. On warm days, outdoor seating is offered. This Juneau hotspot makes a wide selection of entrées, including locally caught halibut and salmon, filet mignon, great burgers, and daily specials. The Hangar serves more than 100 beers, including a few dozen on tap. On Friday and Saturday nights jazz or rock bands take the stage. If you've have had enough salmon, try the prime rib, which the Hangar is known for. ⑤ *Average main: $18* ✉ *2 Marine Way, Merchants Wharf Mall* ☎ *907/586–5018* ⊕ *www. hangaronthewharf.com.*

KETCHIKAN

Ketchikan is famous for its colorful totem poles, rainy skies, steep–as–San Francisco streets, and lush island setting. Some 13,000 people call the town home, and, in summer cruise ships crowd the shoreline, floatplanes depart noisily for Misty Fiords National Monument, and salmon-laden commercial fishing boats motor through Tongass Narrows. In the last decade Ketchikan's rowdy, blue-collar heritage of logging and fishing has been softened by the loss of many timber-industry jobs and the dramatic rise of cruise-ship tourism. With some effort, though, visitors can still glimpse the rugged frontier spirit that once permeated this hardscrabble cannery town.

This town is the first bite of Alaska that many travelers taste. Despite its imposing backdrop, hillside homes, and many staircases, Ketchikan is relatively easy to walk through. Downtown's favorite stops include the Spruce Mill Development shops and Creek Street. A bit farther away you'll find the Totem Heritage Center and Deer Mountain Tribal Hatchery. Out of town (but included on most bus tours) are two longtime favorites: Totem Bight State Historical Park and Saxman Totem Park.

COMING ASHORE

Most ships dock or tender passengers ashore directly across from the Ketchikan Visitors Bureau on Front and Mission streets, in the center of downtown. A new dock, several blocks north on the other side of the tunnel, is still within easy walking distance of most of the town's sights. Walking-tour signs lead you around the city. For panoramic vistas of the surrounding area—and a wee bit of exercise—climb the stairs leading up several steep hillsides.

To reach sights farther from downtown, rent a car, hire a cab, or ride the local buses. Metered taxis meet the ships right on the docks and also wait across the street. Rates are $3.70 for pickup and $3.50 per mile. Up to six passengers can hire a taxi to tour for $75 per hour. Local buses run along the main route through town and south to Saxman. The fare is $1.

VISITOR INFORMATION
The helpful visitors bureau is right next to the cruise-ship docks. Half the space is occupied by day-tour, flightseeing, and boat-tour operators.

Contacts Ketchikan Visitors Bureau ⊠ *131 Front St.* ☏ *907/225–6166, 800/770–3300* ⊕ *www.visit-ketchikan.com.*

KETCHIKAN BEST BETS

■ **Exploring Creek Street.** No visit to Ketchikan would be complete without a stroll along this elevated wooden boulevard, once the site of the town's rip-roaring bordellos.

■ **Totem gazing at Saxman Totem Park.** View one of the best totem collections in all of Southeast Alaska at this must-see stop.

■ **Rain-forest Canopy Tours.** Zip through the towering trees of Ketchikan's coastal rain forest, experiencing the majesty of this unique ecosystem from a bird's-eye view.

EXPLORING

IN TOWN

Cape Fox Lodge. For the town's best harbor views and one of Southeast Alaska's most luxurious lobbies, walk to the top of steep Venetia Avenue or take the funicular ($2) up from Creek Street. Don't miss the totems and other artwork created by master carvers Nathan Jackson and Lee Wallace. ⊠ *800 Venetia Way* ☏ *907/225–8001, 866/225–8001* ⊕ *www. capefoxlodge.com.*

City Park. The Deer Mountain Tribal Hatchery leads into this small but charming park, which has picnic tables, a fountain, and paved paths. Ketchikan Creek runs through it. ⊠ *Park and Fair Sts.*

Creek Street. This was once Ketchikan's infamous red-light district. During Prohibition, Creek Street was home to numerous speakeasies, and in the early 1900s more than 30 houses of prostitution operated here. Today the small, colorful houses, built on stilts over the creek waters, have been restored as trendy shops. ⊕ *creekstreetketchikan.com.*

Creek Street Footbridge. Stand over Ketchikan Creek for good salmon viewing when the fish are running. In summer you can see impressive runs of coho, king, pink, and chum salmon, along with smaller numbers of steelhead and rainbow trout heading upstream to spawn. ■ TIP➔ Keep your eyes peeled for sea lions snacking on the incoming fish.

FAMILY **Deer Mountain Tribal Hatchery.** Tens of thousands of king and coho salmon are raised at this hatchery on Ketchikan Creek owned by the Ketchikan Indian Community. Midsummer visitors can view natural spawning in the creek by pink salmon and steelhead trout as well as workers collecting and fertilizing the salmon eggs for the hatchery. ⊠ *1158 Salmon Rd.* ☏ *907/228–5530, 800/252–5158* ⊕ *kictribe.org/businesses/index. html* ⊙ *Hatchery May–Sept., daily 8–4:30.*

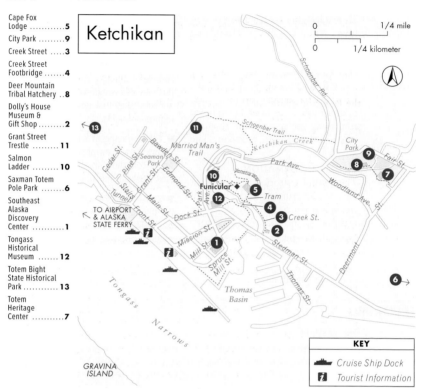

Dolly's House Museum & Gift Shop. Formerly owned by the inimitable Dolly Arthur, this steep-roofed home once housed Creek Street's most famous brothel. The house has been preserved as a museum, complete with furnishings, beds, and a short history of the life and times of Ketchikan's best-known madam. ⊠ *24 Creek St.* ☎ *907/225–6329 (summer only)* ⊕ *www.dollyshouse.com* ⊡ *$5* ⊗ *Daily 8–4 when cruise ships are in port; closed in winter.*

Grant Street Trestle. At one time virtually all of Ketchikan's walkways and streets were made from wooden trestles, but now only one of these handsome wooden streets remains, constructed in 1908.

Salmon ladder. Get out your camera and set it for high speed at the fish ladder, a series of pools arranged like steps that allow fish to travel upstream around a dam or falls. When the salmon start running from June onward, thousands of fish leap the falls (or take the easier fish-ladder route). They spawn in Ketchikan Creek's waters farther upstream. Many can also be seen in the creek's eddies above and below the falls. The falls, fish ladder, and a large carving of a jumping salmon are just off Park Avenue on Married Man's Trail. The trail was once used by married men for discreet access to the red-light district on Creek Street. ⊠ *Married Man's Trail off Park Ave.*

FAMILY **Southeast Alaska Discovery Center.** This impressive public lands interpretive center features exhibits—including one on the rain forest—that focus on the resources, Native cultures, and ecosystems of Southeast Alaska. The U.S. Forest Service and other federal agencies provide information on Alaska's public lands, and a large gift shop sells natural-history books, maps, and videos about the sights in Ketchikan and Southeast. America the Beautiful–National Park and Federal Recreational Land Passes are accepted and sold. ⊠ *50 Main St.* ☎ *907/228–6220* ⊕ *www.alaskacenters. gov/ketchikan.cfm* ⊠ *$5 May–Sept., free Oct.–Apr.* ☉ *May–Sept., weekdays 8–5, weekends 8–4; Oct.–Apr., Fri. and Sat. 10–4.*

Tongass Historical Museum. Native artifacts and pioneer relics revisit the mining and fishing eras at this museum in the same building as the library. Exhibits include a big, brilliantly polished lens from Tree Point Lighthouse, well-presented Native tools and artwork, and photography collections. Other exhibits rotate, but always include Tlingit items. ⊠ *629 Dock St.* ☎ *907/225–5600* ⊕ *www.city.ketchikan.ak.us/ departments/museums/tongass.html* ⊠ *$2* ☉ *May–Sept., daily 8–5; Oct.–Apr., Tues.–Fri. 1–5, Sat. 10–4.*

Totem Heritage Center. Gathered from uninhabited Tlingit and Haida village sites, many of the authentic Native totems in this rare collection are well over a century old—a rare age for cedar carvings, which are frequently lost to decay in Southeast's exceedingly wet climate. The center also features guided tours and displays crafts of the Tlingit, Haida, and Tsimshian cultures. Outside are several more poles carved in the three decades since this center opened. The center offers an annual series of classes, workshops, and seminars related to Northwest Coast Native art and culture. ⊠ *601 Deermount St.* ☎ *907/225–5900* ⊕ *www.city. ketchikan.ak.us/departments/museums/totem.html* ⊠ *$5* ☉ *May–Sept., daily 8–5; Oct.–Apr., weekdays 1–5.*

OUTSIDE TOWN

Saxman Totem Park. A 2.5-mile paved walking path–bike trail parallels the road from Ketchikan to Saxman Native Village, named for a missionary who helped Native Alaskans settle here before 1900. A totem park dominates the center of Saxman, with poles that represent a wide range of human and animal-inspired figures, including bears, ravens, whales, and eagles. There is a $5 charge to enter.

Saxman's Beaver Clan tribal house is said to be the largest in Alaska. Carvers create totem poles and totemic art objects in the adjacent carver's shed. You can get to the park on foot or by taxi, bicycle, or city bus. You can visit the totem park on your own, but to visit the tribal house and theater you must take a tour. Tickets are sold at the gift shop across from the totems. Call ahead for tour schedules. ⊠ *S. Tongass Hwy., 2 miles south of town* ☎ *907/225–4421.*

Totem Bight State Historical Park. Totem Bight State Historical Park has many totem poles and a hand-hewn Native tribal house; it sits on a scenic spit of land facing the waters of Tongass Narrows. The clan house is open daily in summer. About a quarter of the Ketchikan bus tours include Totem Bight. ⊠ *N. Tongass Hwy., approx. 10 miles north of town* ☎ *907/247–8574* ⊠ *Free* ☉ *Dawn–dusk.*

SPORTS AND THE OUTDOORS

CANOPY TOURS

Alaska Canopy Adventures. Often associated with rain forests of the tropical sort, canopy tours are Ketchikan's fastest-growing outdoor activity. Featuring a series of ziplines, aerial boardwalks, and suspension bridges, canopy tours provide an up-close view of the coastal forests. At Alaska Canopy Adventures—a course at the Alaska Rainforest Sanctuary, 8.4 miles south of town—the longest of the tour's eight ziplines stretches more than 800 feet, and whisks you along some 130 feet off the ground. Book online or with your cruise line. ⊠ *116 Wood Rd.* ☎ *907/225–5503* ⊕ *www.alaskacanopy.com.*

Southeast Exposure. A rain-forest zipline and ropes course is offered through Southeast Exposure, a well-known kayaking outfit in the area. ⊠ *37 Potter Rd.* ☎ *907/225–8829* ⊕ *www.southeastexposure.com.*

FLIGHTSEEING

Alaska Travel Adventures. The company's backcountry jeep trips are fun, as are the 20-person canoe outings perfect for people just dipping their toes into (very) soft adventure travel. ☎ *800/323–5757, 907/247–5295* ⊕ *www.bestofalaskatravel.com.*

Allen Marine Tours. One of Southeast's largest and best-known tour operators, Allen Marine Tours leads Misty Fiords National Monument catamaran tours throughout the summer. The company also offers combo motor-coach and walking tours of Ketchikan sites that end with a water-jet-powered cruise into the Tongass Narrows. ⊠ *5 Salmon Landing* ☎ *907/225–8100, 877/686–8100* ⊕ *www.allenmarinetours.com.*

HIKING

Deer Mountain. Get details on hiking around Ketchikan from the Southeast Alaska Discovery Center and Ketchikan Visitors Bureau (⇨ *Exploring, above*). The 3-mile trail from downtown to the 3,000-foot summit of Deer Mountain will repay your efforts with a spectacular panorama of the city below and the wilderness behind. The trail officially begins at the corner of Nordstrom Drive and Ketchikan Lake Road, but consider starting on the paved, 1.5-mile scenic walk on the corner of Fair and Deermount streets. Pass through dense forests before emerging into the alpine country. A shelter cabin near the summit provides a place to warm up. ⊠ *Fair and Deermount Sts..*

LUMBERJACK SHOWS

FAMILY **Great Alaskan Lumberjack Show.** The show consists of a 60-minute lumberjack competition providing a Disneyesque taste of old-time woodsman skills, including ax throwing, bucksawing, springboard chopping, log-rolling duels, and a 50-foot speed climb. It's a little hokey, but it's good fun (and kids will love it). Shows take place in a covered, heated grandstand directly behind the Salmon Landing Marketplace and are presented rain or shine all summer. ⊠ *420 Spruce Mill Way* ☎ *907/225–9050, 888/320–9049* ⊕ *www.lumberjacksports.com* ⌨ *$35* ⊙ *May–Sept., 2–4 times daily; hrs vary.*

CLOSE UP

Common Nautical Terms

Before acquainting yourself with your ship, you should add a few nautical terms to your vocabulary:

Berth. Sleeping space on a ship (literally refers to your bed).

Bow. The pointy end of the ship, also known as forward. Yes, it's also the front of the ship.

Bridge. The navigational control center (where the captain drives the ship).

Bulkhead. A wall or upright partition separating a ship's compartments.

Cabin. Your accommodation on a ship (used interchangeably with *stateroom*).

Course. Measured in degrees, the direction in which a ship is headed.

Debark. To leave a ship (also known as disembarkation).

Draft. The depth of water needed to float a ship; the measurement from a ship's waterline to the lowest point of its keel.

Embark. To go on board a ship.

Galley. The ship's kitchen.

Gangway. The stairway or ramp used to access the ship from the dock.

Hatch. An opening or door on a ship, either vertical or horizontal.

Head. A bathroom aboard a ship.

Helm. The apparatus for steering a ship.

Muster. To assemble the passengers and/or crew on a ship.

Pitch. Plunging in a longitudinal direction; the up-and-down motion of a ship. (A major cause of seasickness.)

Port. The left side of the ship when you're facing forward.

Promenade. Usually outside, a deck that fully or partially encircles the ship, popular for walking and jogging.

Roll. Side-to-side movement of the ship. (Another seasickness culprit.)

Stabilizers. Operated by gyroscopes, these retractable finlike devices below the waterline extend from a ship's hull to reduce roll and provide stability. (Your best friend if you're prone to motion sickness.)

Starboard. The right side of the ship when you're facing forward.

Stern. The rounded end of the ship, also called aft. It's the back end.

Tender. A boat carried on a ship that's used to take passengers ashore when it's not possible to tie up at a dock.

Thrusters. Fanlike propulsion devices under the waterline that move a ship sideways.

Wake. The ripples left on the water's surface by a moving ship.

5

SEA KAYAKING

Southeast Exposure. Southeast Exposure offers a 3½-hour guided Eagle Islands sea-kayak tour and a 4½-hour Tatoosh Islands sea-kayak tour in Behm Canal. ✉ *37 Potter Rd.* ☎ *907/225–8829* ⊕ *www. southeastexposure.com.*

Southeast Sea Kayaks. This company leads kayak tours of Ketchikan and Misty Fiords, and offers kayak lessons and rentals. It specializes in remote day trips and guided multinight trips to Misty Fiords. Travelers with just one day to spend on a Ketchikan adventure should consider the combination tour of kayaking through Orcas Cove and flightseeing Misty Fiord National Monument. It's hard to beat a day that includes a transfer from a boat to a floatplane. ⊠ *3 Salmon Landing* ☎ *907/225–1258, 800/287–1607* ⊕ *www.kayakketchikan.com.*

SHOPPING

Scanlon Gallery. In business since 1972, Scanlon Gallery carries prints from a number of well-known Alaska artists, including Byron Birdsall, John Fehringer, Barbara Lavallee, Rie Muñoz, and Jon Van Zyle. ⊠ *318 Mission St.* ☎ *907/247–4730, 888/228–4730* ⊕ *www. scanlongallery.com.*

Soho Coho Art Gallery. Design, art, clothing, and collectibles converge in the stylish Soho Coho Art Gallery, where you'll find an eclectic collection of art and T-shirts featuring the work of owner Ray Troll—best known for his wacky fish art—and other Southeast Alaska artists. ⊠ *5 Creek St.* ☎ *907/225–5954, 800/888–4070* ⊕ *www.trollart.com.*

WHERE TO EAT

\$\$\$ ✕ **Annabelle's Famous Keg and Chowder House.** Nestled into the ground
SEAFOOD   floor of the historic Gilmore Hotel, this unpretentious Victorian-style restaurant serves a hearty array of seafood and pastas, including several kinds of chowder and steamer clams. Prime rib on Friday and Saturday evenings is a favorite, and the lounge with a jukebox adds a friendly vibe. ⑤ *Average main: \$20* ⊠ *326 Front St.* ☎ *907/225–6009* ⊕ *www. gilmorehotel.com/annabelles.htm.*

\$ ✕ **Diaz Café.** Take a break from salmon saturation at this Old Town
ASIAN   Ketchikan spot. On historic Stedman Street, Diaz Café serves hearty Filipino cuisine that's a favorite of locals and, especially, of cruise-ship staffers hungry for a taste of home. Budget-wary travelers take heart: you don't have to spend much at Diaz to get a really filling meal. And the place is a wonderful time warp; it's straight back to the linoleum-and-tile 1950s inside. ⑤ *Average main: \$8* ⊠ *335 Stedman St.* ☎ *907/225–2257.*

KODIAK ISLAND

On the second-largest island in the United States (Hawaii's Big Island is the largest), the town of Kodiak is the least touristy of all the Alaska port towns. It's an out-of-the-way destination for smaller cruise ships and Alaska state ferries, and despite its small population (just over 6,000 people), there's a lot of "big" stuff here: Kodiak is home to a very large commercial fishing fleet, and is almost always one of the top two or three in the country for tonnage of fish brought in. It's also home to the country's largest Coast Guard base, and the world-famous Kodiak brown bear, billed as the largest land carnivore in the world.

"On a cool spring day, after walking on glaciers and seeing so much wildlife in the Tundra and sea coast, Ketchikan is comfortable and warm." —Sandy Cook, Fodors.com photo contest participant

Today commercial fishing is king in Kodiak. A clearinghouse for fish caught by islanders throughout the Kodiak archipelago—about 15,000 people are scattered among the islands—the city is among the busiest fishing ports in the United States. The harbor is also an important supply point for small communities on the Aleutian Islands and the Alaska Peninsula.

COMING ASHORE

Most cruise ships dock at Pier 2, a half mile south of downtown Kodiak. Most ships offer shuttles into town (about $7 round-trip), but if yours doesn't, it's a 15-minute walk.

TAXIS

Contacts **A&B Taxi.** You can catch a cab ride from A&B Taxi ☎ 907/486–4343, 907/486–2461.

TOURS

Contacts **Kodiak Adventures Unlimited.** Kodiak Adventures Unlimited books charter and tour operators for all of Kodiak. Find their summer kiosk in St. Paul Harbor across from Wells Fargo. ⊠ *105 Marine Way* ☎ *907/486–8766, 907/539–8767* ⊕ *www.kodiakadventuresunlimited.com.*

VISITOR INFORMATION

Pick up maps, details on kayaking trips, bear-viewing flights, marine tours, and more from the local visitors center.

Contacts **Kodiak Island Convention & Visitors Bureau** ⊠ *100 Marine Way, Suite 200* ☎ *907/486–4782, 800/789–4782* ⊕ *www.kodiak.org.*

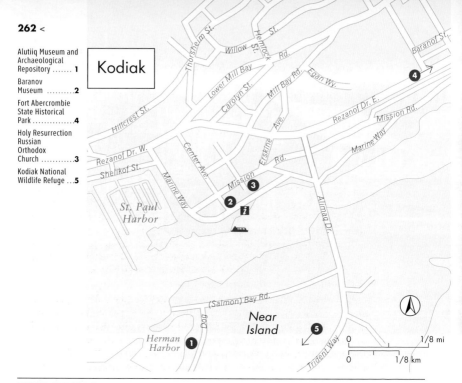

Kodiak

EXPLORING

Alutiiq Museum and Archaeological Repository. The Alutiiq Museum and
Archaeological Repository is home to one of the largest collections
of Alaska Native materials in the world, and contains archaeological
and ethnographic items dating back 7,500 years. The museum displays only a fraction of its more than 150,000 artifacts, including har-
poons, masks, dolls, stone tools, seal-gut parkas, grass baskets, and
pottery fragments. The museum store sells Native arts and educational
materials. ⊠ *215 Mission Rd., Suite 101* ☎ *907/486–7004* ⊕ *www.
alutiiqmuseum.org* ⊠ *$5* ☉ *June–Aug., weekdays 9–5, Sat. 10–5, Sun.
by appointment; Sept.–May, Tues.–Fri. 9–5, Sat. noon–4.*

Baranov Museum. The Baranov Museum presents artifacts from the area's
Russian past. On the National Register of Historic Places, the building
was built in 1808 by Alexander Baranov to warehouse precious sea-
otter pelts. W.J. Erskine made it his home in 1911. On display are samo-
vars, a collection of intricate Native basketry, and other relics from the
early Native Koniags and the later Russian settlers. A collection of 40
albums of archival photography portrays various aspects of the island's
history. Contact the museum for a calendar of events. ⊠ *101 Marine
Way* ☎ *907/486–5920* ⊕ *www.baranovmuseum.org* ⊠ *$5* ☉ *June–
Aug., Mon.–Sat. 10–4; Sept.–May, Tues.–Sat. 10–3.*

FAMILY   **Fort Abercrombie State Historical Park.** As part of America's North Pacific
defense in World War II, Kodiak was the site of an important naval
station, now occupied by the Coast Guard fleet that patrols the

surrounding fishing grounds. Part of the old military installation has been incorporated into Fort Abercrombie State Historical Park, 3½ miles north of Kodiak on Rezanof Drive. Self-guided tours take you past concrete bunkers and gun emplacements, and a network of trails wind through moss-draped spruce forest. There's a spectacular scenic overlook, great for bird- and whale-watching, and a volunteer-run military history museum inside a bunker; call the park for museum hours. ⊠ *Mile 3.7, Rezanof Dr.* ☎ *907/486–6339* ⊕ *www.dnr.alaska. gov/parks/units/kodiak/ftaber.htm* ▬ No credit cards.

Holy Resurrection Russian Orthodox Church. The ornate Holy Resurrection Russian Orthodox Church is a visual feast, both inside and out. The cross-shape building is topped by two onion-shape blue domes, and the interior contains brass candelabra, distinctive chandeliers, and numerous icons representing Orthodox saints. Three different churches have stood on this site since 1794. Built in 1945, the present structure is on the National Register of Historic Places. ⊠ *385 Kashevaroff Rd.* ☎ *907/486–5532 parish priest* ⊕ *oca.org/parishes/oca-ak-kodhrc* ▣ *Donations accepted* ☾ *By appointment.*

FAMILY **Kodiak National Wildlife Refuge Visitor Center.** Whether you're spending time in the Kodiak National Wildlife Refuge itself, make sure you stop by the Kodiak National Wildlife Refuge Visitor Center (located a block from the downtown ferry dock). Wander through exhibits about Refuge flora and fauna, attend an interpretive talk, and marvel at the complete 36-foot hanging skeleton of a male gray whale on the second floor. ⊠ *402 Center Ave.* ☎ *907/487–2626* ⊕ *www.fws.gov/ refuge/kodiak/.*

SPORTS AND THE OUTDOORS

BEAR WATCHING

Kodiak Adventures Unlimited. Kodiak Adventures Unlimited books charter and tour operators for all of Kodiak. Find their summer kiosk in St. Paul Harbor across from Wells Fargo. ⊠ *105 Marine Way* ☎ *907/486–8766, 907/539–8767* ⊕ *www.kodiakadventuresunlimited.com.*

FISHING

Memory Makers Tour and Guide Service. Memory Makers Tour and Guide Service specializes in angling day trips on the local Kodiak road system; guide Dake Schmidt's knowledge and passion for fishing the 15 local rivers are a real find for those not flying off to remote lodges. Fishing gear, lunch, and a comfy van provided, with sightseeing, wildlife-viewing, and photography tours also available. ⊠ *1523 B Mission Rd.* ☎ *907/486–7000* ⊕ *www.memorymakersinak.com*

Rohrer Bear Camp. Rohrer Bear Camp guides both bear viewers and visitors who come to Kodiak seeking the island's abundant sportfishing opportunities. ☎ *907/486–5835* ⊕ *www.sportfishingkodiak.com.*

DID YOU KNOW?

Despite their given names, black and brown bears range in color from pure black to nearly blond. Size is the defining characteristic: male brown bears on Kodiak Island—home to the largest browns on Earth—can reach 1,700 pounds and stand 10 feet tall. Male black bears rarely exceed 500 pounds or 6 feet.

WHERE TO EAT

$$
AMERICAN
✕ **Henry's Great Alaskan Restaurant.** Henry's is a big, boisterous, friendly place at the plaza near the small-boat harbor. The menu is equally big, ranging from fresh local seafood and barbecue to pastas and even some Cajun dishes. Dinner specials, a long list of appetizers, salads, rack of lamb, and a tasty dessert list round out the choices. ⑤ *Average main: $18 ⊠ 512 E. Marine Way ☎ 907/486–8844 ⊕ www.henryskodiak.com ⊘ Closed Sun. Oct.–Apr.*

$$
SEAFOOD
✕ **Old Powerhouse Restaurant.** This converted powerhouse facility allows a close-up view of Near Island and the channel connecting the boat harbors with the Gulf of Alaska. Enjoy fresh sushi and sashimi while watching the procession of fishing boats gliding past on their way to catch or deliver your next meal. Keep your eyes peeled for sea otters, seals, sea lions, and eagles, too. The menu also features tempura, *yakisoba* (fried noodles), and rice specials. ⑤ *Average main: $18 ⊠ 516 E. Marine Way ☎ 907/481–1088 ⊘ Closed Mon. No lunch Sun.*

METLAKATLA

The village of Metlakatla—the name translates roughly as "saltwater passage"—is on Annette Island, just a dozen miles by sea from busy Ketchikan but a world away culturally. A visit to this quiet community offers visitors a chance to learn about life in a small Inside Passage Native community.

In most Southeast Native villages the people are Tlingit or Haida in heritage. Metlakatla is the exception, as most folks are Tsimshian. They moved to the island from British Columbia in 1887, led by William Duncan, an Anglican missionary from England. The town grew rapidly and soon contained dozens of buildings on a grid of streets, including a cannery, a sawmill, and a church that could seat 1,000 people. Congress declared Annette Island a federal Indian reservation in 1891, and it remains the only reservation in Alaska today. Father Duncan continued to control life in Metlakatla for decades, until the government finally stepped in shortly before his death in 1918.

During World War II the U.S. Army built a major air base 7 miles from Metlakatla that included observation towers for Japanese subs, airplane hangars, gun emplacements, and housing for 10,000 soldiers. After the war it served as Ketchikan's airport for many years, but today the long runways are virtually abandoned save for a few private flights.

COMING ASHORE

Cruise ships dock at the Metlakatla dock adjacent to town. There's free Wi-Fi at the Metlakatla Artists' Village on Airport Road.

TOURS

Run by the Metlakatla community, **Metlakatla Tours** leads local tours that include visits to Duncan Cottage, the cannery, and the longhouse, along with a Tsimshian dance performance. Local taxis can take you to other sights around the island, including Yellow Hill and the old Air Force base.

Contacts Metlakatla Tours ☎ *907/886–8687 ⊕ www.metlakatla.com.*

EXPLORING

Longhouse. Father Duncan worked hard to eliminate traditional Tsimshian beliefs and dances, but today the people of Metlakatla have resurrected their past; they perform old dances in traditional regalia. The best place to catch these performances is at the traditional longhouse (known as *Le Sha'as* in the Tsimshian dialect), which faces Metlakatla's boat harbor. Three totem poles stand on the back side of the building, and the front is covered with a Tsimshian design. Inside are displays of Native crafts and a model of the fish traps that were once common throughout the Inside Passage. Native dance groups perform here on Wednesday and Friday in summer. Just next to the longhouse is an **Artists' Village,** where booths display locally made arts and crafts. The village and longhouse open when groups and tours are present.

William Duncan Memorial Church. Metlakatla's religious heritage still shows today. The clapboard William Duncan Memorial Church, topped with two steeples, burned in 1948 but was rebuilt several years later. It is one of nine churches in tiny Metlakatla. **Father Duncan's Cottage** is maintained to appear exactly as it would have in 1891, and includes original furnishings, personal items, and a collection of turn-of-the-20th-century music boxes. ⊠ *Corner of 4th Ave. and Church St.* ☎ *907/886–4441* ⊕ *www.metlakatla.com* ✉ *$2.*

Yellow Hill. Two miles from town is a boardwalk path that leads up the 540-foot Yellow Hill. Distinctive yellow sandstone rocks and panoramic vistas make this a worthwhile detour on clear days.

MISTY FIORDS NATIONAL MONUMENT

Misty Fiords National Monument. Just east of Ketchikan, Misty Fiords National Monument is a wilderness of cliff-faced fjords (or fiords, if you follow the monument's spelling), mountains, and islands with spectacular coastal scenery, wildlife, and recreation. Small boats provide views of breathtaking vistas. Travel on these waters can be an almost mystical experience, with the green forests reflected in the waters of the monument's many fjords. You may find yourself in the company of a whale, see a bear fishing for salmon along the shore, or even pull in your own salmon for an evening meal. ▪ TIP→ Note that the name Misty refers to the weather you're likely to encounter.

Alaska Travel Adventures. Most visitors to Misty Fiords arrive on day trips via floatplane from Ketchikan or on board catamarans run by Alaska Travel Adventures. ☎ *800/323–5757, 907/247–5295 outside Alaska* ⊕ *www.bestofalaskatravel.com.*

Allen Marine Tours. This company offers tours of Misty Fiords. ☎ *907/225–8100, 877/686–8100* ⊕ *www.allenmarinetours.com.*

SPORTS AND THE OUTDOORS

FLIGHTSEEING

The dramatic fjords and isolated alpine lakes of the 2.3-million-acre Misty Fiords National Monument don't exactly lend themselves to pedestrian exploration. But thanks to flightseeing services like **Island Wings Air Service** (☎ *907/225–2444 or 888/854–2444* ⊕ *www.island-wings.com*) and **Southeast Aviation** (☎ *907/225–2900 or 888/359–6478* ⊕ *www.southeastaviation.com*), the sublime splendor of this region doesn't go unseen. Island Wings offers a popular two-hour tour that includes a 35-minute stopover at one of the Monument's many lakes or fjords. Southeast Aviation offers transportation from the cruise-ship pier and a 2½-hour tour that includes a water landing for photos. Both companies are based in Ketchikan.

MISTY FIORDS BEST BETS

■ **Flightsee.** The unspoiled wilderness of Misty Fiords from the air is a sight you won't soon forget. Arrange trips from Ketchikan.

■ **Go Fish.** One of Southeast Alaska's most fertile marine ecosystems, Misty is home to healthy runs of all five salmon species and some excellent fishing.

■ **Watch wildlife.** You may catch a glimpse of Southeast regulars (bears and porpoises) or seldom-seen characters (mountain goats, wolves, killer whales, and wolverines).

PETERSBURG

Only ferries and smaller cruise ships can squeak through Wrangell Narrows with the aid of more than 50 buoys and range markers along the 22-mile waterway, which takes almost four hours. But the inaccessibility of Petersburg is also part of its charm: you'll never be overwhelmed here by hordes of cruise passengers; only smaller ships can reach the town.

The Scandinavian heritage is gradually being submerged by the larger American culture, but you can occasionally hear Norwegian spoken, especially during the Little Norway Festival, held here each year on the weekend closest to May 17 (Norwegian Constitution Day). If you're in town during the festival, be sure to take part in one of the fish feeds that highlight Syttende Mai (aka the Norwegian Constitution Day) celebration. You won't find better folk dancing and beer-batter halibut outside Norway.

One of the most pleasant things to do in Petersburg is to roam among the fishing vessels tied up dockside in the town's expanding harbor. This is one of Alaska's busiest, most prosperous fishing communities, with an enormous variety of seacraft. You'll see small trollers, big halibut vessels, and sleek pleasure craft. By watching shrimp, salmon, or halibut catches being brought ashore (though be prepared for the pungent aroma), you can get a real appreciation for this industry.

DID YOU KNOW?

Lakes like this one in the Rousseau Range in Misty Fiords National Monument make attractive places to contemplate how an area that was covered in glaciers 17,000 years ago is now filled with saltwater fjords, tidewater estuaries, 3,000-foot mist-shrouded mountains, and miles and miles of pristine solitude.

On clear days Petersburg's scenery is second to none. Across Frederick Sound the sawlike peaks of the Stikine Ice Cap scrape clouds from the sky, looking every bit as malevolent as their monikers suggest. (Some of the most wickedly named summits include Devil's Thumb, Kate's Needle, and Witches Tits.) LeConte Glacier, Petersburg's biggest draw, lies at the foot of the ice cap, about 25 miles east of town. Accessible only by water or air, the LeConte is the continent's southernmost tide-water glacier and one of its most active, often calving off so many icebergs that the tidewater bay at its face is carpeted shore to shore with floating bergs.

COMING ASHORE

Cruise companies with stops at Petersburg include: Un-Cruise and Lind-blad Expeditions. These lines operate smaller, adventure-oriented ships that offer complimentary walking and hiking tours ashore led by an onboard guide or naturalist. The ships dock in the South Harbor, which is about a ½-mile walk from downtown.

TOURS

If you want to learn about local history, the commercial fishing industry, and the Tongass National Forest, you can take a guided tour.

VISITOR INFORMATION

Petersburg Visitor Information Center. This small office is a good source for local information, including maps and details on tours, charters, and nearby outdoor recreation opportunities. ✉ *1st and Fram Sts.* ☎ *907/772–4636, 866/484–4700* ⊕ *www.petersburg.org* ⊗ *May–Sept., Mon.–Sat. 9–5, Sun. noon–4; Oct.–Apr., weekdays 10–2.*

EXPLORING

Blind Slough Recreation Area. This recreation area includes a number of sites scattered along the Mitkof Highway 15–20 miles south of Petersburg. Blind River Rapids Trail is a wheelchair-accessible 1-mile boardwalk that leads to a three-sided shelter overlooking the river—one of Southeast's most popular fishing spots—before looping back through the muskeg. Not far away is a bird-viewing area where several dozen trumpeter swans spend the winter. In summer you're likely to see many ducks and other waterfowl. At Mile 18 the state-run Crystal Lake Hatchery releases thousands of king and coho salmon each year. The kings return in June and July, the coho in August and September. Nearby is a popular picnic area. Four miles south of the hatchery is a Forest Service campground. ☎ *907/772–3871 USFS Petersburg Ranger District.*

Clausen Memorial Museum. The museum's exhibits explore commercial fishing and the cannery industry, the era of fish traps, the social life of Petersburg, and Tlingit culture. Don't miss the museum shop; the 126.5-pound king salmon—the largest ever caught commercially—as well as the Tlingit dugout canoe; the Cape Decision lighthouse station lens; and *Earth, Sea and Sky,* a 3-D wall mural outside. ✉ *203 Fram St.* ☎ *907/772–3598* ⊕ *www.clausenmuseum.net* ✉ *$3* ⊗ *May–early Sept., Mon.–Sat. 10–5; early-Sept.–late-Dec., Tues.–Sat. 10–2.*

Petersburg

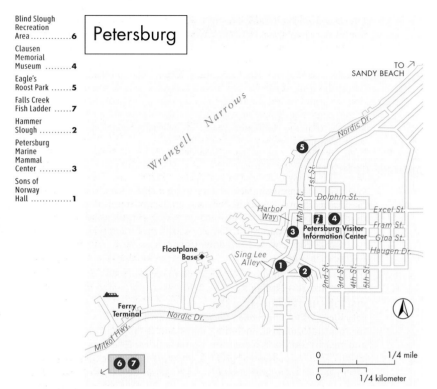

Eagle's Roost Park. Just north of the Petersburg Fisheries cannery, this small roadside park is a great place to spot eagles, especially at low tide. On a clear day you will also discover dramatic views of the sharp-edged Coast Range, including the 9,077-foot summit of Devil's Thumb.

Falls Creek Fish Ladder. Coho and pink salmon migrate upstream in late summer and early fall at this fish ladder south of town. Fish head up the ladder to get around a small falls. ⊠ *Mile 10.8, Mitkof Hwy.*

Hammer Slough. Houses on high stilts and the historic Sons of Norway Hall border this creek that floods with each high tide, creating a photogenic reflecting pool.

Petersburg Marine Mammal Center. Visitors to this nonprofit research and learning center can share and gather information on marine mammal sightings, pick up reference material, and have fun with the interactive educational kiosk. ⊠ *Gjoa St. and Sing Lee Alley, behind Viking Travel* ☎ *907/772–4170 summer only* ⊕ *psgmmc.org* ✉ *Free* ☉ *Mid-June–Aug., Mon.–Sat. 9–5.*

Sons of Norway Hall. Built in 1912, this large, barnlike structure that stands just south of the Hammer Slough is the headquarters of an organization devoted to keeping alive the traditions and culture of Norway. The window shutters are decorated with colorful Norwegian rosemaling designs. Outside sits a replica of a Viking ship that is a featured attraction in the annual Little Norway Festival each May. On the south side of the building is the **Bojer Wikan Fisherman's Memorial,** where deceased local fishermen are honored with a bronze statue. ⊠ *23 S. Sing Lee Alley* ☎ *907/772–4575.*

SPORTS AND THE OUTDOORS

HIKING

For an enjoyable loop hike from town, follow Dolphin Street uphill from the center of town. At the intersection with 5th Street, a board-walk path leads 900 feet through forested wetlands to the baseball fields, where a second boardwalk takes you to 12th Street and Haugen Drive. Turn left on Haugen and follow it past the airport to **Sandy Beach Park,** where picnickers can sit under log shelters and low tide reveals remnants of ancient fish traps and a number of petroglyphs. From here you can return to town via Sandy Beach Road or hike the beach when the tide is out. Along the way is the charming **Outlook Park,** a covered observatory with binoculars to scan for marine life. A pullout at Hungry Point provides views to the Coast Range and Frederick Sound. Across the road the half-mile **Hungry Point Trail** takes you back to the baseball fields—a great spot for panoramic views of the mountains—where you can return downtown on the nature boardwalk. Plan on an hour and a half for this walk.

SHOPPING

Northern Lights Smokeries. Outside of downtown, consider stopping in at Northern Lights Smokeries for owner Thomas Cumps's hot-smoked white king, red king, and sockeye salmon, or a local favorite, cold-smoked black cod. Northern Lights also ships. It's best to call ahead to make sure he'll be around before you stop by. ☎ *907/772–4608* ✍ *wildsalmon@nlsmokeries.com* ⊕ *www.nlsmokeries.com.*

Party House. The Party House sells objects decorated with Norwegian-style rosemaling, including plates, trays, and key chains. ⊠ *14 Sing Lee Alley* ☎ *907/772–2717.*

Tonka Seafoods. At Tonka Seafoods, across the street from the Sons of Norway Hall, check out the gift shop, and sample smoked or canned halibut and salmon. Be sure to taste the white king salmon—an especially flavorful type of Chinook that the locals swear by. Tonka will also ship. ⊠ *22 Sing Lee Alley* ☎ *907/772–3662, 888/560–3662* ☉ *Weekdays 8–6, weekends 9–5.*

WHERE TO EAT

$ ✕**Coastal Cold Storage.** This busy little seafood deli in the heart of
SEAFOOD   Petersburg serves daily lunch specials, including fish chowders and halibut beer bits (a local favorite), along with grilled-chicken wraps, steak sandwiches, breakfast omelets, and waffles. It's a great place for a quick bite en route to your next adventure; there isn't much seating in the shop's cramped interior. On sunny days, place your order and then grab a seat at one of the tables set up out front on the sidewalk.

Live or cooked crab is available for takeout, and the shop can process your sport-caught fish. $ *Average main: $10* ⊠ *306 N. Nordic Dr.* ☎ *907/772–4177, 877/257–4746.*

$ ✕ **Helse Restaurant.** Locals flock to this modest mom-and-pop place for
AMERICAN lunch. It's the closest thing to home cooking Petersburg has to offer, and most days it's open from 8:30 to 4, even in winter. A couple of dozen sandwiches grace the menu, as do rotating soups and homemade bread. The daily specials are a good bet, and the gyros are decent as well. Helse also doubles as an ice-cream and espresso stand. $ *Average main: $7* ⊠ *13 Sing Lee Alley* ☎ *907/772–3444* ⊗ *Closed Sun.*

PRINCE RUPERT, BRITISH COLUMBIA

Just 40 miles (66 km) south of the Alaskan border, Prince Rupert is the largest community on British Columbia's north coast. Set on Kaien Island at the mouth of the Skeena River and surrounded by deep green fjords and coastal rain forest, Prince Rupert is rich in the culture of the Tsimpshian First Nations who have been in the area for thousands of years.

As the western terminus of Canada's second transcontinental railroad and blessed with a deep natural harbor, Prince Rupert was, at the time of its incorporation in 1910, poised to rival Vancouver as a center for trans-Pacific trade. This didn't happen, partly because the main visionary behind the scheme, Grand Trunk Pacific Railroad president Charles Hays, went down with the *Titanic* on his way back from a financing trip to England. Prince Rupert turned instead to fishing and forestry. A port of call for both British Columbia and Alaska ferries, but relatively new to cruise ships, this community of 12,000 retains a laid-back, small-town air.

COMING ASHORE

Large cruise ships calling at Prince Rupert dock at the Northland Cruise Terminal, while smaller ships tie up at Atlin Terminal next door. Both terminals are in the city's historic Cow Bay district, steps from the Museum of Northern British Columbia and about five blocks from the central business district. The terminals for both British Columbia and Alaska ferries as well as the VIA Rail station are grouped together about 2 km (1 mile) from town. ■ **TIP**➔ If you're coming from Alaska, remember to adjust your watch. British Columbia is on Pacific Time, one hour ahead of Alaska Time.

TOURS

Most points of interest are within walking distance of the cruise-ship terminals.

Contacts Skeena Taxi ☎ *250/624–2185.*

VISITOR INFORMATION

Visitor Information Centre. Prince Rupert's Visitor Information Centre is located in the Museum of Northern BC. ⊠ *Museum of Northern British Columbia, 100 1st Ave. W, Prince Rupert, British Columbia, Canada* ☎ *250/624–5637, 800/667–1994* ⊕ *www.visitprincerupert.com.*

Tourism Prince Rupert ⊕ *www.visitprincerupert.com.*

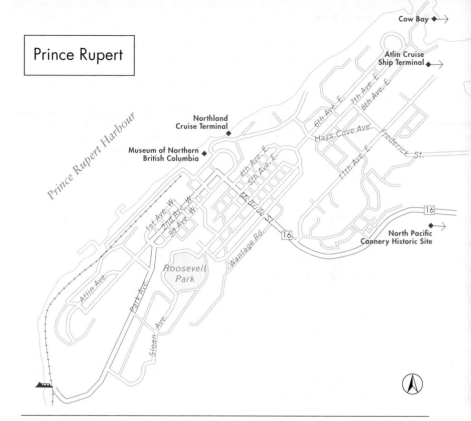

Prince Rupert

Cow Bay

Atlin Cruise
Ship Terminal

Northland
Cruise Terminal

Museum of Northern
British Columbia

Prince Rupert Harbour

Hays Cove Ave.

Frederick St.

6th Ave. E.
7th Ave. E.
8th Ave. E.
11th Ave. E.

4th Ave. E.
5th Ave. E.

1st Ave. W.
2nd Ave. W.
3d Ave. W.

McBride St.

16

North Pacific
Cannery Historic Site

16

Wantage Rd.

Roosevelt
Park

Atlin Ave.

Park Ave.

Sloan Ave.

EXPLORING

Cow Bay. Home to both of Prince Rupert's cruise-ship terminals, Cow Bay is an historic waterfront area of shops, galleries, cozy cafés, seafood restaurants, yachts, and fishing boats. Originally nicknamed for the time when there was no dock and dairy cattle had to swim ashore, Cow Bay has since taken its name very seriously: lampposts, benches, and anything else stationary is painted Holstein-style making for some quirky photo opportunities. ⊠ *Prince Rupert, British Columbia, Canada.*

Museum of Northern British Columbia. The Museum of Northern British Columbia has one of the province's finest collections of coastal First Nations art. Artifacts are showcased within a longhouse-style facility overlooking the waterfront and share 10,000 years of Northwest Coast history. Artisans often work in the nearby carving shed—studio-style—and while there no set schedule, opening hours usually coincide with those of visiting cruise ships. Between June and August, museum staff also operate the **Kwinitsa Railway Museum**, a five-minute walk away on the waterfront. ⊠ *100 1st Ave. W, Prince Rupert, British Columbia, Canada* ☎ *250/624–3207* ⊕ *www.museumofnorthernbc.com* ⊠ *C$6* ⊙ *June–Sept., daily 9–5; Oct.–May, Tues.–Sat. 9–5.*

SHOPPING

Prince Rupert has a great selection of locally made crafts and First Nations artwork. Look for items carved in argillite, a kind of slate unique to this region.

Cow Bay Gift Galley. The Cow Bay Gift Galley has a wide selection of gifts, souvenirs, and local art. ⊠ *24 Cow Bay Rd., Prince Rupert, British Columbia, Canada* ☎ *250/627–1808.*

North Coast Artists' Cooperative Ice House Gallery. An ideal stop for local, First Nations art, this gallery-store represents more than 80 artists from across the Pacific North West. Works sold here are done in a wide variety of media, from paintings, weaving, and pottery to jewelry, wood carvings and glass. ⊠ *Atlin Cruise Ship Terminal, 190–215 Cow Bay Rd., Prince Rupert, British Columbia, Canada* ☎ *250/624–4546* ⊕ *www.icehousegallery.ca.*

PRINCE RUPERT BEST BETS

■ **Wildlife-Viewing.** The area is home to North America's largest concentration of grizzly bears; the nearby waters are alive with seals, humpbacks, and orcas.

■ **Local Interest.** Pay a visit to the excellent Museum of Northern British Columbia, followed by a stroll around the funky Cow Bay neighborhood.

■ **A Cannery Tour.** If you have a little extra time, hit the North Pacific Cannery National Historic Site, in nearby Port Edward (⊕ www.cannery.ca), about 15 miles (24 km) south of Prince Rupert.

WHERE TO EAT

$$ ✕ **Cow Bay Café.** Cow Bay Café has always been the must-do eatery in
CONTEMPORARY   Prince Rupert, with a reputation that meant reservations were often required weeks in advance. At this writing, however, this iconic restaurant was changing ownership and the hope is that the tiny waterfront café will continue to serve some of the just-caught-today seafood dishes, homemade breads, and desserts. Its history alone suggest that the place be given a chance. ⑤ *Average main: C$15* ⊠ *205 Cow Bay Rd., Cow Bay, Prince Rupert, British Columbia, Canada* ☎ *250/627–1212* ⊘ *Closed Sun. and Mon. No dinner Tues.*

$ ✕ **Cowpuccino's Coffee House.** Not only is CowPos (its local moniker) the
CAFÉ   friendliest meeting place in Cow Bay, but the café also pulsates with a local vibe. Bunker down with your laptop and free Wi-Fi, curl up on the sofa with an espresso and a magazine, or pull up a chair for homemade soup, sandwiches, panini, and luscious house-made desserts. Sex in a Pie is chocolate ecstasy! There are plenty of veggie and a growing number of gluten-free options. Hearty breakfasts are served here, too. Outdoor tables are a great place for eagle-watching. ⑤ *Average main: C$10* ⊠ *25 Cow Bay Rd., Prince Rupert, British Columbia, Canada* ☎ *250/627–1395.*

DID YOU KNOW?

Real glacier drama happens in Prince William Sound. The area has the highest concentration of calving tidewater glaciers in the state. Columbia Glacier, the world's fastest retreating glacier, is carving a new fjord in the sound.

PRINCE WILLIAM SOUND

Tucked into the east side of the Kenai Peninsula, the sound is a peaceful escape from the throngs of people congesting the towns and highways. Enhanced with steep fjords, green enshrouded waterfalls, and calving tidewater glaciers, Prince William Sound is a stunning area. It has a convoluted coastline, in that it is riddled with islands, which makes it hard to discern just how vast the area is. The sound covers almost 15,000 square miles—more than 12 times the size of Rhode Island—and is home to more than 150 glaciers. The sound is vibrantly alive with all manner of marine life, including salmon, halibut, humpback and orca whales, sea otters, sea lions, and porpoises. Bald eagles are easily seen soaring above, and often brown and black bears, Sitka black-tailed deer, and gray wolves can be spotted on the shore.

Unfortunately, the *Exxon Valdez* oil spill in 1989 heavily damaged parts of the sound, and oil still washes up on shore after high tides and storms. The original spill had a devastating effect on both animal and human lives. What lasting effect this lurking oil will have on the area is still being studied and remains a topic of much debate.

EXPLORING

The major attraction in Prince William Sound on most Gulf of Alaska cruises is the day spent in **College Fjord**. This deep finger of water boasts the largest collection of tidewater glaciers in the world, and is ringed by 16 glaciers, each named after one of the colleges that sponsored early exploration of the fjord.

A visit to Columbia Glacier, which flows from the surrounding Chugach Mountains, is included on many Gulf of Alaska cruises (often via Valdez). Its deep aquamarine face is 5 miles across, and it calves new icebergs with resounding cannonades. This glacier is one of the largest and most readily accessible of Alaska's coastal glaciers.

SITKA

Sitka was home to the Kiksádi clan of the Tlingit people for centuries prior to the 18th-century arrival of the Russians under the direction of territorial governor Alexander Baranof. The Tlingits attacked Baranof's people and burned his buildings in 1802, but Baranof returned in 1804 with formidable strength, including shipboard cannons. He attacked the Tlingits at their fort near Indian River (site of the present-day, 105-acre Sitka National Historical Park) and drove them to Chichagof Island, 70 miles northwest of Sitka. The Tlingits and Russians made peace in 1821, and eventually the capital of Russian America was shifted from Kodiak to Sitka.

Today Sitka is known for its beautiful setting and some of Southeast Alaska's most famous landmarks: the onion-dome St. Michael's Cathedral; the Alaska Raptor Center, where you can come up close to ailing and recovering birds of prey; and Sitka National Historical Park, where you can see some of the oldest and most skillfully carved totem poles in the state.

COMING ASHORE

Only the smallest excursion vessels can dock at Sitka. Medium to large cruise ships must drop anchor in the harbor and tender passengers ashore near Harrigan Centennial Hall. You can recognize the hall by the big Tlingit war canoe to the side of the building. Sitka is an extremely walkable town, and the waterfront attractions are all fairly close to the tender landing. At this writing, a privately owned dock capable of accommodating large cruise ships is in the works about 5 miles north of town at Halibut Point. Highliner Coffee on Seward Street offers free Wi-Fi with a coffee purchase.

TOURS

Sitka Tours. Sitka Tours meets ferries and cruise ships and leads both bus tours and historical walks. ☎ 907/747–5800.

Tribal Tours. Tribal Tours emphasizes Sitka's rich Native culture, with bus or walking tours and dance performances at the Tribal Community House. ☎ 907/747–7290, 888/270–8687 ⊕ www.sitkatours.com.

VISITOR INFORMATION

Sitka Convention and Visitors Bureau. The Harrigan Centennial Hall has a volunteer-staffed information desk provided by the Sitka Convention and Visitors Bureau, whose headquarters are a short walk away on Lincoln Street. ✉ 303 Lincoln St. ☎ 907/747–5940 ⊕ www.sitka.org.

EXPLORING

FAMILY **Alaska Raptor Center.** The only full-service avian hospital in Alaska, the Raptor Center rehabilitates 100 to 200 birds each year. Situated just above Indian Creek, the center is a 20-minute walk from downtown. Well-versed guides provide an introduction to the rehabilitation center (including a short video), and guests are able to visit with one of these majestic birds. The Raptor Center's primary attraction is an enclosed 20,000-square-foot flight training center, built to replicate the rain forest, where injured eagles relearn survival skills, including flying and catching salmon. Visitors watch through one-way glass windows. A large deck out back faces an open-air enclosure for eagles and other raptors whose injuries prevent them from returning to the wild. Additional mews with hawks, owls, and other birds are along a rain-forest path. The gift shop sells all sorts of eagle paraphernalia, the proceeds from which fund the center's programs. ✉ 1000 Raptor Way, off Sawmill Creek Rd. ☎ 907/747–8662, 800/643–9425 ⊕ www.alaskaraptor. org ☞ $12 ⊙ Mid-May–Sept., daily 8–4.

St. Michael's Cathedral. This cathedral, one of Southeast Alaska's best-known national landmarks, is treasured by visitors and locals alike—so treasured that in 1966, as a fire engulfed the building, townspeople risked their lives and rushed inside to rescue the cathedral's precious Russian icons, religious objects, and vestments. Using original blueprints, an almost exact replica of onion-dome St. Michael's was completed in 1976. Today you can see what could possibly be the largest collection of Russian icons in the United States, among them the much-prized *Our Lady of Sitka* (also known as the *Sitka Madonna*) and the

Continued on page 282

DID YOU KNOW?

The blue glow of a glacier is caused by the light-absorbing properties of glacial ice. Ice readily absorbs long-wavelength frequencies of light (associated with the color red) but reflects short-wavelength frequencies, which, you guessed it, are blue.

ALASKA'S GLACIERS
NOTORIOUS LANDSCAPE ARCHITECTS

(opposite) Facing the Taku Glacier challenge outside of Juneau. (top) River of ice

Glaciers—those massive, blue-hued tongues of ice that issue forth from Alaska's mountain ranges—perfectly embody the harsh climate, unforgiving terrain, and haunting beauty that make this state one of the world's wildest places. Alaska is home to roughly 100,000 glaciers, which cover almost 5% of the state's land.

FROZEN GIANTS
A glacier occurs where annual snowfall exceeds annual snowmelt. Snow accumulates over thousands of years, forming massive sheets of compacted ice. (Southeast Alaska's **Taku Glacier,** popular with flightseeing devotees, is one of Earth's meatiest: some sections measure over 4,500 feet thick.) Under the pressure of its own weight, the glacier succumbs to gravity and begins to flow downhill. This movement results in sprawling masses of rippled ice (Alaska's **Bering Glacier,** at 127 miles, is North America's longest). When glaciers reach the tidewaters of the coast, icebergs calve, or break off from the glacier's face, plunging dramatically into the sea.

THE RAPIDLY RETREATING GLACIERS IN KENAI FJORDS NATIONAL PARK

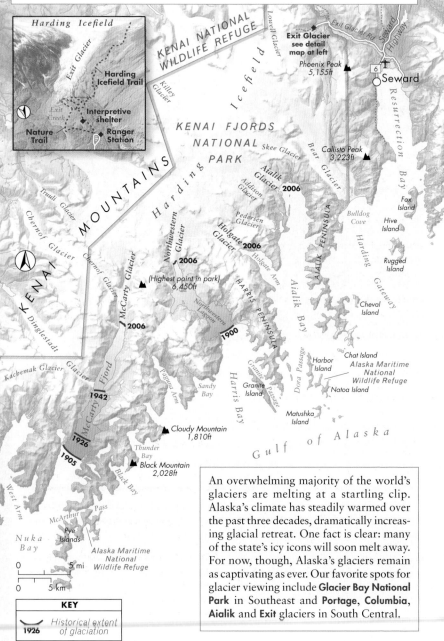

Harding Icefield

Exit Glacier

Harding Icefield Trail

Interpretive shelter

Nature Trail

Exit Creek

Ranger Station

KENAI NATIONAL WILDLIFE REFUGE

Lowell Glacier

Exit Glacier see detail map at left

Exit Glacier Rd

Seward Highway

Phoenix Peak 5,155ft

6 Seward

Killey Glacier

Icefield

KENAI FJORDS NATIONAL PARK

Skee Glacier

Bear Glacier

Callisto Peak 3,223ft

Resurrection Bay

Truuli Glacier

Harding

Aialik Glacier 2006

Addison Glacier

Fox Island

Bulldog Cove

Hive Island

Chernof Glacier

Northwestern Glacier

Pedersen Glacier

Holgate Glacier 2006

Holgate Arm

Harding Gateway

Rugged Island

Chernof Glacier

2006

(Highest point in park) 6,450ft

AIALIK PENINSULA

Cheval Island

KENAI MOUNTAINS

McCarty Glacier

Northwestern Lagoon

HARRIS PENINSULA

Aialik Bay

Dinglestadt Glacier

2006

Paguna Arm

Dora Passage

Chat Island

Harbor Island

Alaska Maritime National Wildlife Refuge

Natoa Island

Kachemak Glacier

McCarty Fiord

Glacier

1900

Sandy Bay

Harris Bay

Granite Passage

Granite Island

Matushka Island

1942

1926

Cloudy Mountain 1,810ft

Gulf of Alaska

1905

Thunder Bay

Black Bay

Black Mountain 2,028ft

West Arm

McArthur

Pass

Nuka Bay

Pye Islands

Alaska Maritime National Wildlife Refuge

0   5 mi

0   5 km

KEY

1926   *Historical extent of glaciation*

An overwhelming majority of the world's glaciers are melting at a startling clip. Alaska's climate has steadily warmed over the past three decades, dramatically increasing glacial retreat. One fact is clear: many of the state's icy icons will soon melt away. For now, though, Alaska's glaciers remain as captivating as ever. Our favorite spots for glacier viewing include **Glacier Bay National Park** in Southeast and **Portage, Columbia, Aialik** and **Exit** glaciers in South Central.

ICY BLUE HIKES & THUNDEROUS BOATING EXCURSIONS

Glaciers enchant us with their size and astonishing power to shape the landscape. But let's face it: nothing rivals the sheer excitement of watching a bus-size block of ice burst from a glacier's face, creating an unholy thunderclap that resounds across an isolated Alaskan bay.

Most frequently undertaken with a seasoned guide, **glacier trekking** is becoming increasingly popular. Many guides transport visitors to and from glaciers (in some cases by helicopter or small plane), and provide ski excursions, dogsled tours, or guided hikes on the glacier's surface. Striding through the surreal landscape of a glacier, ice crunching underfoot, can be an otherworldly experience. Whether you're whooping it up on a dogsled tour, learning the fundamentals of glacier travel, or simply poking about on a massive field of ice, you're sure to gain an acute appreciation for the massive scale of the state's natural environment.

You can also experience glaciers **via boat**, such as the Alaska Marine Highway, a cruise ship, a small chartered boat, or even your own bobbing kayak. Our favorite out of Seward is the ride with Kenai Fjords Tours. Don't be discouraged by rainy weather. Glaciers often appear even bluer on overcast days. When piloting your own vessel, be sure to keep your distance from the glacier's face.

Taking in the sights at Mendenhall Glacier

DID YOU KNOW?

What do glaciers and cows have in common? They both *calve*. While bovine calving refers to actual calf-birth, the word is also used to describe a tidewater glacier's stunning habit of rupturing icebergs from its terminus. When glacier ice meets the sea, steady tidal movement and warmer temperatures cause these frequent, booming deposits.

GLACIER-VIEWING TIPS

- The most important rule of thumb is never to venture onto a glacier without proper training or the help of a guide.

- Not surprisingly, glaciers have a cooling effect on their surroundings, so wear layers and bring gloves and rain gear.

- Glaciers can powerfully reflect sunlight, even on cloudy days. Sunscreen, sunglasses, and a brimmed hat are essential.

- Warm, thick-soled waterproof footwear is a must. Crampons are highly recommended.

- Don't forget to bring a camera and binoculars (preferably waterproof).

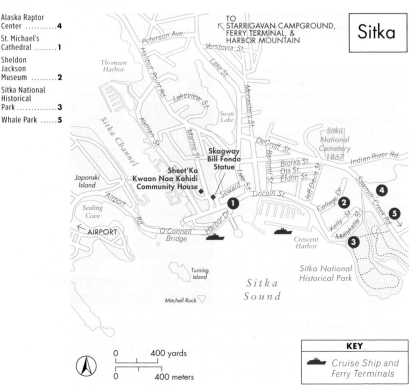

Christ Pantocrator (*Christ the World Judge*), displayed on the altar screen. ⊠ *240 Lincoln St.* ☎ *907/747–8120* ⊕ *www.oca.org/parishes/ oca-ak-sitsmk* ⊒ *$2 requested donation* ☉ *May–Sept., daily 9–4; Oct.– Apr., hrs vary.*

Sheldon Jackson Museum. Near the campus of the former **Sheldon Jackson College,** this octagonal museum, which dates from 1895, contains priceless Native Alaskan items collected by Dr. Sheldon Jackson (1834– 1909), who traveled the remote regions of Alaska as an educator and missionary. This state-run museum features artifacts from every Native Alaska culture; on display are carved masks, Chilkat blankets, dogsleds, kayaks, and even the impressive helmet worn by Chief Katlean during the 1804 battle against the Russians. The museum's small but well-stocked gift shop, operated by the Friends of the Sheldon Jackson Museum, carries books, paper goods, and handicrafts created by Alaska Native artists. ▉TIP➜ If you open the drawers under the glass cases all around the main room of the museum, you'll find on-exhibit artifacts. ⊠ *104 College Dr.* ☎ *907/747–8981* ⊕ *www.museums.state. ak.us/sheldon_jackson/sjhome.html* ⊒ *$5 mid-May–mid-Sept., $3 mid- Sept.–mid-May* ☉ *Mid-May–mid-Sept., daily 9–5; mid-Sept.–mid-May, Tues.–Sat. 10–4.*

Fodor's Choice **Sitka National Historical Park.** The main building at this 113-acre park
★ houses a small museum with fascinating historical exhibits and photos
of Tlingit Native culture. Highlights include a brass peace hat given
to the Sitka Kiksádi by Russian traders in the early 1800s and Chilkat
robes. Head to the theater to watch a 12-minute video about Russian–
Tlingit conflict in the 19th century. Ask a ranger to point you toward
the Centennial Totem Pole, installed in honor of the park's 100th anni-
versary in 2011. Also here is the **Southeast Alaska Indian Cultural
Center,** where Native artisans demonstrate silversmithing, weaving,
wood carving, and basketry. Make sure you strike up a conversation
(or two) with the artists; they're there to showcase and talk about their
work as well as Tlingit cultural traditions. At the far end of the building are seven totems (some more than a century old) that have been
brought indoors to protect them from decay. Behind the center a wide,
2-mile path takes you through the forest and along the shore of Sitka
Sound. Scattered along the way are some of the most skillfully carved
Native totem poles in Alaska. Keep going on the trail to see spawning
salmon from the footbridge over Indian River. Park Service rangers lead
themed walks in summer, which focus on the Russian–Tlingit conflict,
the area's natural history, and the park's totem poles. ☒ *106 Metlakatla
St.* ☎ *907/747–0110 visitor center* ⊕ *www.nps.gov/sitk* ☒ *$4* ☽ *May–
Sept., daily 8–5; Oct.–Apr., Tues.–Sat. 9–3.*

FAMILY **Whale Park.** This small waterside park sits in the trees 4 miles east of
Sitka right off Sawmill Creek Road. Boardwalk paths lead to five viewing platforms and steps take you down to the rocky shoreline. A gazebo
next to the parking area contains signs describing the whales that visit
Silver Bay, and you can listen to their sounds from recordings and an
offshore hydrophone here. ▉**TIP➜** Tune your radio to FM 88.1 anywhere
in Sitka to hear a broadcast of humpback whale sounds picked up by
the hydrophone. ☒ *Sawmill Creek Rd.*

SPORTS AND THE OUTDOORS

FOUR-WHEELING

Alaska ATV Tours. Departing from Sitka aboard two-person Yamaha
ATVs, Alaska ATV Tours' half-day tour of remote Kruzof Island
includes a scenic 30-minute boat transfer through the islands and channels of Sitka Sound. Stops include Iris Meadows Estuary, a black-sand
beach, and one of Kruzof's numerous salmon-laden creeks. ☎ *907/966–
2301, 877/966-2301* ⊕ *www.alaskaatvtours.com.*

SEA KAYAKING

Sitka Sound Ocean Adventures. The guide company's waterfront operation is easy to find: just look for the big blue bus it uses as its base at
Crescent Harbor next to Harrigan Centennial Hall. Sitka Sound runs
a variety of guided kayak trips through the mysterious and beautiful
outer islands off the coast of Sitka. Experienced paddlers who want to
go it on their own can rent gear from the company. Sitka Sound's guides
quickly help new-to-the-area paddlers understand its wonders (and, for
day trips, Sitka Sound packs a great picnic). ☒ *Harbor Dr. at Centennial
Hall* ☎ *907/752–0660* ⊕ *www.kayaksitka.com.*

5

WHALE WATCHING

Allen Marine Tours. One of Southeast's largest and best-known tour operators, Allen Marine Tours leads different boat-based Sitka Sound tours throughout the summer, such as the Wildlife Quest tours, which are a fine opportunity to view humpback whales, sea otters, puffins, eagles, and brown bears in a spectacular setting. When seas are calm enough, Allen Marine offers a tour to the bird sanctuary at **St. Lazaria Islands National Wildlife Refuge.** ⊠ *1512 Sawmill Creek Rd.* ☎ *907/747–8100, 888/747–8101* ⊕ *www.allenmarinetours.com.*

SHOPPING

Fishermen's Eye Fine Art Gallery. This tasteful downtown gallery prides itself on its vibrant collection of made-in-Sitka art, including silver jewelry, Native masks, and carved bowls. ⊠ *239 Lincoln St.* ☎ *907/747–6080.*

Fresh Fish Company. This company sells and ships fresh locally caught salmon, halibut, and shrimp. ⊠ *411 DeGroff St.* ☎ *907/747–5565, 888/747–5565 outside Alaska* ⊕ *www.akfreshfishinc.com.*

Sitka Rose Gallery. Housed within a Victorian-style 1895 home next to the Bishop's House, Sitka Rose Gallery is the town's most charming shop, and features Alaskan paintings, sculptures, Native art, and jewelry. ⊠ *419 Lincoln St.* ☎ *907/747–3030, 888/236–1536* ⊕ *www. sitkarosegallery.com.*

WinterSong Soap Company. Behind the Sitka Rose Gallery, WinterSong Soap Company sells colorful and scented soaps that are handcrafted on the premises. ⊠ *321 Lincoln St.* ☎ *907/747–8949, 888/819–8949* ⊕ *www.wintersongsoap.com.*

WHERE TO EAT

$$
AMERICAN
✗ **Nugget Restaurant.** Travelers flying out from Sitka head here while hoping their jet will make it through the pea-soup fog outside. The setting is standard, and the menu encompasses burgers (15 kinds), sandwiches, tuna melts, salads, steaks, pasta, seafood, and Friday-night prime rib. There's a big breakfast menu, too, but the real attraction is the range of homemade pies, which are known throughout Southeast Alaska. ▪ TIP→ The lemon custard pie is a local favorite. Get a slice à la mode, or buy a whole pie to take with you. Reservations are recommended. ⑤ *Average main: $12* ⊠ *Sitka Airport Terminal* ☎ *907/966–2480.*

$$
SEAFOOD
✗ **Van Winkle & Sons.** This restaurant's somewhat lackluster ambience (Formica tabletops, paper napkins, vinyl swivel-chair seating) doesn't quite match up to the gorgeous water views and upscale fare but, really, you won't mind. One of Sitka's largest eateries, it bills itself as "Frontier Cuisine," which translates to a seafood-heavy menu. But Van Winkle also serves pizzas, chicken, and duck. The create-your-own pastas are excellent (a half order is plenty for normal-size appetites), and the rich desserts necessitate sharing. There's no elevator to the restaurant's second-floor location, but a stair lift assists customers with disabilities. The water view is good. ⑤ *Average main: $15* ⊠ *205 Harbor Dr.* ☎ *907/747–7652.*

Sitka in wintry late-morning dawn light

SKAGWAY

Located at the northern terminus of the Inside Passage, Skagway is only a one-hour ferry ride from Haines. The town is an amazingly preserved artifact from North America's biggest, most-storied gold rush. Most of the downtown district forms part of the Klondike Gold Rush National Historical Park, a unit of the national park system dedicated to commemorating and interpreting the frenzied stampede of 1897 that extended to Dawson City in Canada's Yukon.

Nearly all the historic sights are within a few blocks of the cruise-ship and ferry dock, allowing visitors to meander through the town's attractions at whatever pace they choose. Whether you're disembarking from a cruise ship, a ferry, or a dusty automobile fresh from the Golden Circle, you'll quickly discover that tourism is the lifeblood of this town. Unless you're visiting in winter or hiking into the back-country on the Chilkoot Trail, you aren't likely to find a quiet Alaska experience around Skagway.

COMING ASHORE

Skagway is a major stop for cruise ships in Alaska, and this little town sometimes has four large ships in port at once. Some dock a short stroll from downtown, others ½ mile away at the Railroad Dock, where city buses are waiting to provide transportation to the center of town. The charge is $2 one-way, or $5 for a day pass.

Virtually all the shops and gold-rush sights are along Broadway, the main strip that leads from the visitor center through the middle of town. It's a nice walk from the docks up through Broadway, but you can also take tours in horse-drawn surreys, antique limousines, and modern vans. Glacial Smoothies on 3rd Avenue has Wi-Fi.

TOURS

Skagway Street Car Company. Revisit the gold-rush days in modern restorations of the bright-yellow 1920s sightseeing buses with Skagway Street Car Company. Costumed conductors lead these popular two-hour tours, but advance reservations are recommended for independent travelers, since most seats are sold aboard cruise ships. Call a week ahead in peak season to reserve a space. ⊠ *270 2nd Ave.* ☎ *907/983–2908* ⊕ *www.skagwaystreetcar.com.*

TRAIN EXCURSIONS

Skagway offers one of the few opportunities to drive in the region. Take the Alaska Highway to the Canadian Yukon's Whitehorse and then drive on Klondike Highway to the Alaska Panhandle. Southeast Alaska's only railroad, the White Pass and Yukon Route, operates several different tours departing from Skagway, Fraser, British Columbia, and on some days, Carcross, Yukon. The tracks follow the historic path over the White Pass summit—a mountain-climbing, cliff-hanging route of as far as 67½ miles each way. Bus connections are available at Fraser to Whitehorse, Yukon. While the route is primarily for visitors, some locals use the service for transportation between Skagway and Whitehorse.

Contacts White Pass and Yukon Route ☎ *907/983–2217, 800/343–7373* ⊕ *www.wpyr.com.*

VISITOR INFORMATION

Contacts Skagway Convention and Visitors Bureau ☎ *907/983–2854, 888/762–1898* ⊕ *www.skagway.com.*

SKAGWAY BEST BETS

■ **Riding the White Pass and Yukon Route.** Wending upward through unparalleled scenery and steep-sided gorges to the breathtaking summit of White Pass, the route remains an engineering marvel.

■ **Klondike Gold Rush National Historical Park.** This marvelous collection of museums and landmarks spread throughout downtown will immerse you in the rough-and-tumble spirit of yesteryear.

■ **Shopping.** From scrimshaw to silver, Skagway's shops offer huge collections of art, jewelry, and crafts.

DID YOU KNOW?

Individual elements of totem poles can be interpreted with some specificity—the two bottom faces on this Heida house post in Sitka, for example, represent the passing of information between generations—but traditionally, it's thought that no one can fully interpret a single totem's interconnected stories except the carver.

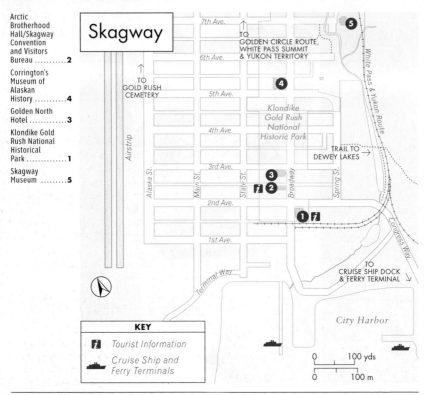

Skagway

7th Ave.

TO
GOLDEN CIRCLE ROUTE,
WHITE PASS SUMMIT
& YUKON TERRITORY

6th Ave.

TO
GOLD RUSH
CEMETERY

5th Ave.

Klondike
Gold Rush
National
Historic Park

4th Ave.

3rd Ave.

2nd Ave.

1st Ave.

Airstrip

Alaska St.

Main St.

State St.

Broadway

Spring St.

White Pass & Yukon Route

TRAIL TO
DEWEY LAKES

Congress Way

Terminal Way

TO
CRUISE SHIP DOCK
& FERRY TERMINAL

City Harbor

KEY

🛈 *Tourist Information*

⛴ *Cruise Ship and
Ferry Terminals*

0   100 yds

0   100 m

EXPLORING

Arctic Brotherhood Hall. The Arctic Brotherhood was a fraternal organization of Alaska and Yukon pioneers. Local members of the Brotherhood built the building's (now renovated) false front out of 8,833 pieces of driftwood and flotsam gathered from local beaches. The result: one of the most unusual buildings in all of Alaska. The AB Hall now houses the **Skagway Convention and Visitors Bureau,** along with public restrooms. ✉ *Broadway between 2nd and 3rd Aves., Box 1029* ☎ *907/983–2854, 888/762–1898 message only* ⊕ *www.skagway.com* ☉ *May–Sept., daily 8–6; Oct.–Apr., weekdays 8–noon and 1–5.*

Corrington's Museum of Alaskan History. Inside a gift shop, this impressive (and free) scrimshaw museum highlights more than 40 exquisitely carved walrus tusks and other exhibits that detail Alaska's history. Dennis Corrington, a onetime Iditarod Race runner, and the founder of the museum, is often present. A bright flower garden decorates the exterior. ✉ *5th Ave. and Broadway* ☎ *907/983–2579* 🎫 *Free* ☉ *Open when cruise ships are in port.*

Golden North Hotel. Built during the 1898 gold rush, the Golden North Hotel was—until closing in 2002—Alaska's oldest hotel. Despite the closure, the building has been lovingly maintained and still retains its gold rush–era appearance; a golden dome tops the corner cupola. Today the downstairs houses shops. ✉ *3rd Ave. and Broadway.*

Continued on page 294

GOLD! GOLD! GOLD!

At the end of the 19th Century, scoundrels and starry-eyed gold seekers alike made their way from Alaska's Inside Passage to Canada's Yukon Territory, with high hopes for heavy returns.

"There are strange things done in the midnight sun
By the men who moil for gold...."
—*Robert Service, "The Cremation of Sam McGee"*

Miners have moiled for gold in the Yukon for many centuries, but the Klondike Gold Rush was a particularly strange and intense period of history. Within a decade, the towns of Skagway, Dyea, and Dawson City appeared out of nowhere, mushroomed to accommodate tens of thousands of people, and just about disappeared again. At the peak of the rush, Dawson City was the largest metropolis north of San Francisco. Although only a few people found enough gold even to pay for their trip, the rush left an indelible mark on the nation's imagination.

An 1898 photograph shows bearded miners using a gold pan and sluice as they search for riches.

(above) Rush hour on Broadway, Skagway, 1898.

A GREAT STAMPEDE

Historians squabble over who first saw the glint of Yukon gold. All agree that it was a member of a family including "Skookum" Jim Mason (of the Tagish tribe), Kate and George Carmack, and Dawson Charlie, who were prospecting off the Klondike River in 1896. Over the following months, word spread and claims were quickly staked. When the first boatload of gold reached Seattle in July 1897, gold fever ignited with the *Seattle Post-Intelligencer's* headline: "GOLD! GOLD! GOLD! Sixty-Eight Rich Men On the Steamer Portland." Within six months, 100,000 people had arrived in Southeast Alaska, intent upon making their way to the untold riches.

Skagway had only a single cabin standing when the gold rush began. Three months after the first boat landed, 20,000 people swarmed its raucous hotels, saloons, gambling houses, and dance halls. By spring 1898, the town was labeled "little better than a hell on earth." When gold was discovered in Nome the next year and in Fairbanks in the early 1900s, Skagway's population dwindled to 700 souls.

A GRITTY REALITY

To reach the mining hub of Dawson City, prospectors had to choose between two risky routes from the Inside Passage. From Dyea, the Chilkoot Trail was steep and bitterly cold. The longer, bandit-ridden White Pass Trail from Skagway killed so many pack animals that it earned the nickname Dead Horse Trail. After the mountains, there were still over 500 mi to travel. For those who arrived, dreams were quickly washed a w a y, as most promising claims had already been staked by the Klondike Kings. Many ended up working as labor. The disappointment was unbearable.

KLONDIKE KATE

The gold rush was profitable for clever entrepreneurs. Stragglers, outfitters, and outlaws took advantage of every opportunity to make a buck. Klondike Kate, a brothel keeper and dance-hall gal, had an elaborate song-and-dance routine that involved 200 yards of bright red chiffon.

TWO ENEMIES DIE IN A SKAGWAY SHOWDOWN

CON ARTIST "SOAPY" SMITH

Claim to Fame: Skagway's best-known gold-rush criminal, Soapy was the de facto leader of the town's loosely organized network of criminals and spies.

Cold-Hearted Snake: Euphemistically referred to as "colorful," he ruthlessly capitalized on the naïveté of prospectors.

Famous Scheme: Soapy charged homesick miners $5 to wire a message home in his counterfeit Telegraph Office (the wires ended in a tangled pile behind a shed).

Shot Through the Heart: In 1898, just days after he served as grand marshal of Skagway's 4th of July parade, Soapy barged in on a meeting set up by his rival, Frank Reid. There was a scuffle, and they shot each other.

Famous Last Words: When he saw Reid draw his gun, Soapy shouted, "My God, don't shoot!"

R.I.P.: Soapy's tombstone was continually stolen by vandals and souvenir seekers; today's grave marker is a simple wooden plank in Skagway's Gold Rush Cemetery.

GOOD GUY FRANK REID

Claim to Fame: Skagway surveyor and all-around good fellow, Frank Reid was known for defending the town against bad guys.

The Grid Man: A civil engineer, Reid helped to make Skagway's streets wide and gridlike.

Thorn in My Side: Reid set up a secret vigilante meeting to discuss one very thorny topic: Soapy Smith.

In Skagway's Honor: Reid killed Soapy during the shootout on the city docks, breaking up Soapy's gang and freeing the town from its grip.

Dyin' Tryin': Reid's heroics cost him his life—he died some days later from the injuries he sustained.

R.I.P.: The town built a substantial monument in Reid's memory in the Gold Rush Cemetery, which you can visit to this day; the inscription reads: "He gave his life for the honor of Skagway."

(above) Soapy Smith (front), so named for his first con, which involved selling "lucky soap," stands with five friends at his infamous saloon.

FOLLOWING THE GOLD TRAIL TODAY

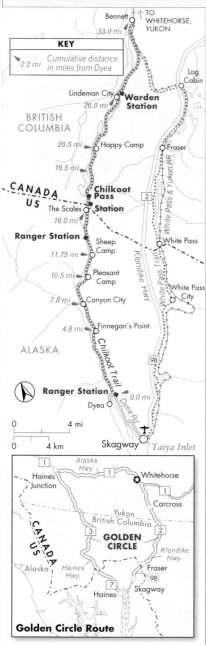

KEY

2.2 mi Cumulative distance in miles from Dyea

Bennett → TO WHITEHORSE, YUKON
33.0 mi
Log Cabin
Lindeman City — Warden Station
26.0 mi

BRITISH COLUMBIA

20.5 mi — Happy Camp — Fraser
16.5 mi

CANADA
US
The Scales — Chilkoot Pass — Station
2
16.0 mi

Ranger Station — Sheep Camp — White Pass
11.75 mi

Klondike Hwy
10.5 mi — Pleasant Camp
White Pass City
7.8 mi — Canyon City
4.8 mi — Finnegan's Point

White Pass Trail
White Pass & Yukon RR

ALASKA
98
Ranger Station
0.0 mi
Chilkoot Trail
Dyea — Dyea Rd.

0   4 mi
0   4 km
Skagway — Taiya Inlet

Golden Circle Route

1 Alaska Hwy.
Haines Junction — 1 — Whitehorse
1
Carcross
Yukon
British Columbia
CANADA
US
GOLDEN CIRCLE
3   2
Klondike Hwy.
Alaska — Haines Hwy.
7   Fraser
98
Haines — Skagway

THE HISTORIC CHILKOOT TRAIL

If you're an experienced backpacker, consider hiking the highly scenic Chilkoot Trail, the 33-mi route of the 1897–98 prospectors from Skagway into Canada. Most hikers will need four to five days. The trail is generally in good condition, with primitive campsites strategically located along the way. Expect steep slopes and wet weather, along with exhilarating vistas at the summit. Deep snow often covers the pass until late summer. The trail stretches from Dyea (just outside of Skagway) to Lake Bennett. The National Park Service maintains the American side of the pass as part of **Klondike Gold Rush National Historical Park;** the Canadian side is part of the **Chilkoot Trail National Historic Site.** A backcountry permit is required.

■ **TIP ➔** To return to Skagway, hikers usually catch the White Pass & Yukon Route train from Lake Bennett. The fare is $95. For more information, visit www.upyr.com/chilkoottrail.html.

For more details, including backcountry permits (C$55), contact the summer-only **Chilkoot Trail Center** ☎ 907/983–9234 ⊕ www.nps.gov/klgo. Or you can call Parks Canada ☎ 800/661–0486 ⊕ www. pc.gc.ca/chilkoot.

GOLDEN DRIVES

The Golden Circle Route starts in Skagway on the Klondike Highway, then travels to Whitehorse. The route continues to Haines Junction, and then south to Haines. On the much longer Klondike Loop, you'll take Klondike Highway past Whitehorse, all the way to Dawson City, where the Klondike Highway meets the Alaska Highway. From start to finish, this segment covers 435 miles. From there, you can continue west and then south on the Alaska Highway, past Kluane National Park, and back down to Haines, a total distance of 890 miles. If you're taking the Klondike Highway north from Skagway, you must stop at Canadian customs, Mile

(top left) Trekking the Chilkoot Trail (right) White Pass & Yukon Route (bottom left) A bridge on Chilkoot Trail

22. If you're traveling south to Skagway, check in at U.S. Customs, Mile 6. For more on these drives, visit travelyukon.com/discover-yukon/scenic-drives.

WHITE PASS & YUKON ROUTE

You can travel the gold-rush route aboard the historic White Pass & Yukon Route (WP & YR) narrow-gauge railroad. The diesel locomotives tow vintage-style viewing cars up steep inclines, hugging the walls of precipitous cliffs with views of craggy peaks, forests, and plummeting waterfalls. It's open mid-May to late September only, and reservations are highly recommended.

▮▮▮**TIP➜** Most of the commentary is during the first half of the trip and relates to sights out of the left side of the train, so sit on this side. A "seat exchange" at the summit allows all guests a canyonside view.

Several options are available, including a fully narrated 3-hour round-trip excursion to White Pass summit (fare: $115). Sights along the way include Bridal Veil Falls, Inspiration Point, and Dead Horse Gulch. Through service to Whitehorse, Yukon (4 hours), is offered daily as well—in the form of a train trip to Fraser, where bus connections are possible on to Whitehorse (entire one-way fare to Whitehorse: $120). Also offered are the Chilkoot Trail hikers' service and a 4-hour roundtrip to Fraser Meadows on Friday and Monday (fare: $155).

Call ahead or check online for details and schedules. ☎ 907/983–2217 or 800/343–7373 ⊕ www.wpyr.com.

Klondike Gold Rush National Historical Park. Housed in the former White Pass and Yukon Route Depot, this wonderful museum contains exhibits, photos, and artifacts from the White Pass and Chilkoot trails. It's a must-see for anyone planning on taking a White Pass train ride, driving the nearby Klondike Highway, or hiking the Chilkoot Trail. Films, ranger talks, and walking tours are offered. Special free Robert Service poetry performances by Buckwheat Donahue—a beloved local character and head of the Skagway Convention and Visitors Bureau— occasionally take place at the visitor center. ⊠ *2nd Ave. at Broadway* ☏ *907/983–2921, 907/983–9224* ⊕ *www.nps.gov/klgo* ⊠ *Free* ☉ *Visitor center May–Sept., daily 8–6; museum May–Sept., daily 7:30–6; Oct.–Apr., daily 8–5.*

Skagway Museum. This nicely designed museum—also known as the Trail of '98 Museum—occupies the ground floor of the beautiful building that also houses Skagway City Hall. Inside, you'll find a 19th-century Tlingit canoe (one of only two like it on the West Coast), historic photos, a red-and-black sleigh, and other gold rush–era artifacts, along with a healthy collection of contemporary local art and post–gold rush history exhibits. ⊠ *7th Ave. and Spring St.* ☏ *907/983– 2420* ⊠ *$2* ☉ *Mid-May–Sept., weekdays 9–5, Sat. 10–5, Sun. 1–4; Oct.–mid-May, hrs vary.*

SPORTS AND THE OUTDOORS

DOG-SLEDDING

Temsco Helicopters. Fly to Denver Glacier for an hour of learning about mushing and riding on a dogsled with Temsco Helicopters. The company also offers guided glacier discovery tours to other locations in the area. ⊠ *901 Terminal Way* ☏ *907/983–2900, 866/683–2900* ⊕ *www. temscoair.com.*

HIKING

Packer Expeditions. This company offers guided hikes on wilderness trails not accessible by road. One trip includes a helicopter flight, a 2-mile hike toward the Laughton Glacier, and a one-hour ride back to town on the White Pass Railroad. A longer hike on the same trail uses the train for access in both directions and includes time hiking on the glacier. ⊠ *9th Ave. and State St.* ☏ *907/983–3005* ⊕ *www. packerexpeditions.com.*

SHOPPING

Alaska Artworks. For those in search of locally produced silver jewelry, watercolor prints, and other handmade crafts, the artist-owned Alaska Artworks can't be beat. ⊠ *555C Broadway* ☏ *907/983–3443* ⊕ *www. inspiredartworks.com.*

Corrington's Alaskan Ivory. Corrington's Alaskan Ivory is the destination of choice for scrimshaw seekers; it has one of the state's best collections of ivory art. ⊠ *525 Broadway* ☏ *907/983–2579.*

Travel the White Pass and Yukon route via train out of Skagway.

Skaguay News Depot & Books. This small but quaint bookstore carries books on Alaska, magazines, children's books, maps, and gifts. Its moniker is a throwback to the town's old spelling. ⊠ *264 Broadway* ☎ *907/983–3354* ⊕ *www.skagwaybooks.com.*

WHERE TO EAT

$ ✕ **Glacial Smoothies and Espresso.** This local hangout is the place to
CAFÉ go for a breakfast bagel or a lunchtime soup-and-sandwich combo. Prices are steeper than at some coffee shops, but the ingredients are fresh and local, and nearly everything on the menu is made on-site. Customers can cool down with a Mango Madness or Blueberry Blues smoothie, and soft-serve ice cream in summer. $ *Average main: $7* ⊠ *3rd Ave. between Main and State Sts.* ☎ *907/983–3223* ⊕ *www. glacialsmoothies.com* ☾ *No dinner.*

$ ✕ **Skagway Pizza Station.** Housed in a former gas station, this year-
PIZZA round restaurant is known for its comfort-food specials. The huge calzones are stuffed and served piping hot with sides of house marinara and ranch dressing—build your own or choose one of the chef's creations, like the Chicken Hawk Squawk with pineapple and jalapeños. Or do as the Skagwegians do and wash down one of the 14-inch pizzas with a pint or two of Alaskan Summer Ale. For dog-tired travelers who can't walk another block, the Pizza Station delivers for free. $ *Average main: $10* ⊠ *4th Ave. between Main and State Sts.* ☎ *907/983–2200* ⊕ *pizzastation.eskagway.com.*

HAINES FROM SKAGWAY

If your cruise ship only stops in Skagway, you can catch a fast catamaran to Haines for a delightful day away from the crowds. **Haines-Skagway Fast Ferry** (☎ *907/766–2100 or 888/766–2103*) provides a passenger catamaran ferry between Skagway and Haines ($68 round-trip, and 45 minutes each way), with several runs a day in summer. **Alaska Fjordlines** (☎ *907/766–3395 or 800/320–0146* ⊕ *www.alaskafjordlines.com*) operates a high-speed catamaran from Skagway and Haines to Juneau and back ($155 round-trip), stopping along the way to watch whales and other marine mammals in Lynn Canal. The morning catamaran leaves Haines at 8:45 am, and the connecting bus from Auke Bay arrives in Juneau at noon. Passengers are back in Haines by 7:30 pm. Check your itinerary carefully to make sure you'll return before your ship's scheduled departure.

TRACY ARM

Tracy Arm and its sister fjord, Endicott Arm, have become staples on many Inside Passage cruises. Ships sail into the arm just before or after a visit to Juneau, 50 miles to the north. A day of scenic cruising in Tracy Arm is a lesson in geology and the forces that shape Alaska. The fjord was carved by a glacier eons ago, leaving behind sheer granite cliffs. Waterfalls continue the process of erosion that the glaciers began. Very small ships may nudge their bows under the waterfalls so crew members can fill pitchers full of glacial runoff. It's a unique Alaska refreshment. Tracy Arm's glaciers haven't disappeared, though; they've just receded, and at the very end of Tracy Arm you'll come to two of them, known as the twin Sawyer Glaciers. Because the glaciers constantly shed enormous blocks of ice, navigating the passage is sometimes difficult, which can prevent ships from reaching the glacier's face.

VALDEZ

Valdez (pronounced val-*deez*) is the largest of the Prince William Sound communities. This year-round ice-free port was the entry point for people and goods going to the Interior during the gold rush. Today that flow has been reversed, as Valdez Harbor is the southern terminus of the Trans-Alaska Pipeline, which carries crude oil from Prudhoe Bay and surrounding oil fields nearly 800 miles to the north. This region, with its dependence on commercial fishing, is still feeling the aftereffects of the massive oil spill in 1989. Much of Valdez looks modern, because the business area was relocated and rebuilt after its destruction by the 1964 Good Friday earthquake. Even though the town is younger than the rest of developed Alaska, it's acquiring a lived-in look.

COMING ASHORE

Ships tie up at the world's largest floating container dock. About 3 miles from the heart of town, the dock is used not only for cruise ships but also for cargo ships loading with timber and other products bound for markets "outside" (that's what Alaskans call the rest of the world). Ship-organized motor coaches meet you on the pier and provide transportation into town. Cabs and car-rental services will also provide transportation from the pier, and individualized tours of the area can be arranged with the cab dispatcher. Several local ground- and adventure-tour operators meet passengers as well. At this writing, no cruise ships call in Valdez, but it is still a popular excursion from Anchorage, about 5½ hours away by car.

VISITOR INFORMATION

Once in town, you find that Valdez is a very compact community. Motor coaches generally drop passengers at the Visitor Bureau.

Valdez Convention and Visitors Bureau ⊠ *200 Chenega St., Valdez* ☎ *907/835–4636* ⊕ *www.valdezalaska.org.*

EXPLORING

FAMILY **Valdez Museum.** The Valdez Museum explores the lives, livelihoods, and events significant to Valdez and surrounding regions. Exhibits include a restored 1880s Gleason & Baily hand-pump fire engine, a 1907 Ahrens steam fire engine, a 19th-century saloon, information on the local Native peoples, and a recently updated exhibit on the 1989 oil spill. Every summer the museum hosts an exhibit of quilts and fiber arts made by local and regional artisans. ⊠ *217 Egan Dr., Valdez* ☎ *907/835–2764* ⊕ *www.valdezmuseum.org* ⊠ *$7* ⊘ *Oct.–Apr., Tues.–Sun. noon–5; May–Sept., daily 9–5.*

Historical Old Town Valdez. At a separate site, a 35- by 40-foot model of Historical Old Town Valdez depicts the original town, which was devastated by the 1964 earthquake. There's also an operating seismograph and an exhibit on local seismic activity. A Valdez History Exhibits Pass includes admission to both the museum and the annex. ⊠ *436 S. Hazlet Ave., Valdez* ⊕ *www.valdezmuseum.org.*

OFF THE BEATEN PATH

Columbia Glacier. A visit to Columbia Glacier, which flows from the surrounding Chugach Mountains, should certainly be on your Valdez agenda. Its deep aquamarine face is 5 miles across, and it calves icebergs with resounding cannonades. This glacier is one of the largest and most readily accessible of Alaska's coastal glaciers. The state ferry travels past the face of the glacier, and scheduled tours of the glaciers and the rest of the sound are available by boat and aircraft from Valdez, Cordova, and Whittier. ⊠ *Valdez* ⊕ *www.dot.state.ak.us/amhs.*

SPORTS AND THE OUTDOORS

GLACIER TRIPS

H2O Guides. Whether you're looking for a full-on winter backcountry heli-ski excursion (in winter) or a half-day walk on a glacier, H2O Guides can hook you up. For most visitors, the day trips to Worthington Glacier State Park will suffice. It can set up any level of icy adventure you desire, from a half-day walk on the glacier to a multiday ice-climbing trip. The company is in the Valdez Harbor Inn, and can arrange fishing, flight-seeing, multiday, multisport, and otherwise-customized trips as well. ✉ *Valdez* 🕾 *907/835–8418* ⊕ *www. alaskahelicopterskiing.com.*

SEA KAYAKING

Anadyr Adventures. Anadyr Adventures has 20 years' experience leading sea-kayak trips into Alaska's most spectacular wilderness, Prince William Sound. Guides will escort you on day trips, multiday camping trips, "mother ship" adventures based in a remote anchorage, or lodge-based trips for the ultimate combination of adventure by day and comfort by night. If you're already an experienced kayaker, it'll outfit you and you can travel on your own. Also available are guided hiking and glacier trips, ice caving at Valdez Glacier, soft-adventure charter-boat trips in the sound, and water-taxi service to or from anywhere on the eastern side of the sound. ✉ *Valdez* 🕾 *907/835–2814, 800/865–2925* ⊕ *www.anadyradventures.com.*

WILDLIFE-VIEWING

Lu-Lu Belle. Valdez-based Lu-Lu Belle leads small-group whale-watching and wildlife-viewing cruises, and sailings past the Columbia Glacier, the largest glacier in Prince William Sound. The 11 am departure boards promptly at 10:45. Ice conditions and whale sightings can be unpredictable so cruises can often run long. ✉ *Valdez* 🕾 *800/411–0090* ⊕ *www. lulubelletours.com.*

VALDEZ BEST BETS

■ **Touring the Sound.** Take a tour of Prince William Sound and get a seaside view of the Alyeska Pipeline terminal, where the 800-mile-long Trans-Alaska Pipeline loads oil into huge tanker ships.

■ **Kayaking.** Several local companies offer sea-kayaking tours of varying lengths and degrees of difficulty.

■ **Glacier Hiking.** Worthington Glacier State Park at Thompson Pass is a roadside attraction. If you want to learn glacier travel or ice climbing, H2O Guides can hook you up.

WHERE TO EAT

$$ ✕ **MacMurray's Alaska Halibut House.** At this very casual family-owned
SEAFOOD establishment you order at the counter, sit at the Formica-covered tables, and check out the photos of local fishing boats. The battered halibut is excellent—light and not greasy. Other menu items include homemade clam chowder, but if you're eating at the Halibut House, why try anything else? ⑤ *Average main: $15* ✉ *208 Meals Ave., Valdez* 🕾 *907/835–2788.*

VICTORIA, BRITISH COLUMBIA

Although Victoria isn't in Alaska, it's a port of call for many ships cruising the Inside Passage. Despite its role as the provincial capital, Victoria was largely bypassed, economically, by Vancouver throughout the 20th century. This, as it turns out, was all to the good, helping to preserve Victoria's historic downtown and keeping the city free of freeways. For much of the 20th century Victoria was marketed to tourists as "The Most British City in Canada," and it still has more than its share of Anglo-themed pubs, tea shops, and double-decker buses. These days, however, Victorians prefer to celebrate their combined indigenous, Asian, and European heritage, and the city's stunning wilderness backdrop. Locals do often venture out for afternoon tea, but they're just as likely to nosh on dim sum or tapas. Decades-old shops sell imported linens and tweeds, but newer upstarts offer local designs in hemp and organic cotton. And let's not forget that fabric favored by locals: Gore-Tex. The outdoors is ever present here. You can hike, bike, kayak, sail, or whale-watch straight from the city center, and forests, beaches, offshore islands, and wilderness parklands lie just minutes away.

COMING ASHORE

Only the smallest excursion vessels dock downtown in Victoria's Inner Harbour. Cruise ships tie up at the Ogden Point cruise-ship terminal (⊕ *www.victoriaharbour.org*), 2.4 km (1½ miles) from the Inner Harbour, and a few pocket cruise ships moor at Sidney, 29 km (18 miles) north of Victoria. When ships are in port a shuttle bus makes trips between Ogden Point and downtown Victoria at least every 20 minutes; the last shuttle from downtown leaves one hour prior to scheduled ship departures from the port. The C$10 (US$10) shuttle fare allows you to make as many return trips as you like. The walk downtown is pleasant and will take 20 to 30 minutes.

GETTING AROUND

Most points of interest are within walking distance of the Inner Harbour. For those that aren't, public and private transportation is readily available. The public bus system is excellent; pick up route maps and schedules at the Tourism Victoria Visitor InfoCentre. City tours by horse-drawn carriage, pedicab, and double-decker bus, as well as limousine service, are available at the cruise-ship terminal. ■ **TIP→ If you're coming from Alaska, remember to adjust your watch.** British Columbia is on Pacific Time, one hour ahead of Alaska Time.

Taxis also meet each ship, and fares run about C$1.97 per kilometer; the meter starts at C$3.40. A cab from Ogden Point to the downtown core will cost about C$10–C$12.

Contacts Bluebird Cabs ☎ *250/382–2222* ⊕ *www.taxicab.com.* **Yellow Taxi** ☎ *250/381–2222.*

VISITOR INFORMATION

Contacts **Victoria Visitor Information Centre.** Tourism Victoria also has event listings, and you can buy tickets for many events at the Victoria Visitor Information Centre. ⊠ *812 Wharf St.* ☎ *250/953–2033, 800/663–3883* ⊕ *www.tourismvictoria.com.*

EXPLORING

Victoria's heart is the Inner Harbour, always bustling with ferries, seaplanes, and yachts. In summer the waterfront comes alive with strollers, artists, and street entertainers.

IN TOWN

Abkhazi Garden. Called "the garden that love built," this once-private garden is as fascinating for its history as for its innovative design. The seeds were planted, figuratively, in Paris in the 1920s, when Englishwoman Peggy Pemberton-Carter met exiled Georgian Prince Nicholas Abkhazi. World War II internment camps (his in Germany, hers near Shanghai) interrupted their romance, but they reunited and married in Victoria in 1946. They spent the next 40 years together cultivating their garden. Rescued from developers and now operated by the Land Conservancy of British Columbia, the 1-acre site is recognized as a leading example of West Coast horticultural design, resplendent with native Garry Oak trees, Japanese maples, and mature rhododendrons. The tearoom, in the sitting parlor of the modest, modernist home, serves lunch and afternoon desserts, as well as breakfast on weekends. Watch for evening concerts in the garden. ⊠ *1964 Fairfield Rd., Fairfield* ☎ *250/598–8096* ⊕ *www.conservancy.bc.ca* ☎ *Mar.–Oct. C$10; Nov.–Feb. by donation* ⊘ *Daily 11–5.*

FAMILY **Chinatown.** Chinese immigrants built much of the Canadian Pacific Railway in the 19th century, and their influence still marks the region. Victoria's Chinatown, founded in 1858, is the oldest such district in Canada. If you enter from Government Street, you'll pass under the elaborate **Gate of Harmonious Interest,** made of Taiwanese ceramic tiles and decorative panels. Along Fisgard Street, merchants display paper lanterns and exotic produce. Mah-jongg, fan-tan, and dominoes were games of chance played on **Fan Tan Alley,** said to be the narrowest street in Canada. Once the gambling and opium center of Chinatown, it's now lined with offbeat shops, few of which sell authentic Chinese goods. Look for the alley on the south side of Fisgard Street between Nos. 545½ and 549½. At just two square blocks, Victoria's Chinatown is much smaller than Vancouver's. It's still pleasant to stroll through, particularly as hip boutiques and eateries have moved into the district. ⊠ *Fisgard St. between Government and Store Sts., Chinatown.*

Craigdarroch Castle. This resplendent mansion complete with turrets and Gothic rooflines was built as the home of one of British Columbia's wealthiest men, coal baron Robert Dunsmuir, who died in 1889, just a few months before the castle's completion. Now a museum depicting life in the late 1800s, the castle's 39 rooms have ornate Victorian furnishings, stained-glass windows, carved woodwork, and a

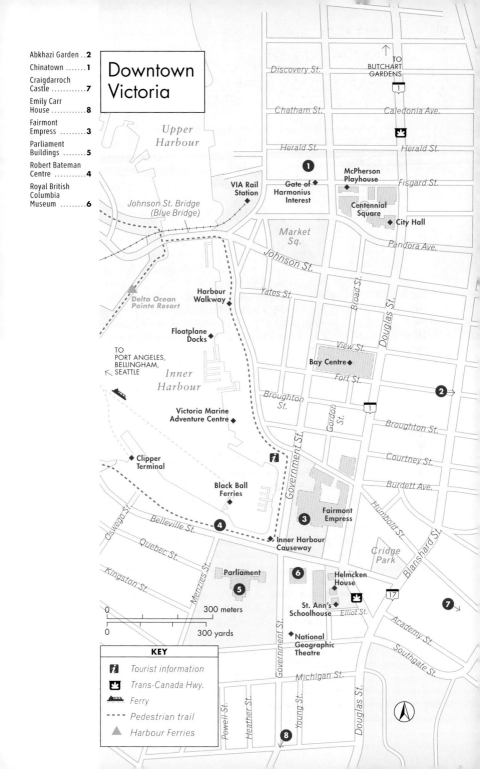

Downtown Victoria

Upper Harbour

Discovery St.

TO
BUTCHART
GARDENS

Chatham St.

Caledonia Ave.

Herald St.

Herald St.

1

McPherson
Playhouse

Fisgard St.

VIA Rail
Station

Gate of
Harmonius
Interest

Centennial
Square

City Hall

*Johnson St. Bridge
(Blue Bridge)*

*Market
Sq.*

Pandora Ave.

Johnson St.

Yates St.

Broad St.

Douglas St.

*Delta Ocean
Pointe Resort*

Harbour
Walkway

Floatplane
Docks

View St.

Bay Centre

Fort St.

2

TO
PORT ANGELES,
BELLINGHAM,
SEATTLE

*Inner
Harbour*

Broughton
St.

Gordon St.

Broughton St.

Victoria Marine
Adventure Centre

Courtney St.

Burdett Ave.

Clipper
Terminal

Black Ball
Ferries

Belleville St.

4

3

Fairmont
Empress

Humboldt St.

Blanshard St.

Oswego St.

Quebec St.

Inner Harbour
Causeway

*Cridge
Park*

Kingston St.

Menzies St.

Parliament

5

6

Helmcken
House

17

7

300 meters

300 yards

St. Ann's
Schoolhouse

Government St.

Elliot St.

Academy St.

National
Geographic
Theatre

Michigan St.

Powell St.

Heather St.

Young St.

Douglas St.

Southgate St.

8

KEY

- **i** *Tourist information*
- **W** *Trans-Canada Hwy.*
- **⛴** *Ferry*
- - - - *Pedestrian trail*
- **▲** *Harbour Ferries*

The Butchart Gardens, Victoria, British Columbia

beautifully restored painted ceiling in the drawing room. A winding staircase climbs four floors to a tower overlooking Victoria. Castles run in the family: son James went on to build the more lavish Hatley Castle west of Victoria. The castle is not wheelchair accessible and has no elevators. ⊠ *1050 Joan Crescent, Rockland* ☎ *250/592–5323* ⊕ *www.thecastle.ca* ◲ *C$13.75* ⊗ *Mid-June–early Sept., daily 9–7; early Sept.–mid-June, daily 10–4:30.*

Emily Carr House. One of Canada's most celebrated artists and a respected writer, Emily Carr (1871–1945) lived in this extremely proper, wooden Victorian house before she abandoned her middle-class life to live in the wilds of British Columbia. Carr's own descriptions, from her autobiography *Book of Small*, were used to restore the house. Art on display includes reproductions of Carr's work—visit the Art Gallery of Greater Victoria or the Vancouver Art Gallery to see the originals. ⊠ *207 Government St., James Bay* ☎ *250/383–5843* ⊕ *www.emilycarr. com* ◲ *C$6.75* ⊗ *May–Sept., Tues.–Sat. 11–4.*

Fairmont Empress. Opened in 1908 by the Canadian Pacific Railway, the Empress is one of the grand château-style railroad hotels that grace many Canadian cities. Designed by Francis Rattenbury, who also designed the Parliament Buildings across the way, the solid Edwardian grandeur of the Empress has made it a symbol of the city. The elements that made the hotel an attraction for travelers in the past—old-world architecture, ornate decor, and a commanding view of the Inner Harbour—are still here. Nonguests can reserve ahead for afternoon tea (the dress code is smart casual), meet for a curry under the tiger skin in the Bengal Room, enjoy a treatment at the hotel's

Willow Stream spa, or sample the superb Pacific Northwest cuisine in the Empress Room, where afternoon tea is served from 11:30 to 5. In summer, lunch, snacks, and cocktails are served on the Terrace Verandah overlooking the Inner Harbour. ✉ *721 Government St., Downtown* ☎ *250/384–8111, 250/389–2727 tea reservations* ⊕ *www.fairmont. com/empress* ✎ *Free; afternoon tea C$59.95.*

VICTORIA BEST BETS

■ Most cruise ships visit Victoria in the late afternoon and evening, which is an ideal time for a stroll around the city's compact downtown or a visit to the splendid 55-acre Butchart Gardens.

■ Victoria's other main attraction is the city center itself, with its street entertainers, yachts at harbor, cafés, funky little shops, intriguing museums, and illuminated Victorian architecture.

■ A promenade around the Inner Harbour with, perhaps, a carriage ride for two (available at the corner of Belleville and Menzies streets, next to the Parliament Buildings) is a romantic option.

Parliament Buildings. Officially the British Columbia Provincial Legislative Assembly Buildings, these massive stone structures are more popularly referred to as the Parliament Buildings. Designed by Francis Rattenbury (who also designed the Fairmont Empress Hotel) when he was just 25 years old, and completed in 1897, they dominate the Inner Harbour. Atop the central dome is a gilded statue of Captain George Vancouver (1757–98), the first European to sail around Vancouver Island. A statue of Queen Victoria (1819–1901) reigns over the front of the complex. More than 3,300 lights outline the buildings at night. The interior is lavishly done with stained-glass windows, gilt moldings, and historic photographs, and in summer actors play historic figures from B.C.'s past. When the legislature is in session, you can sit in the public gallery and watch British Columbia's democracy at work (custom has the opposing parties sitting 2½ sword lengths apart). Free, informative, 30- to 45-minute tours run every 20 to 30 minutes in summer and several times a day in the off-season (less frequently if school groups or private tours are coming through). Tours are obligatory on summer weekends (mid-May until Labor Day) and optional the rest of the time. ✉ *501 Belleville St., Downtown* ☎ *250/387–3046* ⊕ *www. leg.bc.ca* ✎ *Free* ⊗ *Mid-May–early Sept., daily 9–5; early Sept.–mid-May, weekdays 9–5.*

Robert Bateman Centre. Robert Bateman is Canada's foremost wildlife artist and advocate, naturalist, and educator who is intent on reconnecting people—and especially children—to the magic of nature. This new gallery cum educational center has taken over the former Steamship Terminal Building on the Inner Harbour. Many exhibits are interactive (some pictures even "talk"), especially if you bring along a smartphone or tablet. ✉ *470 Belleville St., Downtown* ☎ *250/940–3630* ⊕ *www. batemancentre.org* ✎ *C$12.50* ⊗ *June–Sept., Sun.–Wed. 10–6, Thurs.– Sat. 10–9; Oct.–May, Tues.–Sun. 10–5.*

5

FAMILY

Fodor's Choice

★

Royal British Columbia Museum. This excellent museum, one of Victoria's leading attractions, traces several thousand years of British Columbian history. Especially strong is its First Peoples Gallery, home to a genuine Kwakwaka'wakw big house and a dramatically displayed collection of masks and other artifacts. The Environmental History Gallery traces B.C.'s natural heritage, from prehistory to modern-day climate change, in realistic dioramas. An Ocean Station exhibit gets kids involved in running a Jules Verne–style submarine. In the Modern History Gallery, a replica of Captain Vancouver's HMS *Discovery* creaks convincingly, and a re-created frontier town comes to life with cobbled streets, silent movies, and the rumble of an arriving train. An IMAX theater presents films on a six-story-tall screen.

Optional one-hour tours, included in the admission price, run roughly twice a day in summer and less frequently in winter. Most focus on a particular gallery, though the 90-minute Highlights Tour touches on all galleries. Special exhibits, usually held between April and October, attract crowds despite the higher admission prices. Skip (sometimes very long) ticket lines by booking online.

The museum complex has several more interesting sights, beyond the expected gift shop and café. In front of the museum, at Government and Belleville streets, is the **Netherlands Centennial Carillon.** With 62 bells, it's the largest bell tower in Canada; the Westminster chimes ring out every hour, and free recitals are occasionally held on Sunday afternoons. Behind the main building, bordering Douglas Street, are the grassy lawns of **Thunderbird Park,** home to 10 totem poles (carved replicas of originals that are preserved in the museum). One of the oldest houses in B.C., **Helmcken House** (☉ *Late May–early Sept., daily noon–4*) was built in 1852 for pioneer doctor and statesman John Sebastian Helmcken. Inside are displays of the family's belongings, including the doctor's medical tools. Behind it is **St. Ann's School House,** built in 1858. One of British Columbia's oldest schools, it is thought to be Victoria's oldest building still standing. Both buildings are part of the Royal British Columbia Museum. ⊠ *675 Belleville St., Downtown* ☎ *250/356–7226, 888/447–7977, 877/480–4887 theater show times* ⊕ *www.royalbcmuseum.bc.ca* ✆ *C$21.60, IMAX theater C$11.80; combination ticket C$31.40* ☉ *Oct.–May, daily 9–5; June–Sept., Sun.–Wed. 9–5, Thurs.–Sat. 10–10.*

OUTSIDE TOWN

Home to the B.C. and Washington State ferry terminals as well as the Victoria International Airport, the Saanich Peninsula, with its rolling green hills and small family farms and wineries, is the first part of Vancouver Island that most visitors see. Bus tours to the Butchart Gardens run several times a day, and many tours take in other sights in the area; several companies also offer winery tours.

FAMILY

Fodor's Choice

★

Butchart Gardens. This stunning 55-acre garden and National Historic Site has been drawing visitors since it was planted in a limestone quarry in 1904. Highlights include the dramatic 70-foot Ross Fountain, the formal Japanese garden, and the intricate Italian garden complete with a gelato stand. Kids will love the old-fashioned carousel and will likely enjoy the 45-minute mini-boat tours around Todd Inlet.

From mid-June to mid-September the gardens are illuminated at night with hundreds of hidden lights. In July and August, kids' entertainers perform Sunday through Friday afternoons; jazz, blues, and classical musicians play at an outdoor stage each evening; and fireworks draw crowds every Saturday night. The wheelchair- and stroller-accessible site is also home to a seed-and-gift shop, a plant identification center, two restaurants (one offering traditional afternoon tea), and a coffee shop; you can even call ahead for a picnic basket on fireworks nights. To avoid crowds, come at opening time, in the late afternoon or evening (except ultrabusy fireworks Saturday evenings), or between September and June, when the gardens are still stunning. The grounds are especially magical at Christmas, with themed lighting and an ice rink.

The gardens are a 20-minute drive north of downtown; parking is free but fills up on fireworks Saturdays. You can get here by city Bus 75 from Douglas Street in downtown Victoria, but service is slow and infrequent. CVS Cruise Victoria (☎ 877/578–5552 ⊕ *www.cvscruisevictoria.com*) runs shuttles from downtown Victoria as well as from Swartz Bay ferry terminal. ⊠ *800 Benvenuto Ave., Brentwood Bay* ☎ *250/652–5256, 866/652–4422* ⊕ *www.butchartgardens.com* ⊠ *C$30.20* ☾ *Mid-June–Aug., daily 9 am–10 pm; Sept.–mid-June, daily 9 am–dusk.*

FAMILY **Shaw Ocean Discovery Centre.** A simulated ride underwater in a deep-sea elevator is just the beginning of a visit to this fun and educational marine interpretive center. Devoted entirely to the aquatic life and conservation needs of the Salish Sea—the waters south and east of Vancouver Island—the small but modern center displays local sea life, including luminous jellyfish, bright purple starfish, wolf eels, rockfish, and octopi. Hands-on activities and touch tanks delight kids, who also love the high-tech effects, including a floor projection that ripples when stepped on and a pop-up tank you can poke your head into. ⊠ *9811 Seaport Pl., Sidney* ☎ *250/665–7511* ⊕ *www.oceandiscovery.ca* ⊠ *$14* ☾ *July and Aug., daily 10–5; Sept.–June daily 10–4.*

SHOPPING

Shopping in Victoria is easy: virtually everything is in the downtown area on or near Government Street stretching north from the Fairmont Empress hotel. Victoria stores specializing in English imports are plentiful, though Canadian-made goods, including B.C. jade and First Nations work, are usually a better buy.

Artina's. Canadian-made jewelry—all handmade, one-of-a-kind pieces—fills the display cases at this unique jewelry shop. ⊠ *1002 Government St., Downtown* ☎ *250/386–7000* ⊕ *www.artinas.com.*

Design District. The area where Wharf Street runs into Store Street contains a cluster of Victoria's home decor shops. ⊕ *www.victoriadesign district.com.*

Fodor's Choice
★ **Lower Johnson Street.** This row of candy-color Victorian-era shop fronts in LoJo (Lower Johnson) is Victoria's hub for independent fashion boutiques. Storefronts—some closet size—are filled with local designers' wares, funky boutiques, and no fewer than three shops selling ecologically friendly clothes of hemp and organic cotton. ⊠ *Johnson St., between Government and Store Sts., Downtown.*

Munro's Books. Move over, Chapters: this beautifully restored 1909 former bank now houses one of Canada's best-stocked independent bookstores. Deals abound in the remainders' bin. ⊠ *1108 Government St., Downtown* ☎ *250/382–2464* ⊕ *www.munrobooks.com.*

Fodor's Choice
★ **Silk Road.** Tea aspires to new heights in this chic emporium. Shelves are stacked with more than 300 intriguing varieties; some you can enjoy in flights at an impressive tasting bar, and others have been restyled into aromatherapy remedies and spa treatments, including a green tea facial, which you can try out in the tiny spa downstairs. ⊠ *1624 Government St., Downtown* ☎ *250/704–2688* ⊕ *www.silkroadtea.com.*

WHERE TO EAT

The foodie vibe and eat-local ethos here is extraordinary, and although some restaurants along the Inner Harbour lean on views over service, chances are you'll find something to please.

$$$
MODERN
CANADIAN
Fodor's Choice
★ ✕ **Aura.** When an award-winning chef names "imagination" as his most treasured possession, you know the food here is likely to be creative, if not exquisite. The seasonal menu uses only local ingredients, revealing Asian influences. Think poached B.C. salmon paired with barbecued eel and a Japanese rice-cabbage roll; buffalo short ribs braised with fennel and star anise and served with wild-mushroom bread pudding; or free-range chicken with a wasabi-pea crust. The wine cellar is full of hard-to-find Vancouver Island wines and Okanagan labels. Sleek lines, warm colors, and water-view windows create a room that's both stylish and cozy. Plus, Aura has the city's best waterfront patio when the weather is cooperative. ⑤ *Average main: C$26* ⊠ *Inn at Laurel Point, 680 Montreal St., James Bay* ☎ *250/414–6739* ⊕ *www.aurarestaurant.ca.*

$$$$
MODERN
CANADIAN
Fodor's Choice
★ ✕ **Cafe Brio.** This intimate yet bustling Italian villa–style room has long been a Victoria favorite, mainly because of its Mediterranean influence in both atmosphere and mostly organic food. You might find local rockfish pan roasted and paired with chickpea polenta, grilled albacore tuna with an olive vinaigrette, or braised duck legs with a red wine risotto. Most dishes come in full or half sizes, which are ideal for smaller appetites or for those who want to sample the menu more widely. However, the Family Meal (C$24/person) is the choice for sharing, comprising six chef's choice-of-the-day dishes. Virtually everything, including the bread, pasta, charcuterie, and desserts, is made in-house. The 400-label wine list has a top selection of B.C. choices. ⑤ *Average main: C$28* ⊠ *944 Fort St., Downtown* ☎ *250/383–0009, 866/270–5461* ⊕ *www.cafe-brio.com* ⊗ *No lunch.*

$
ASIAN ✕ **The Noodle Box.** Noodles, whether Indonesian style with peanut sauce, thick Japanese udon in teriyaki, or Thai-style chow mein, are scooped straight from the open kitchen's steaming woks into bowls or cardboard

take-out boxes. Malaysian-, Singapore-, and Cambodian-style curries tempt those who like it hot. The brick, rose, and lime walls keep things modern and high energy at the Douglas Street location near the Inner Harbour. There are half a dozen "boxes" around town; the branch at 626 Fisgard Street is a tiny hole-in-the-wall near Chinatown. $ *Average main: C$12* ⊠ *818 Douglas St., Downtown* ☎ *250/384–1314* ⊕ *www. thenoodlebox.net* ⤸ *Reservations not accepted.*

WRANGELL

A small, unassuming timber and fishing community, Wrangell sits on the northern tip of Wrangell Island, near the mouth of the fast-flowing Stikine River—North America's largest undammed river. The Stikine plays a large role in the life of many Wrangell residents, including those who grew up homesteading on the islands that pepper the area. Trips on the river with local guides are highly recommended as they provide, basically, an insider's guide to the Stikine and a very Alaskan way of life. Like much of Southeast, Wrangell has suffered in recent years from a declining resource-based economy. But locals are working to build tourism in the town. Bearfest, which started in 2010, celebrates Wrangell's proximity to Anan Creek, where you can get a close-up view of both brown and black bears.

COMING ASHORE

Cruise ships calling in to Wrangell dock downtown, within walking distance of the museum and gift stores. Greeters welcome you and are available to answer questions. Wrangell's few attractions—the most notable being totem-filled Chief Shakes Island—are within walking distance of the pier. The Nolan Center houses an excellent museum, and Petroglyph Beach, where rocks are imprinted with mysterious prehistoric symbols, is 1 mile from the pier. Most cruise-ship visitors see it on guided shore excursions or by taxi.

TAXIS
Contacts **Northern Lights Taxi.** Call Northern Lights Taxi ☎ *907/874–4646.* **Star Cab** ☎ *907/874–3622.*

TOURS
Contacts **Sunrise Aviation.** This charter-only air carrier flies to the Anan Creek Wildlife Observatory, LeConte Glacier, and Forest Service cabins. ☎ *907/874–2319, 800/874–2311* ⊕ *www.sunriseflights.com.*

VISITOR INFORMATION
Contacts **Wrangell Visitor Center** ⊠ *296 Campbell Dr., in Nolan Center* ☎ *907/874–2829, 800/367–9745* ⊕ *www.wrangellalaska.org.*

EXPLORING

Chief Shakes's Grave Site. Buried here is Shakes V, who led the local Tlingit during the first half of the 19th century. A white picket fence surrounds the grave, and two killer-whale totem poles mark his resting spot overlooking the harbor. Find the grave on Case Avenue. ⊠ *Case Ave.*

Chief Shakes Island. This small island sits in the center of Wrangell's protected harbor, and is accessible by a footbridge from the bottom of Shakes Street. The Tribal House, constructed in 1940 as a replica of the original 19th century structure, was completely restored by local carvers in 2012 and 2013, as were the surrounding totem poles. ⊠ *Off Shakes St.* ☎ *907/874–4304* ⊕ *www.shakesisland.com* ☜ *$3.50* ◷ *Daily when cruise ships are in port (ask at Wrangell Visitor Center) or by appointment.*

Nolan Center. Wrangell's museum moved into a building that acts as a centerpiece for cultural life in Wrangell. Exhibits provide a window on the region's rich history. Featured pieces include the oldest known Tlingit house posts dating from the late 18th century, decorative posts from Chief Shakes's clan house, petroglyphs, century-old spruce-root and cedar-bark baskets, masks, gold-rush memorabilia, and a fascinating photo collection. If you're spending any time in town, don't pass this up. ⊠ *296 Campell Dr.* ☎ *907/874–3770* ⊕ *www.wrangell.com/cc/welcome-nolan-center* ◷ *May–Sept., Mon.–Sat. 10–5, and when ferry or cruise ships are in port; Oct.–Apr., Tues.–Sat. 1–5.*

Civic Center. Also in the building are the town's Civic Center, a 200-seat movie theater–performance space–convention center, and the **Wrangell Visitor Center.** The latter is staffed when the museum is open, and has details on local adventure options. ⊠ *296 Campbell Dr.* ☎ *907/874–2829, 800/367–9745* ⊕ *www.wrangellalaska.org.*

Petroglyph Beach State Historic Park. Scattered among other rocks at this public beach are three dozen or more large stones bearing designs and pictures chiseled by unknown ancient artists. No one knows why the rocks at this curious site were etched the way they were, or even exactly how old these etchings are. You can access the beach via a boardwalk, where you'll find signs describing the site along with carved replicas of the petroglyphs. Most of the petroglyphs are to the right between the viewing deck and a large outcropping of rock in the tidal beach area. Because the original petroglyphs can be damaged by physical contact, only photographs are permitted. But you are welcome to use the replicas to make a rubbing from rice paper and charcoal or crayons (available in local stores). ⊠ *0.6 mile north of ferry terminal off Evergreen Ave.*

OFF THE BEATEN PATH

Anan Creek Wildlife Observatory. About 30 miles southeast of Wrangell in the Tongass National Forest, Anan is one of Alaska's premier black- and brown-bear–viewing areas. Each summer, from early July to late August, as many as 30 to 40 bears gather at this Southeast stream to feed on huge runs of pink salmon. On an average visit of about three hours you might spot bears while strolling the ½-mile viewing boardwalk. Once on the platform, you will likely see many bears at the same time. There is a photo blind accessible from the viewing

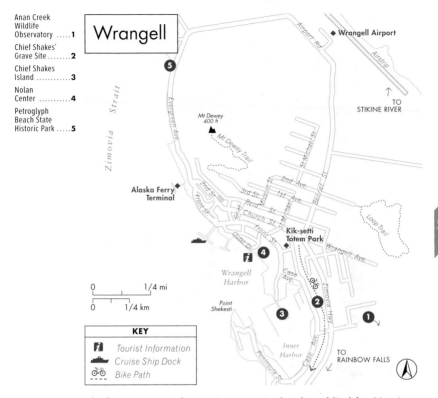

Wrangell

♦ **Wrangell Airport**

↑
TO
STIKINE RIVER

Mt Dewey
400 ft

Zimovia Strait

**Alaska Ferry
Terminal** ♦

**Kik-setti
Totem Park**

Loop Trail

*Wrangell
Harbor*

*Case
Ave.*

*Point
Shekesti*

0 ———— 1/4 mi

0 ———— 1/4 km

KEY

🛈 *Tourist Information*
⚓ *Cruise Ship Dock*
🚲 *Bike Path*

*Inner
Harbor*

TO
RAINBOW FALLS

platform. Five people at a time can use the photo blind for 30-minute intervals, which provides photo opportunities of bears at less than 11 yards. The photo blind provides stream-level photo ops of bears catching salmon. Forest Service interpreters are on hand to answer questions. The site is accessible only by boat or floatplane. From July 5 to August 25 you must have a pass to visit Anan; the U.S. Forest Service places a limit on the number of people who can visit the site each day. Unless you have experience navigating the Stikine by boat and in walking through bear country, it's highly recommended that you go to Anan with a local guide. The guide companies provide passes to Anan for their guests. ☎ *907/874–2323.*

SPORTS AND THE OUTDOORS

Alaska Vistas and Stikine Wilderness Adventures. Take jet-boat trips to Anan Creek Wildlife Observatory that depart from Wrangell, plus a variety of guided sea-kayak adventures and rafting trips. Alaska Vistas and Stikine Wilderness Adventures also offers custom tours and itinerary planning. ☎ *907/874–3006, 866/874–3006* ⊕ *www. alaskavistas.com.*

Breakaway Adventures. This outfitter leads a variety of jet-boat trips, including a tour to Chief Shakes Glacier and the nearby hot springs. You can catch one of its water taxis to Petersburg or Prince of Wales Island. ☎ 907/874–2488, 888/385–2488 ⊕ www.breakawayadventures.com.

FLIGHTSEEING

Alaska Charters and Adventures. Wildlife viewing, bear photography trips, fishing, glacier tours, and a Stikine River jet-boat wilderness tour are offered by Alaska Charters and Adventures. ☎ 888/993–2750 ⊕ www. alaskaupclose.com.

SHOPPING

Garnet Ledge. Garnet Ledge, a rocky ledge at the mouth of the Stikine River, is the source for garnets sold by local children for 25¢ to $50. The site was deeded to the Boy Scouts in 1962 and to the Presbyterian Church in Wrangell in 2006, so only children can collect these colorful but imperfect stones, the largest of which are an inch across. You can purchase garnets at a few covered shelters near the city dock when cruise ships are in, at the Wrangell Museum, or at the ferry terminal when a ferry is in port.

Brenda Schwartz-Yeager. Local artist Brenda Schwartz-Yeager creates watercolor scenes of the Alaskan coast on navigational charts of the region. Schwartz-Yeager, who grew up in Wrangell, is also a boat captain and local guide who, with her husband, owns Alaska Charters and Adventures. ✉ 7 Front St. ☎ 907/874–3508 ⊕ www.marineartist.com.

WHERE TO EAT

$ ✕ **Diamond C Cafe.** The big breakfasts at the Diamond C are just part of
CAFÉ the attraction. The café also serves as the gathering place for a group of local guys and, really, it's fun to just sit back and listen. As you dig into the breakfast hash and other goodies, though, there's a chance you'll only have eyes for your plate. $ Average main: $10 ✉ 223 Front St. ☎ 907/874–3677 ☾ No dinner.

$$ ✕ **Stikine Inn Restaurant.** With views overlooking the water, the restaurant
AMERICAN at the Stikine Inn is, easily, the prettiest place to dine in town. Considering the sparse number of restaurants in town, the Stikine could just serve a get-by menu, but the restaurant's salads, pizzas, burgers, and hearty soups go far beyond—it serves seriously tasty dishes. Portions tend to be oversized, especially on the dessert front. Consider splitting that dessert you eyeballed on the menu with at least one other person (if not two). The Stikine also has a full bar and serves good coffee drinks. $ Average main: $15 ✉ 107 Stikine Ave. ☎ 907/874–3388 ⊕ www. stikineinn.com/dining.html.

INLAND
CRUISE TOUR
DESTINATIONS

By Edward
Readicker-
Henderson

Alaska's Interior remains the last frontier, even for the Last Frontier state. The northern lights sparkle above a vast, mostly uninhabited landscape that promises adventure for those who choose to traverse it. Come here for wildlife-rich, pristine land and hardy locals, a rich and quirky history, gold panning, nonstop daylight in the summer, or ice-sculpting competitions under the northern lights in winter. Outdoors enthusiasts can enjoy hiking, rafting, fishing, skiing, and dogsledding. And don't forget to top off the experience with a soak in the hot springs.

The geology of the Interior played a key role in human history at the turn of the 20th century. The image of early-1900s Alaska, set to the harsh tunes of countless honky-tonk saloons and the clanging of pans, is rooted in the Interior's goldfields. Gold fever struck in Circle and Eagle in the 1890s, spread into Canada's Yukon Territory in the big Klondike Gold Rush of 1898, headed as far west as the beaches of Nome in 1900, then came back to Alaska's Interior when Fairbanks hit pay dirt in 1903. Through it all, the broad, swift Yukon River was the rush's main highway. Flowing almost 2,300 miles from Canada to the Bering Sea, just below the Arctic Circle, it carried prospectors across the north in search of instant fortune.

Although Fairbanks has grown into a small, bustling city with some serious attractions, many towns and communities in the Interior seem little changed from the gold-rush days. While soaking in the water of the Chena Hot Springs Resort, you can almost hear the whispers of gold seekers exaggerating their finds and claims, ever alert for the newest strike. When early missionaries set up schools in the Bush, the Native Alaskan peoples were herded to these regional centers for schooling and "salvation," but that stopped long ago, and today Interior Alaska's Native villages are thriving, with their own schools and a particularly Alaskan blend of modern life and tradition. Fort Yukon, on the Arctic Circle, is the largest Athabascan village in the state.

Alaska's current gold rush—the pipeline carrying (a little less each year) black gold from the oil fields in Prudhoe Bay south to the port of Valdez—snakes its way through the Interior. The Richardson Highway, which started as a gold stampeders' trail, parallels the Trans-Alaska Pipeline on its route south of Fairbanks. And gold still glitters in the Interior: Fairbanks, the site of the largest gold production in Alaska in pre–World War II days, is home to the Fort Knox Gold Mine, which has approximately doubled Alaska's gold production. Throughout the region, as the price of gold continues to climb to record highs on an almost daily basis, hundreds of tiny mines—from one-man operations to full-scale works—are starting up again, proving that what Robert Service wrote more than a hundred years ago still holds true: "There are strange things done in the midnight sun/ by the men who moil for gold."

PLANNING

WHEN TO GO
June and July bring near-constant sun (nothing quite like walking out of a restaurant at 11 pm into broad daylight), sometimes punctuated by afternoon cloudbursts. Like most of Alaska, many of the Interior's main attractions are seasonal, May into mid-September. A trip in May avoids the rush, but it can snow in Fairbanks in spring. Late August brings fall colors, ripe berries, active wildlife, and the start of northern lights season, with marvelous shows if you hit the right night.

GETTING HERE AND AROUND
AIR TRAVEL
Beyond the highways are many Native villages reached by small airplanes making daily connections out of Fairbanks, which is the regional hub and the thriving commercial center of the Interior. Delta offers seasonal nonstop service from Fairbanks to the Lower 48. Alaska Airlines and ERA Alaska fly the Anchorage–Fairbanks route. There are hotel shuttles, rental cars, and taxis available at the Fairbanks airport.

Contacts Alaska Airlines ☎ 800/252–7522 ⊕ www.alaskaair.com. **ERA Alaska** ☎ 907/266–8394, 800/866–8394 ⊕ www.flyera.com.

BUS TRAVEL
Alaska/Yukon Trails runs between Fairbanks, Denali, Anchorage, Talkeetna, Whitehorse, and Dawson City.

City Bus Fairbanks MACS Bus System ☎ 907/459–1011 ⊕ www.co.fairbanks.ak.us/transportation 🚌 $1.50/ride or $3/day.

Commuter Buses Alaska/Yukon Trails ☎ 800/770–7275 ⊕ www.alaskashuttle.com.

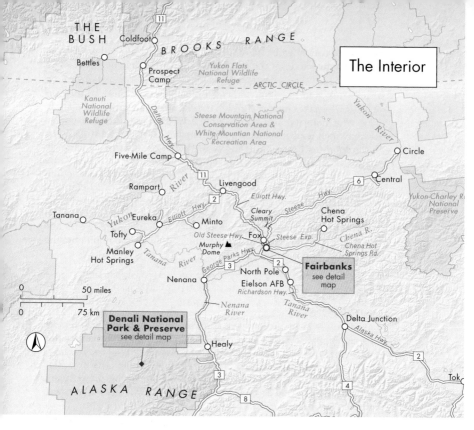

CAR TRAVEL

Interior Alaska is sandwiched between two monumental mountain ranges: the Brooks Range to the north and the Alaska Range to the south. In such a vast wilderness many of the region's residents define their area by a limited network of two-lane highways. You really need a car in the Interior, even if you're based in Fairbanks.

Fairbanks is a sprawling city. Things are too spread out for walking; public transportation is good but service is limited. Hotels run shuttle buses to and from the airport, and you can get around by taxi, but that's going to add up fast. Save yourself some frustration and just rent a car.

The Steese Highway, the Dalton Highway, and the Taylor Highway (which is closed in winter) are well-maintained gravel roads. However, summer rain can make them slick and dangerous. ■TIP➔ Rental-car companies have varying policies on whether they allow travel on gravel roads, so check in advance.

The George Parks Highway runs south to Denali National Park and Preserve and on to Anchorage, the state's largest city, 360 miles away on the coast. The Richardson Highway extends to the southeast to Delta Junction before turning south to Valdez, which is 368 miles from Fairbanks.

Two major routes lead north. You can take the Elliott Highway to the Dalton Highway, following the Trans-Alaska Pipeline to its origins at Prudhoe Bay on Alaska's North Slope (you can't drive all the way to the end, but you can get close). Alternatively, explore the Steese Highway to its termination at the Yukon River and the town of Circle.

Car Rentals Budget Rent-A-Car ☎ *907/474–0855, 800/474–0855 in Alaska* ⊕ *www.budget.com.* **Dollar Rent A Car** ☎ *907/451–4360, 800/800–4000* ⊕ *www.dollar.com.* **Hertz** ☎ *907/452–4444, 800/654–3131* ⊕ *www.hertz.com.*

TRAIN TRAVEL

Between late May and early September, Alaska Railroad's daily passenger service runs between Seward, Anchorage, and Fairbanks, with stops at Talkeetna and Denali National Park and Preserve. Standard trains have dining, lounge, and dome cars, plus the only outdoor viewing platform of its kind. Holland America and Princess offer luxurious travel packages as well.

Contacts Alaska Railroad ☎ *907/458–6025, 800/544–0552* ⊕ *www.alaskarailroad.com.* **Holland America Tours/Gray Line of Alaska** ☎ *800/544–2206* ⊕ *www.graylinealaska.com.* **Princess Tours** ☎ *800/426–0500* ⊕ *www.princesslodges.com.*

TOURS

Especially if you're interested in getting out into the wilderness or out to one of the villages, we recommend a tour—it's far less stressful, particularly if you'd otherwise be faced with tasks that you've never undertaken before, such as driving remote unpaved roads without knowing how to change a tire or, worse, wandering the backcountry with limited previous Alaska experience.

Tour Contacts Go North Alaska Adventure Travel Center ☎ *907/479–7272, 855/236–7271* ⊕ *www.gonorth-alaska.com.* **Northern Alaska Tour Company** ☎ *907/474–8600, 800/474–1986* ⊕ *www.northernalaska.com.*

RESTAURANTS

Even in the most elegant establishments Alaskans sometimes sport sweats or Carhartts. Most restaurants fly in fresh salmon and halibut from the coast. Meat-and-potatoes main courses and the occasional pasta dish fill menus, but most restaurants offer palatable vegetarian choices, too. The food isn't the only thing full of local flavor: walls are usually decked out in some combination of snowshoes, caribou and bear hides, the state flag, and historic photos.

HOTELS

You won't find ultraluxury hotels, but you can find a range of bed-and-breakfasts, rustic-chic lodges, and national chains, as well as local spots that will please even the most discriminating travelers. For interaction with Alaskans, choose a B&B, as they're usually locally owned; proprietors tend to be eager to provide travel tips or an unforgettable story. The cheapest options are tents or RVs, and there is no shortage of campgrounds here.

Prices in the reviews are the lowest cost of a standard double room in high season.

HEALTH AND SAFETY

To keep yourself from going insane when you're being attacked by a cloud of mosquitoes—and they grow them big in the Interior—DEET, and lots of it, is your best bet. And don't wear blue. Mosquitoes really like blue.

FAIRBANKS

At first glance Fairbanks appears to be little more than a sprawling conglomeration of strip malls, chain stores, and other evidence of suburbia (or, as a local writer once put it, "su-brrr-bia"). But look beyond the obvious in the Interior's biggest town and you'll discover why thousands insist that this is the best place to live in Alaska.

The hardy Alaskans who refuse to leave during the cold and dark winters share a strong camaraderie. To live here, you really have to want to live here, which gives the whole city a relaxed, happy vibe. The fight to stave off cabin fever leads to creative festivals, from winter solstice celebrations to midnight baseball in summer. And isn't there something marvelous about people who, if their car breaks down and it's cold enough to freeze the tires and make them explode, still know what to do? It takes a special kind of confidence to live here, and that adds to the town's attractions.

Many of the old homes and commercial buildings trace their history to the city's early days, especially in the downtown area, with its narrow, winding streets following the contours of the Chena River. Even if each year brings more chain stores, the beautiful hillsides and river valleys remain. And of course there is Fairbanks's fall, winter, and spring bonus: being able to see the aurora borealis, or northern lights, an average of 243 nights a year.

As you walk the streets of Fairbanks today, it takes a good imagination to envision the rough-and-tumble gold-mining camp that first took shape along the Chena River in the early 1900s. Although a few older neighborhoods have weathered log cabins, the rest is a Western hodgepodge that reflects the urge to build whatever one wants, wherever one wants—a trait that has long been a community standard (and sometimes leads to really interesting roof angles as the house sinks in permafrost).

The city is making some real efforts to preserve what's left of its gold-rush past, most notably in the 44-acre Pioneer Park, where dozens of cabins and many other relics were moved out of the path of progress. Downtown Fairbanks began to deteriorate in the 1970s, before and after the boom associated with the building of the Trans-Alaska Pipeline. But the downward spiral ended long ago, and most of downtown has been rebuilt.

ESSENTIALS

VISITOR INFORMATION

Make the **Morris Thompson Cultural and Visitors Center** your first stop in Fairbanks, where you can plan your whole trip, from a quick visit to a local attraction or a backcountry adventure. This center is also home to the **Fairbanks Convention and Visitors Bureau** and the **Alaska**

Public Lands Information Center. While you're here, browse the free exhibits on Interior Alaska's environment and people, as well as the recently opened, fantastic displays of both gold-rush and Native history. In the summer, the center hosts Alaska Native art, music, storytelling, and dance. Don't forget to enjoy the free films, use the Wi-Fi and Internet access, or peruse the literature at the Alaska Geographic Bookstore.

FAIRBANKS GOLD

The gold strike by Felix Pedro in 1902 is commemorated annually in late July with the celebration of Golden Days, marked by a parade and several days of gold rush–inspired activities.

Contacts Alaska Department of Fish and Game ⊠ *1300 College Rd.* ☎ *907/459-7207* ⊕ *www.adfg.alaska.gov.* **Alaska Public Lands Information Center** ⊠ *101 Dunkel St., Downtown* ☎ *907/459-3730* ⊕ *www.alaskacenters. gov/fairbanks.cfm.* **Fairbanks Convention and Visitors Bureau** ⊠ *101 Dunkel St., Downtown* ☎ *907/456-5774, 800/327-5774 recording* ⊕ *www.explorefairbanks.com.* **Morris Thompson Cultural and Visitors Center** ⊠ *101 Dunkel St.* ☎ *907/459-3700* ⊕ *www.morristhompsoncenter.org* ▣ *Free* ☽ *Summer, daily 8–9; winter, daily 8–5.*

TOURS
Gray Line of Alaska. Gray Line of Alaska runs scenic and informative trips through the Fairbanks area, including an eight-hour Discover the Gold sightseeing tour of the *Gold Dredge Number 8*, a stern-wheeler cruise, and a lunch of miner's stew for $130. ☎ *800/544-2206* ⊕ *www. graylinealaska.com.*

EXPLORING

Fodor'sChoice ★ **"Fountainhead" Antique Automobile Museum.** Located on the property of the Wedgewood Resort, this museum features automobiles from 1898 to 1938—all of which run, the curators taking them out on the roads regularly. The museum also has the first car ever made in Alaska, built in Skagway out of sheet metal and old boat parts, all to impress a girl (didn't work). Alongside the cars are displays of vintage clothing and historical photographs. It's widely considered one of the best auto museums in the world, and incredibly interesting, even if you're not interested in old cars. ⊠ *212 Wedgewood Dr.* ☎ *907/450-2100* ⊕ *fountainhead-museum.com* ▣ *$10; $5 for guests of Wedgewood Resort, Sophie Station Suites, or Bridgewater Hotel* ☽ *Mid-May–mid-Sept., Sun.–Thurs. 11–10, Fri. and Sat. 11–6; mid-Sept.– mid-May, Sun. noon–6.*

FAMILY **Large Animal Research Station.** Out on the fringes of the University of Alaska campus is a 134-acre home to about 50 musk ox, 45 caribou, and 40 domestic reindeer (those last two are actually the same animal from most standpoints; they can interbreed, and the main difference comes down to the fact that reindeer, having been domesticated, are lazier and fatter than caribou). Resident and visiting scientists study these large ungulates to better understand their physiologies and how they adapt to Arctic conditions. The station also serves as a valuable outreach program. Most people have little chance to see these animals in their natural habitats, especially the musk ox. Once nearly eradicated

6

from Alaska, these shaggy, prehistoric-looking beasts are marvels of adaptive physiques and behaviors. Their qiviut, the delicate musk ox undercoat of hair that is so soft it makes cashmere feel like steel wool, is combed out (without harming the animals) and made into yarn for scarves, hats, and gloves. The station has this unprocessed wool and yarn for sale to help fund the care of the animals. On tours you visit the pens for a close-up look at the animals and their young, while learning about the biology and ecology of the animals from a naturalist. The tours are a very good deal, and the best way to learn about the animals, but you can also just come by any time of day, and usually see musk ox from the parking lot; they sometimes come quite close to the fence. ✉ *Yankovich Rd. off Ballaine Rd., behind University of Alaska Fairbanks* ☎ *907/474–5724 tour information* ⊕ *www.lars.uaf.edu* ✆ *Tours $10; free general viewing year-round* ☉ *Jun.–Aug., grounds daily 9:30– 4:30, tours Tues.–Sat. at 10, 12, and 2.*

FAMILY   **Pioneer Park.** The 44-acre park is along the Chena River near downtown Fairbanks, and has several museums, an art gallery, theater, civic center, Native village, large children's playground, miniature-golf course, antique merry-go-round, and restaurants. The park also has a re-created gold-rush town with historic buildings saved from urban renewal, log-cabin gift shops, and **Mining Valley,** an outdoor museum of mining artifacts surrounding an indoor-outdoor Alaska Salmon Bake restaurant. The 227-foot stern-wheeler *Nenana* is the second-largest wooden vessel in existence and a national historic landmark. A diorama inside the stern-wheeler details the course the riverboat took on the Yukon and Tanana rivers around the turn of the 20th century. The **Crooked Creek and Whiskey Island Railroad,** a narrow-gauge train, circles the park. The newest addition to the park is a museum housing the first locomotive in Fairbanks, which has been restored to its 1905 condition and is run on special occasions. This is one of the best places in Fairbanks to bring kids and let them run off some energy. ■TIP➔ **No-frills (dry) RV camping is available for $12 a night in the west end of the large parking lot on Airport Way.** ✉ *2300 Airport Way(Airport Way and Peger Rd.)* ☎ *907/459–1087* ⊕ *www.fnsb.us/ pioneerpark* ✆ *Free* ☉ *Park 24 hrs; museum and shops Memorial Day–Labor Day, daily noon–8.*

Fodor'sChoice   **University of Alaska Museum of the North.** This museum has some of the
★   most distinctive architecture in the state, with sweeping curves and graceful lines that evoke glaciers, mountains, and a fluke of a diving whale. Inside, two-story viewing windows look out on the Alaska Range and the Tanana Valley. Otto, the 8-foot, 9-inch brown bear, greets visitors to the entrance of the Gallery of Alaska, also featuring Blue Babe, a mummified steppe bison that lived 36,000 years ago during the Pleistocene epoch. The museum has several "please touch" items, including the molars of a mammoth and a mastodon, a gray whale skull, and a 5,495-pound copper nugget. Also in the gallery is a fantastic collection of Native clothes, tools, boats, and more from around the state, offering a chance to see how different groups came to terms with climatic extremes; other dioramas show the state's animals and how they interact. And don't miss the treasured Rose Berry Alaska

DID YOU KNOW?

The University of Alaska Museum of the North is pure Alaska inside and out: the exterior was inspired by the state's alpine ridges, glaciers, Yukon River, and northern lights, and the interior houses thousands of years of Alaskan art, culture, and nature. Don't miss Blue Babe, the 36,000-year-old steppe bison. Also inside is one of the best gift shops in the city.

Art Gallery, representing 2,000 years of Alaska's art, from ancient to modern, or the year-round special exhibits. In the Place Where You Go to Listen, ever-changing light and sound, composed by the real-time movements of the sun, moon, aurora, and seismic activity, create a mesmerizing effect. This is one of the best museums in Alaska, and a can't-miss stop. The gift shop also has one of the better selections of Alaskana in town. ⊠ *University of Alaska Fairbanks, 907 Yukon Dr.* ☎ *907/474–7505* ⊕ *www.uaf.edu/museum* 🍴 *$12 general admission and additional charges for 30-min summer auditorium shows* ⊘ *Mid-May–mid-Sept., daily 9–7; mid-Sept.–mid-May, Mon.–Sat. 9–5.*

WHERE TO EAT

$$$
SEAFOOD
✕ **Alaska Salmon Bake.** Salmon cooked over an open fire with a lemon-and-brown-sugar sauce is a favorite at this indoor-outdoor restaurant in Pioneer Park's Mining Valley. Halibut, cod, prime rib, a salad bar, and dessert are also available at the nightly all-you-can-eat dinner. ⑤ *Average main: $33* ⊠ *Airport Way and Peger Rd., Pioneer Park* ☎ *907/452–7274, 800/354–7274* ⊕ *www.akvisit.com/salmon.html* ⊘ *Closed Oct.–mid-May. No lunch.*

$$$
AMERICAN
✕ **Pike's Landing.** Enjoy lunch on a huge outside deck (it seats 420) over-looking the Chena River, or inside in the elegant dining room of an extended log cabin. The meals cost up to $47 for steak and lobster and rank with the best in the Interior. For a dinner in the $15 to $20 range, relax in the sports bar and catch a view of the river. The palate-pleasing Sunday brunch has an irresistible dessert table. ⑤ *Average main: $25* ⊠ *4438 Airport Way* ☎ *907/479–6500* ⊕ *www.pikeslodge.com.*

$$
AMERICAN
✕ **Sam's Sourdough Cafe.** Although Sam's serves meals all day, Fairbank-sans know it as the best breakfast place in town. Sourdough recipes are a kind of minor religion in Alaska, and Sam's serves an extensive menu of sourdough specialties, including hotcakes and French toast, as well as standard meat-and-eggs options, all at reasonable prices. On week-ends get here early or be prepared for a wait. The address says Cameron Street, but it's really fronted on University, just over the railroad tracks. ⑤ *Average main: $12* ⊠ *3702 Cameron St.* ☎ *907/479–0523.*

$$
AMERICAN
✕ **Silver Gulch Brewing and Bottling Co.** You'll find some unique souvenirs and an interesting collection of Fairbanks citizens at North America's northernmost brewery. Founded in 1998, Silver Gulch is probably best known for its pilsner and lager brews, carried throughout the state. The brewery is in the Fox Roadhouse building. A preserved section of the old roadhouse's exterior still stands in the second floor of the res-taurant. This hot spot is 10 miles north of Fairbanks on the Old Steese Highway, across from the Howling Dog Saloon. After your brewery tour (make sure to call ahead to arrange it), satisfy your hunger with I.P.A.–battered fish-and-chips or fresh Alaskan seafood, or enjoy a brew while sitting in the outdoor beer garden. ⑤ *Average main: $15* ⊠ *2195 Old Steese Hwy., Fox* ☎ *907/452–2739* ⊕ *www.silvergulch.com* ⊘ *No lunch weekdays* ☞ *Free brewery tours available in summer.*

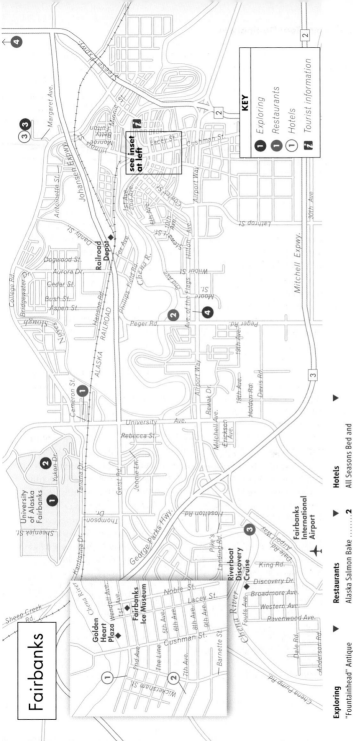

Fairbanks

KEY

- **1** Exploring
- **1** Restaurants
- **1** Hotels
- **i** Tourist information

see inset at left

Exploring ▶

"Fountainhead" Antique Automobile Museum **3**
Large Animal Research Station **2**
Pioneer Park **4**
University of Alaska Museum of the North **1**

Restaurants ▶

Alaska Salmon Bake **2**
Pike's Landing **3**
Sam's Sourdough Cafe **1**
Silver Gulch Brewing and Bottling Co. **4**

Hotels ▶

All Seasons Bed and Breakfast Inn **2**
Bridgewater Hotel **1**
Wedgewood Resort **3**

WHERE TO STAY

For expanded hotel reviews, visit Fodors.com.

$$
B&B/INN

All Seasons Bed and Breakfast Inn. In a quiet residential neighborhood within walking distance of downtown, this nicely furnished inn provides relaxation and privacy. **Pros:** close to downtown; clean rooms; trip planning help available. **Cons:** lacks Alaskan ambience. *$ Rooms from: $169* ✉ *763 7th Ave., Downtown* ☎ *907/451–6649* ⊕ *www. allseasonsinn.com* ⮌ *8 rooms* ⦿ *Breakfast.*

$$
HOTEL

Bridgewater Hotel. In the heart of downtown Fairbanks, just above the Chena River, this hotel has gone through a number of incarnations and is now a thoroughly modern, European-style hotel. **Pros:** good location; weekend specials available; downtown hotel with the most character; free trolley. **Cons:** small and modest rooms; no kitchen or refrigerators; restaurant serves breakfast only. *$ Rooms from: $145* ✉ *723 1st Ave., Downtown* ☎ *907/452–6661, 800/528–4916* ⊕ *www. fountainheadhotels.com/bridgewater/bridgewater.htm* ⮌ *93 rooms* ⊗ *Closed mid-Sept.–mid-May* ⦿ *Breakfast.*

$$
RESORT
Fodor's Choice
★

Wedgewood Resort. Both wild and cultivated flowers adorn the landscaped grounds of the Wedgewood Resort, which borders on Creamer's Field Migratory Waterfowl Refuge. **Pros:** courteous staff; 4 miles of trails through 76 acres of wildlife sanctuary; antique automobile museum; elegant banquet halls; free shuttle. **Cons:** a bit far from most of Fairbanks's other attractions. *$ Rooms from: $175* ✉ *212 Wedgewood Dr.* ☎ *907/456–3642, 800/528–4916* ⊕ *www.fountainheadhotels.com* ⮌ *307 suites.*

NIGHTLIFE

Check the "Kaleidoscope" section in the Thursday *Fairbanks Daily News–Miner* for current nightspots, plays, concerts, and art shows.

Blue Loon. The Blue Loon, between Ester and Fairbanks, presents year-round entertainment and great grill food. Movies are nightly at 5:30 and 8. Catch national touring bands, comedy, outdoor summer concerts, DJ dancing late nights on weekends, and much more, including free Wi-Fi. ✉ *Mile 353.5, Parks Hwy.* ☎ *907/457–5666* ⊕ *www.theblueloon.com* ⊗ *Closed Mon.*

Midnight Mine. Don't be alarmed by the exterior of the Midnight Mine. It's a friendly neighborhood bar with darts, foosball, a pool table, and a big-screen TV, and it's within walking distance of downtown. Cleo the dog is likely to greet you as you come in—be sure to ask to see her trick. It'll cost you a buck, but it's worth it. ✉ *308 Wendell St.* ☎ *907/456–5348.*

Senator's Saloon. The Senator's Saloon at the Pump House Restaurant, is the place to hear easy-listening music alongside the Chena River on a warm summer evening. ✉ *796 Chena Pump Rd.* ☎ *907/479–8452* ⊕ *www.pumphouse.com.*

SHOPPING

Alaska Rag Company. Known for handwoven rugs, the Alaska Company pany carries the work of many local artists. ⊠ *603 Lacey St., Downtown* ☎ *907/451–4401* ⊕ *www.alaskaragco.com.*

Beads and Things. Beads and Things sells Native handicrafts from around the state. ⊠ *537 2nd Ave., Downtown* ☎ *907/456–2323.*

Great Alaskan Bowl Company. The Great Alaskan Bowl Company sells lathe-turned bowls made out of Alaskan birch. Open every day of the year, except New Year's, Thanksgiving, and Christmas, this is the big one-stop shop for pretty much any kind of Alaskan thing you need– more than 90 vendors are selling out of the place. They have on the spot engraving, plenty of Alaskan goodies to sample, and they'll ship just about anything. ⊠ *4630 Old Airport Rd.* ☎ *907/474–9663* ⊕ *www. woodbowl.com.*

Judie Gumm Designs. In her small, eponymous shop Ms. Gumm fashions stunning (and moderately priced) silver and gold designs best described as sculptural interpretations of Northern images. Ester is 6 miles south of Fairbanks off the George Parks Highway. ⊠ *3600 Main St., Ester* ☎ *907/479–4568, 800/478–4568* ⊕ *www.judiegumm.com.*

A Weaver's Yarn. A Weaver's Yarn has musk-ox qiviut to spin. This is undoubtedly the softest stuff imaginable. ⊠ *1810 Alaska Way, College* ☎ *907/374–1995* ⊕ *www.aweaversyarn.com.*

SPORTS AND THE OUTDOORS

ADVENTURE TOURS

Northern Alaska Tour Company. Northern Alaska Tour Company leads year-round half- and full-day excursions to the Arctic Circle and the Yukon River and (in summer) two- and three-day fly-drive tours to Prudhoe Bay, Barrow, and the Brooks Range. Aurora-watching trips are available in winter. ☎ *907/474–8600, 800/474–1986* ⊕ *www.northern alaska.com.*

BOATING

For relaxing boating in or near Fairbanks, use Chena River access points at Nordale Road east of the city, at the Cushman and Wendell Street bridges near downtown, in Pioneer Park above the Peger River Bridge, at the state campground, and at the University Avenue Bridge.

The Tanana River, with a current that is fast and often shallow, is ideally suited for riverboats. On this river and others in the Yukon River drainage, Alaskans use long, wide, flat-bottom boats powered by one or two large outboard engines. The boats include a lift to raise the engine a few inches, allowing passage through the shallows; lately, it's more common just to get a jet boat, which doesn't have a propeller and so can go into much shallower waters. Arrangements for riverboat charters can be made in almost any river community. Ask at the Fairbanks Convention and Visitors Bureau.

CLOSE UP

Celestial Rays of Light: Aurora Borealis

The light show often begins simply, as a pale yellow-green luminous band that arches across Alaska's night sky. Sometimes the band will quickly fade and disappear. Other nights, however, it may begin to waver, flicker, and pulsate. Or the quiescent band may explode and fill the sky with curtains of celestial light that ripple wildly above the northern landscape. Growing more intense, these dancing lights take on other colors: pink, red, blue, or purple. At times they appear to be heavenly flames, leaping across the sky, or perhaps they're exploding fireworks, or cannon fire.

The Fairbanks area is one of the best places in the world to see the aurora borealis—commonly called the northern lights. Here they may appear more than 200 nights per year; they're much less common in Anchorage, partly because of urban glare.

As you watch these dazzling lights swirling from horizon to horizon, it is easy to imagine why many Northern cultures, including Alaska's Native peoples, created myths to explain auroral displays. What start out as patches, arcs, or bands can be magically transformed into vaporous, humanlike figures. Some of Alaska's Native groups have traditionally believed the lights to be spirits of their ancestors. According to one belief, the spirits are celebrating with dance and drumming; another says they're playing games. Yet another tradition says the lights are torches, carried by spirits who lead the souls of recently deceased people to life in the afterworld.

During Alaska's gold-rush era some non-Native stampeders supposed the aurora to be reflections of ore deposits. Even renowned wilderness explorer John Muir allowed the northern lights to spark his imagination. Once, while traveling through Southeast Alaska in 1890, Muir stayed up all night to watch a gigantic, glowing auroral bridge and bands of "restless electric auroral fairies" who danced to music "too fine for mortal ears."

Scientists have a more technical explanation for these heavenly apparitions. The aurora borealis is an atmospheric phenomenon that's tied to explosive events on the sun's surface, known as solar flares. Those flares produce a stream of charged particles, the "solar wind," which shoots off into space. When such a wind intersects with Earth's magnetic field, most of the particles are deflected; some, however, are sent into the upper atmosphere, where they collide with gas molecules such as nitrogen and oxygen. The resulting reactions produce glowing colors. The aurora is most commonly a pale green, but its borders are sometimes tinged with pink, purple, or blue. Especially rare is the all-red aurora, which appears when charged solar particles collide with oxygen molecules from 50 to 200 miles above Earth's surface.

■TIP➔ Alaska's long hours of daylight hide the aurora in summer, so the best viewing is from September through March. Scientists at the University of Alaska Geophysical Institute give a daily forecast from late fall to spring of when the lights will be the most intense at ⊕ *www.gedds. alaska.edu/auroraforecast* and in the *Fairbanks Daily News–Miner.*

Fodor's Choice
★
Alaska Outdoor Rentals and Guides. Alaska Outdoor Rentals and Guides rents gear and arranges pickups and drop-offs for the Class I waters of the lower Chena River (the only real challenge for canoeists on the lower river is watching out for powerboats), as well as other local rivers. ⊠ *Pioneer Park Boat Dock, along Chena River next to Peger Rd.* ☎ *907/457–2453* ⊕ *www.akbike.com.*

Fodor's Choice
★
Riverboat *Discovery.* The city's riverboat history and the Interior's cultural heritage are relived each summer aboard the Riverboat *Discovery*, a 3½-hour narrated trip by stern-wheeler along the Chena and Tanana rivers to a rustic Native village on the Tanana River. The cruise provides a glimpse of the lifestyle of the dog mushers, subsistence fishermen, traders, and Native Alaskans who populate the Yukon River drainage. Sights along the way include operating fish wheels, a bush airfield, floatplanes, a smokehouse and cache, log cabins, and dog kennels once tended by the late Susan Butcher, the first person to win the Iditarod four times. The Binkley family, with four generations of river pilots, has run the great rivers of the north for more than 100 years. Cruises are $59.95 and run twice daily (at 8:45 am and 2 pm) mid-May to mid-September. ⊠ *1975 Discovery Dr.* ☎ *907/479–6673, 866/479–6673* ⊕ *www.riverboatdiscovery.com.*

DOG MUSHING

Throughout Alaska, sprint races, freight hauling, and long-distance endurance runs are held in late February and March, during the season when longer days afford enjoyment of the remaining winter snow. Men and women often compete in the same classes in the major races. For children, various racing classes are based on age, starting with the one-dog category for the youngest. The Interior sees a constant string of sled-dog races from November to March, which culminates in the **North American Open Sled-Dog Championship,** attracting international competition to Fairbanks.

Paws for Adventure Sled Dog Tours. Offering a mix of trips, Paws for Adventure Sled Dog Tours is a good choice. The most adventurous can embark on multiday trips, but other options include a mushing school or a short sled ride. ☎ *907/378–3630* ⊕ *www.pawsforadventure.com* ☉ *Oct.–Apr., weather permitting.*

GOLD PANNING

Alaskan Prospectors. The gold information center for Interior Alaska, Alaskan Prospectors is the oldest mining and prospecting supply store in the state, also featured on the Travel Channel. Stop here for gold pans and books or videos, or to visit the rocks and minerals museum. Employees have valuable advice for the neophyte gold bug. ⊠ *504 College Rd.* ☎ *907/452–7398.*

Gold Dredge 8 and El Dorado Gold Mine. Gold Dredge 8 offers a two-hour tour of a seasonal mining operation, all from the comfort of a narrow-gauge railroad. Miners demonstrate classic and modern techniques, and at the end, you get to try your own luck panning for gold. They've also brought over a lot of the historic elements from the old El Dorado Gold Mine, so it's a pretty complete look at how Fairbanks got rich. ⊠ *1603 N. Old Steese Hwy.* ☎ *907/479–6673, 866/479–6673* ⊕ *www. golddredge8.com* ☒ *$39.95.*

6

NORTHERN LIGHTS TOURS

Aurora Borealis Lodge. The Aurora Borealis Lodge has late-night tours to a log lodge on Cleary Summit, with big picture windows to see the sky. The $75–$85 tour includes hot drinks and transportation from Fairbanks. With independent transportation, admission is $25 per person. Four spacious rooms in the two-story building are also available for overnight accommodation (call ahead in the summer season), each with large, north-facing windows, Wi-Fi, private bath, and kitchen. Aurora tours run from August 20 to April 1. If space is available, snowshoe tours are $95 for four hours, with transportation. Rooms range $199–$224 per night, with discounts for longer stays. ⊠ *Mile 20.5, Steese Hwy., Cleary Summit* ☎ *907/389–2812* ⊕ *www.auroracabin.com.*

Chena Hot Springs Resort. About 60 miles northeast of Fairbanks, the Chena Hot Springs Resort treats guests to a Sno-Cat ride to a yurt with a 360-degree panoramic vista of nothing but wilderness. Open every day of the year. ⊠ *End of Chena Hot Springs Rd., Chena Hot Springs* ☎ *907/451–8104* ⊕ *www.chenahotsprings.com.*

Mount Aurora Skiland. Visitors fill the two warm mountaintop lodges at Mount Aurora Skiland after 10 pm on winter nights. Images from an aurora Web cam are shown on a large-screen TV. Admission is $30 and includes hot drinks. ⊠ *Mile 20.5, Steese Hwy., Cleary Summit* ☎ *907/389–2314* ⊕ *www.skiland.org.*

DENALI NATIONAL PARK AND PRESERVE

More than 6 million acres of wilderness, Denali National Park and Preserve is the heart of Alaska: the biggest mountains, the wildest rivers, and so much wildlife, you'll probably end up frying your camera trying to catch it all. Founded in 1917 as Mt. McKinley National Park (despite the fact that the park's then borders went right across the mountain), government caught up with thousands of years of Native tradition and renamed the park Denali in 1980. One road in, the tallest mountain on the continent, and endless possibilities await you.

Although it isn't technically a port of call, Denali National Park and Preserve is, quite understandably, one of the most popular land extensions to an Alaska cruise. Anchorage, 240 miles south of the park, serves as a point of departure.

GEOLOGY AND TERRAIN

The most prominent geological feature of the park is the Alaska Range, a 600-mile-long crescent of mountains that separates South Central Alaska from the Interior. Mt. Hunter (14,573 feet), Mt. Foraker (17,400 feet), and Mt. McKinley (20,320 feet) are the mammoths of the group. Glaciers flow from the entire Alaska Range.

Another, smaller group of mountains—the Outer Range, north of Denali's park road—is a mix of volcanics and heavily metamorphosed sediments. Though not as breathtaking as the Alaska Range, the Outer Range is popular with hikers and backpackers because its summits and ridges are not as technically difficult to reach.

Several of Denali's most spectacular landforms are deep in the park, but are still visible from the park road. The multicolor volcanic rocks at Cathedral Mountain and Polychrome Pass reflect the vivid hues of the American Southwest. The braided channels of glacially fed streams such as the Teklanika, Toklat, and McKinley rivers serve as highway routes for both animals and hikers. The debris- and tundra-covered ice of the Muldrow Glacier, one of the largest glaciers to flow out of Denali National Park's high mountains, is visible from Eielson Visitor Center, at Mile 66 of the park road. Wonder Lake, a dark and narrow kettle pond that's a remnant from Alaska's ice ages, lies at Mile 85, just a few miles from the former gold-boom camp of Kantishna.

EXPLORING DENALI

You can take a tour bus or the Alaskan Railroad from Anchorage to the Denali National Park entrance. Princess, Holland America, and Royal Caribbean attach their own railcars behind the trains for a more luxurious experience. Most cruise passengers stay one or two nights in hotels at a riverside settlement called Denali Park, just outside the park entrance. Shuttle buses provide transportation from your hotel to the park's busy visitor center, where you can watch slide shows on the park, purchase maps and books, or check the schedule for naturalist presentations and sled-dog demonstrations. Access to the park itself is by bus on day tours. If you aren't visiting Denali as part of your cruise package, make reservations for a tour or outdoor adventure that fits your style *(see Outdoor Activities, below)*. All the major hotels in the Denali Park area have good restaurants on the premises, and most travelers choose to dine there.

The 90-mile Denali Park Road winds from the park entrance to Wonder Lake and Kantishna, the historic mining community in the heart of the park. Public access along this road is limited to tour and shuttle buses that depart from the Wilderness Access Center. The Park Road is paved for the first 15 miles and gravel the rest of the way.

The Wilderness Access Center near the park's entrance (at Mile 237 of the Parks Highway, or Mile 1 of the Park Road) is the transportation hub, with bus and campsite reservations. The adjacent backcountry information building has hiking details for those heading into the wilderness, including current data on animal sightings, river-crossing conditions, weather, and closed areas.

PARK BASICS

Wilderness Access Center. The Wilderness Access Center near the park's entrance at Mile 237.3, George Parks Highway, is where you can handle reservations for roadside camping and bus trips into the park. A smaller building nearby is the **Backcountry Information Center,** for those visitors who want to travel and stay overnight in the wilderness. The Backcountry Information Center has backcountry permits and hiking information, including current data on animal sightings (remember the whole park is bear territory), river-crossing conditions, weather, and closed areas. The center is closed in winter (mid-September through mid-May). ■TIP→ **Free permits are required for overnight backpacking trips, but you won't need one for day hiking.** ✉ *Mile 1, Park Rd., Denali National Park* ☎ *907/683–9274.*

Denali National Park and Preserve

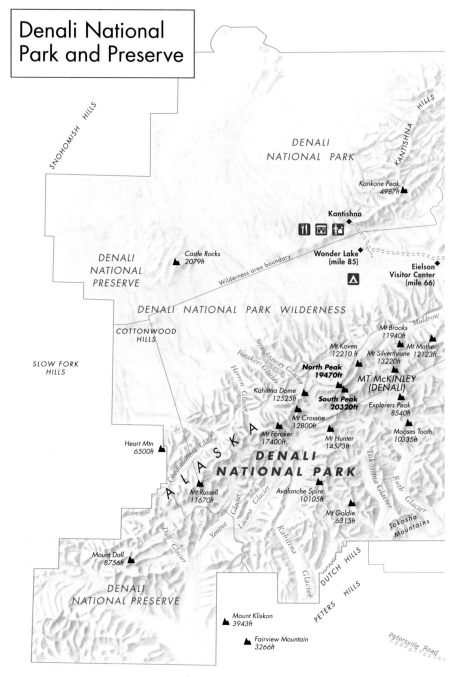

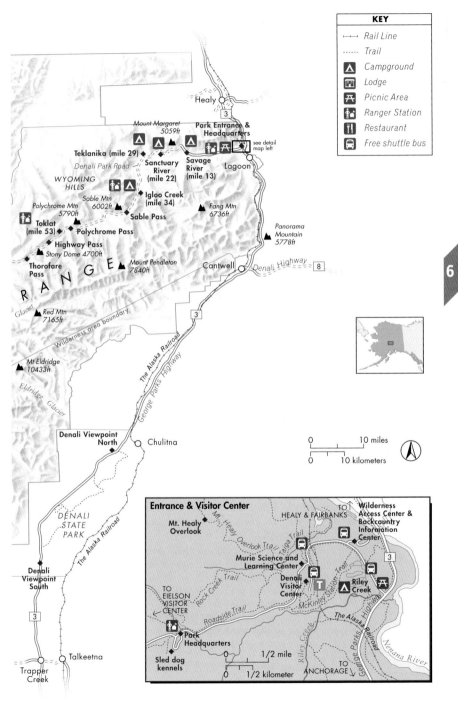

KEY

⊢─⊣	Rail Line
······	Trail
🅰	Campground
🏠	Lodge
🎋	Picnic Area
🚻	Ranger Station
🍴	Restaurant
🚌	Free shuttle bus

Healy

Mount Margaret
5059ft

Park Entrance &
Headquarters

see detail
map left

Teklanika (mile 29)

Denali Park Road

Sanctuary
River
(mile 22)

Savage
River
(mile 13)

Lagoon

WYOMING
HILLS

Sable Mtn
6002ft

Igloo Creek
(mile 34)

Polychrome Mtn
5790ft

Sable Pass

Fang Mtn
6736ft

Toklat
(mile 53)

Polychrome Pass

Panorama
Mountain
5778ft

Highway Pass

Stony Dome 4700ft

Mount Pendleton
7840ft

Cantwell

Denali Highway

8

Thorofare
Pass

R A N G E

3

Red Mtn
7165ft

The Alaska Railroad

Wilderness area boundary

Mt Eldridge
10433ft

Eldridge Glacier

George Parks Highway

6

Denali Viewpoint
North

Chulitna

0 ————— 10 miles
0 ————— 10 kilometers

DENALI
STATE
PARK

The Alaska Railroad

Denali
Viewpoint
South

3

Talkeetna

Trapper
Creek

Entrance & Visitor Center

TO
HEALY & FAIRBANKS

Mt. Healy
Overlook

Mt. Healy Overlook Trail

Taiga Trail

Wilderness
Access Center &
Backcountry
Information
Center

3

Murie Science and
Learning Center

Rock Creek Trail

Denali
Visitor
Center

Riley
Creek

TO
EIELSON
VISITOR
CENTER

Roadside Trail

McKinley Station Trail

The Alaska Railroad

Park
Headquarters

Riley Creek

George Parks Highway

Nenana River

Sled dog
kennels

1/2 mile

0 ——— 1/2 kilometer

TO
ANCHORAGE

Denali Visitor Center. Open from mid-May to mid-September, the Denali Visitor Center exhibits beautiful displays about the park's natural and cultural history, and holds regular showings of *Heartbeats of Denali* in the Karstens Theater. In addition, the center offers a wide variety of interpretive programs and a chance to browse the nearby Denali Bookstore, a great source for wildlife guides, birding guides, and picture books; send some to relatives to make them jealous of your trip. While the park itself is open year-round with limited vehicle access, everything is up and running from mid-May through mid-September. ☎ *907/683–2294* ⊕ *www.nps.gov/dena.*

Eielson Visitor Center. At Mile 66 on the Park Road is the Eielson Visitor Center, the park's pride and joy. LEED certified as a green building, Eielson offers amazing views of the mountain, the glaciers, and what happens to a landscape when glaciers go away. Inside is the usual interpretive material. Starting around the beginning of June, the center offers a daily guided walk at 1 pm, an easy 45-minute exploration of the landscape. Another hike each day takes on a little rougher terrain. Guided hikes vary from day to day to minimize the impact on the surroundings. Guided snowshoe walks are also offered January–March on Saturday and Sunday, weather permitting. ⊠ *Mile 66 on Park Rd., Denali National Park* ⊕ *www.nps.gov/dena/planyourvisit/the-eielson-visitor-center.htm* ⊗ *June–mid-Sept., daily 9–7.*

Murie Science and Learning Center. Next to the Denali Visitor Center, Murie Science and Learning Center is the foundation of the park's science-based education programs, and also serves as the winter visitor center when the Denali Visitor Center is closed. This center has basic but good displays, and is a good option when the main visitor center is closed. ⊠ *Mile 1.5, Park Rd., Denali National Park* ☎ *907/683–1269* ⊕ *www.murieslc.org.*

TRANSPORTATION AND TOURS

Don't be alarmed by the crowded park entrance; that gets left behind very quickly. After the chaos of private businesses that line the George Parks Highway and the throngs at the visitor center, there's pretty much nothing else in the park but wilderness. From the bus you'll have the opportunity to see Denali's wildlife in natural settings, as the animals are habituated to the road and vehicles, and go about their daily routine with little bother. In fact, the animals really like the road: it's easier for them to walk along it than to work through the tundra and tussocks.

Bus trips take time. The maximum speed limit is 35 mph, and the buses don't hit that very often. Add in rest stops, wildlife sightings, and slowdowns for passing, and it's an 8- to 11-hour day to reach the heart of the park and the best Denali views from Mile 62 to 85. *All prices listed below are for adults and include the $10 park admission fee, unless otherwise noted.* ■TIP→ If you decide to tour the park by bus, you have two choices: a sightseeing bus tour offered by a park concessionaire or a ride on the shuttle bus. The differences between the two are significant.

Alaskans call Mt. McKinley by its original name, Denali, which means "the High One."

Tour buses. Tour buses offer a guided introduction to the park. Advance reservations are required for the tour buses and are recommended for the park shuttles. Reservations for the following season become available on December 1, so if you have only a small window to see Denali, plan far ahead. If you're not organized enough to think six months or more out, you can usually get on the bus of your choice with less than a week's notice—and you can almost always get on a shuttle bus within a day or two—but try not to count on that. Work as far ahead as you can to avoid disappointment.

Rides through the park include a 5-hour Natural History Tour ($77.50), a 6- to 8-hour Tundra Wilderness Tour ($125.50), and an 11- to 12-hour Kantishna Experience ($169). These prices include the park entrance fee, and kids are half price. Trips are fully narrated by the driver-guides and include a snack or box lunch and hot drinks. Although the Natural History Tour lasts five hours, it goes only 17 miles into the park (2 miles beyond the private-vehicle turnaround), emphasizing Denali's human and natural history. Do not take this tour if you want the best wildlife- or Mt. McKinley–viewing opportunities. You might see a moose or two but not much else. The Tundra Wilderness Tour is a great way to go for a fun, thorough introduction to the park, but if it leaves you wanting more, the Kantishna Experience travels the entire length of the road, features an interpretive guide and ranger, lunch, and some walking. Note, though, that none of the tours allows you to leave the bus without the group or to travel independently through the park. ⊠ *Denali National Park* ☎ *800/622–7275, 907/272–7275 in Alaska or outside U.S.* ⊕ *www.reservedenali.com.*

Shuttle buses. The park's own shuttle buses don't include a formal interpretive program or food and drink. ■ TIP→ They're less expensive, and you can get off the bus and take a hike or just stop and sightsee almost anywhere you like, then catch another bus along the road. Most of the drivers are well versed in the park's features and will point out plant, animal, and geological sights. The shuttles are less formal than the tour buses, and generally less comfortable (converted school buses). They do stop to watch and photograph wildlife, but with a schedule to keep, time is sometimes limited. Shuttle-bus round-trip fares are $26.25 to the Toklat River at Mile 53; $33.50 to Eielson Visitor Center at Mile 66; and $46 to Wonder Lake at Mile 85. They also run a shuttle to Kantishna, for $50; the trip takes about 13 hours. Kids 15 and under ride free on the shuttles; shuttle bus prices do not include the $10 park admission fee.

Also, obviously, the farther out you're going, the earlier in the day you'll need to be starting; the last bus for Wonder Lake leaves at 10:15 am; the last one for Toklat, at 5 pm. Check with the park for the current schedule.

If you decide to get off the shuttle bus and explore the tundra, just tell the driver ahead of time where you'd like to get out. Some areas are closed to hiking, so check with the rangers at the visitor center before you decide where to go. Some areas are closed permanently, such as Sable Pass, which is heavily traveled by bears; others close as conditions warrant, such as when there's been a wolf kill nearby.

When it's time to catch a ride back, just stand next to the road and wait; it's seldom more than 30 minutes or so between buses. The drivers stop if there is room on board. However, during the mid- and late-summer peak season, an hour or more may pass between stopping buses, as they are more likely to be full. Be prepared to split up if you are in a big group in order to fit on crowded buses during peak times. ✉ *Denali National Park* ☎ *800/622–7275, 907/272–7275* ⊕ *www. reservedenali.com.*

WHERE TO STAY

$$ ▤ **Denali Cabins.** Cedar cabins built within the taiga forest have all the
RENTAL basic amenities (including TV and phone), private baths, and shared hot tubs at this complex along the highway 8 miles south of the park entrance. **Pros:** quiet location; offers National Park day trips; sauna and hot tub to relax in. **Cons:** not on the river; few amenities offered. ⑤ *Rooms from: $179* ✉ *Mile 229, Parks Hwy.* ☎ *907/683–2643, 800/808–8068* ⊕ *www.denali-cabins.com* ⇨ *45 cabins* ☉ *Closed mid-Sept.–June 1* ❙◎❙ *Breakfast.*

$$ ▤ **McKinley Creekside Cabins & Creekside Café.** This nice spot sits on 10
HOTEL acres along Carlo Creek. **Pros:** great location by the water. **Cons:** no TV may lead to withdrawal symptoms in some. ⑤ *Rooms from: $169* ✉ *Mile 238.5, Parks Hwy.* ☎ *888/533–6254* ⊕ *www.mckinleycabins. com* ⇨ *32 cabins* ☉ *Closed mid-Sept.–mid-May.*

SPORTS AND THE OUTDOORS

GUIDED TOURS

In addition to exploring the park on your own, you can take free ranger-guided discovery hikes and learn more about the park's natural and human history. Rangers lead daily hikes throughout summer. Inquire at the visitor center.

Denali Park Resorts. Privately operated, three- to four-hour, 4-mile-round-trip guided hikes are available through Denali Park Resorts. ✉ *Mile 238.5, Parks Hwy., at the entrance to Denali National Park, Denali National Park* ☎ *907/276–7234, 800/276–7234* ⊕ *www.denaliparkresorts.com.*

NATURE TRAILS AND SHORT WALKS

The park offers plenty of options for those who prefer to stay on marked and groomed pathways. The entrance area has more than a half dozen forest and tundra trails. These range from easy to challenging, so there's something suitable for all ages and hiking abilities. Some, like the **Taiga Loop Trail** and **McKinley Station Loop Trail,** are less than 1½ miles; others, like the **Rock Creek Trail** and **Triple Lakes Trail,** are several miles round-trip, with an altitude gain of hundreds of feet. Along these paths you may see beavers working on their lodges in Horseshoe Lake, red squirrels chattering in trees, red foxes hunting for rodents, sheep grazing on tundra, golden eagles gliding over alpine ridges, and moose feeding on willow.

The **Savage River Trail,** farthest from the park entrance and as far as private vehicles are allowed, offers a 1¾-mile round-trip hike along a raging river and under rocky cliffs. Be on the lookout for caribou, Dall sheep, foxes, and marmots.

The only relatively long, marked trail for hiking in the park, **Mt. Healy Overlook Trail,** is accessible from the entrance area; it gains 1,700 feet in 2½ miles and takes about four hours round-trip, with outstanding views of the Nenana River below and the Alaska Range, including the upper slopes of Mt. McKinley.

FORTYMILE COUNTRY

A trip through the Fortymile Country up the Taylor Highway will take you back in time more than a century—when gold was the lure that drew hardy travelers to Interior Alaska. It's one of the few places to see active mining without leaving the road system. In addition, remote wilderness experiences and float trips abound.

RICHARDSON HIGHWAY

If you're headed to Fortymile Country from Fairbanks, you'll drive along the historic Richardson Highway, once a pack-train (think mules with bags) trail and dogsled route for mail carriers and gold miners in the Interior. As quirky places to turn off a highway go, North Pole and Delta Junction are up there with the best of them.

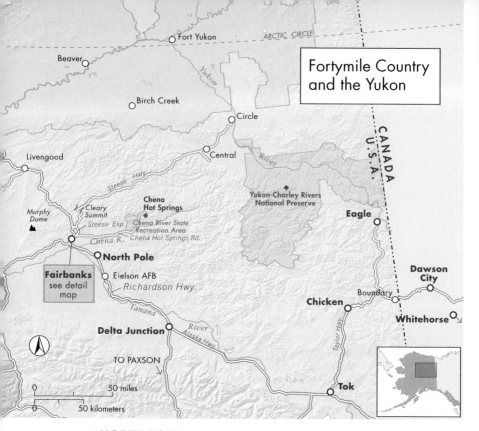

NORTH POLE

It may be a featureless suburb of Fairbanks, but you'd have to be a Scrooge not to admit that this town's year-round acknowledgment of the December holiday season is at least a little bit fun to take in.

Knotty Shop. The Knotty Shop has a large selection of Alaskan handicrafts as well as a mounted wildlife display and a yard full of spruce-burl sculptures, including a 6-foot mosquito and other wooden animals that photographers find hard to resist. Get served soft drinks, coffee, and ice cream over a spruce-burl counter. Burls are actually caused by parasites in the living tree, and they create beautiful patterns in the wood. ✉ *Mile 332, 6565 Richardson Hwy., 32 miles south of Fairbanks, Tok* ☎ *907/488–3014* ⊕ *www.alaskaknottyshop.com.*

Santa Claus House Gift Shop. If you stop in North Pole, don't skip the Santa Claus House Gift Shop. Look for the giant Santa statue and the Christmas mural on the side of the building. You'll find toys, gifts, and Alaskan handicrafts; Santa is often on duty to talk to children. And yes, you can get your mail sent with a genuine North Pole postmark. ✉ *101 St. Nicholas Dr., Tok* ☎ *907/488–2200, 800/588–4078* ⊕ *www.santaclaushouse.com.*

DELTA JUNCTION

A good 100 miles southeast of Fairbanks, Delta is not only a handy stop on the Richardson Highway but also the official western terminus of the Alaska Highway (when the Alcan was built, although Fairbanks was the ultimate destination, there was already a road from Fairbanks down to Delta). It's no surprise, then, that in summer Delta becomes a bustling rest stop for road-weary travelers. On top of this, it's the largest agricultural center in Alaska, boasting a local farmers' market, meat-and-sausage company, and dairy. Delta is also known for its access to good fishing and its proximity to the Delta Bison Range. Don't expect to see the elusive 500-strong bison herd, though, as they roam free and generally avoid people.

Delta Chamber of Commerce. At the actual junction of the Alaska and Richardson highways, stop in the Delta Chamber of Commerce for more information on the area. This is also where you can get your "I Drove the Alaska Highway" certificates—technically, the Alcan ends here, in Delta, since there was already an extant road this far from Fairbanks. It's also worth the stop to see the chunk of pipeline outside, just to get an idea of what's carrying all that oil across the state. ⊠ *2855 Alaska Hwy., Suite 1B, Tok* ☎ *907/895–5068, 877/895–5068* ⊕ *www. deltachamber.org.*

Rika's Roadhouse. Historic landmark Rika's Roadhouse, part of Big Delta State Historical Park, is a good detour for the free tours of the beautifully restored and meticulously maintained grounds, gardens, and historic buildings. Roadhouses were once stretched out at pretty regular intervals in the north, providing everything a traveler might need. You can use your imagination for what that must have been like in the old days. But Rika's is far and away the prettiest, best preserved of what's left, and it's a great place to get out, stretch and snack on some of their wonderful baked goods. ⊠ *Mile 275, Richardson Hwy., Tok* ☎ *907/895–4201* ⊕ *www.rikas.com.*

TOK

12 miles west of Tetlin Junction, 175 miles southwest of Dawson City.

Loggers, miners, old sourdoughs (Alaskan for "colorful local curmudgeons"), and hunting guides who live and work along Tok's streams or in the millions of acres of spruce forest nearby come here for supplies, at the junction of the Glenn Highway and the Alaska Highway. Each summer the city, with a resident population of fewer than 1,500, becomes temporary home to thousands of travelers, including adventurers journeying up the Alaska Highway from the Lower 48.

After crossing into Alaska from the Yukon Territory on the Alaska Highway, the first vestiges of what passes for civilization in the Far North are found in the town of Tok. Here you'll find a visitor center (one of the biggest in Alaska, since it serves as a center for roads branching across the state), food, fuel, hotels, a couple of restaurants, and the need to make a decision.

Staying on the Alaska Highway and heading roughly west will take you into the Interior and to Fairbanks, whereas heading south on the Tok Cutoff will aim you toward South Central Alaska and the population center of Anchorage. Or you can make a huge loop tour, covering most of the paved highway in the state, taking in much of the terrific variety of landscapes and terrain that the 49th state has to offer. Head down the Tok Cutoff to the Richardson Highway (no one in Alaska uses the highway route numbers, and if you try to, you'll most likely just get blank stares), and then keep going south to Valdez. From there, catch the ferry to Whittier, Cordova, or Seward,

> ## BORDER CROSSING
>
> Crossing into Interior Alaska from the Lower 48 or from the ferry terminals in the Southeast requires border crossings into Canada and then into Alaska. Be very certain of all the requirements for crossing an international border before you travel, including restrictions on pets and firearms and the need for adequate personal identification for every member of the party. Know that even citizens of Canada and the United States traveling between Alaska and Canada are now required to have a passport.

explore the Kenai and Anchorage, then head north on the Seward Highway to the parks, to Denali, Fairbanks, and beyond. Loop back to Tok and you've seen most of what can be seen from the road system.

EXPLORING

Taylor Highway. The 160-mile Taylor Highway runs north from the Alaska Highway at Tetlin Junction, 12 miles east of Tok. It's a narrow rough-gravel road that winds along mountain ridges and through valleys of the Fortymile River. The road passes the tiny community of Chicken and ends in Eagle at the Yukon River. This is one of only three places in Alaska where the Yukon River can be reached by road. A cutoff just south of Eagle connects to the Canadian Top of the World Highway leading to Dawson City in the Yukon Territory, which is the route many Alaskans take to Dawson City—far more scenic, and shorter, than the alternative of taking the Alcan to Whitehorse and then turning north, but it's another of those places where it's good to check your insurance policy's attitude towards towing and windshield replacement. ⚠ The highway is not plowed in winter, so it is snowed shut from fall to spring. Watch for road equipment. If you're roughing it, know that in addition to the lodging listed below, the Alaska Bureau of Land Management also maintains three first-come, first-served campsites (as all BLM campsites are) on the Taylor Highway between Tetlin Junction and Eagle at Miles 48.5, 82, and 160.

Tetlin National Wildlife Refuge. The Tetlin National Wildlife Refuge parallels the Alaska Highway for the first 65 highway miles after leaving Canada and offers two basic and seasonal campgrounds at Mileposts 1,249 and 1,256, or take a break from driving at Mile 1,240 and hike 1 mile over a raised-plank boardwalk to Hidden Lake. This 700,000-acre refuge has most of the charismatic megafauna that visitors travel to Alaska to see, including black and grizzly bears, moose, Dall sheep, wolves, caribou, and tons of birds. The visitor center at Mile 1,229 has a large deck with spotting scopes, and inside are maps, wildlife exhibits, books, and interpretive information, as well as a board with information on current road conditions. ✉ *Mile 1,229, Alaska Hwy.* ☎ *907/883–5312* ⊕ *tetlin.fws.gov* ✎ *Free* ⊙ *Closed mid-Sept.–mid-May.*

Tok Main Street Visitors Center. To help with your planning, stop in at the Tok Main Street Visitors Center, which has travel information covering the entire state, as well as wildlife and natural-history exhibits. The staff is quite helpful. This is one of the largest info centers in all of Alaska—no matter what direction you want to go from Tok, you'll find something here to help you along the way. ✉ *Mile 1,314, Alaska Hwy.* ☎ *907/883–5775* ⊕ *www. tokalaskainfo.com.*

ON THE DEFENSIVE

Ft. Greely, which is 5 miles south of Tok toward Valdez, contains a growing number of underground silos with missiles that are part of the Ballistic Missile Defense System. The missiles are connected to tracking stations elsewhere and would be launched to try to shoot down enemy missiles in space if the United States were ever so attacked.

WHERE TO EAT

$$$

AMERICAN

✕ **Fast Eddy's Restaurant.** It's much better than the name would indicate: the chef makes his own noodles for chicken noodle soup, and the homemade hoagies and pizza are a welcome relief from the roadhouse hamburgers served by most Alaska Highway restaurants. It's open late, but the soup is usually gone by 5. ⑤ *Average main: $20* ✉ *Mile 1,313.3, Alaska Hwy.* ☎ *907/883–4411.*

WHERE TO STAY

$

B&B/INN

▦ **Burnt Paw.** One of the nicer places to stay in Tok, the Burnt Paw offers seven comfortable, sod-roofed cabins, each with two beds, private bath, microwaves and fridges, Wi-Fi, satellite TV, and adorable sled-dog puppies. **Pros:** cozy cabins; good breakfast; best location in town; puppies. **Cons:** not the place to be if you object to falling asleep to the sound of happy dogs barking. ⑤ *Rooms from: $99* ✉ *Mile 1,314.3, Alaska Hwy.* ☎ *907/883–4121* ⊕ *www.burntpawcabins.com* ⤵ *7 cabins.*

$$

HOTEL

▦ **Westmark Inn Tok.** Made up of a series of interconnected buildings, the hotel has been updated and has decent accommodations for this remote part of Alaska. **Pros:** satellite TV; margaritas to get lost in; some pets allowed. **Cons:** not for those looking for lots of in-room character; frequently booked up with tour groups. ⑤ *Rooms from: $120* ✉ *Junction of Alaska and Glenn Hwys.* ☎ *907/883–5174, 800/544–0970* ⊕ *www. westmarkhotels.com* ⤵ *97 rooms* ⊙ *Closed mid-Sept.–mid-May.*

SHOPPING

Naabia Niign. In Northway, south of Tok, Naabia Niign is a Native-owned crafts gallery with an excellent selection of authentic, locally made birch baskets, beadwork items, fur moccasins, and gloves. The friendly staff also operate a general store, gas station, bar, and RV park. Hours can be a little unpredictable so call ahead. ✉ *Mile 1,264, Alaska Hwy.* ☎ *907/778–2234.*

CHICKEN

78 miles north of Tok, 109 miles west of Dawson City.

Chicken was, and still is, the heart of the southern Fortymile Mining District, and many of these works are visible along the highway. Chicken (the story goes that they wanted to name the town "Ptarmigan," but nobody knew how to spell that), the second town in Alaska to be incorporated (Skagway was the first), has only a handful of permanent residents, mostly miners and trappers, creating an authentic frontier atmosphere. Do not encroach on private property, as miners rarely have a sense of humor about trespassing. Overland travel to Dawson City winds along a gravel road. Some drivers love it, some white-knuckle it. The road still closes for the entire winter, but in February and March snowmachiners hold a "poker run" on the road from Tok to Dawson City (⊕ *www. alaskatrailblazers.com*). Chicken has only three businesses in town, but what it lacks in infrastructure, it makes up for in atmosphere.

Get a feel for the past on a gold-mining adventure, where finder's keepers is the name of the game (in 2008 one participant walked away with a 1.4-ounce nugget), or tour the historic Pedro Dredge at 9 am and 1 pm daily at the Chicken Gold Camp & Outpost. The Gold Camp also provides meals, drinks, cabins, a campground–RV park, showers, free Wi-Fi, firewood, and espresso, as well as kayaking and other activities. Bluegrass lovers will appreciate the Chickenstock Music Festival on the second weekend in June.

Downtown Chicken, the longest-running business in town, has classic wooden porches and provides multiple services: the Chicken Creek Café; a saloon; a liquor store; an emporium with gifts and odds and ends; free Wi-Fi; and overnight parking, rental cabins, and wall tents, along with gas and diesel service. Wild Alaskan baked salmon is available for lunch and dinner.

All in one establishment, you'll find Chicken Creek RV Park & Cabins, the Historic Town of Chicken, and the Goldpanner Gift Shop, which offers free Wi-Fi and an ATM. The RV park has gas and diesel, cabins, hotel rooms, and camping sites. Activities include gold panning and daily tours of Tisha's Schoolhouse at 9 am and 2 pm.

SPORTS AND THE OUTDOORS
CANOEING

Fortymile River. The beautiful Fortymile River offers everything from a 38-mile run to a lengthy journey to the Yukon and then down to Eagle. Its waters range from easy Class I to serious Class IV (possibly Class V) stretches. Only experienced canoeists should attempt boating on this river, and rapids should be scouted beforehand. Several access points can be found off the Taylor Highway.

Canoe Alaska. Since 1980 Canoe Alaska has conducted guided canoe and raft trips on Interior Alaska rivers. Trips (mid-May–Labor Day) range from two to eight days on rivers that vary in difficulty and remoteness. Evening interpretive tours in the *Arctic Voyageur*, a replica of a 34-foot voyageur canoe, are offered on a lake. Multiday *Voyageur* trips, canoe instruction, and rentals to qualified paddlers are also available. ☎ *907/883–2628* ⊕ *www.canoealaska.net*.

YUKON TERRITORY

Gold! The happy, shining promise of gold is what called Canada's Yukon Territory to the world's attention with the Klondike Gold Rush of 1897–98. Maybe as many as 100,000 people set off for the confluence of the Yukon and Klondike rivers, on the promise of gold nuggets the size of basketballs just waiting to be picked up. In the end, roughly a dozen of them went home rich, but they all went home rich in memories and stories that are still being told.

Though the international border divides Alaska from Yukon Territory, the Yukon River tends to unify the region. Early prospectors, miners, traders, and camp followers moved readily up and down the river with little regard for national boundaries. An earlier Alaska strike preceded the Klondike find by years, yet Circle was all but abandoned in the stampede to the creeks around Dawson City. Later gold discoveries in the Alaskan Fortymile Country, Nome, and Fairbanks reversed that flow across the border into Alaska.

DAWSON CITY

109 miles east of Chicken.

Dawson City, one of the coolest, most beautiful towns in the north, is the prime specimen of a Yukon gold-rush town. Since the first swell of hopeful migrants more than 100 years ago, many of the original buildings have disappeared, victims of fire, flood, and weathering. But plenty remain, and it's easy to step back in time, going to a performance at the Palace Theatre, originally built in 1899, or stepping into a shop whose building originally went up to serve stampeders. In modern Dawson City street paving seems erratic at best, and the place maintains a serious frontier vibe. But it's also a center for the arts—the Dawson City Music Festival, held each summer, is one of the biggest in Canada, as the whole town turns into one big party and all kinds of music echo under the midnight sun—and as the last touch of civilization before the deep wild, hikers share tables with hard-core miners at the local restaurants.

In the years leading up to the turn of the 20th century, Dawson was transformed from a First Nations camp into the largest, most refined city north of Seattle and west of Winnipeg. It had grand buildings with running water, telephones, and electricity. In 1899 the city's population numbered almost 30,000—a jump of about 29,900 over the previous few years—which all but overwhelmed the Tr'ondëk Hwëch'in, the First Nations Hän-speaking people who inhabited the area. Their chief, a man named Isaac, who is still revered as the savior of the culture, packed his people up and moved them from the confluence, where they had hunted and fished for thousands of years, to the village of Moosehide a few miles downstream. The town he left behind grew into a place where a fresh egg could cost the equivalent of a day's salary down south, and where one of the most profitable jobs was panning gold dust out of the sawdust scattered on saloon floors.

Today Dawson City is home to about 1,800 people, 400 or so of whom are of First Nation descent. The city itself is now a National Historic Site of Canada. Besides being one of the coolest, funkiest towns in the north, Dawson also serves as a base from which to explore the Tombstone Territorial Park on the Dempster Highway, a region sometimes referred to as the "Patagonia of the Northern Hemisphere": a natural wonderland, with plants and animals found nowhere else, living in the spaces between high, steep mountain ranges.

> ## DAWSON CITY MUSIC FESTIVAL
>
> The Dawson City Music Festival, held every July, is the town's biggest party: at venues across town, from a big tent near the museum to inside the beautiful Palace Theatre, musicians from around Canada and around the world get together to jam. The entire town turns out, every hotel room is full, every camping spot is taken, and there is no better time to be in Dawson. ⊕ *www.dcmf.com.*

GETTING HERE AND AROUND

The Alaska Highway starts in Dawson Creek, British Columbia, and goes almost 1,500 miles to Fairbanks. Drivers traveling north and south on the Alaska Highway can make a loop with the Taylor Highway route. This adds 100 miles to the trip, but is worth it. Part with the Alaska Highway at Tetlin Junction and wind through the Fortymile Country past the little communities of Chicken and Jack Wade Camp into Canada. The border is open from 8 am to 8 pm in summer. The Canadian section of the Taylor Highway is called Top of the World Highway, and with most of it on a ridgeline between two huge valleys, it really does feel like the top of the world, opening broad views of range after range of tundra-covered mountains stretching in every direction. Join back with the Alaska Highway at Whitehorse.

Numerous bus companies offer package tours or simple shuttle services (⇨ *see Whitehorse, below)*. Regular air service to Dawson flies from Fairbanks in summer. **Air North, Yukon's Airline,** based in Whitehorse, offers direct air service from Whitehorse to Dawson City in summer.

Airline Contacts Air North, Yukon's Airline ☎ *800/661–0407* ⊕ *www.flyairnorth.com.*

VISITOR INFORMATION

Contacts Klondike Visitors Association ✉ *1102 Front St., Dawson City, Yukon, Canada* ☎ *867/993–5575* ⊕ *www.dawsoncity.ca* ☺ *Year-round.* **Visitor Information Centre** ✉ *1102 Front St., Dawson City, Yukon, Canada* ☎ *867/993–5566* ☺ *Early May–late Sept.*

EXPLORING

Dänojà Zho Cultural Centre. Dänojà Zho Cultural Centre creates an inviting atmosphere in which to explore the Tr'ondëk Hwëch'in First Nation heritage. For countless generations this group of Hän-speaking people lived in the Yukon River drainage of western Yukon and eastern Alaska. This specific language group settled around the mouth of the Klondike River. Through seasonal displays, tours, cultural activities, films, and performances, learn about the traditional and contemporary life of "the people of the river." The gift shop celebrates fine First Nations art, offering unique First Nations clothing, beaded footwear, music, and books. The displays are kind of sparse, but it's good to stop in and see what the gold rush was like for the people who were here first and saw there was more value to a good caribou hunt than a bunch of shiny stuff in the ground. ⊠ *1131 Front St., across from Visitor Information Centre, Dawson City, Yukon, Canada* ☎ *867/993–6768* ⊕ *www.trondekheritage.com* ⊴ *$6* ☯ *May–Sept., Mon.–Sat. 10–6.*

Dawson City Museum. The Dawson City Museum, housing the Yukon's largest collection, presents exhibits focusing on the gold rush, but also includes the geology and prehistory of the Klondike, as well as of the First Nations. Downstairs offers excellent displays of gold rush material; it might surprise you just how luxurious Dawson managed to be for the lucky few. Upstairs are more household goods, which most people skim through, but don't miss the piece of mammoth meat on the stairway landing. Not many places where you'll see that. Four restored locomotives and other railway cars and gear from the Klondike Mines Railway are housed in an adjacent building, which tends to open at odd hours. The museum also features a library and archives, helpful for visitor's hoping to find their gold rush ancestors. Daily programs include justice in the Klondike before the arrival of the NWMP, and "Camp Cheechacko," which gives you a chance to test your skills with a rocker box, finding out if you could have made it as a miner. During the summer season, the museum features costumed interpreters, and don't miss the "City of Gold," a fascinating documentary on the region, narrated by Pierre Berton, perhaps Canada's foremost historian of the gold rush and Yukon. ⊠ *Territorial Administration Bldg., 5th Ave., Dawson City, Yukon, Canada* ☎ *867/993–5291* ⊕ *www.dawsonmuseum.ca* ⊴ *C$9* ☯ *Mid-May–Labor Day, daily 10–6; call ahead for winter visits.*

Diamond Tooth Gerties Gambling Hall. Diamond Tooth Gerties Gambling Hall, for adults 19 and over only, presents nightly live entertainment and high-energy performances, including cancan, seven days a week from May until late September. It is also the only authentic, legal gambling establishment operating in all of the North and the oldest in Canada, although it's mostly just slots and a few table games. Yes, there really was a Diamond Tooth Gertie—Gertie Lovejoy, a prominent dance-hall queen who had a diamond between her two front teeth. ⊠ *Queen and 4th Sts., Dawson City, Yukon, Canada* ☎ *867/993–5525* ⊕ *www.dawsoncity.ca* ⊴ *C$10.*

Gold Dredge Number 4. Gold Dredge Number 4, a wooden-hull gold dredge along Bonanza Creek, is about 20 minutes outside town. The site is currently in transition; Parks Canada used to offer tours, now they offer a brochure for what's billed as "the largest wooden hulled, bucket line gold dredge in North America." When it was in operation the dredge ate rivers whole, spitting out gravel and keeping gold for itself. (To get an idea of how much area the dredge affected, think of the economics of this: hauling this enormous piece of machinery this far into the middle of nowhere, at a time when gold was worth less than $20 per ounce, and still making money.) Pan for gold yourself in Bonanza Creek, where the Klondike Visitors Association offers a free claim for visitors. Be sure to bring your own supplies (almost every gift shop in town sells gold pans). Exit the Klondike Highway at Km Marker 74. ✉ *Mi 8, Bonanza Creek Rd., Dawson City, Yukon, Canada* ☎ *867/993–7200* ⊕ *www.pc.gc.ca.*

Jack London Museum. Jack London Museum is literally a stone's throw from Robert Service's cabin. This reproduction of London's home from 1897 to 1898 is constructed with half of the wood from his original wilderness home that was found south of Dawson in the 1930s. The other half was sent to Oakland, California, where a similar structure sits at Jack London Square. The small museum contains photos, documents, and letters from London's life and the gold-rush era. Half-hour talks are given twice daily during peak season. ✉ *8th Ave. and Firth St., Dawson City, Yukon, Canada* ☎ *867/993–5575* 🏷 *C\$5* ☉ *May–Sept., daily interpretation presentations.*

Robert Service Cabin. Scholars still argue the precise details of the lives of writers Robert Service (1874–1958) and Jack London (1876–1916) in Dawson City, but no one disputes that between Service's poems and London's short stories the two did more than anyone else to popularize and romanticize the Yukon. Service lived in his Dawson cabin from 1909 to 1912. The Robert Service Cabin is open for visitors Memorial Day to Labor Day, and holds multiple daily readings in season. ✉ *8th Ave. and Hanson St., Dawson City, Yukon, Canada* ☎ *867/993–7200* 🏷 *C\$6.*

WHERE TO STAY

For expanded hotel reviews, visit Fodors.com.

\$\$\$
B&B/INN
🏨 **Bombay Peggy's.** Named and fashioned after one of the last of Dawson's legal madams, Peggy's is done in elaborate Victorian gold-rush style, with heavy, plush draperies and rich color schemes. **Pros:** little imagination is needed to step back in time thanks to elaborate refurbishing; nice touches like fresh croissants and the "Sherry Hour." **Cons:** no elevator; not all rooms have air-conditioning. ⑤ *Rooms from: C\$175* ✉ *2nd Ave. and Princess St., Dawson City, Yukon, Canada* ☎ *867/993–6969* ⊕ *www.bombaypeggys.com* ↪ *9 rooms* ⑩ *Breakfast.*

\$\$
HOTEL
🏨 **Eldorado Hotel.** The pioneer-style front to this hotel may be misleading, as the modern rooms, some with kitchenettes, are outfitted with decidedly non-1898 amenities such as cable TV. **Pros:** in-hotel bar and restaurant; top off the evening with a drink at the Sluice Box Lounge. **Cons:** no elevator. ⑤ *Rooms from: C\$150* ✉ *3rd Ave. and Princess St., Dawson City, Yukon, Canada* ☎ *867/993–5451, 800/764–3536 from Alaska and Canada* ⊕ *www.eldoradohotel.ca* ↪ *46 rooms, 16 suites.*

SPORTS AND THE OUTDOORS
BOATING

Klondike River Float Trip. The Klondike River Float Trip offers a chance to relax on a Class I river. You can put in at the Dempster Highway Bridge or Rock Creek. The journey ends when the Klondike spits you into the Yukon River at Dawson. Don't forget to take advantage of photo ops along the way. Other options include a guided 3½-hour float trip for \$75 or a 3½-hour jeep tour for \$95. Pickup is at Westmark Dawson City. ✉ *Dawson City, Yukon, Canada* ☎ *867/993–5599, 800/544–2206* ⊕ *www.graylineyukon.com.*

HIKING

Tombstone Territorial Park. Tombstone Territorial Park, located 1½ hours north of Dawson City and bisected by the Dempster Highway, is a 2,200-square-km (850-square-miles) area dubbed the "Patagonia of the northern hemisphere." Here you'll find some of the best hiking and views of granite peaks in the Yukon. The unique geology and geography of this wilderness supports a vast array of wildlife and vegetation. The park maintains four day-use trails at Km markers 58, 72, 75, and 78, along with one campground and an interpretation center at Km Marker 71.4, with good displays and great views of the mountains. It's worth stopping in to see how animals make it through the winter here. Throughout the park, backcountry mountaineering and wildlife-viewing options are endless. The new Visitor Center is a great place to get a handle on everything the park has to offer. You can book flightseeing trips over the jagged Tombstones from Dawson City. ⊠ *Box 600, Dawson City, Yukon, Canada* ☎ *867/993–6850 in Dawson City, 866/617–2757 toll-free* ⊕ *www.yukonparks.ca* ☽ *Interpretation center late May–mid-Sept.*

WHITEHORSE

6

337 miles southeast of Dawson City, 600 miles southeast of Fairbanks.

Near the White Horse Rapids of the Yukon River, Whitehorse began as an encampment in the late 1890s, a logical layover for gold rushers heading north along the Chilkoot Trail toward Dawson. The next great population boom came during World War II with the building of the Alcan—the Alaska-Canada Highway. Today this city of more than 22,000 residents is Yukon's center of commerce (the only Walmart and Tim Horton's for hundreds of miles), communication, and transportation, and the seat of the territorial government.

Besides being a great starting point for explorations of other areas of the Yukon, the town has plenty of diversions and recreational opportunities. You can spend a day exploring its museums and cultural displays—research the Yukon's mining and development history, look into the backgrounds of the town's founders, learn about its indigenous First Nations people, and gain an appreciation of the Yukon Territory from prehistoric times up to the present.

GETTING HERE AND AROUND

Air Canada flies in summer from Anchorage through Vancouver to Whitehorse. **Air North, Yukon's Airline** (yes, that's really the name), based in Whitehorse, offers direct, seasonal air service between Alaska and Canada, flying regular runs from Fairbanks (summer only), Dawson City, and Whitehorse.

To take in all the scenery along the way, you can drive yourself up the Alcan Highway or let someone else do the driving on a bus tour. Alaska/Yukon Trails provides tours from Whitehorse to Dawson City to Fairbanks. MGM Bus Services offers service from Inuvik to Whitehorse year-round when weather permits; charter trips are available. There are multiple rental-car companies, buses, and taxis in Whitehorse; Whitehorse Transit has a city bus circuit that will get you where you need to go.

Airline Contacts Air Canada ☎ *888/247–2262* ⊕ *www.aircanada.com.*
Air North, Yukon's Airline ☎ *800/661–0407* ⊕ *www.flyairnorth.com.*

Bus Contacts Alaska/Yukon Trails ☎ *800/770–7275*
⊕ *www.alaskashuttle.com.* **Atlin Express** ☎ *866/651–7575*
⊕ *www.atlinexpress.ca.* **MGM Bus Services** ☎ *867/777–4295, 867/678–0129.*

City Bus Whitehorse Transit ⊠ *139 Tlingit St., Whitehorse, Yukon, Canada*
☎ *867/668–8394* ⊕ *www.whitehorse.ca* 🎫 *C$2.50.*

VISITOR INFORMATION

Contacts City Hall ⊠ *2121 2nd Ave., Whitehorse, Yukon, Canada* ☎ *867/668–8325* ⊕ *www.visitwhitehorse.com.* **Yukon Visitor Information Centre** ⊠ *100 Hanson St., Whitehorse, Yukon, Canada* ☎ *867/667–3084, 800/661–0494* ⊕ *www.travelyukon.com* ☉ *Mid-May–mid-Sept., daily 8–8; mid-Sept.–mid-May, weekdays 8:30–5, Sat. 10–2.*

EXPLORING

Canyon City Archaeological Dig. The Canyon City Archaeological Dig provides a glimpse into the past of the local First Nations people. Long before the area was developed by Western civilizations, the First Nations people used the Miles Canyon area as a seasonal fish camp. The Yukon Conservation Society conducts free tours of the area twice a day on weekdays in summer; it also leads two-hour hikes Tuesday through Saturday in July and August. All the hikes are free and provide a great way to see the surrounding countryside with local naturalists. The society office houses a bookstore on Yukon history and wilderness and sells souvenirs, maps, and posters. Check the website or call before you go out; funding cuts have hurt some of their programs. ⊠ *302 Hawkins St., Whitehorse, Yukon, Canada* ☎ *867/668–5678* ⊕ *www.yukonconservation.org* 🎫 *Free* ☉ *Tours July–late Aug., weekdays at 10 and 2.*

MacBride Museum of Yukon History. From gold-rush fever to the birth of Whitehorse, the MacBride Museum of Yukon History offers a comprehensive view of the colorful characters and groundbreaking events that shaped the territory. Follow the Yukon River through the history of Whitehorse in the Gold to Government exhibition. The museum also boasts a unique collection of wildlife, geology, historic artifacts, and photographs, alongside fine First Nations beadwork. The gold-rush displays are particularly telling of just what people went through to find a little glint of color. Outdoor artifacts include the cabin of Sam McGee, who was immortalized in Robert Service's famous poem "The Cremation of Sam McGee." MacBride also offers guided tours and a chance to try your hand at one of the Yukon's oldest professions—gold panning. ⊠ *1124 1st Ave., and Wood St., Whitehorse, Yukon, Canada* ☎ *867/667–2709* ⊕ *www.macbridemuseum.com* 🎫 *C$10* ☉ *Mid-May–Aug., daily 9:30–5; Sept.–mid-May, Tues.–Sat. 10–4 or by appointment.*

Miles Canyon. Miles Canyon, a 10-minute drive south of Whitehorse, is both scenic and historic. Although the dam below it makes the canyon seem relatively tame, it was this perilous stretch of the Yukon River that determined the location of Whitehorse as the starting point for river travel north. In 1897 Jack London won the admiration—and cash—of fellow stampeders headed north to the Klondike goldfields because of his steady hand as pilot of hand-hewn wooden boats here. You can hike on trails along the canyon or take a two-hour cruise aboard the MV *Schwatka* and experience the canyon from the waters of Lake Schwatka. This lake was created by the dam built in 1958, putting an end to the infamous White Horse Rapids. ⊠ *68 Miles Canyon Rd., 1 mile from Whitehorse city center, Whitehorse, Yukon, Canada* ☎ *867/668–4716* ⊕ *www.yukonrivercruises.com* ⊙ *Cruises depart daily early June–mid-Sept.*

SS Klondike. You can't really understand the scale of the gold rush without touring a riverboat. The SS *Klondike*, a national historic site, is dry-docked on the bank of the Yukon River in central Whitehorse's Rotary Park, just a minute from downtown. The 210-foot stern-wheeler was built in 1929, sank in 1936, and was rebuilt in 1937. In the days when the Yukon River was the transportation link between Whitehorse and Dawson City, the SS *Klondike* was the largest boat plying the river. Riverboats were as much a way of life here as on the Mississippi of Mark Twain, and the tour of the Klondike is a fascinating way to see how the boats were adapted to the north; as an added bonus, in the old days they were also one of the few places where First Nations men could get paying jobs, so there's a rich Native history to the riverboats as well. ⊠ *Robert Service Way and 2nd Ave., Whitehorse, Yukon, Canada* ☎ *867/667–4511 mid-May–mid-Sept., 867/667–3910 mid-Sept. –mid-May* ⊕ *www.pc.gc.ca/lhn-nhs/yt/ssklondike/index.aspx* ⊡ *C$6* ⊙ *Mid-May–mid-Sept., daily 9:30–5.*

Waterfront Walkway. The Waterfront Walkway along the Yukon River will take you past a few points of interest. Your walk starts on the path along the river just east of the MacBride Museum entrance on 1st Avenue. Traveling upstream (south), you'll go by the old White Pass and Yukon Route Building on Main Street. It's a good way to get an overview of the old town site, and just stretch your legs if you've been driving all day. ⊠ *Whitehorse, Yukon, Canada.*

Whitehorse Rapids Dam and Fish Ladder. The Chinook (king) salmon hold one of nature's great endurance records: the longest fish migration in the world, which is more than 2,000 miles from the Bering Sea to Whitehorse. The Whitehorse Rapids Dam and Fish Ladder (founded 1958–59) has interpretive exhibits, talks by local First Nations elders, display tanks of freshwater fish and salmon fry, and a platform for viewing the fish ladder. ▦ TIP➔ The best time to visit is August, when between 150 and 2,100 salmon (average count is 800) use the ladder to bypass the dam. ⊠ *End of Nisutlin Dr., Whitehorse, Yukon, Canada* ☎ *867/633–5965* ⊕ *www.yukonenergy.ca* ⊡ *$3 suggested donation* ⊙ *June–Aug., daily; hrs vary, so call ahead.*

Yukon Beringia Interpretive Centre. Near the Whitehorse Airport is the Yukon Beringia Interpretive Centre, which presents the story of the Yukon during the last Ice Age. Beringia is the name given to the large subcontinental landmass of eastern Siberia and Interior Alaska and the Yukon, which stayed ice-free and were linked by the Bering Land Bridge during the latest Ice Age (although Whitehorse wasn't actually part of this; it was glaciated; farther north, say, Dawson City, was right in the center of it, and miners are still turning up mammoth bones). Large dioramas depict the lives of animals in Ice Age Beringia, and there are replicas of skeletons and a 26,000-year-old horsehide; horses weren't as big back then. ⊠ *Mile 886, Alaska Hwy., Whitehorse, Yukon, Canada* ☎ *867/667–8855* ⊕ *www.beringia.com* ✉ *C$6* ☼ *Mid-May–Sept., daily 9–6; Oct.–mid-May, Sun. and Mon. noon–5.*

Yukon Permanent Art Collection. The lobby of the Yukon Government Building displays the Yukon Permanent Art Collection, featuring traditional and contemporary works by Yukon artists, including a 24-panel mural by artist David MacLagan depicting the historical evolution of the Yukon. In addition to the collection on the premises, the brochure *Art Adventures on Yukon Time,* available at visitor reception centers throughout the Yukon, guides you to artists' studios as well as galleries, festivals, and public art locations. ⊠ *2071 2nd Ave., Whitehorse, Yukon, Canada* ☎ *867/667–5811* ✉ *Free* ☼ *Weekdays 8:30–5.*

Yukon Transportation Museum. The Yukon Transportation Museum, next door to the Yukon Beringia Interpretive Centre, takes a great look at the planes, trains, trucks, and snowmachines that opened the North. Even if you're not interested in big machines, it's a pretty cool place to see the adaptations that transport in the north has required. ⊠ *Mile 886, Alaska Hwy., Whitehorse, Yukon, Canada* ☎ *867/668–4792* ⊕ *www. goytm.ca* ✉ *C$6.*

Yukon Wildlife Preserve. The Yukon Wildlife Preserve provides a fail-safe way of photographing rarely spotted animals in a natural setting. Animals roaming freely here include elk, caribou, mountain goats, musk oxen, bison, mule deer, and Dall and Stone sheep. ⊠ *HAPAY, 2nd Ave. at Steele St., Whitehorse, Yukon, Canada* ☎ *867/668–3225* ⊕ *www. yukonwildlife.ca* ✉ *C$15* ☼ *Tours mid-May–mid-Sept., daily 9:30–4.*

WHERE TO EAT

$$$$
EUROPEAN

✕ **The Cellar Steakhouse and Wine Bar.** In the Edgewater Hotel in downtown Whitehorse, this intimate two-room spot—down some stairs, as the name implies—is touted by the locals as the place to go for special occasions. The front room is less formal, with a bar and TV, while the back room, separated by an etched-glass partition, is quieter. The menu offers seafood and meat dishes, complemented by a decent wine list. $ *Average main: C$30* ⊠ *101 Main St., Whitehorse, Yukon, Canada* ☎ *867/667–2572* ⊕ *www.edgewaterhotelwhitehorse.com* ☼ *Closed Mon. and Tues.*

$$$$
AMERICAN
Fodor's Choice
★

✕ **Klondike Rib & Salmon BBQ.** If you're in the mood for something completely different, this is the place. It's known not just for its wild-game dishes such as musk ox, caribou, and bison, but also for its halibut, salmon, Arctic char, and killer ribs. It's open for lunch, but the famous rib dishes are served only at dinner. Due to its popularity, there's almost always a line, but it's worth the wait—for the best food in town, yes, but also for the chance to dine in the oldest operating building in Whitehorse. $ *Average main: C$30* ⊠ *2116 2nd Ave., Whitehorse, Yukon, Canada* ☎ *867/667–7554* ⊕ *www.klondikerib.com* ☼ *Closed mid-Sept.–mid-May.*

WHERE TO STAY

$$
HOTEL
⊞ **Edgewater Hotel.** On a quiet end of Main Street, this corner hotel, first built during the 1898 gold rush, is in its third incarnation (the first two burned down). **Pros:** rich history; borders the Yukon River. **Cons:** small lobby and hallways to rooms; no Continental breakfast. ⑤ *Rooms from: C$149* ⊠ *101 Main St., Whitehorse, Yukon, Canada* ☎ *867/667–2572, 877/484–3334* ⊕ *www.edgewaterhotelwhitehorse. com* ⤵ *32 rooms, 4 suites.*

$$
HOTEL
⊞ **Westmark Whitehorse Hotel and Conference Center.** You can catch a nightly Klondike vaudeville show, the *Frantic Follies*, in summer at this full-service hotel in the heart of downtown, the largest hotel in the Yukon. **Pros:** laundry facilities; some pets allowed; breakfast buffet available in the summer season. **Cons:** not the place to go to escape the action; no air-conditioning. ⑤ *Rooms from: C$149* ⊠ *201 Wood St., Whitehorse, Yukon, Canada* ☎ *867/393–9700, 800/544–0970 reservations* ⊕ *www.westmarkhotels.com* ⤵ *180 rooms, 8 suites.*

SPORTS AND THE OUTDOORS

HIKING

Kluane National Park and Reserve. The Kluane National Park and Reserve, about 170 km (100 miles) west of Whitehorse, has millions of acres for hiking. This is a completely roadless wilderness, with so many mountains over 14,000 feet that they haven't even bothered to name most of them, along with hundreds of glaciers. Together with the neighboring Wrangell-St. Elias National Park in Alaska and a couple smaller parks, this is the largest protected wilderness on the entire continent. The visitor center has a few short guided hikes, and it's easy to book flightseeing into the park in Haines Junction. ⊠ *Visitor center, 119 Logan St., Haines Junction, Yukon, Canada* ☎ *867/634–7207.*

Yukon Conservation Society. The Yukon Conservation Society leads natural and historical hikes from July through August of varying lengths and difficulty. ⊠ *Whitehorse, Yukon, Canada* ☎ *867/668–5678* ⊕ *www. yukonconsevation.org.*

SLED-DOG RACING

Yukon Quest International Sled-Dog Race. Whitehorse and Fairbanks organize the Yukon Quest International Sled-Dog Race in February. The race's starting line alternates yearly between the two cities. This is one of the longest and toughest races in the north—a thousand miles, and considered by mushers to be much harder than the Iditarod, as the terrain is rougher and the checkpoints fewer. ⊠ *Whitehorse, Yukon, Canada* ☎ *867/668–4711* ⊕ *www.yukonquest.com.*

6

INDEX

PHOTO CREDITS

Front cover: Danny Lehman/Corbis [Description: Cruise ship in College Fjord in Prince William Sound]. 1, alaskarap, Fodors.com member. 3, Stephen Frink Collection / Alamy. Chapter 1: Experience an Alaska Cruise:. 6-7, Papilio / Alamy. 8, BrianEmbacher, Fodors.com member. 9 (left), Dale Walsh/iStockphoto. 9(right), Brian Ray/iStockphoto. 10 (left), Tammy Wolfe/iStockphoto. 10 (top right), Nelson Sirlin/Shutterstock. 10 (bottom right), Tracy Hardy/iStockphoto. 11 (top left), Sam Chadwick Photography/iStockphoto. 11 (bottom left), Princess Cruises. 11 (right), marleneawe, Fodors.com member. 12, Photodisc. 13 (left), Clint Henrie/iStockphoto. 13 (right), SrA Joshua Strang/wikipedia.org. 18 (left), David Davis/Shutterstock. 18 (top center), Ianar. S.vi/wikipedia. 18 (bottom center), buchan/Shutterstock. 18 (top right), Ainars Aunins/Shutterstock. 18 (bottom right), Bruce MacQueen/Shutterstock. 19 (top left), Dawn Nichols/iStockphoto. 19 (bottom left), Dennis Donohue/Shutterstock. 19 (center), andre st-louis/Shutterstock. 19 (right), Andrew Howe/iStockphoto. 20, David McMaster/wikipedia.org. 21 (left), Mirek Srb/Shutterstock, 21 (right), Steve Bower/Shutterstock. 22 (left), Arthur van der Kooij/Shutterstock. 22 (top center), Bob Blanchard/Shutterstock. 22 (bottom), UnGePhoto/Shutterstock. 22 (right), neelsky/Shutterstock. 23 (left), Linda Macpherson/Shutterstock. 23 (top center), naturediver/Shutterstock. 23 (bottom center), Bill Hickey/wikipedia.org. 23 (right), TTphoto/Shutterstock. 24, Michael Zahniser/wikipedia.org. 25 (left), scattoselvaggio/Shutterstock. 25 (right), Serg Zastavkin/Shutterstock. 26, American Safari Cruises. Chapter 2: Planning Your Alaska Cruise: 27, American Safari Cruises. 28, Princess Cruises. Chapter 3: Cruise Lines and Cruise Ships: 59, Visual&Written SL / Alamy. 60, Jon Arnold Images Ltd / Alamy. 64-66, Courtesy of American Cruise Lines. 68-73, Courtesy of Carnival Cruise Lines. 74-83, Courtesy of Celebrity Cruises. 84-89, © Disney. 90-101, Courtesy of Holland America Line. 102-04, Courtesy of Lindblad Expeditions. 106-13, Courtesy of Norwegian Cruise Line. 114-19, Courtesy of Oceania Cruises. 120-31, Courtesy of Princess Cruises. 132-37, Courtesy of Regent Seven Seas. 138-45, Courtesy of Royal Caribbean International. 146-51, Courtesy of Silversea Cruises. 152-55, Courtesy of InnerSea Discoveries. 156, SuperStock/age fotostock. Chapter 4: Ports of Embarkation: 157, Agua Verde Paddle Club. 158, Lara Swimmer Photography. 166, Anchorage Museum of History and Art. 171, Jos. Fuste Raga / age fotostock. 178, Yusia/Shutterstock. 181, Richard Cummins / age fotostock. 189, Mark Newman/age fotostock. 195, Chris Cheadle / age fotostock. 200-01, Steve Rosset/iStockphoto. 203, SuperStock / age fotostock. 206, Hannamariah/Shutterstock. 209 (bottom), ImageState / Alamy. 209 (top), Stephen Frink Collection / Alamy. 210 (bottom), Pieter Folkens. 210 (top), Andoni Canela/age fotostock. 211, Pieter Folkens. 212 (top), Michael S. Nolan/age fotostock. 212 (bottom), Pieter Folkens. Chapter 5: Ports of Call: 215, Alaska Stock LLC/Alamy 216, Ladd Bodem, Fodors.com member. 222, Bryan Busovicki/Shutterstock. 233, Bryan & Cherry Alexander Photography / Alamy. 234 (left), Jeff Greenberg/age fotostock. 234 (right), Robert Mitchell. 235 (left), Sitka National Historical Park. 235 (right), Tracy Ferrero / Alamy. 236-37, Alaska State Museum, Juneau. 250, Chris Marlow, Fodors.com member. 261, Sandy Cook, Fodors.com member. 264, FLPA/Mark Newman / age fotostock. 268, Chip Porter / age fotostock. 275, True North Images/age fotostock. 278, Don B. Stevenson / Alamy. 279, Robert Mitchell. 281 (left), Renaud Visage/age fotostock. 281 (right), Alaska Stock LLC / Alamy. 285, Brandon Laufenberg/iStockphoto. 287, Nancy Nehring/iStockphoto. 289, University of Washington Libraries. Special Collections Division, Alaska Photograph Collection, UW7326. 290 (top), University of Washington Libraries. Special Collections Division, Eric A. Hegg Photograph Collection. PH Coll 274, Hegg20a. 290 (bottom), Alaska and Polar Regions Collections, Elmer E. Rasmuson Library, University of Alaska Fairbanks. 291, P277-001-009, Alaska State Library, James Wickersham/State Historic Sites Collection. 293 (top left), Pep Roig/Alamy. 293 (bottom left), Alaska Stock LLC/Alamy. 293 (right), Christian Racich. 295, Tammy Wolfe/iStockphoto. 302, Xuanlu Wang/Shutterstock. Chapter 6: Inland Cruise Tour Destinations: 311, crmarlow, Fodors.com member. 312, Liz Gruder, Fodors.com member. 319: Patricia Fisher/Fisher Photography. 331, PhotoDisc. Back cover: (from left to right), CAN BALCIOGLU/Shutterstock; Princess Cruises; David Davis/Shutterstock. Spine: Ruth Peterkin/Shutterstock.

ABOUT OUR WRITERS

Linda Coffman, our resident cruise diva, wrote the Top Attractions, If You Like, and Best Bets sections of Chapter 1, Experience; she also wrote our Planning chapter and all the cruise line and ship reviews. She is a freelance travel writer who has been dishing out cruise-travel advice and information for nearly two decades. Her articles have appeared online and in national magazines and newspapers, including *Porthole*, *Consumer's Digest*, the *Chicago Sun-Times*, and *USA Today*. An avid cruiser, she spends most of her time cruising in the Caribbean when she's not at home in Augusta, Georgia.

Non-cruise Alaska content in this book was updated by various writers, who also worked on the Fodor's Alaska guide. Teeka Ballas updated our South Central Alaska port coverage. Amy Fletcher updated all the Southeast Alaska port coverage and contributed new coverage of Icy Strait Point. Sarah Henning updated Anchorage. Lisa Hupp updated Kodiak. E. Readicker-Henderson updated Denali National Park and Preserve as well as the remaining coverage of the interior.

Finally, our Canada and Seattle content was also a team effort. Cedar Burnett updated our Seattle content, while Chris McBeath updated Vancouver, Victoria, and Prince Rupert.

NOTES